The Reckoning

Photographs Of Disability Activism In The Age Of Austerity

By

Christopher John Ball

'The Reckoning - Photographs Of Disability Activism In The Age Of Austerity' was first published, in the United Kingdom, in 2024 as an original Paperback by

Britannia Street Theatre and Arts Publishing
3/50 Britannia Street,
London,
WC1X 9JH
United Kingdom

Email: britanniastreetartspublishing@gmail.com

ISBN No: 978-0-9926899-4-0

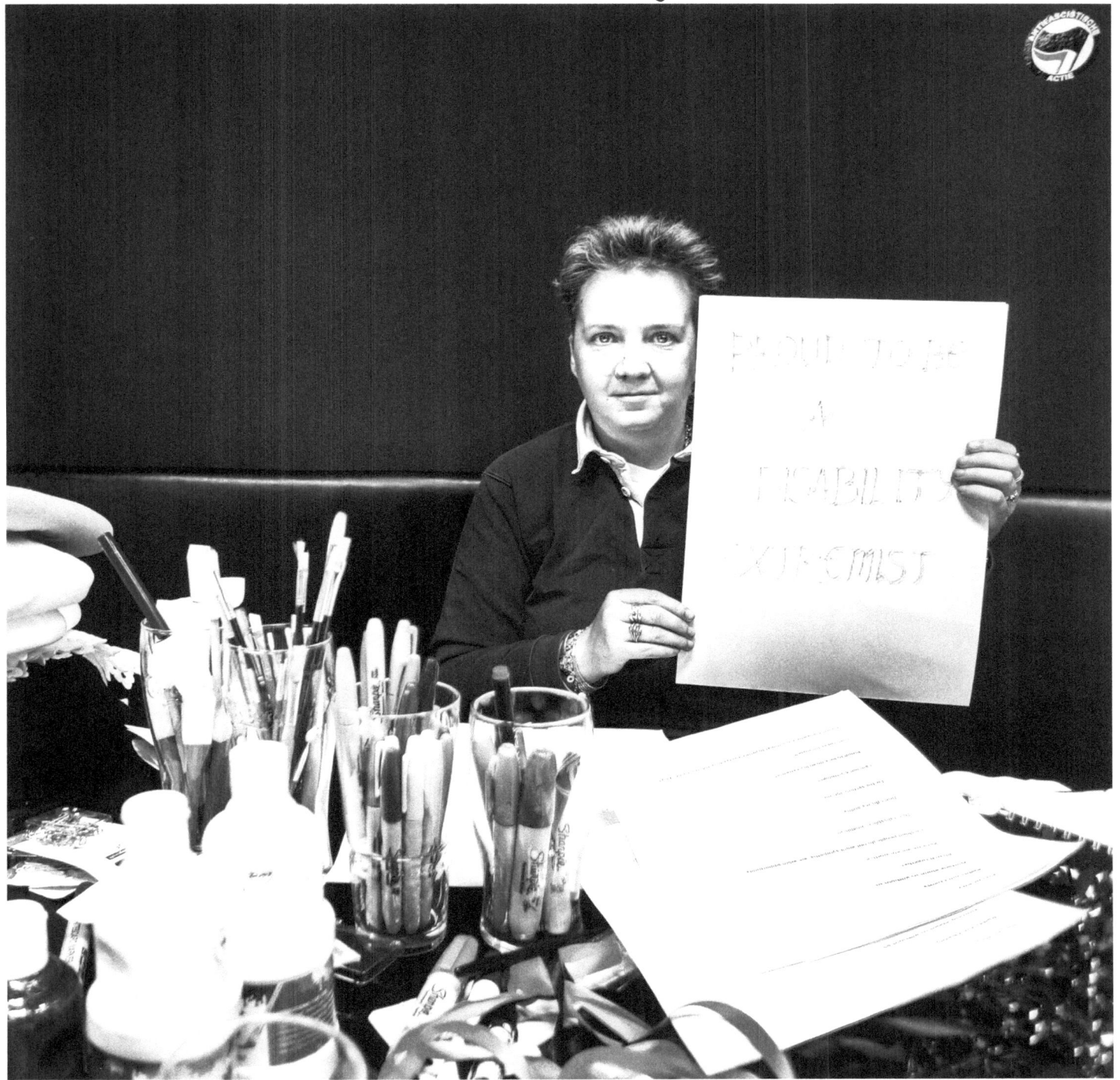

The Birth of a Resistance Movement.

These photographs chart the birth of a movement that for the first time in the history of the UK mobilised disabled people on a mass scale to resist the brutality meted out to them by government.

They portray the heroes and heroines of that resistance movement and the ferocity of the struggles in which they participated.

For many engaged in these campaigns it literally was a life and death battle to secure the means to survive in a brutally harsh political environment. Tragically some of the campaigners did not survive and so this book is also a tribute to them.

The origins of this struggle lie in the financial crisis of 2008, when years of deregulation turned the banks and finance sector into a casino that eventually crashed.

The Conservatives aided by their allies in the media were able to spin the lie that it wasn't the greed of the bankers that caused the crisis but it was overspending on our public services and our welfare state.

So, when the Conservatives were elected in 2010 they decided that it wouldn't be the bankers who were to pay for the crash, it would be all those who depended on our welfare state.

An austerity programme was rapidly introduced to cut public services, especially health, education and council budgets, and to freeze wages and savage social security benefits.

There was clearly a conscious decision taken by government ministers and Conservative strategists to target the sick and disabled. The view in government was that these were easy to pick off with the least resistance. Of course, the media played its role in echoing the Conservative smears about scroungers, malingerers and dependency on benefits being a lifestyle choice.

The frenzy of abuse and hate stirred up against disabled people reached such a height that people with a visible disability were frequently the victims of hate crime and were so often unsafe on the streets. The social security system was transformed into a weapon to be used to harass, denigrate and humiliate disabled people and the sick.

Stories were emerging of people not being able to endure this brutal treatment.

I remember crying when I heard of a young man, a poet, who took his own life and poignantly left by his bed the letter from the DWP withdrawing his benefits.

At this stage people had just had enough and small number of courageous disabled people came together and decided it was time to fight back.

A conference was called, which I was proud to attend, and Disabled People Against the Cuts, DPAC, was formed.

A whirlwind was launched.

This resistance movement broke the mould.

It was not pleading for charity or begging to be listened to.

It was demanding change and was willing to use whatever means it thought justifiable to secure that change.

It's message was clear.

The rights of disabled people must be upheld.

Politicians must listen or if they don't they will be forced to listen.

Advocacy will be reinforced by direct action whenever needed.

And an early principle was established, that disabled people are part of a movement of solidarity mutually supporting all working class struggles from demonstrations to picket lines and occupations.

This series of photographs explains better than any words the breadth and intensity of the DPAC struggles over the last decade.

They portray the emotions of the campaigners often in the toughest of situations, their determination, their bravery, their eloquence and their spirit.

At a closer look what is evident also is the pride that all of us have in being part of this expression of humanity.

John McDonnell MP

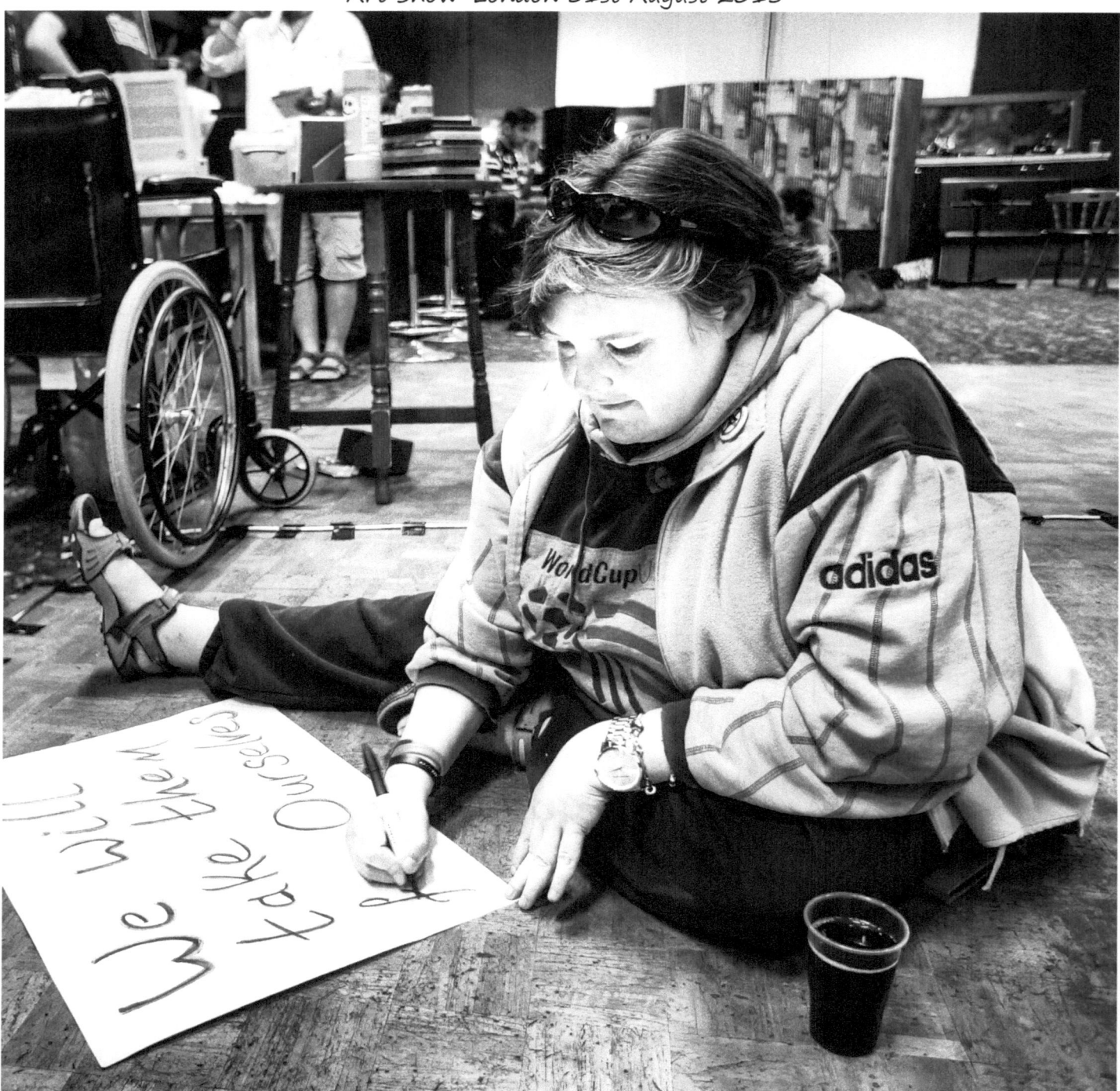

The 2010 General Election saw the Conservative Party, in coalition with their Liberal Democrat partners, come to power in the UK. David Cameron and Nick Clegg imposed a series of deleterious, ideologically driven, austerity policies upon the country.

Cameron saw the 2008 international banking crisis as an opportunity to undo the post war settlement, that had ushered in the modern welfare system, and the moment he took up office as PM he put his plans into place.

The man Cameron selected for the job of dismantling the welfare state was Iain Duncan Smith. Duncan Smith had been leader of the Conservative Party until being ousted, by his own MP's and Party Membership, in a vote of no confidence. The Tory Party didn't have confidence in him to lead them but Cameron expected the British people to have confidence in Duncan Smith with their Social Security.

Throughout his period in office as 'Secretary of State for Work and Pensions', Iain Duncan Smith was repeatedly accused of obfuscation, hubris, discourtesy, manipulating statistics, ignoring warnings and dismissing the mounting evidence of the suffering that resulted from the policies he pushed.

Iain Duncan Smith's policies were not driven by facts or social justice, but by a misplaced messianic belief in himself and his mission. Many criticised his intellect and understanding of his brief. In my opinion, he would have difficulty writing his own name in the sand with a stick. He is a prime example of the Dunning-Kruger effect, and this made him dangerous.

In addition, Duncan Smith was often denounced for his rhetoric about welfare recipients. His policies are based upon a false stereotype of disabled people as lazy and undeserving, as being burdens incapable of contributing to society.

This 'othering' of disabled people, much of which would not have been out of place in 30's Germany 'Aktion T4' program, has been seen as dehumanising and harmful to disabled people and fuelled hostility towards us.

The thin veneer of protection that civilisation brings is easy to break, especially in times of hardship, and the Tory Government austerity policies served to do just that. I'm often the target of abuse directed at my disability but the frequency and nature of said abuse changed during this period. I believe that much of this was fuelled by the scrounger rhetoric being pushed by

Government as a means to 'nudge' people into accepting, indeed wanting, the 'reforms' despite them not being in their own interest.

The Tory Government placed scapegoating at the heart of its economic and social policy; it is what drove much of it, therefore its consequences surely cannot have come as a surprise. I believe that Ministers, MP's and many within the client media were well aware of what they were doing; were aware of the pernicious impact upon disabled individuals and, as such, cannot claim unintended consequences.

Austerity cuts have had a disproportionate impact on disabled people. Despite repeated requests and the success of the 'WOW Petition', the Tory government refused to undertake a cumulative impact assessment of policy forced upon disabled people and carers.

Personal Independence Payments (PIP), which replaced Disability Living Allowance, was a much more stringent assessment process, with a stated aim of cutting disability benefits by 20%.

Disabled people often faced assessors, supplied by private companies ATOS and MAXIMUS, who had no understanding of the health conditions they were assessing. Indeed it was found that some assessors lied during the PIP examination, falsifying the reports, and were even found to talk disparagingly about their 'clients' behind their backs. This resulted in a high percentage of disabled people winning appeals against the DWP.

Iain Duncan Smith responded to this, not by accepting that there were faults in the assessment process and putting in changes, but rather introducing a new attempt to delay justice with the creation of the Mandatory Reconsideration process.

Other policies that disproportionately impacted disabled people and carers were the Bedroom Tax, the removal of the Independent Living Fund and Universal Credit.

Studies have shown that poverty increases wherever Universal Credit is rolled out. A particularly malevolent element of Universal Credit is the sanctions regime. A sanction is the removal of benefit, in part or whole, from an individual for having transgressed some arbitrary DWP rule.

Let us be clear, a sanction is state sponsored terrorism. It is the removal of the means to access food, utilities or housing. We do not deprive convicted murderers of food nor shelter, and we certainly do not punish the murderers family in the same manner, but the Tory Government thought it perfectly correct to do just that for someone who has committed that most heinous of crimes, being a tad late for an appointment or lying in a hospital bed.

Since 2010 the following people have held the post of 'Minster For Disabled People' - Maria Miller, Esther McVey, Mike Penning, Mark Harper, Justin Tomlinson, Penny Mordaunt, Sarah Newton, Chloe Smith, Claire Coutinho and Tom Pursglove. In 2023 PM Rishi Sunak scrapped the post. After outcry from disabled people, charities and activists, Sunak did u-turn but, still showing Tory contempt for disabled people, he downgraded the role before giving it to Mims Davies.

Each of the aforementioned Ministers shared one thing in common and that is their refusal to engage with disabled people in an honest manner. None of them seemed to have understood what the 'For' part of their job title meant.

Disabled people often felt these Ministers actively worked against them rather than representing them. Several of these Ministers and MP's blocked disabled people, on social media, for having had the audacity to point out to them the impact of these pernicious policies. Can you imagine a 'Minister for Business' ignoring businesses or blocking business people?

In response to these cuts, and the attacks upon disabled people in the Tory supporting media, disability campaigners came together to fight back. As a disabled individual, who is also a carer, I became a member of one of these groups, Disabled People Against Cuts (DPAC). DPAC organised protests, demonstrations, events, occupations and organised conferences in an attempt to raise awareness of the terrible impact of austerity.

The UN 'Convention On The Rights Of Persons With Disabilities' (CRPD) undertook several investigations into the policies of the UK government which resulted in the publication of a damning and critical report in 2016.

In 2017 the UN followed up and produced a study which further criticised austerity policies as having created a "human catastrophe" for disabled people. They found evidence of 'grave and systematic violations of disabled people's rights'.

Further investigations by the UN found little attempt by the Tory government to address their concerns. With the UN further condemning the UK Governments "lack of recognition of the findings and recommendations of the (2016) Inquiry". In 2022 a study led by the 'University of Glasgow and the Glasgow Centre for Population Health' and published in the 'Journal of Epidemiology and Community Health', found over 330,000 excess deaths in the UK linked to Tory austerity policies!

The photographs within this book, made over a ten year period, are a powerful reminder of the human cost of austerity. Cuts to services continue to have a catastrophic impact upon the lives of disabled people. These images are a testament to the determination, courage and resilience of disabled people who continue to campaign and fight for our rights. A tribute to those who will not give up until all disabled people have the support they need to live full and independent lives.

The fight against austerity is not just a fight for disabled people. Disability doesn't care if you are in work or out of work. It will show you no favours whichever party you vote for, be it Labour, Conservative, Liberal Democrat, Reform or UKIP. Disability can strike anyone, including YOU!

I have been critical of many governments in the past, but it was the successive Conservative administrations, from 2010 onward, that truly eroded my trust in my own government and made me feel unsafe in my own country. Tory austerity policies have disproportionately harmed the most vulnerable members of society, while their rhetoric has sown division and hatred.

I've seen first-hand the devastating impact of Tory cuts to public services, which have left many people struggling to make ends meet. I have also witnessed the rise in hate crimes and discrimination since they came to power. As a result, I now live in fear of my own government.

The Conservatives deliberately placed our Social Security Safety Net so close to the ground, it was rendered fatal for many.

When the history books are finally written, the likes of David Cameron, Nick Clegg, Esther McVey, Iain Duncan Smith etc will not be seen as the heroes within this sorry narrative — far from it.

One day, there will a reckoning!

Christopher John Ball- Photographer, writer, campaigner and member of DPAC.

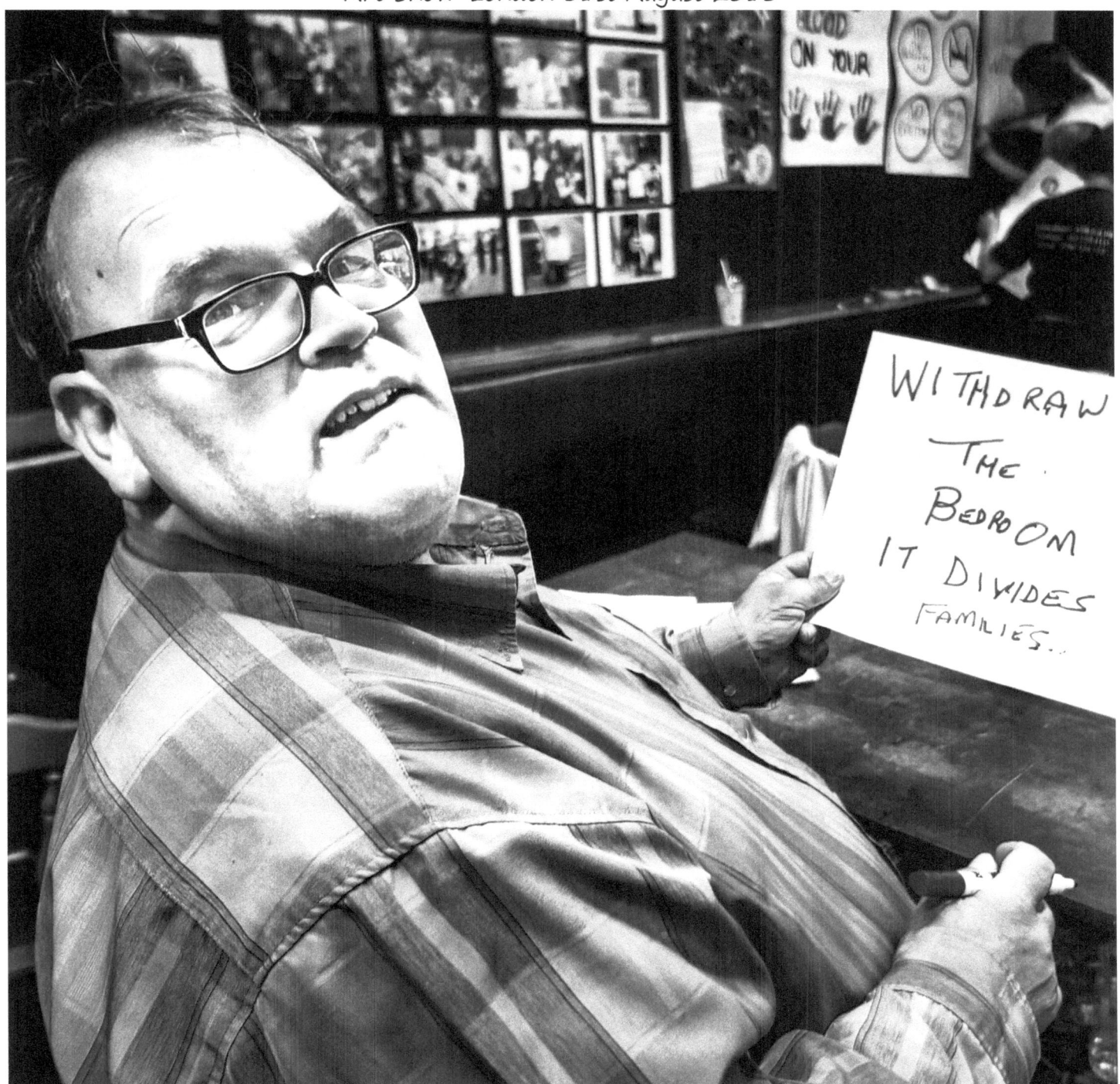

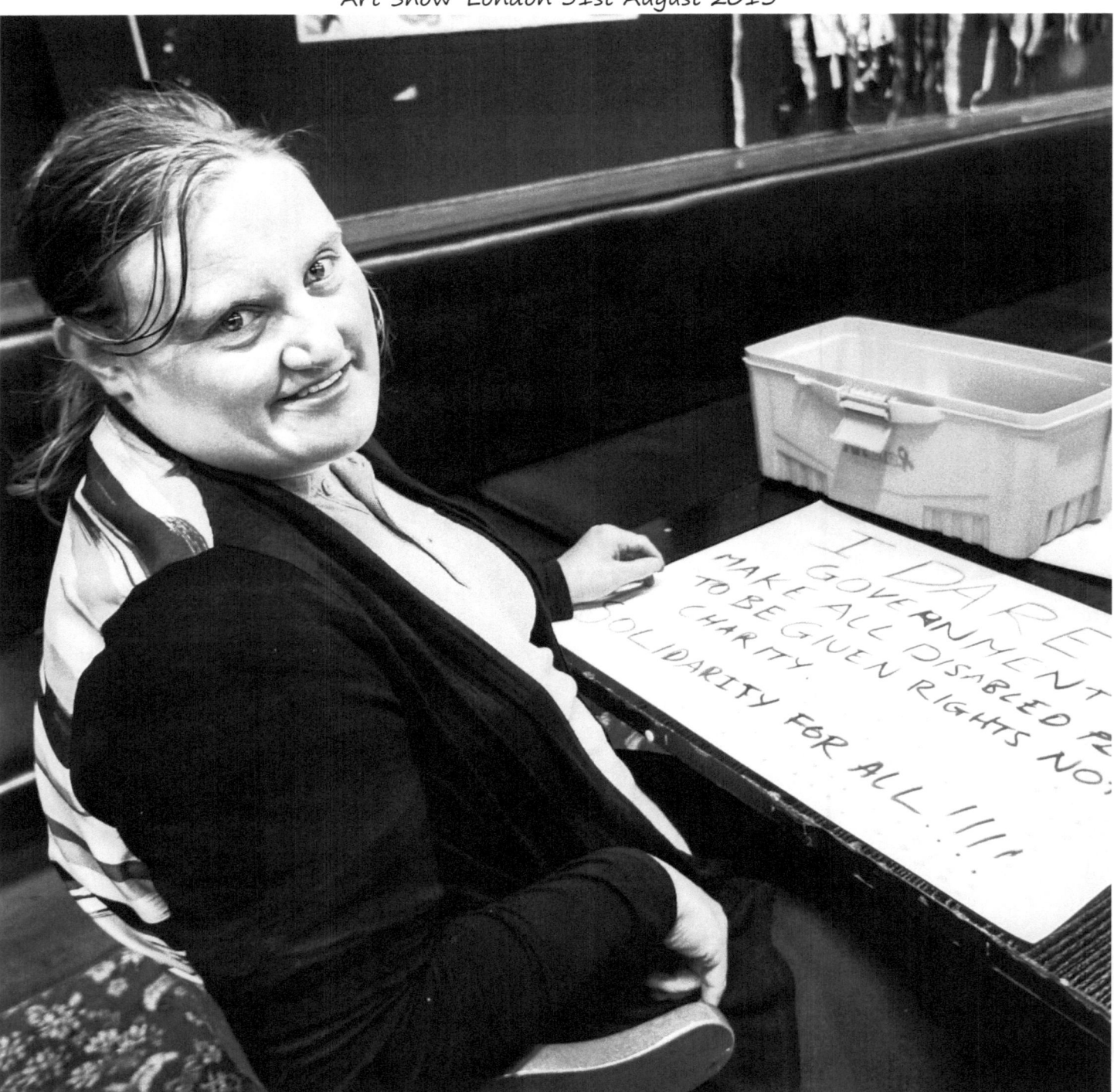

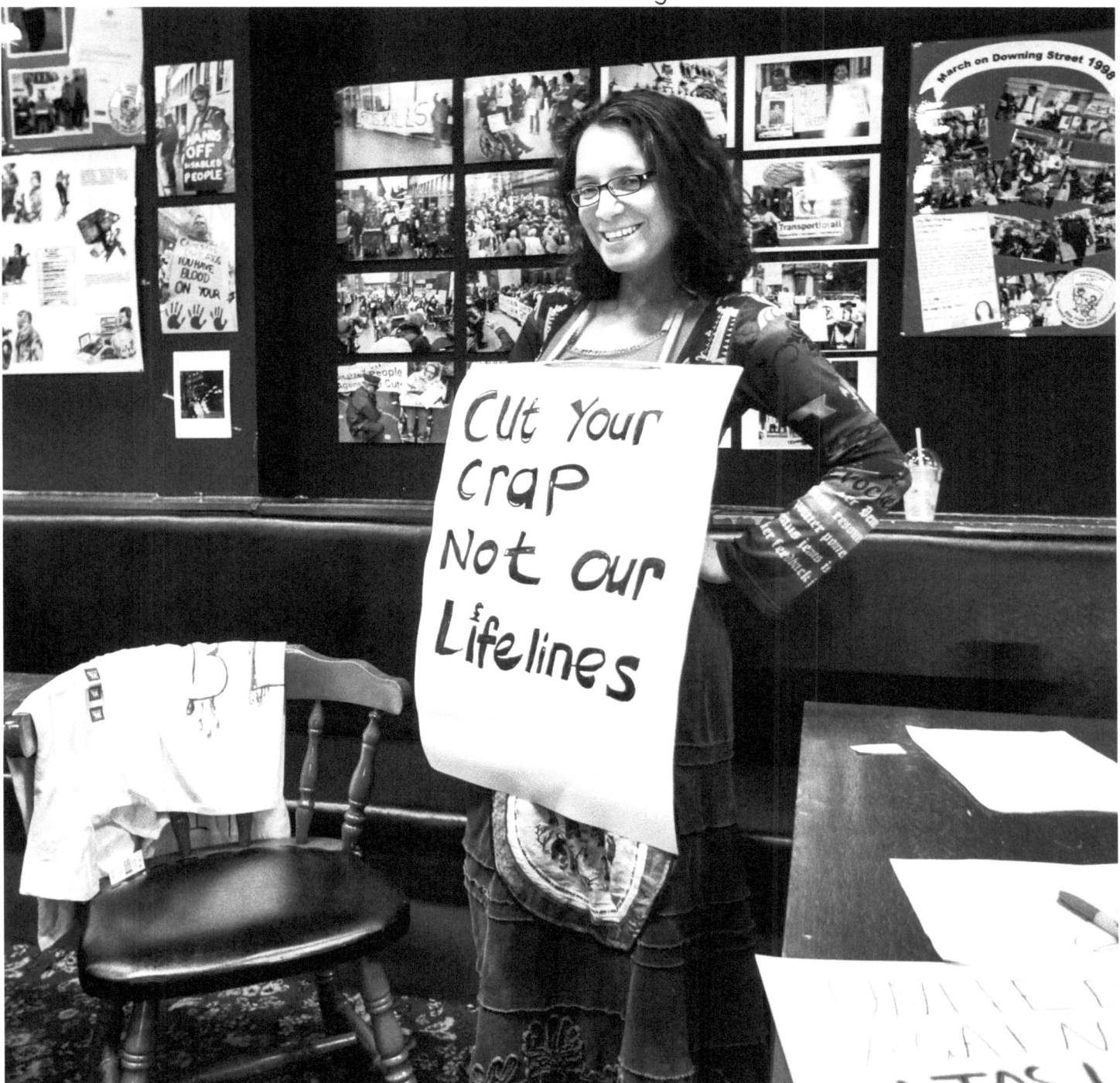

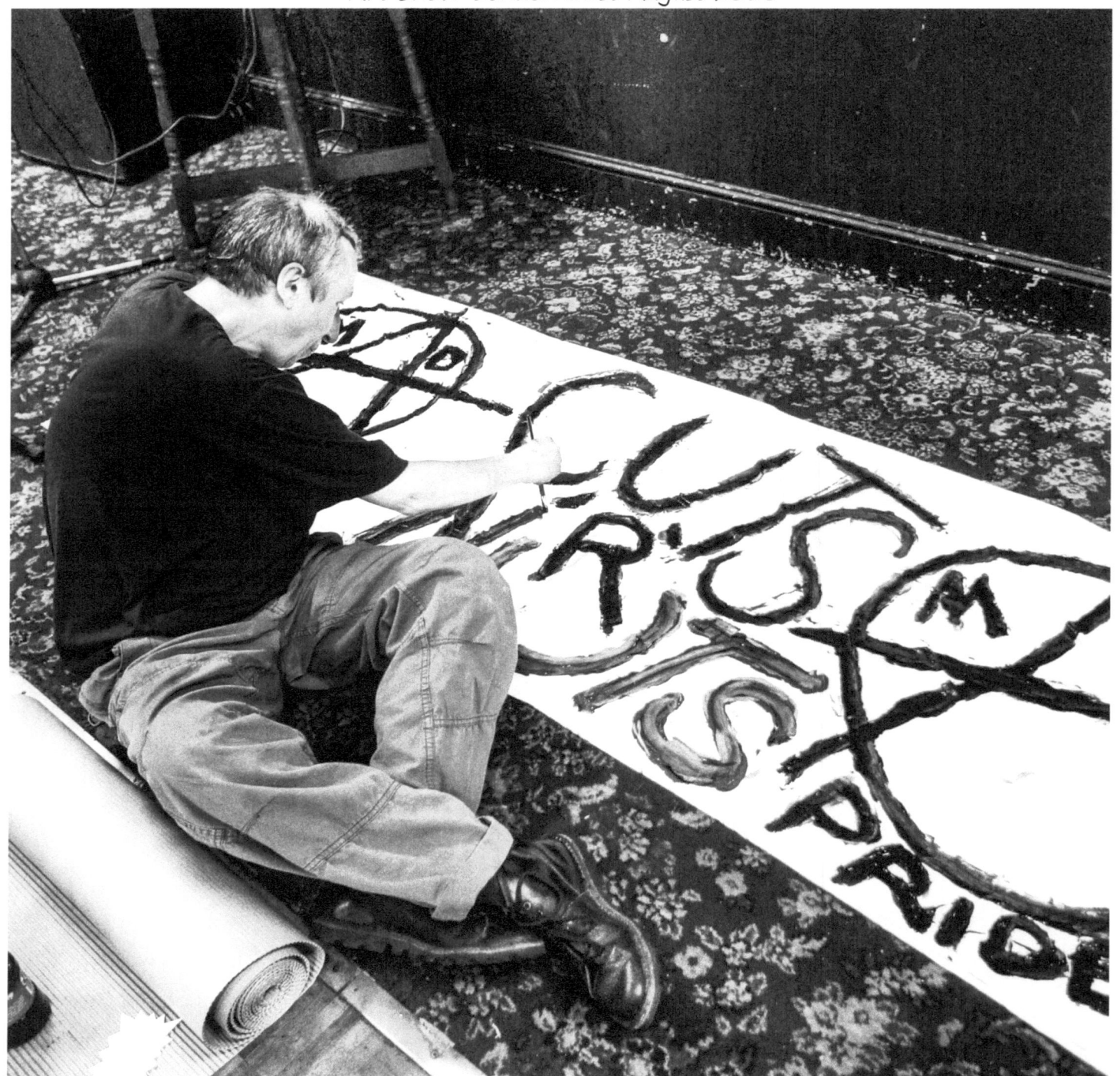

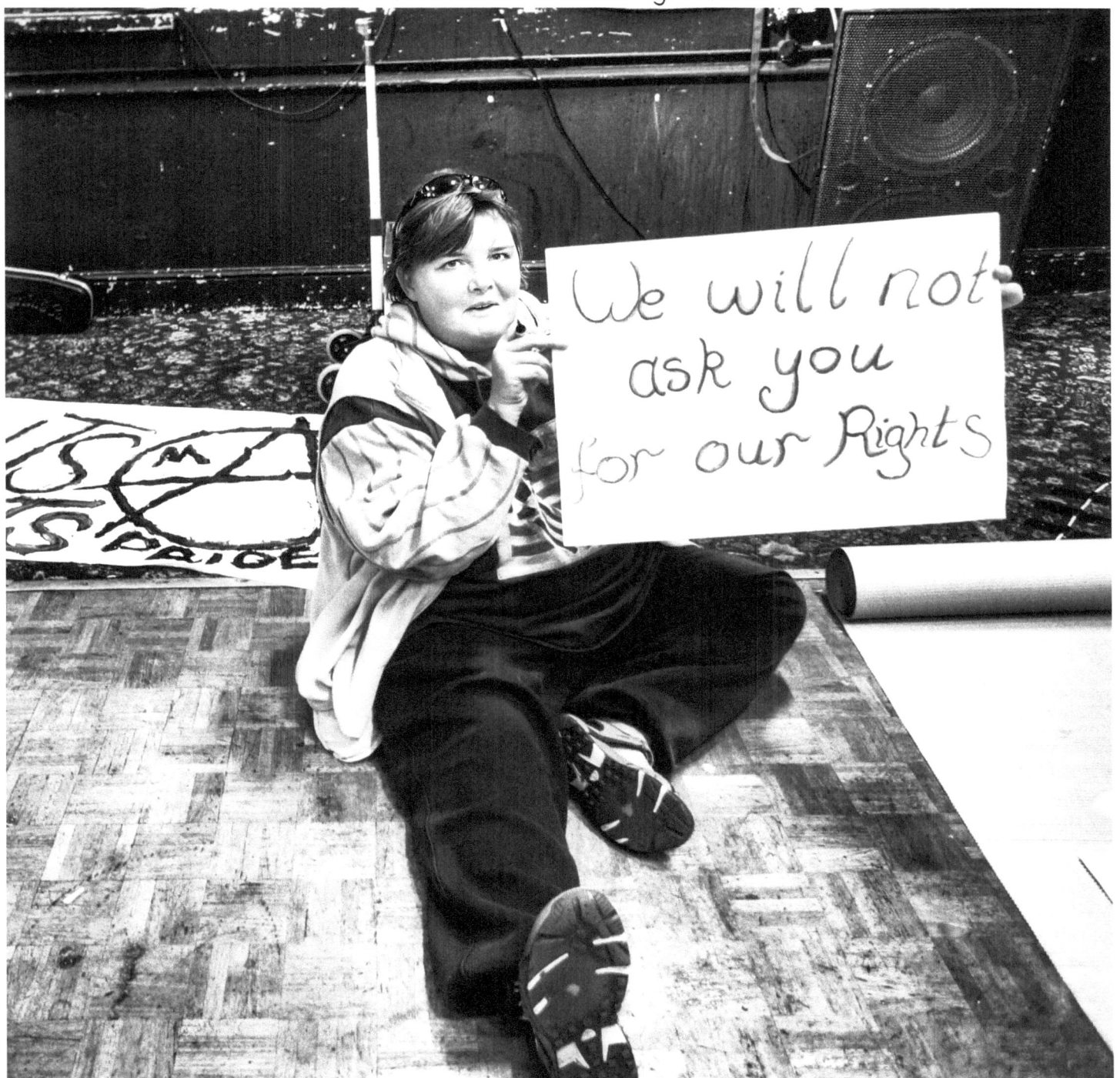

Each picture in this book is a poignant memory seeing comrades like Sean McGovern, Padraig Lynch and Sophie Partridge wonderful disabled activists who were part of the disability resistance and no longer with us today.

Each action I was involved in gave a clear message; from no more benefit deaths, to stopping the segregation in education, to no work coaches in GP surgeries. There were very many campaign tactics & strategies used, occupying Westminster Abbey grounds back in 2014 to fight for independent living, being outside ATOS assessment offices highlighting ATOS appalling involvement in Work Capability Assessments.

We've used art work to make placards and voice our anger, made huge banners as part of a collective to block a bridge.

Each action showed the collective need to be as visible as possible on the streets fighting back against the attacks on our human rights, the services we use and to give other disabled people hope that something was being done to fight back and empower others to join our movement. On every DPAC action, I've needed a bottle of water, a poncho, it rains on 80% of DPAC actions, some chocolate and something to eat to share with my comrades as it's hungry work blocking roads and being tied to the railings in the fight for human rights.

I've got so many memories; the occupation of Westminster Bridge, the occupation of Westminster Abbey grounds. The storming of Parliament amongst many others. I'm humbled to be a part of these actions. But I'm also angry and sad too.

We shouldn't be in a war with this government but we are and on a daily basis. We should have full equality, dignity and respect and be treated like the beautiful human beings we are. Not marginalised even further, having our rights violated and losing so many disabled people to the constant stress and worry of losing their support.

But while we fight back and resist this government. We highlight the appalling truth what this government are doing to us.

This is a powerful social history document of disabled people resisting the Conservative government and fighting back

Paula Peters - (Disabled People Against Cuts) DPAC

Demonstration at 'Department for Education' London 4th September 2013

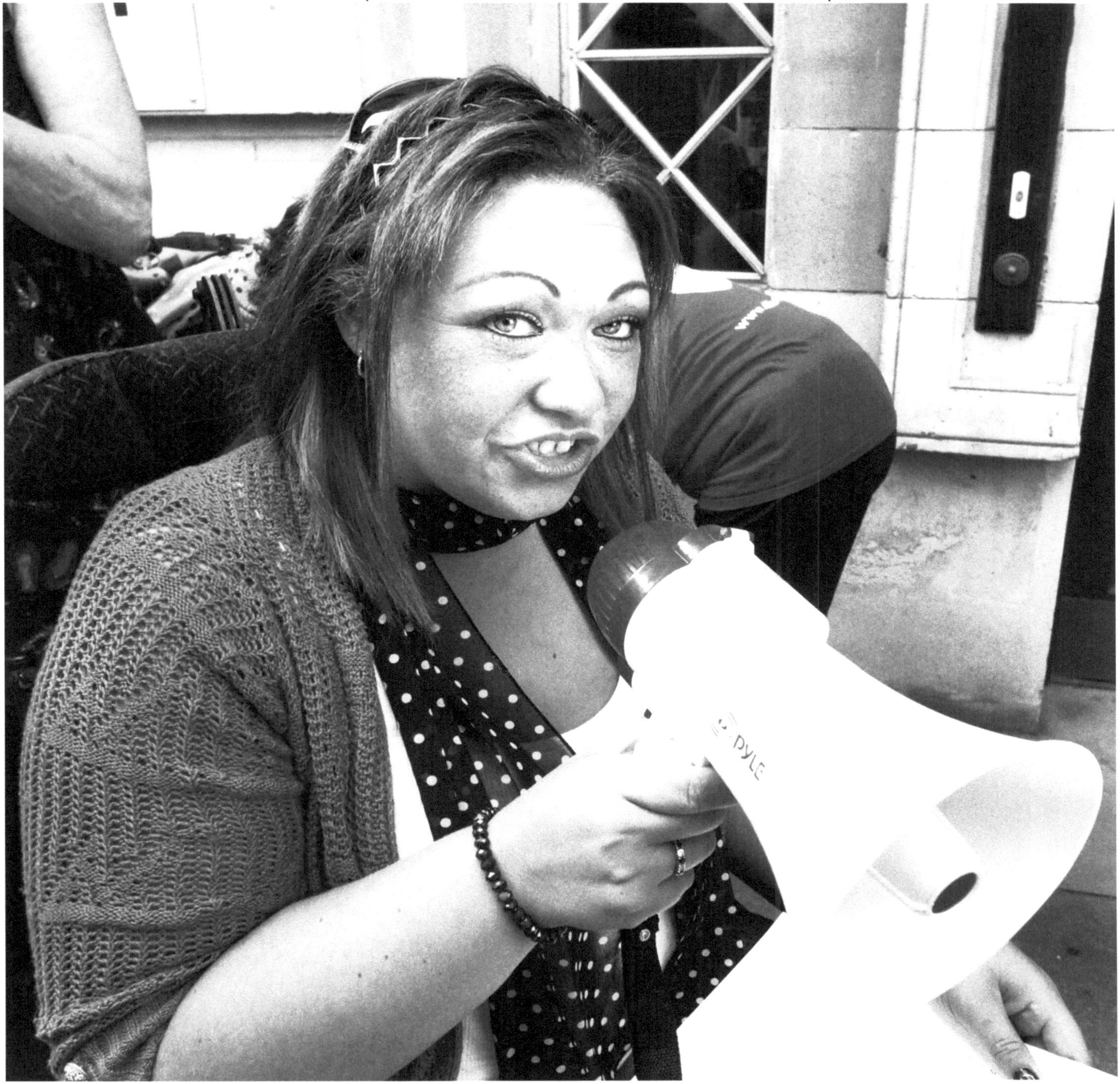

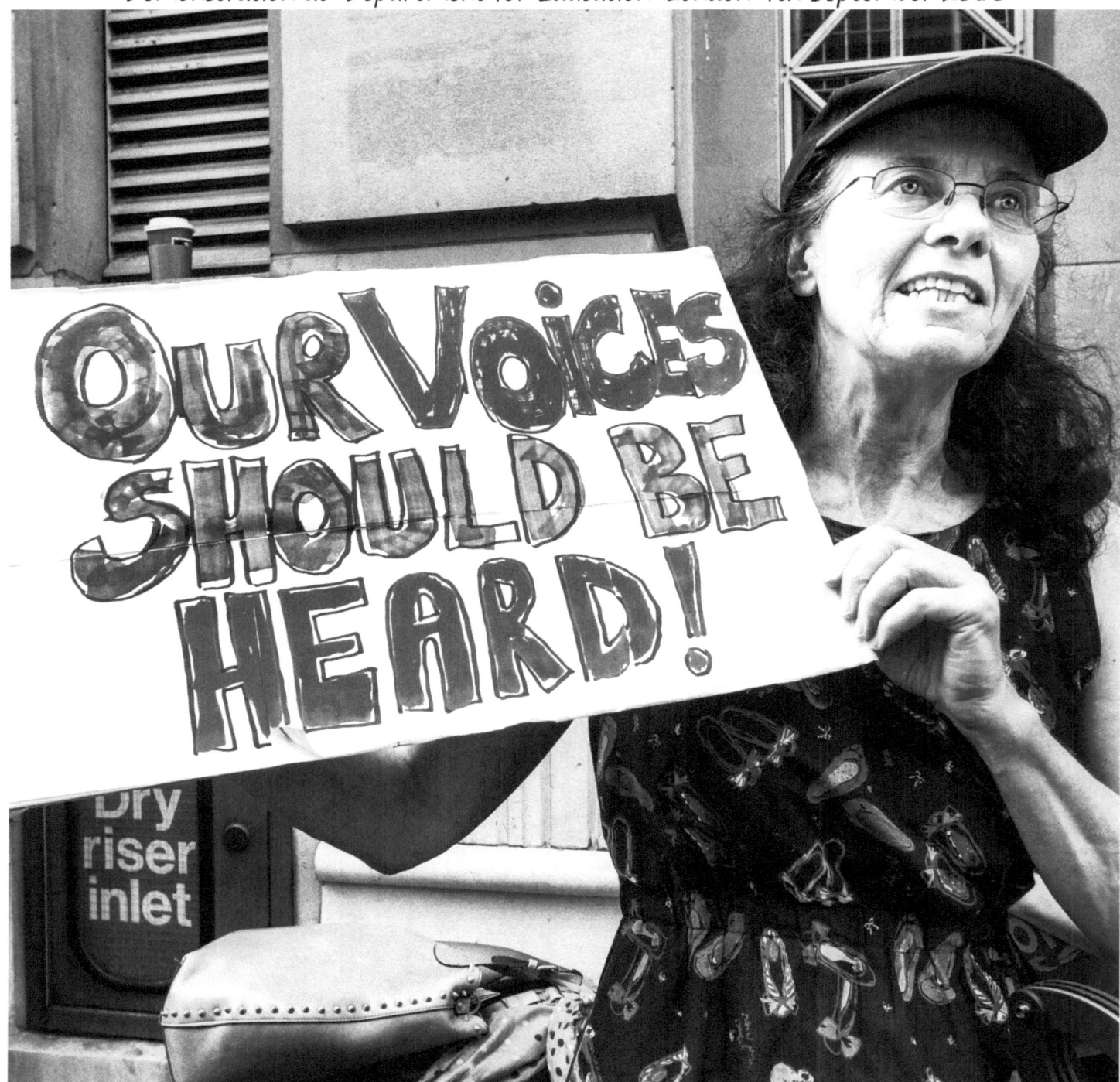

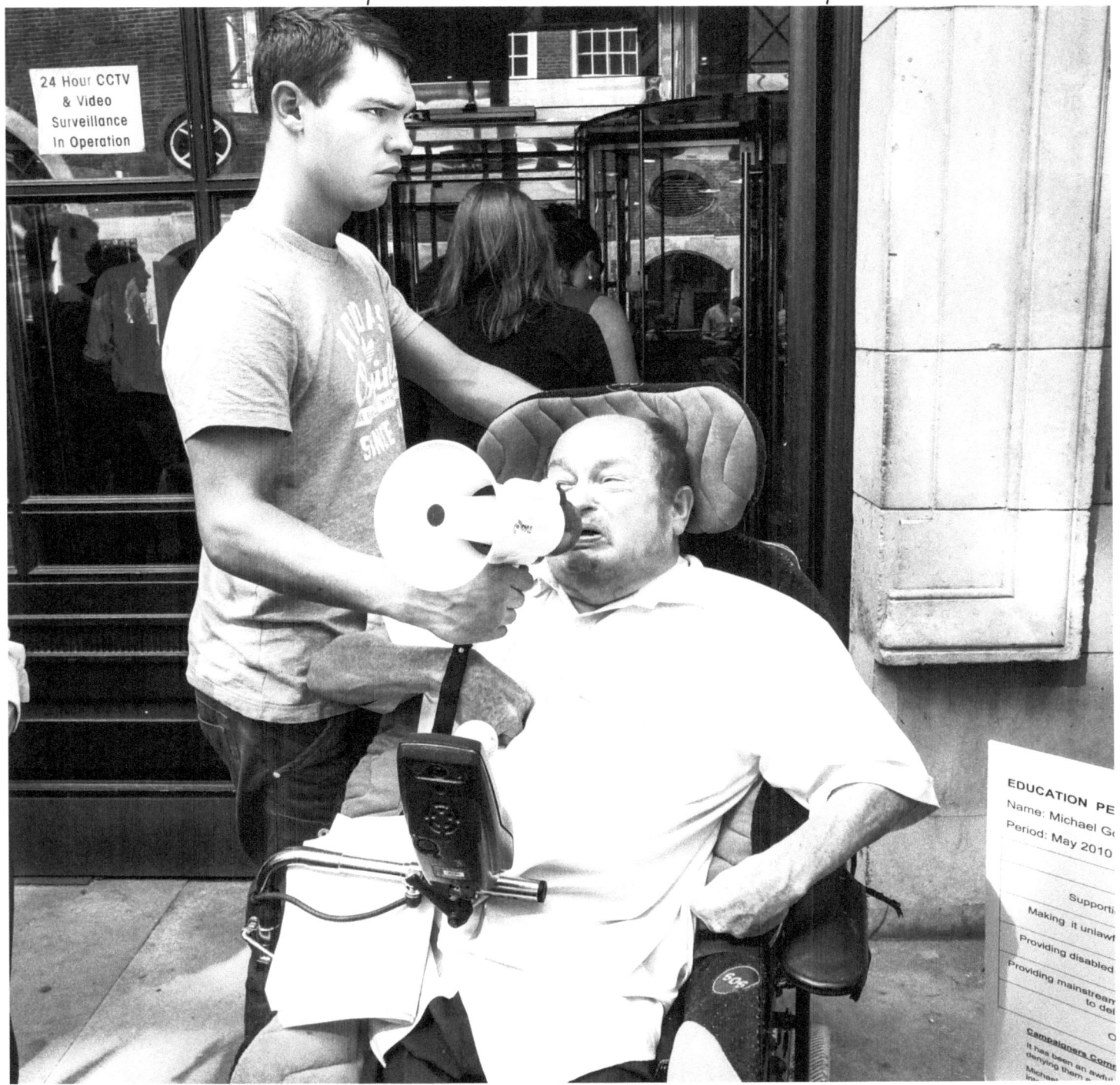

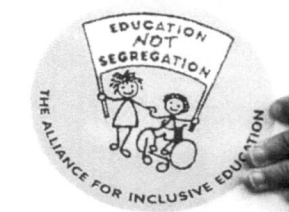

EDUCATION PERFORMANCE REPORT CARD

Name: Michael Gove & the Coalition Government

Period: May 2010 – July 2013

SUBJECT	GOOD	FAIR	FAILED
Supporting CHOICE of mainstream education			
Making it unlawful to force disabled learners into segregated education			✗
Providing disabled learners with the support they need to access mainstream education			✗
Providing mainstream schools with the money and support they need to deliver inclusive education practice			✗
OVERALL PERFORMANCE			✗
			✗
			✓

Campaigners Comments:

It has been an awful year for Michael Gove and the Coalition Govt w
denying them a right to choose to be included in mainstr

Michael Gove and the Coalition Govt
international obligations (U

Signed

20

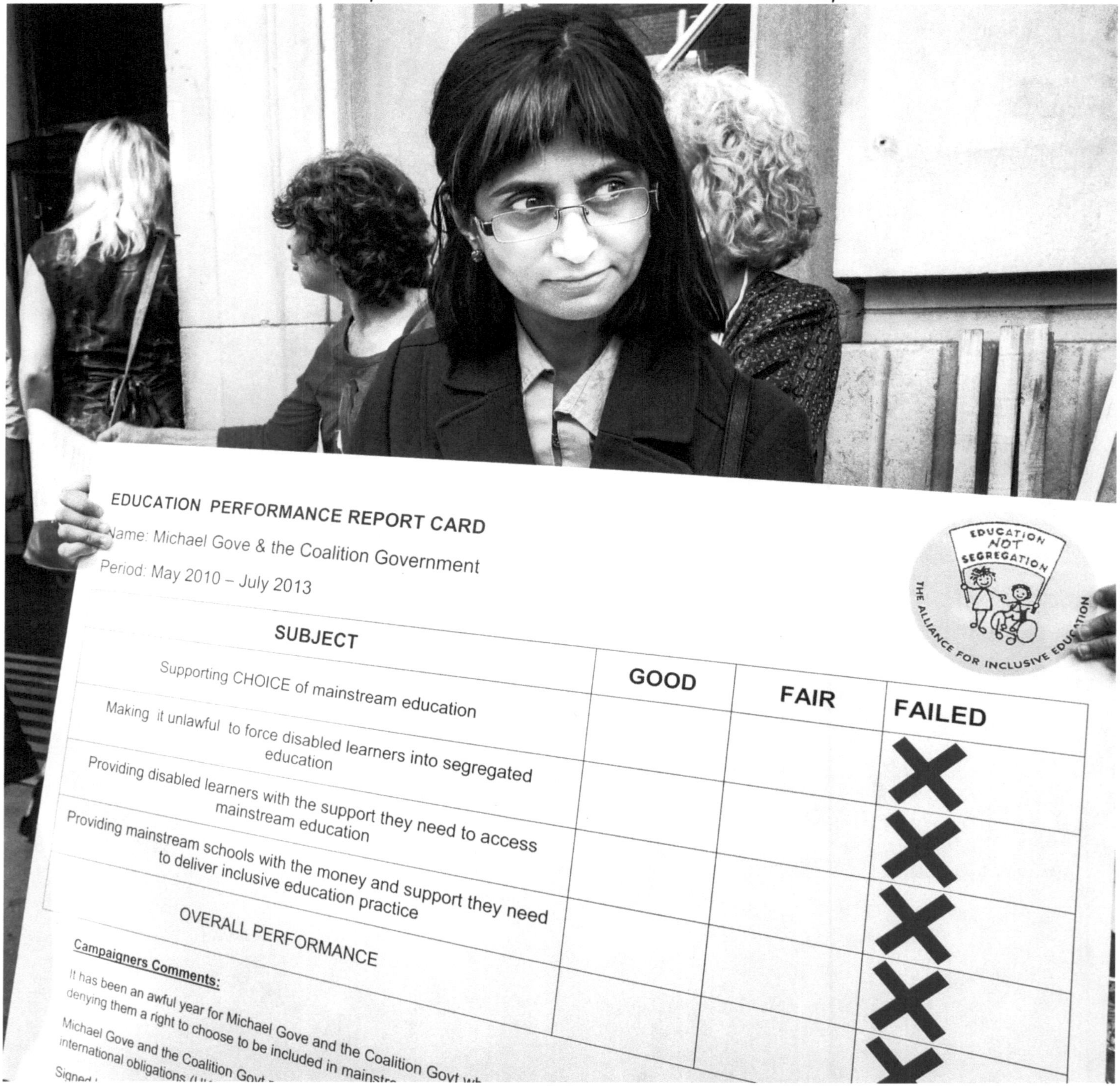

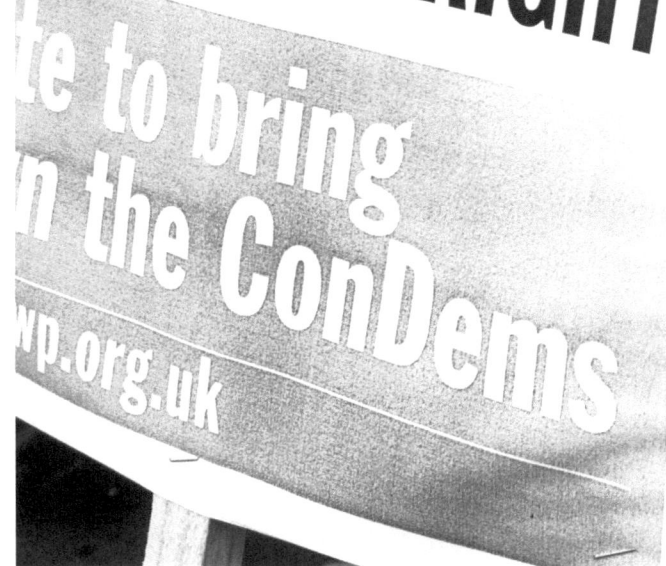

DEFEND DISABLED PEOPLE'S

BENEFITS ●JOBS
SERVICES ●RIGHTS

...te to bring
...n the ConDems

...wp.org.uk

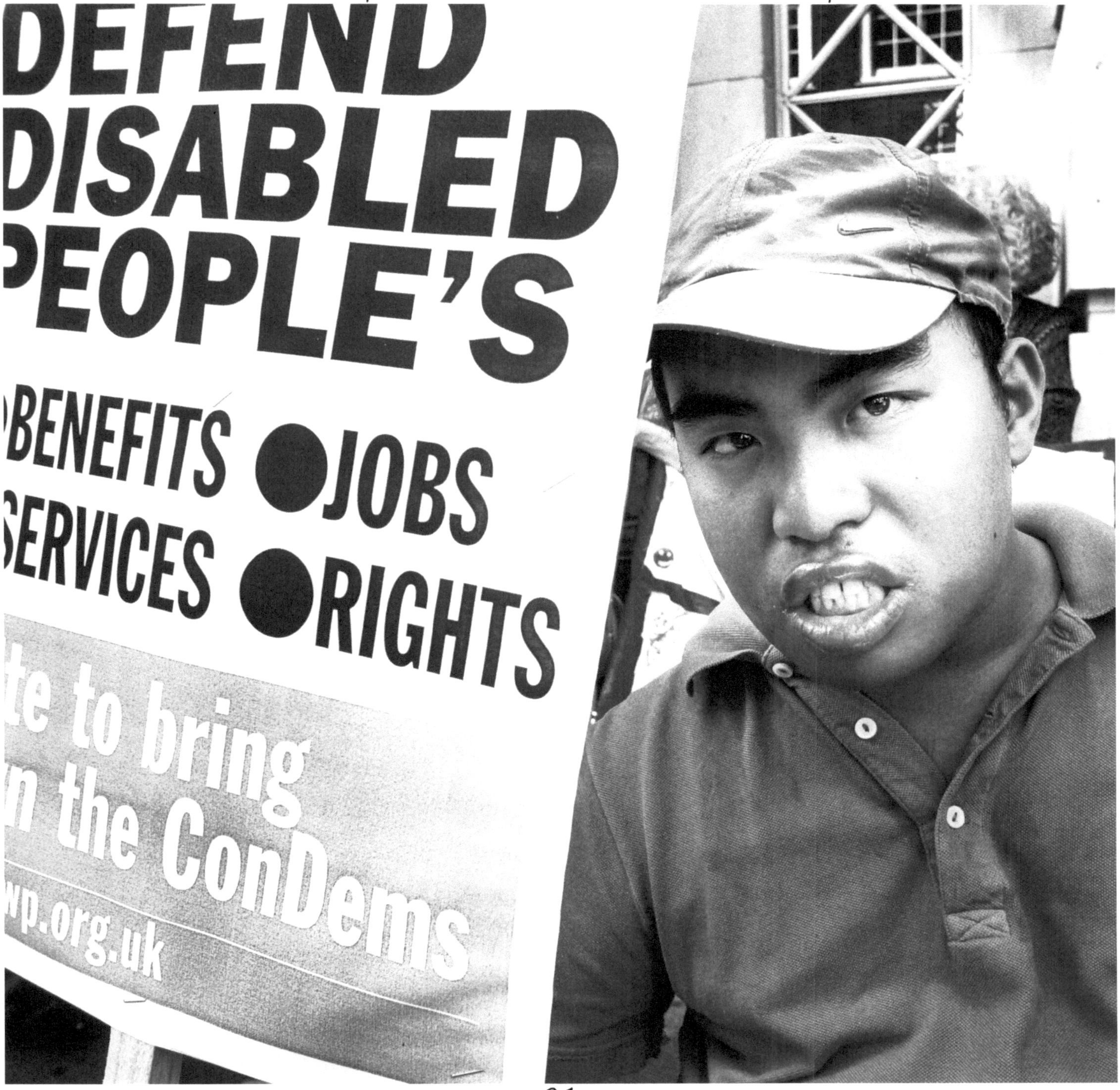

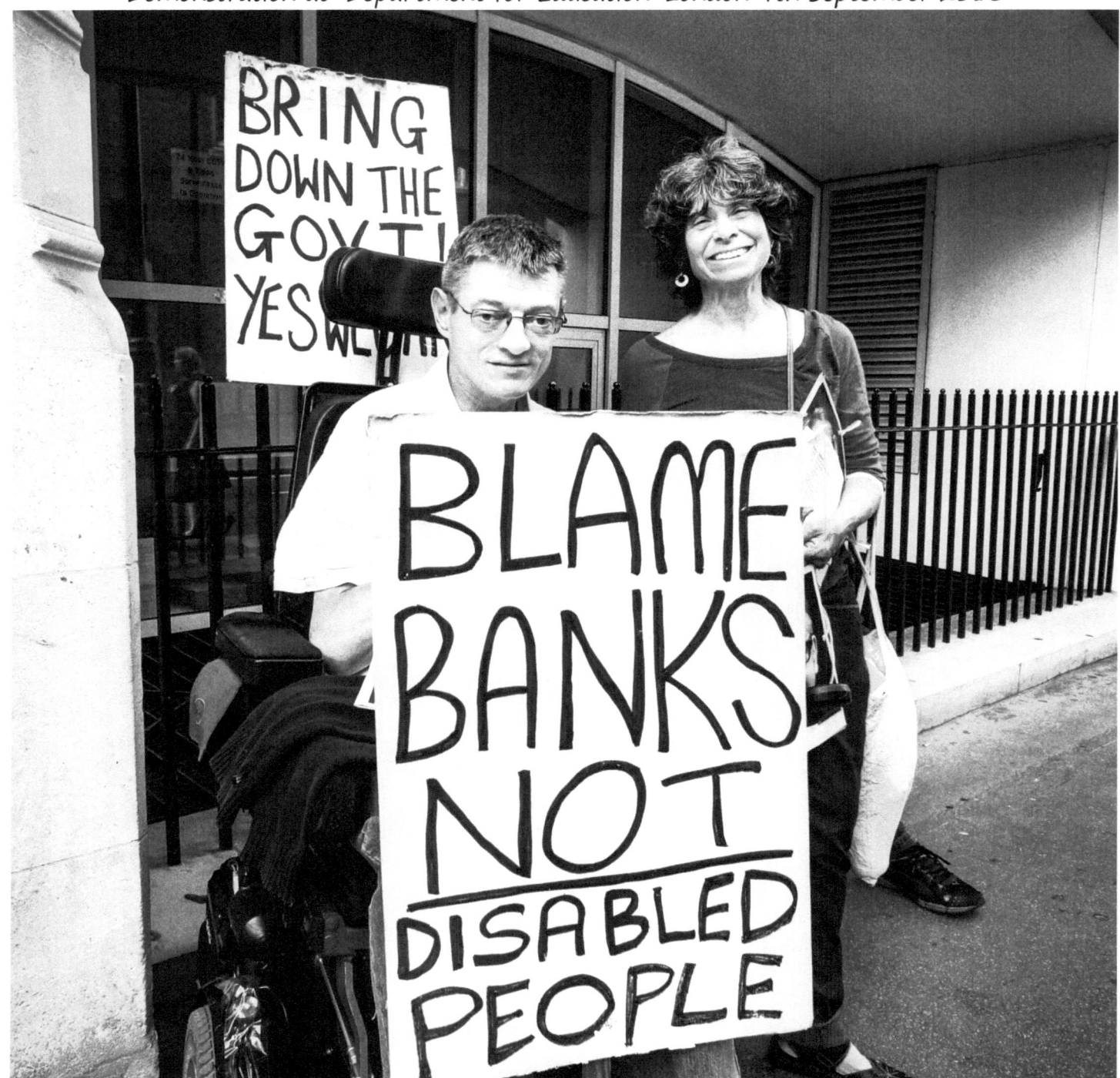

Demonstration at 'Department for Work and Pensions' London 4th September 2013

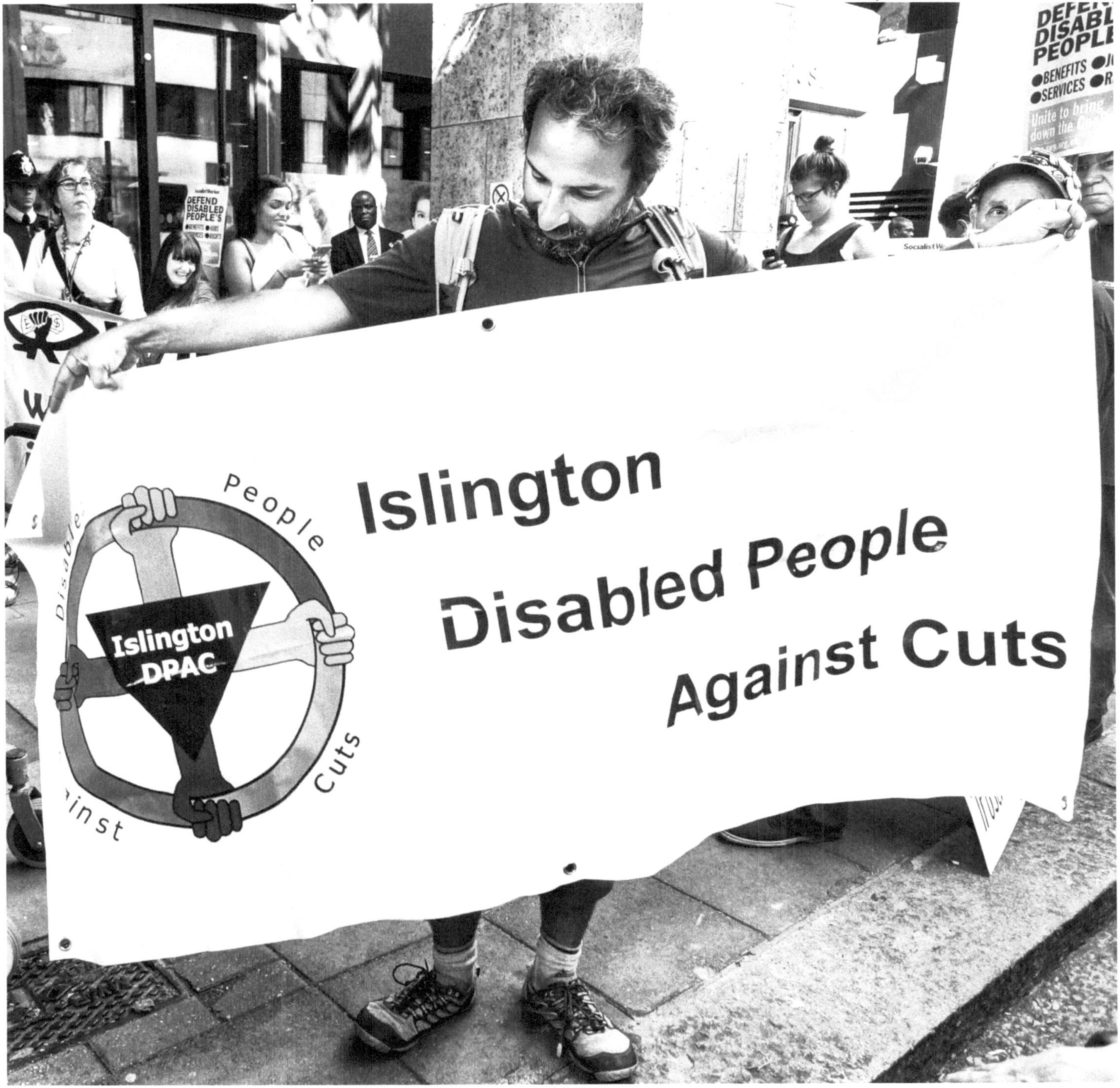

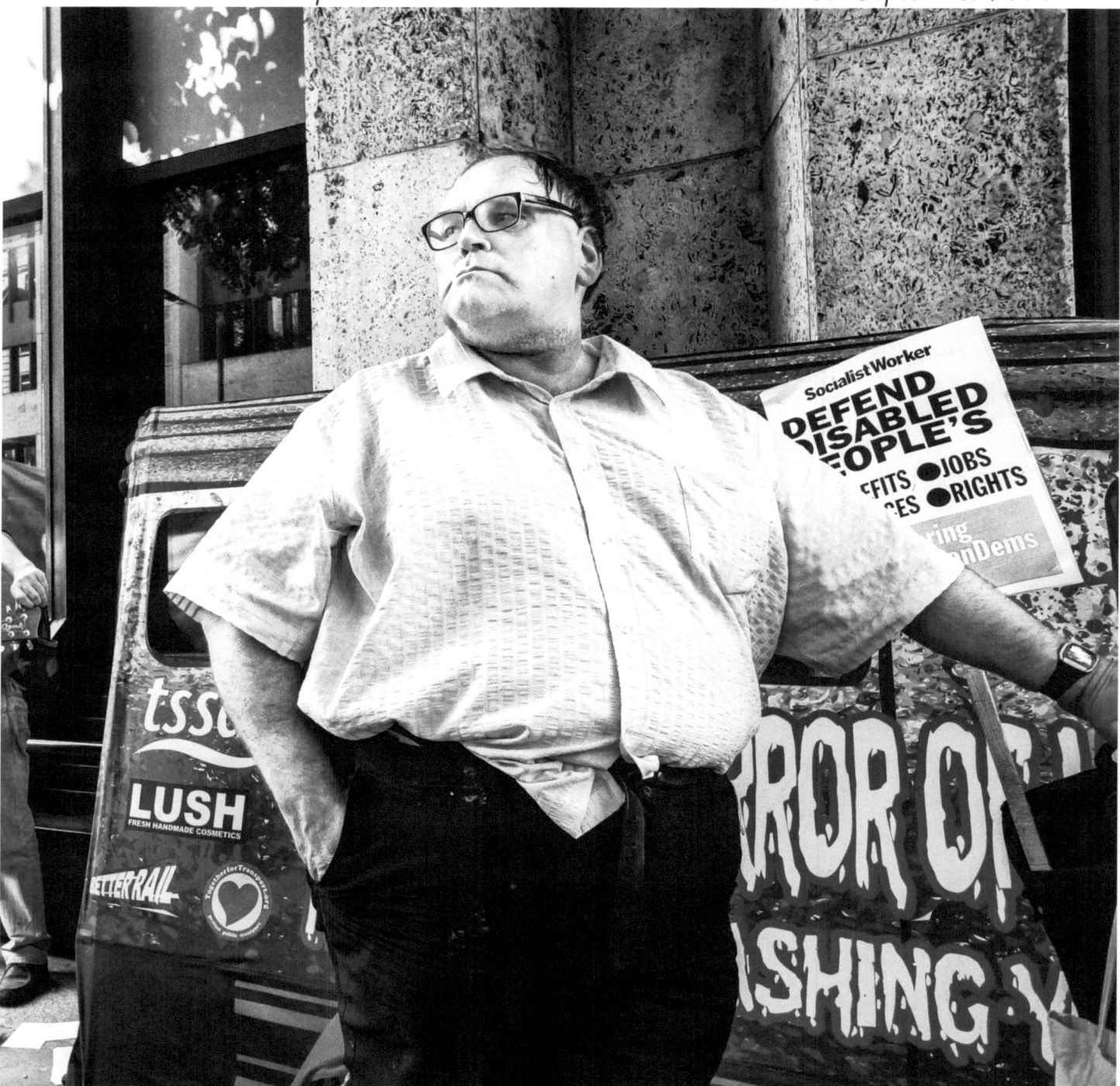

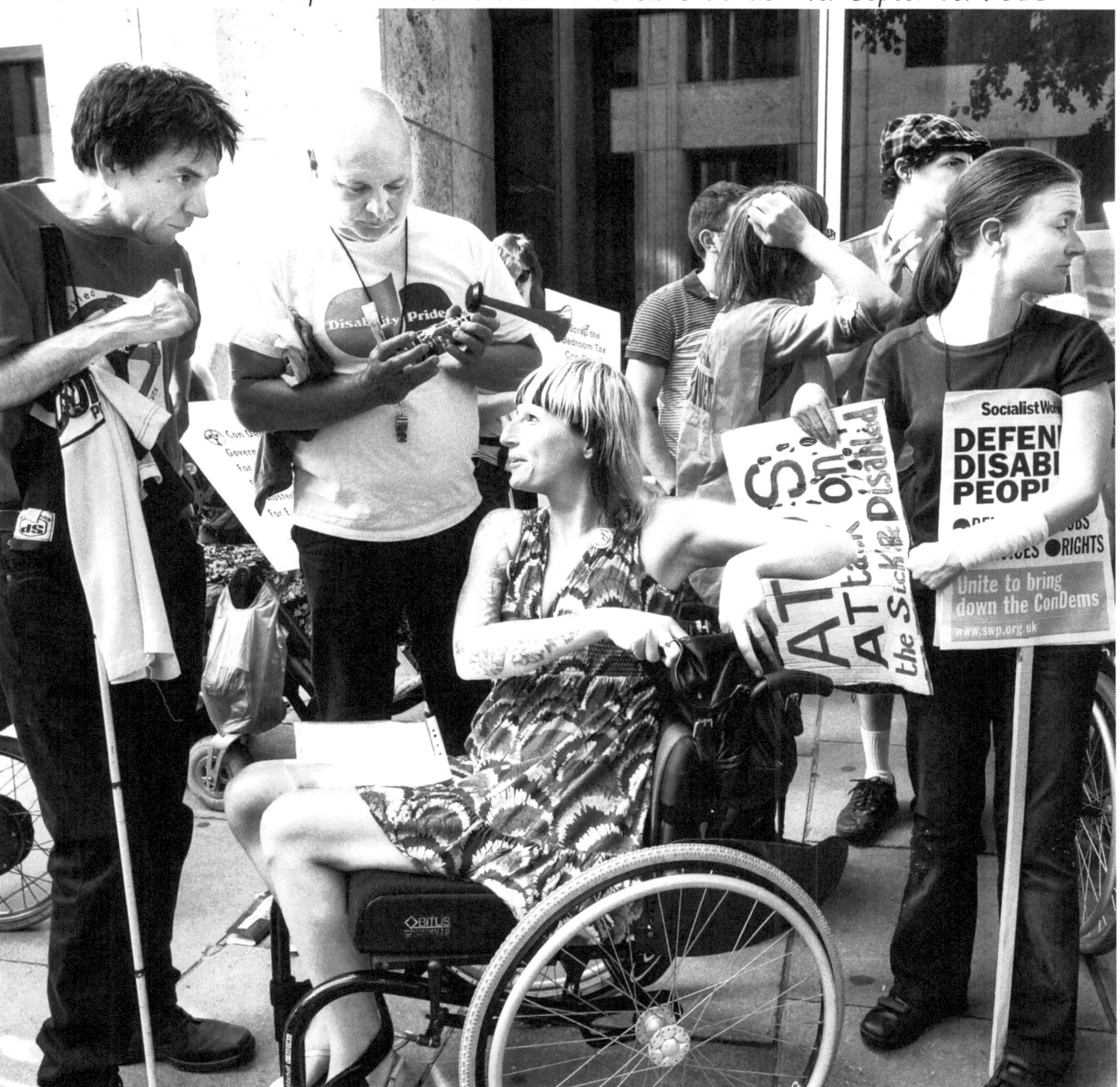

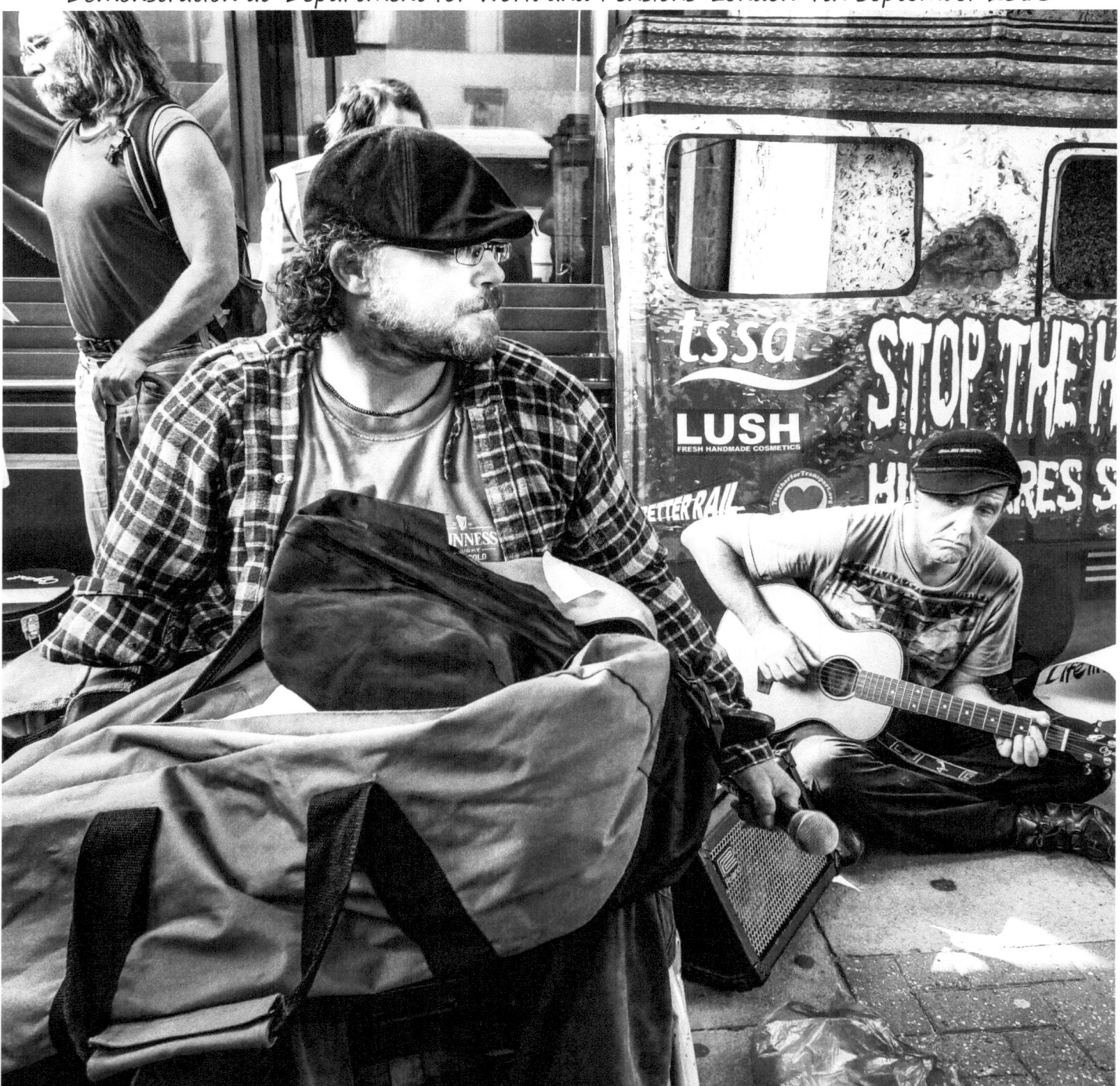

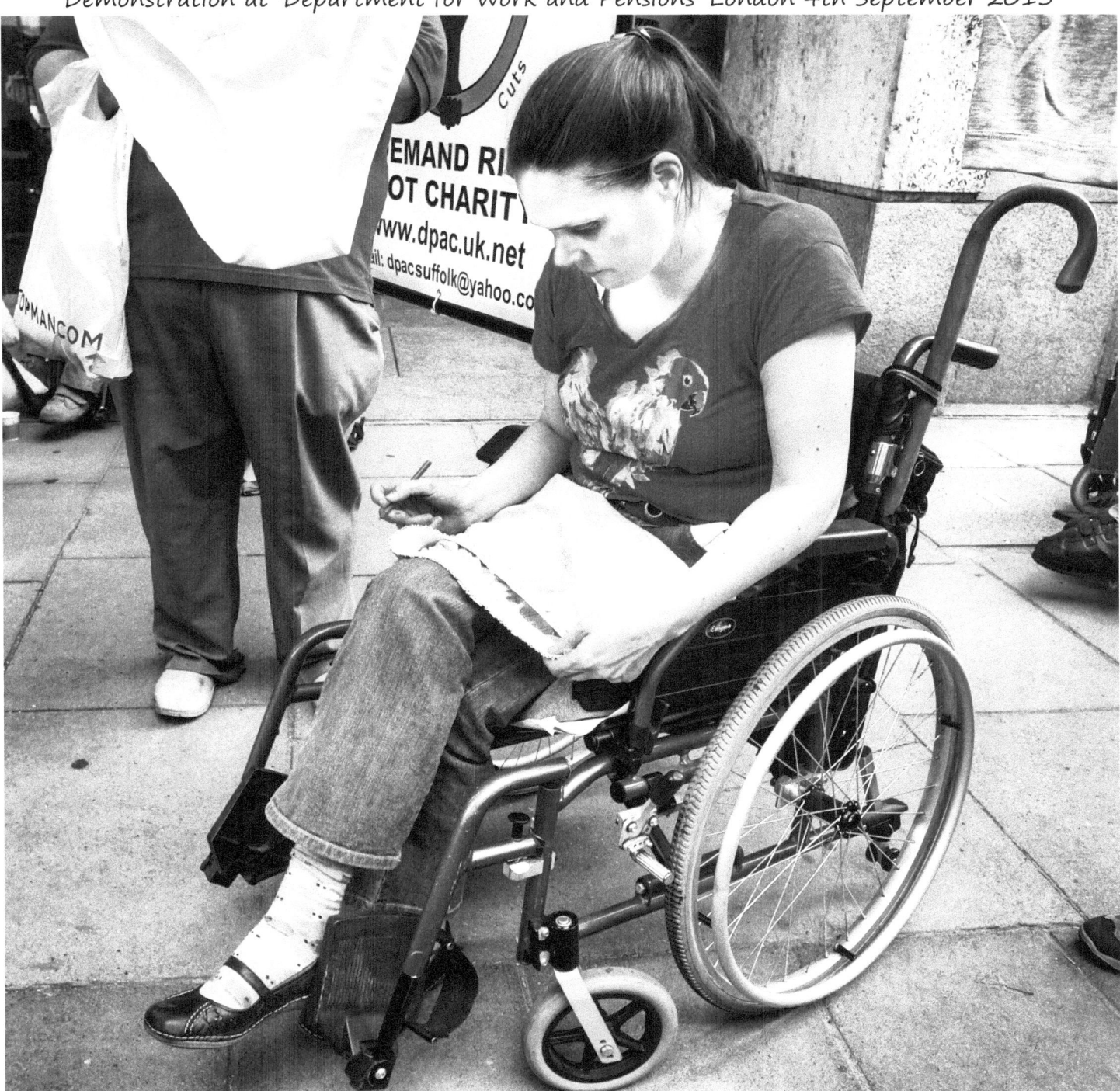

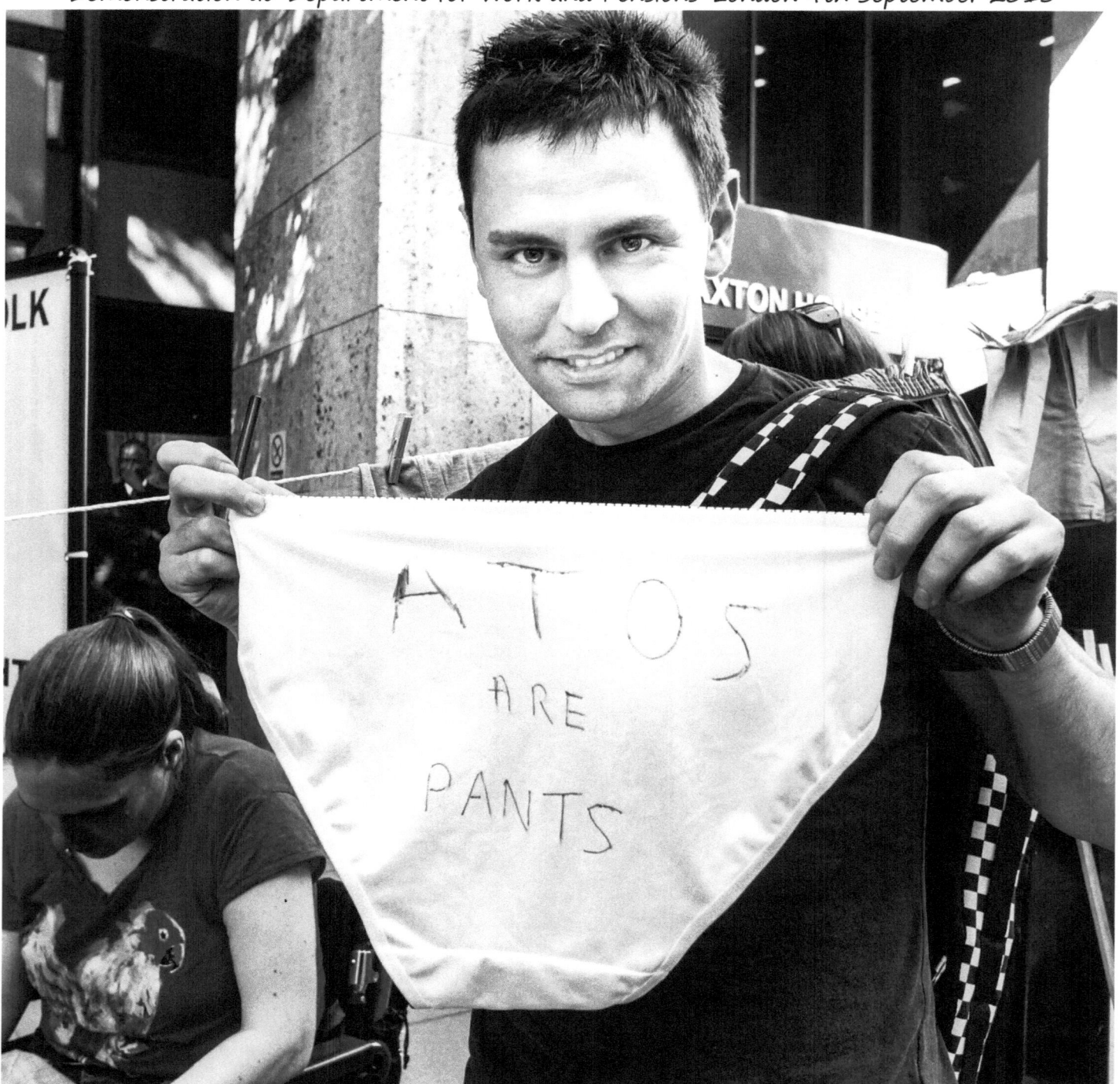

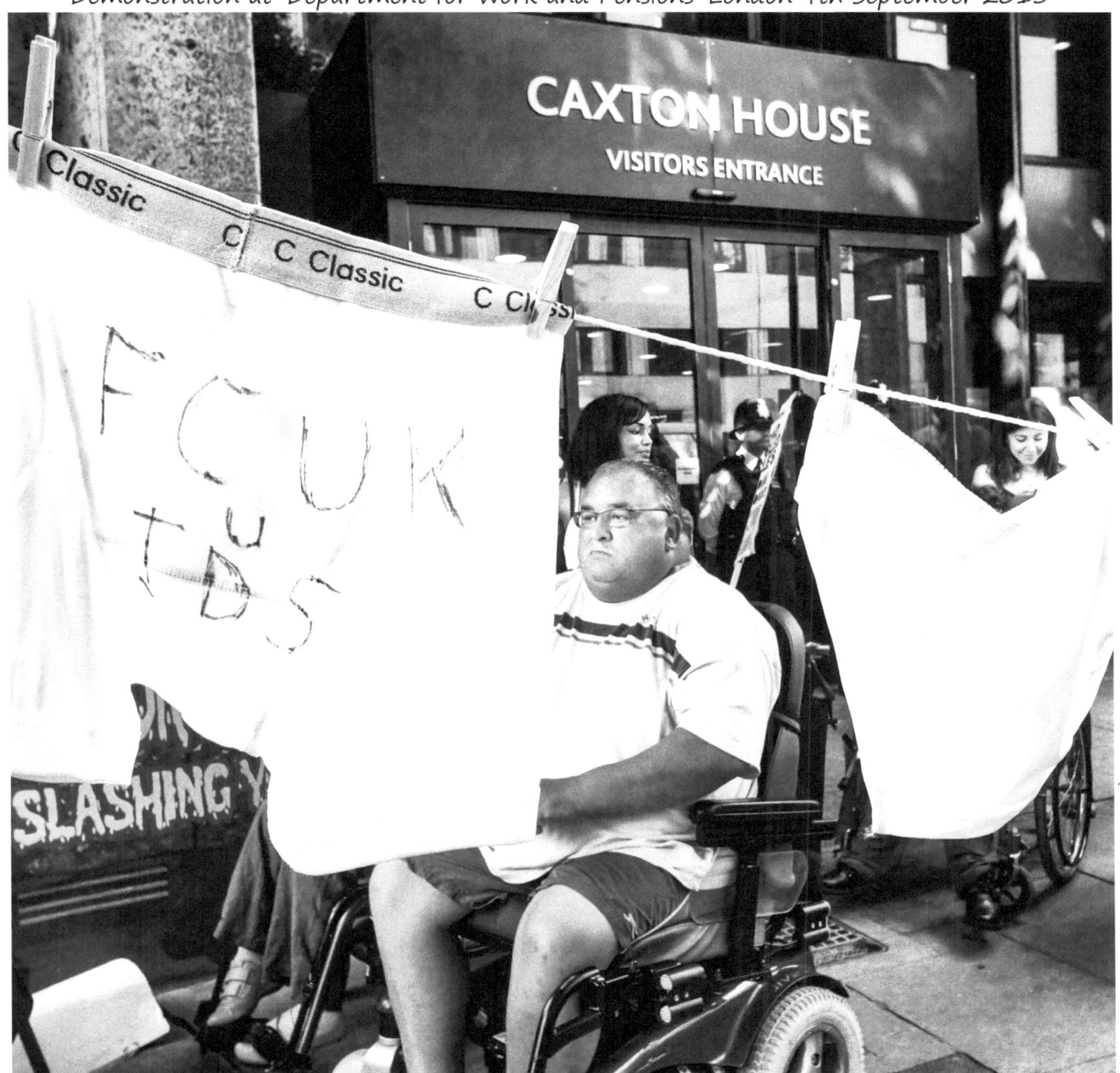

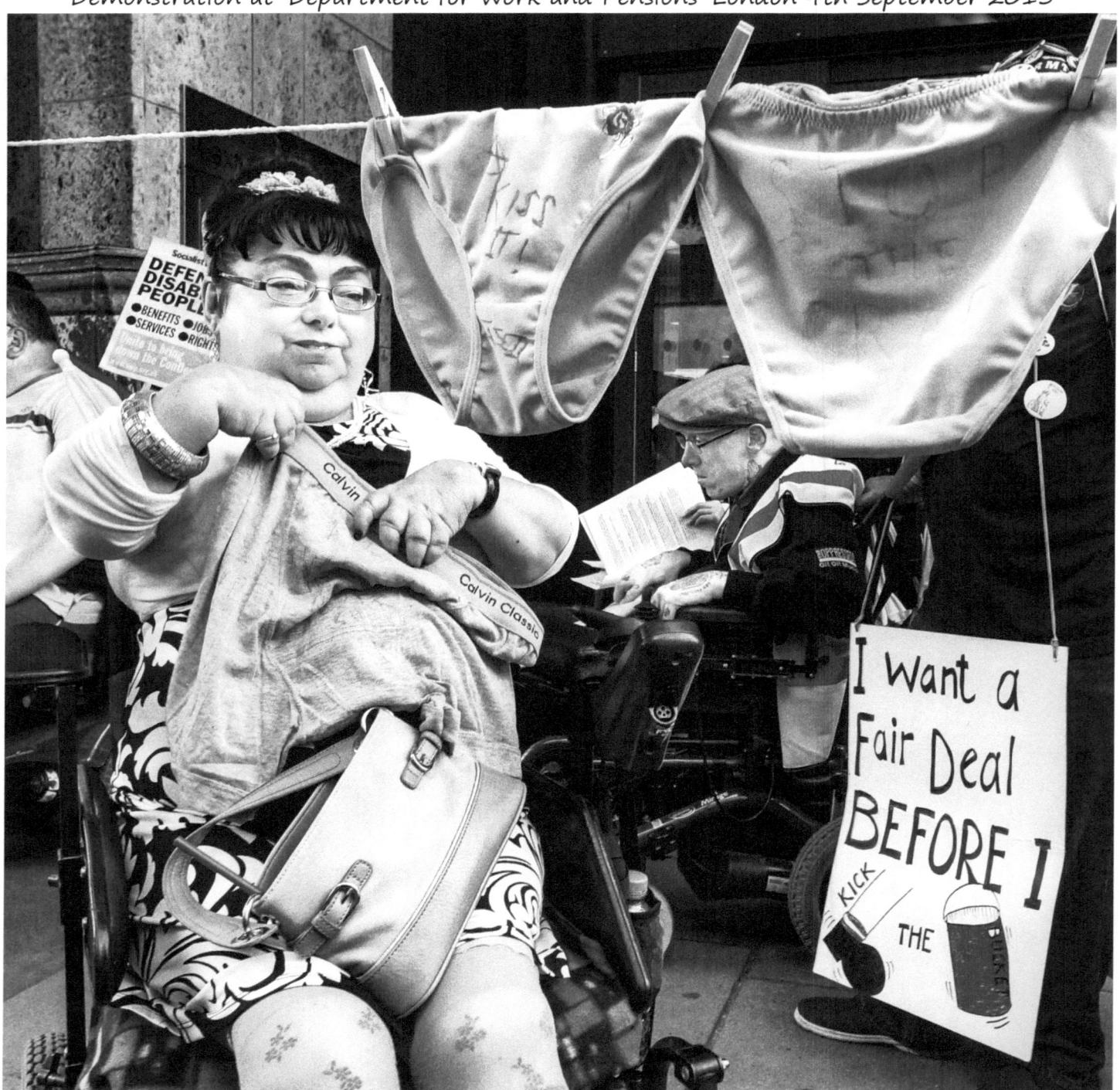

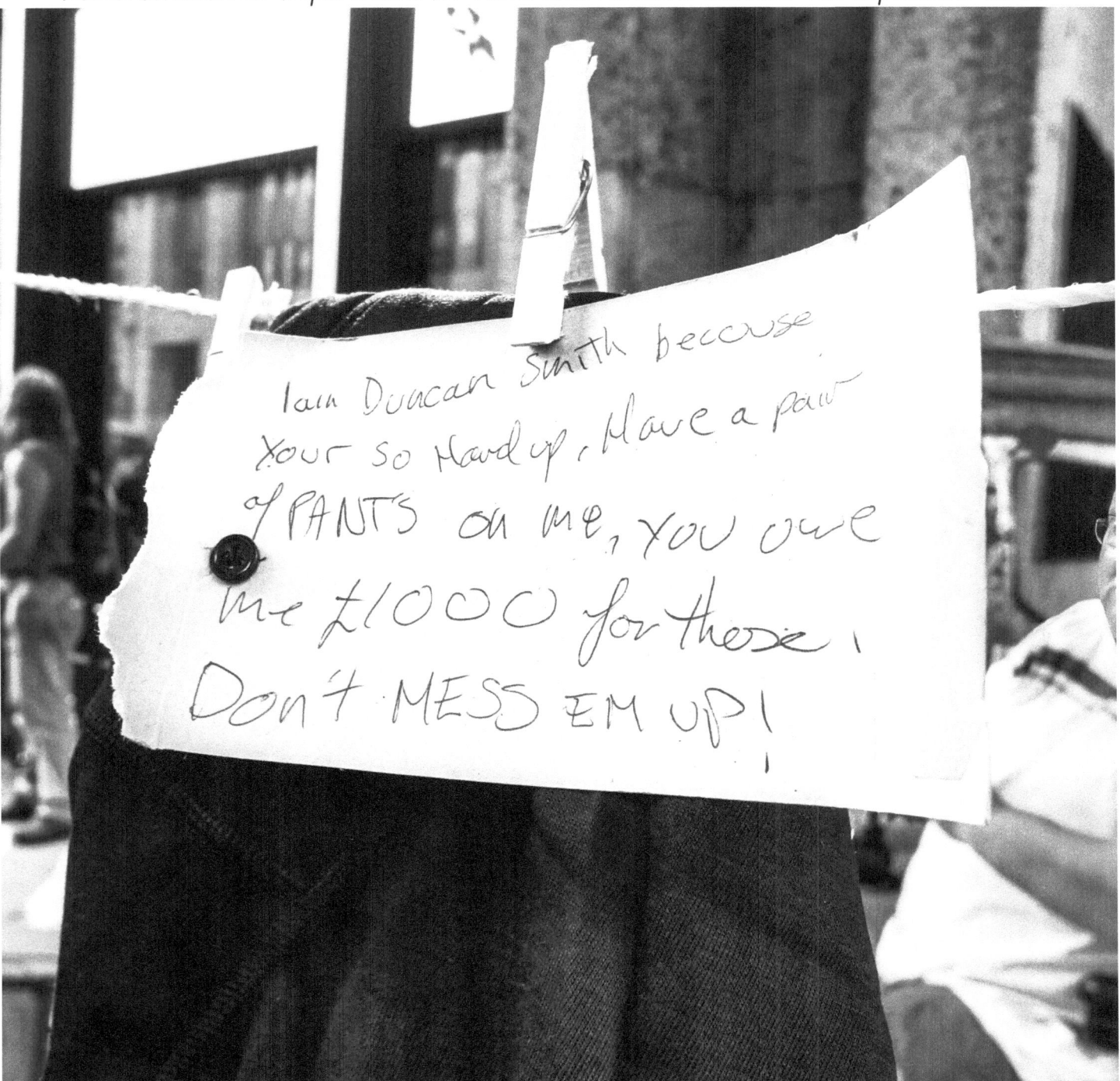

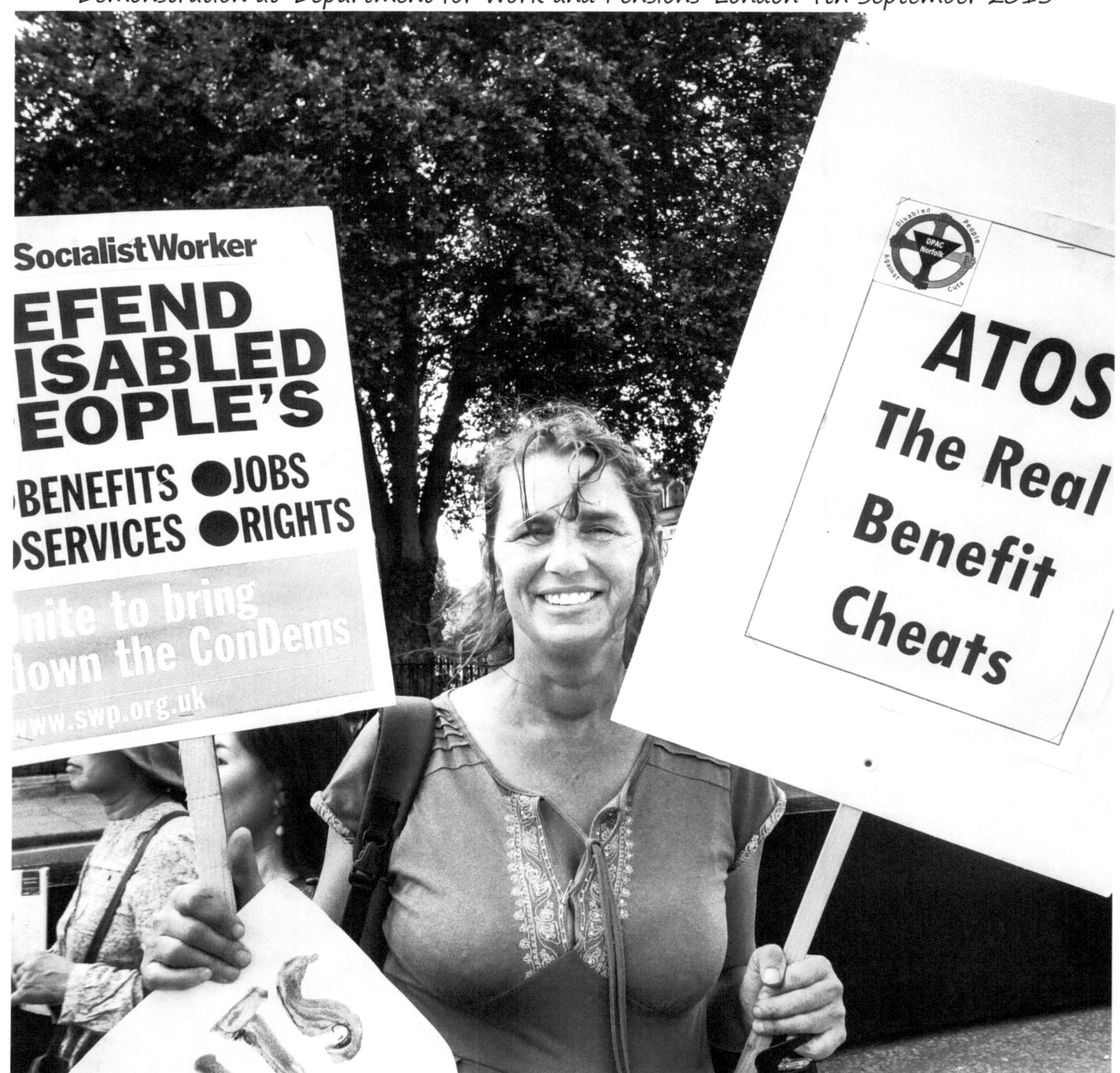

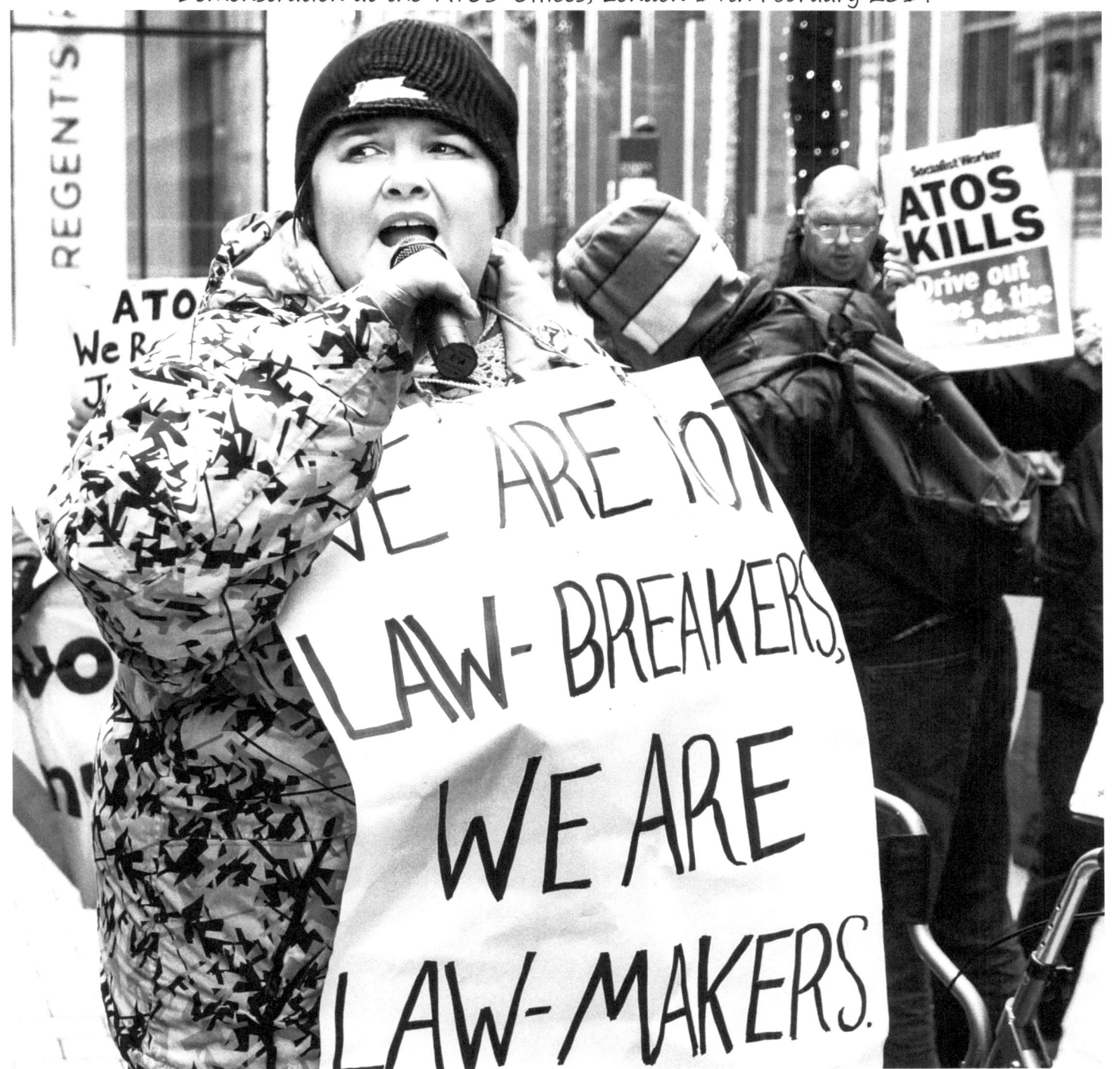

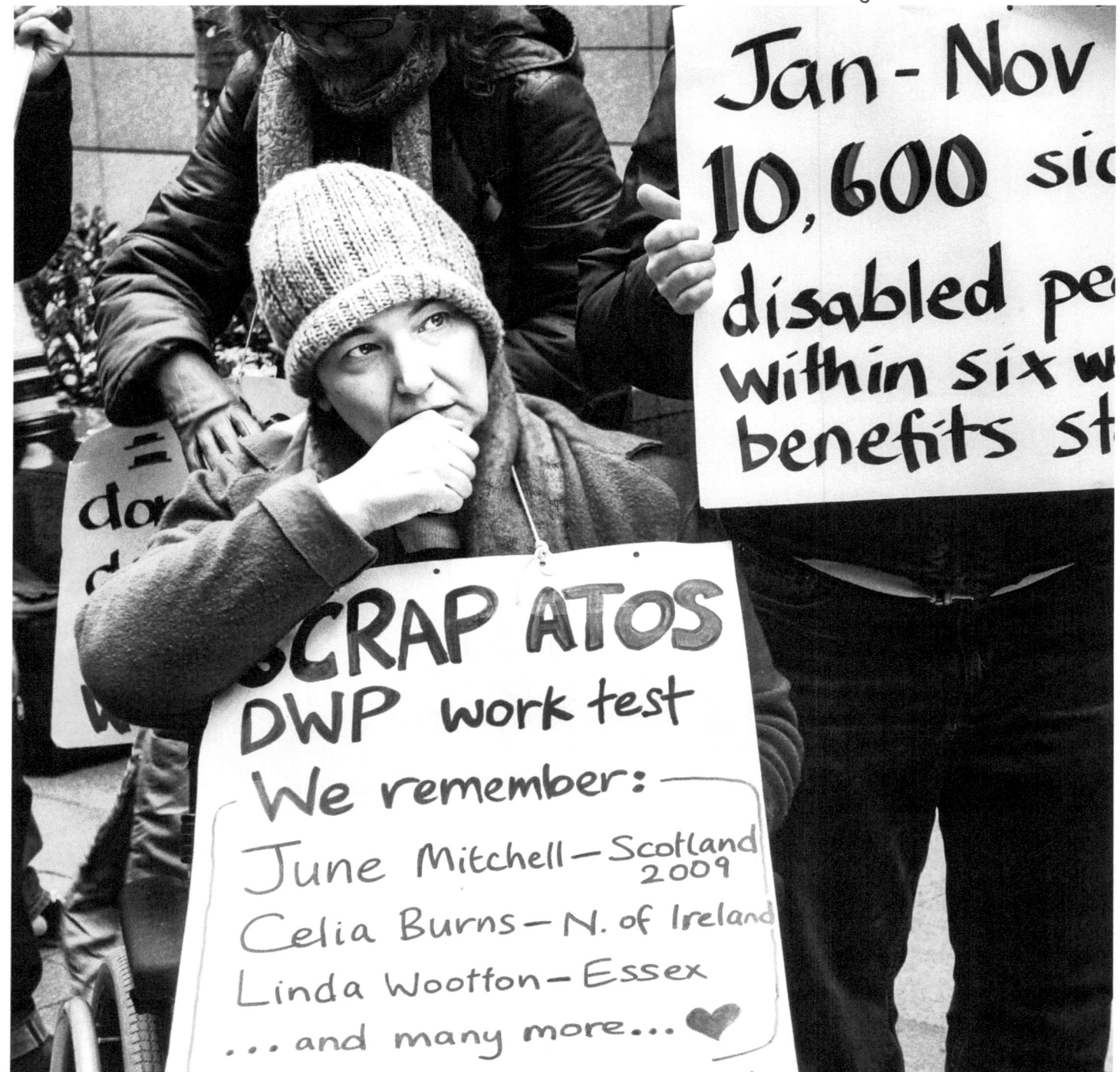

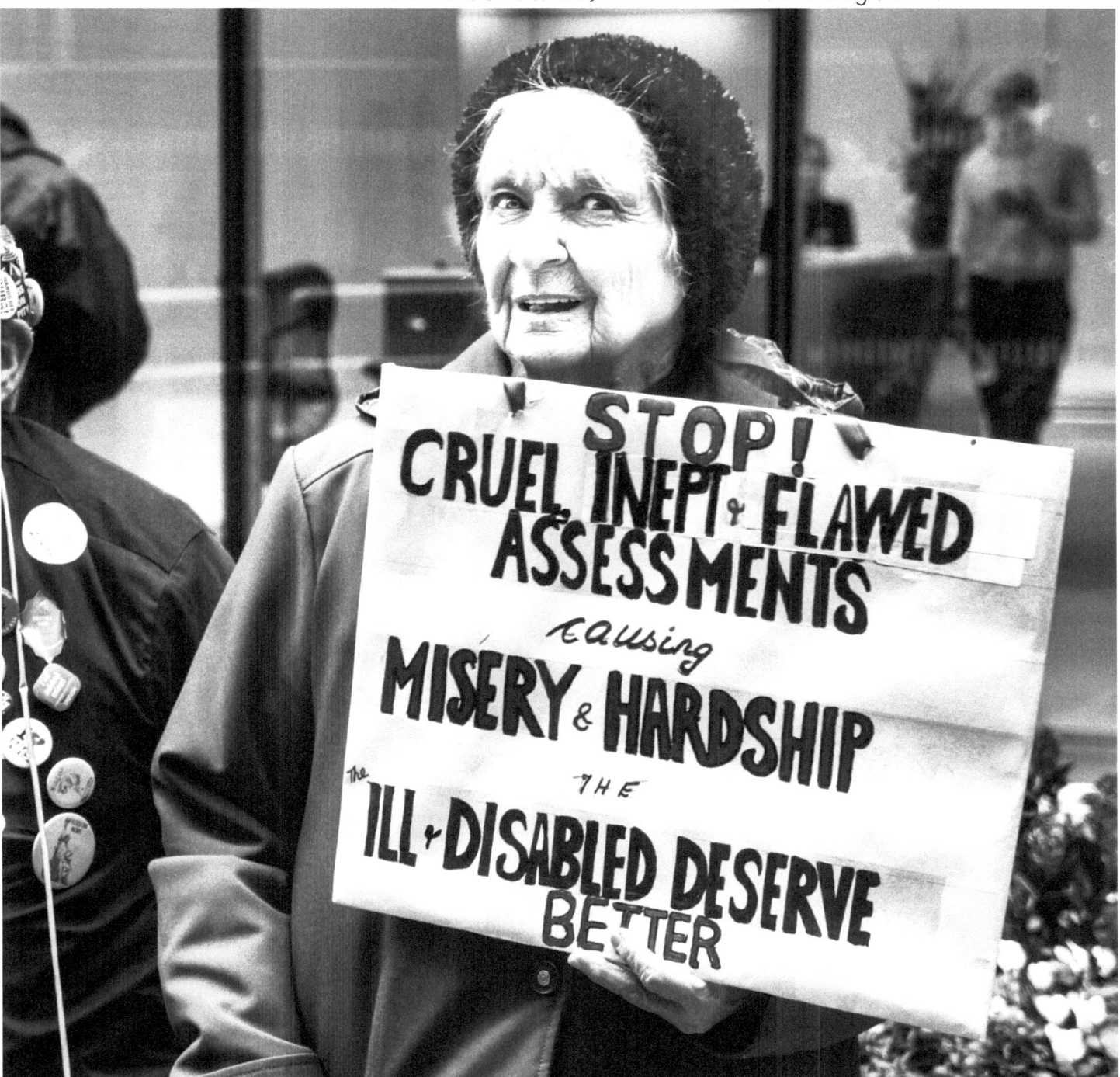

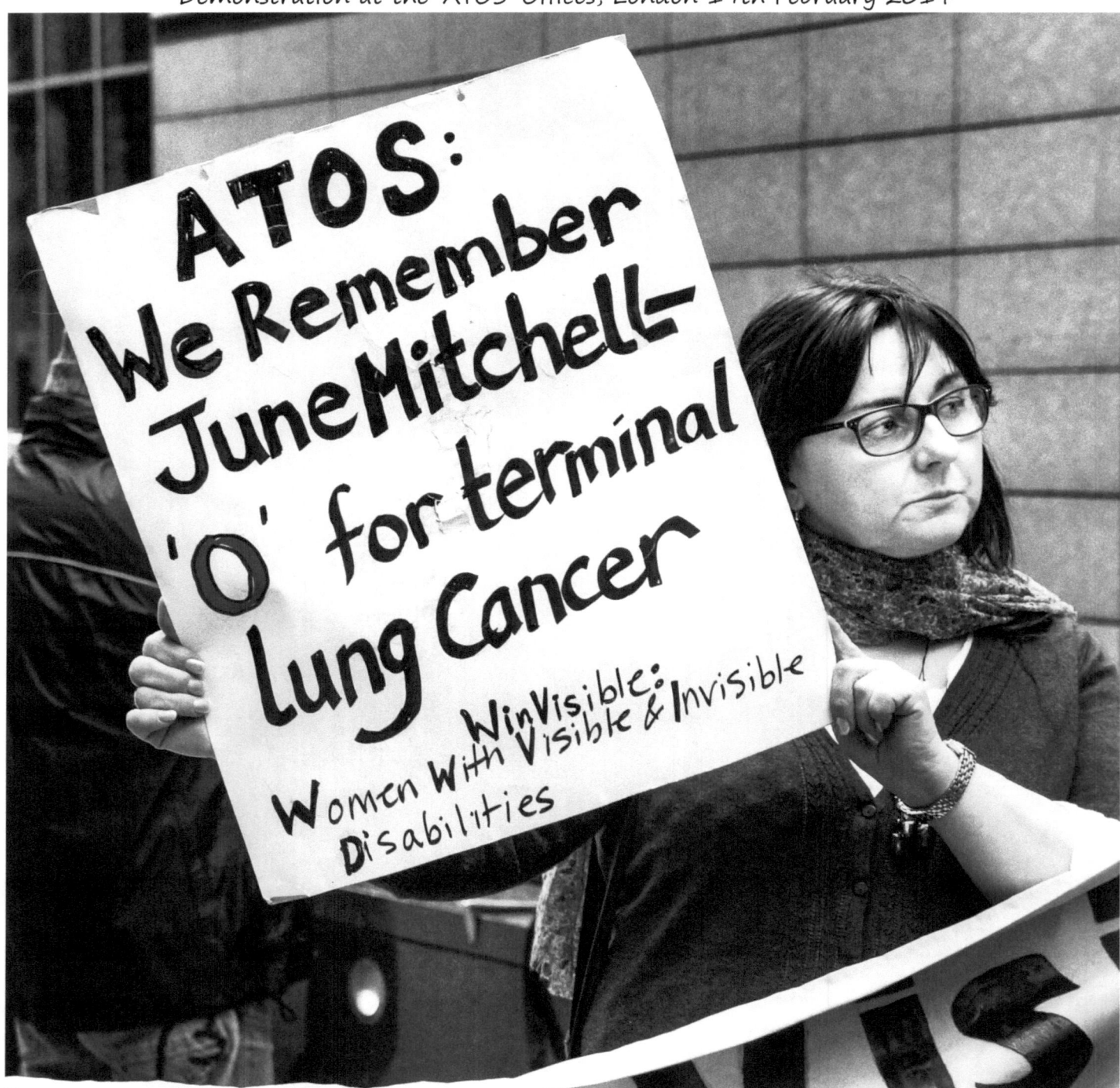

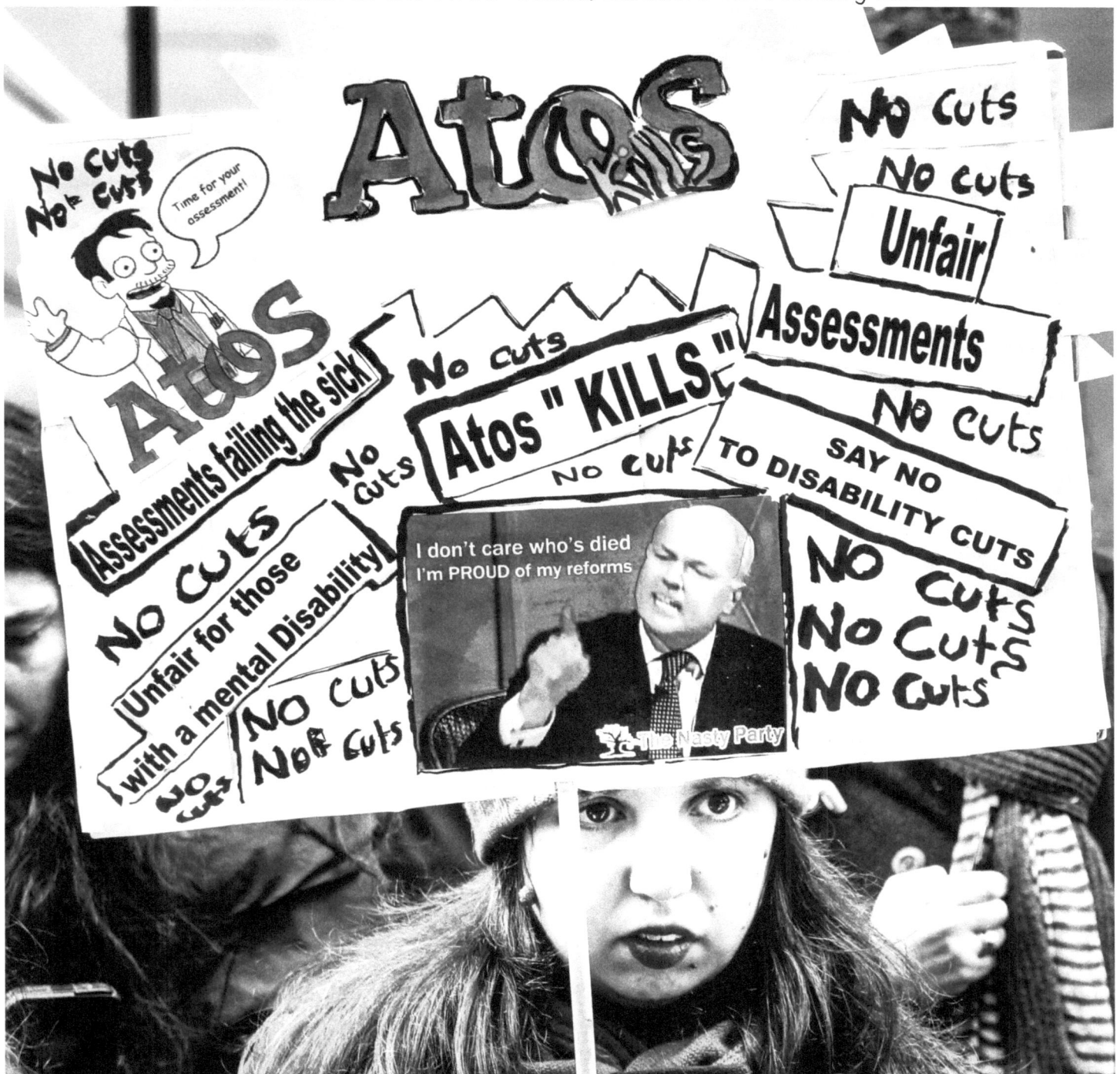

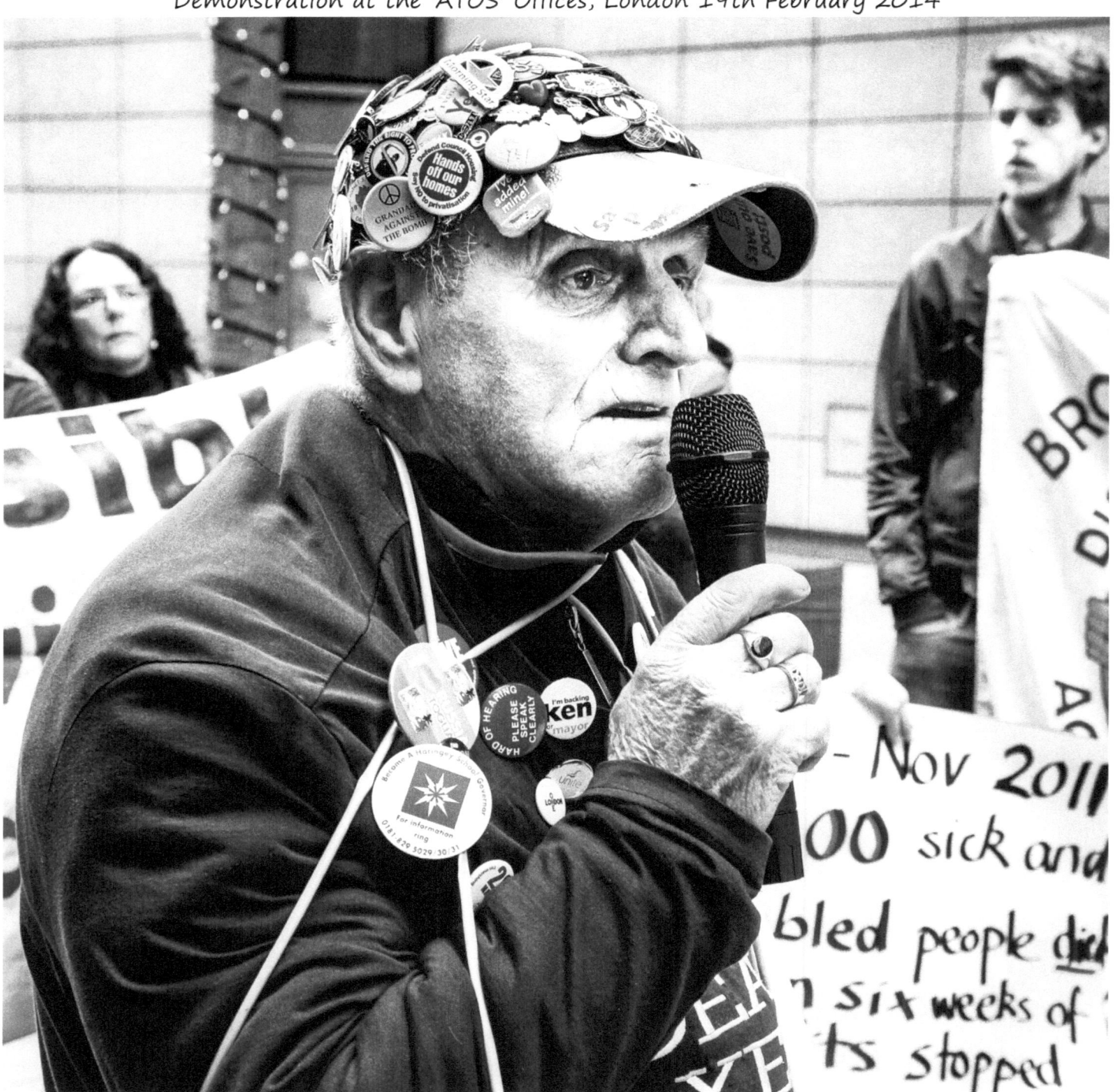

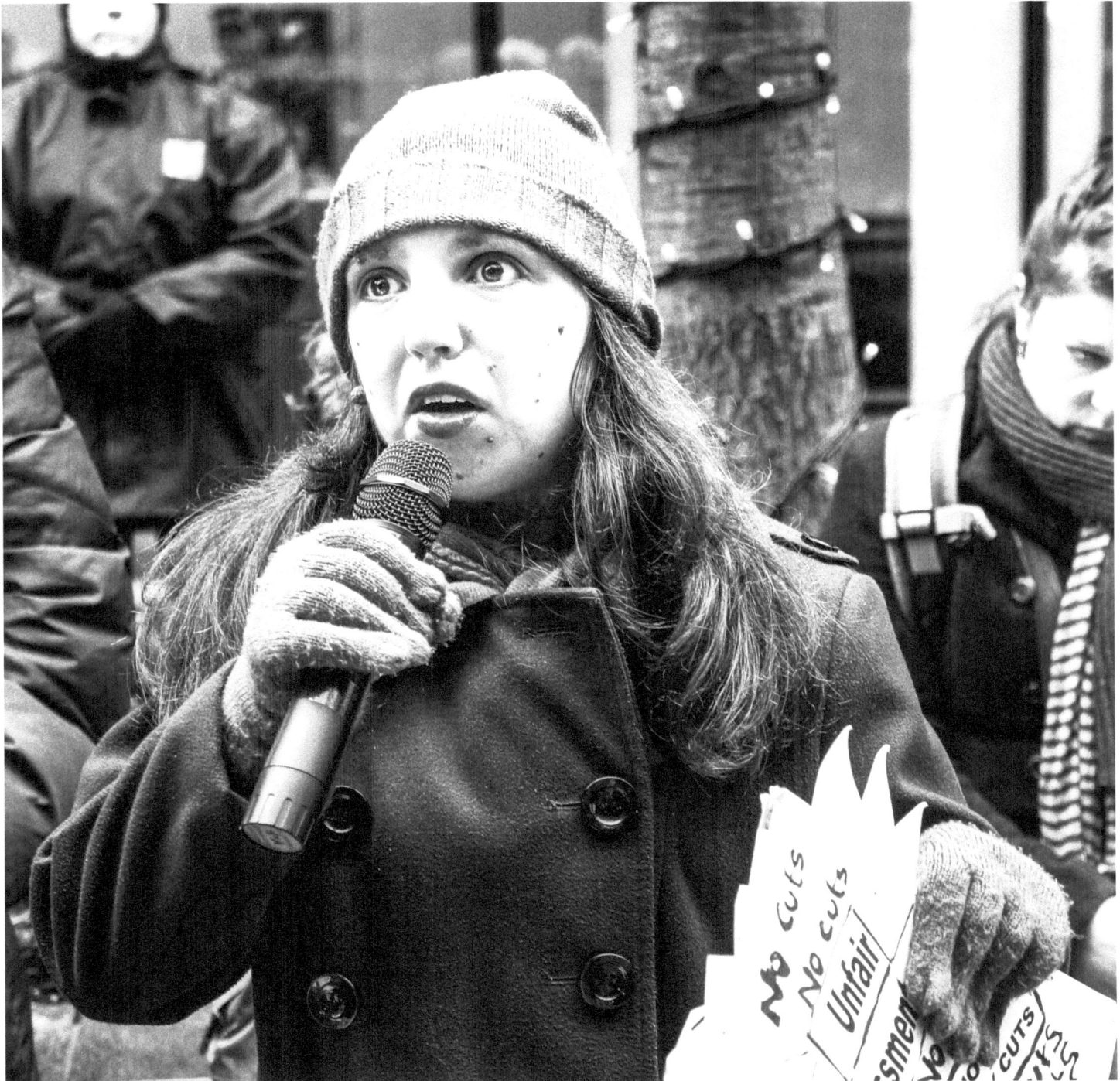

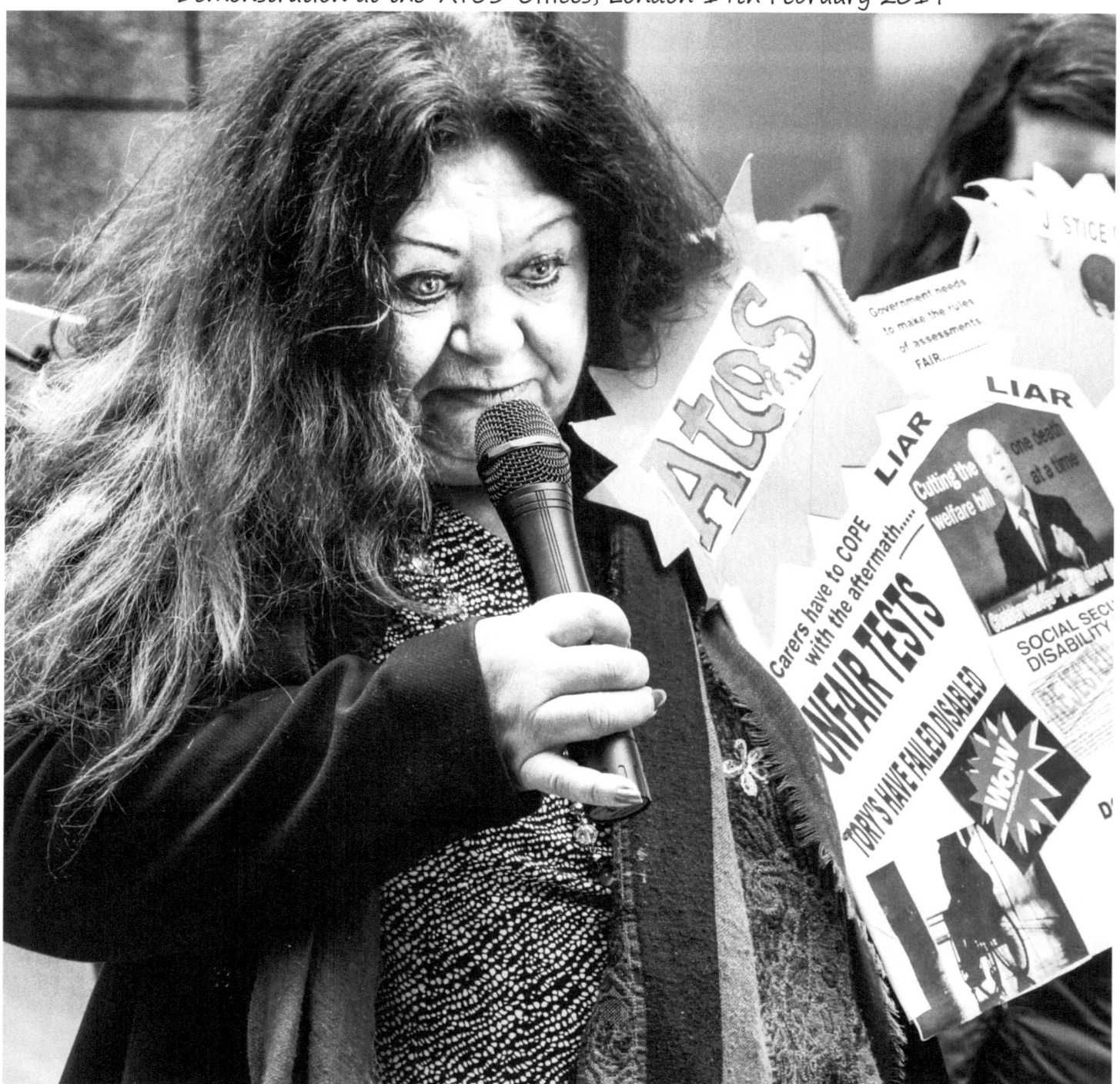

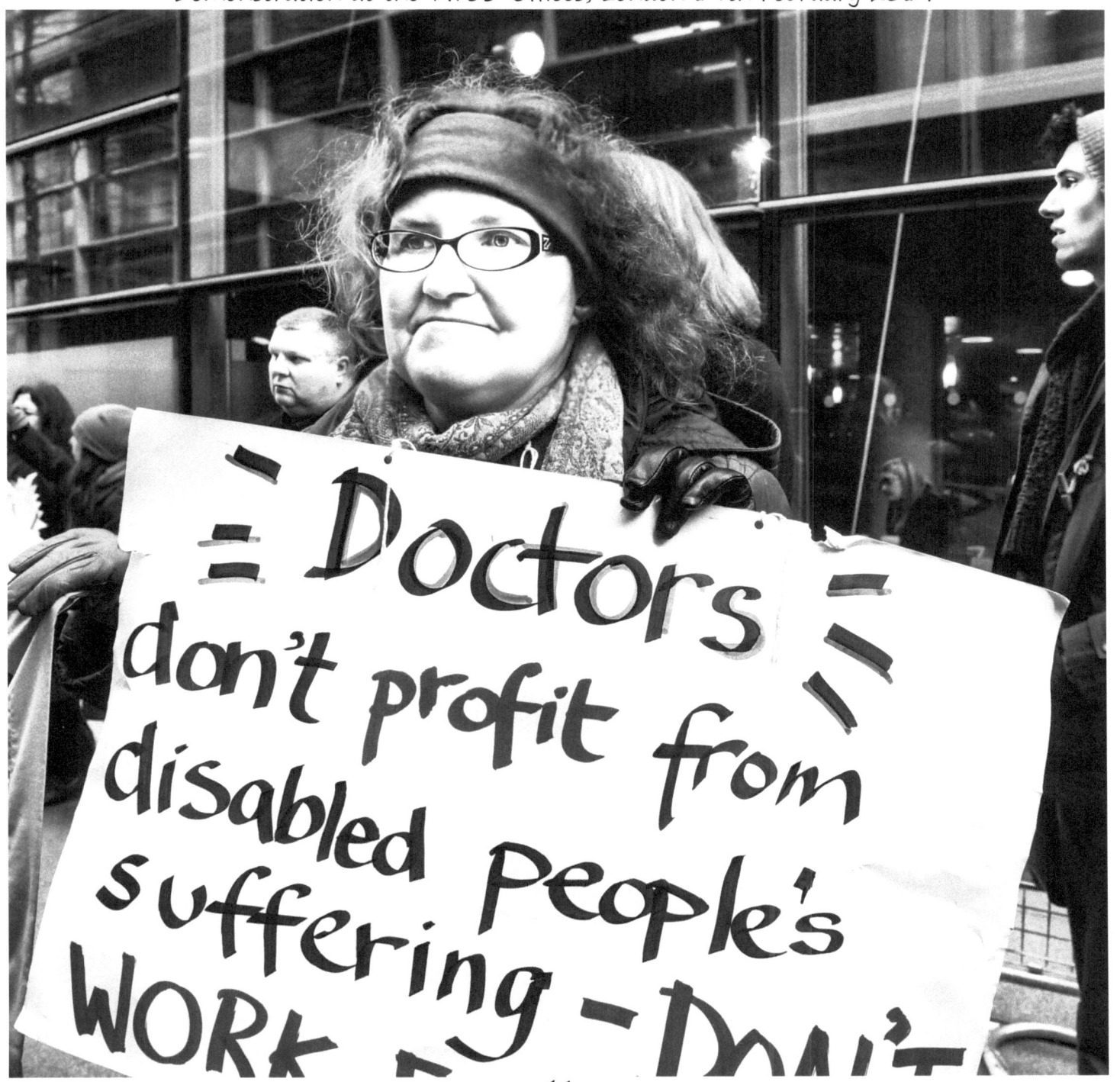

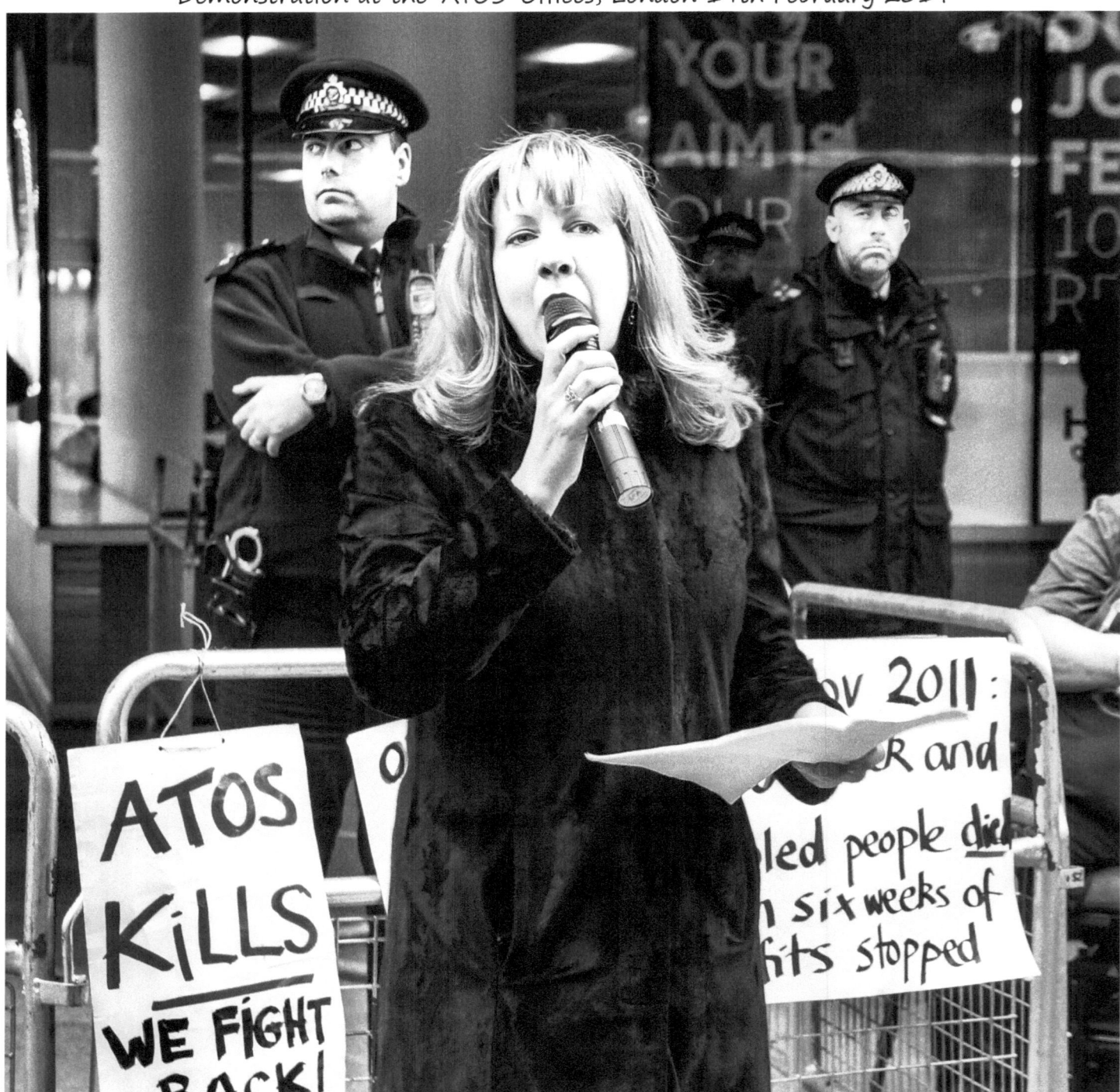

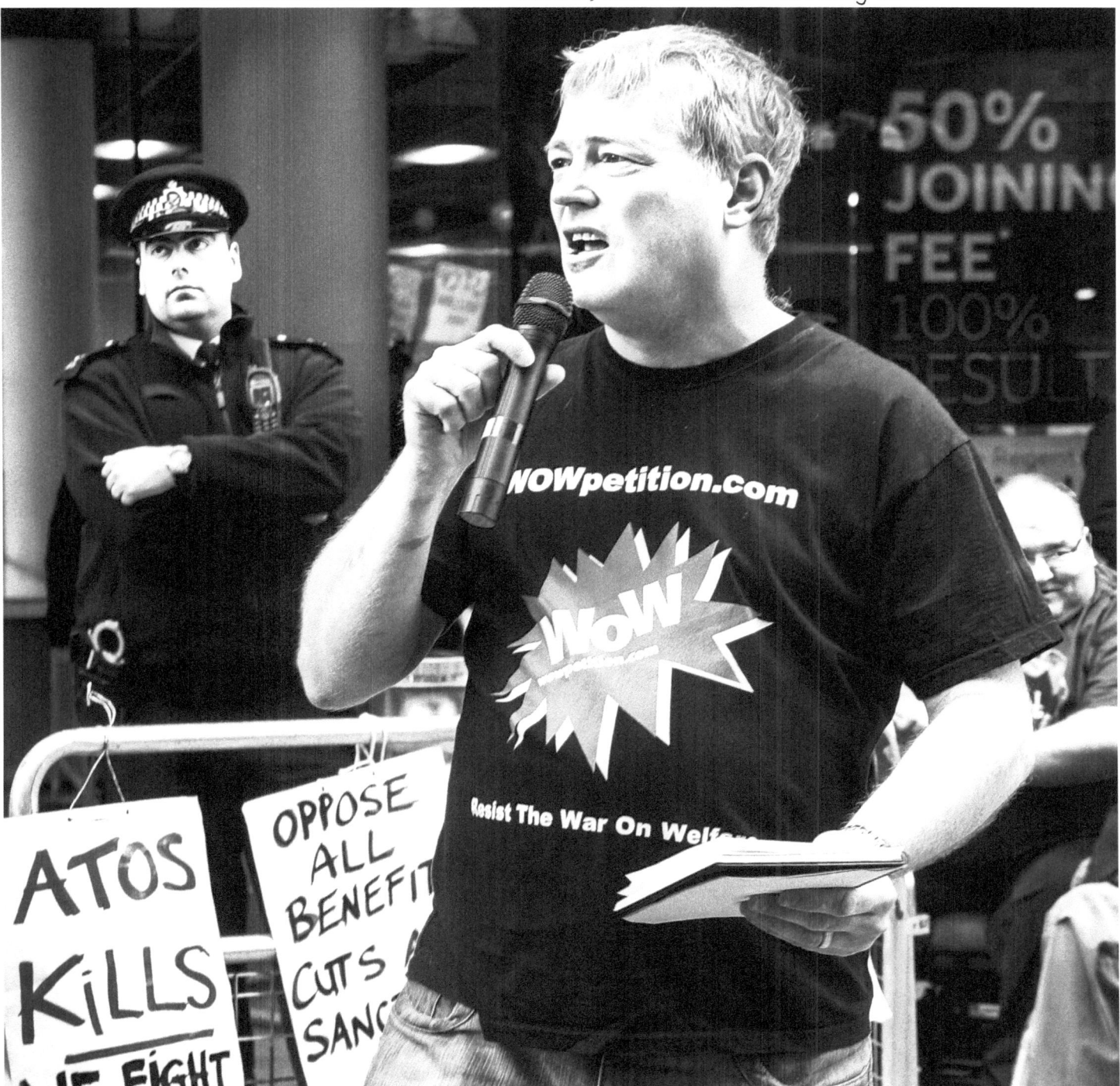

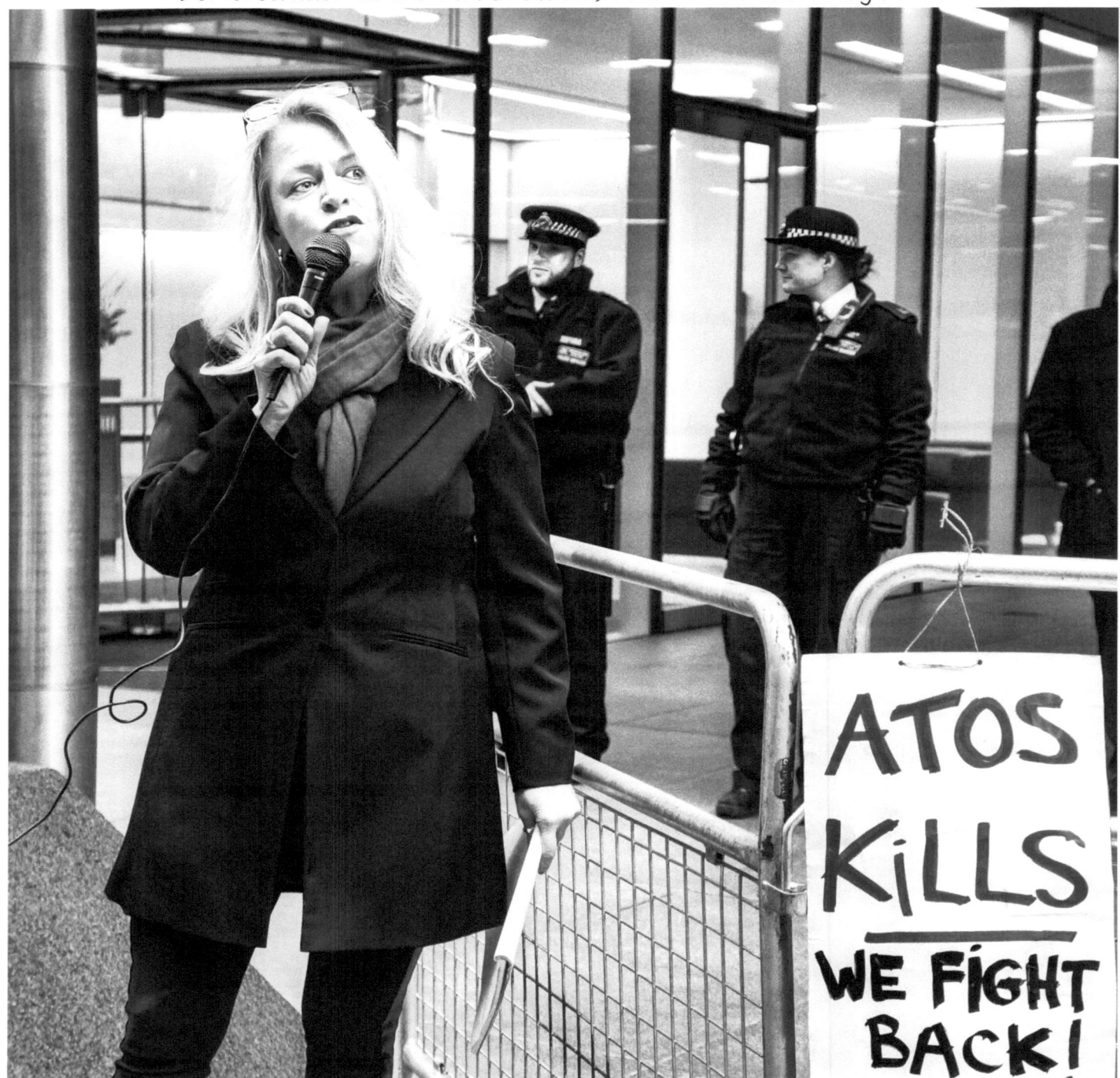

ATOS KILLS
WE FIGHT BACK!

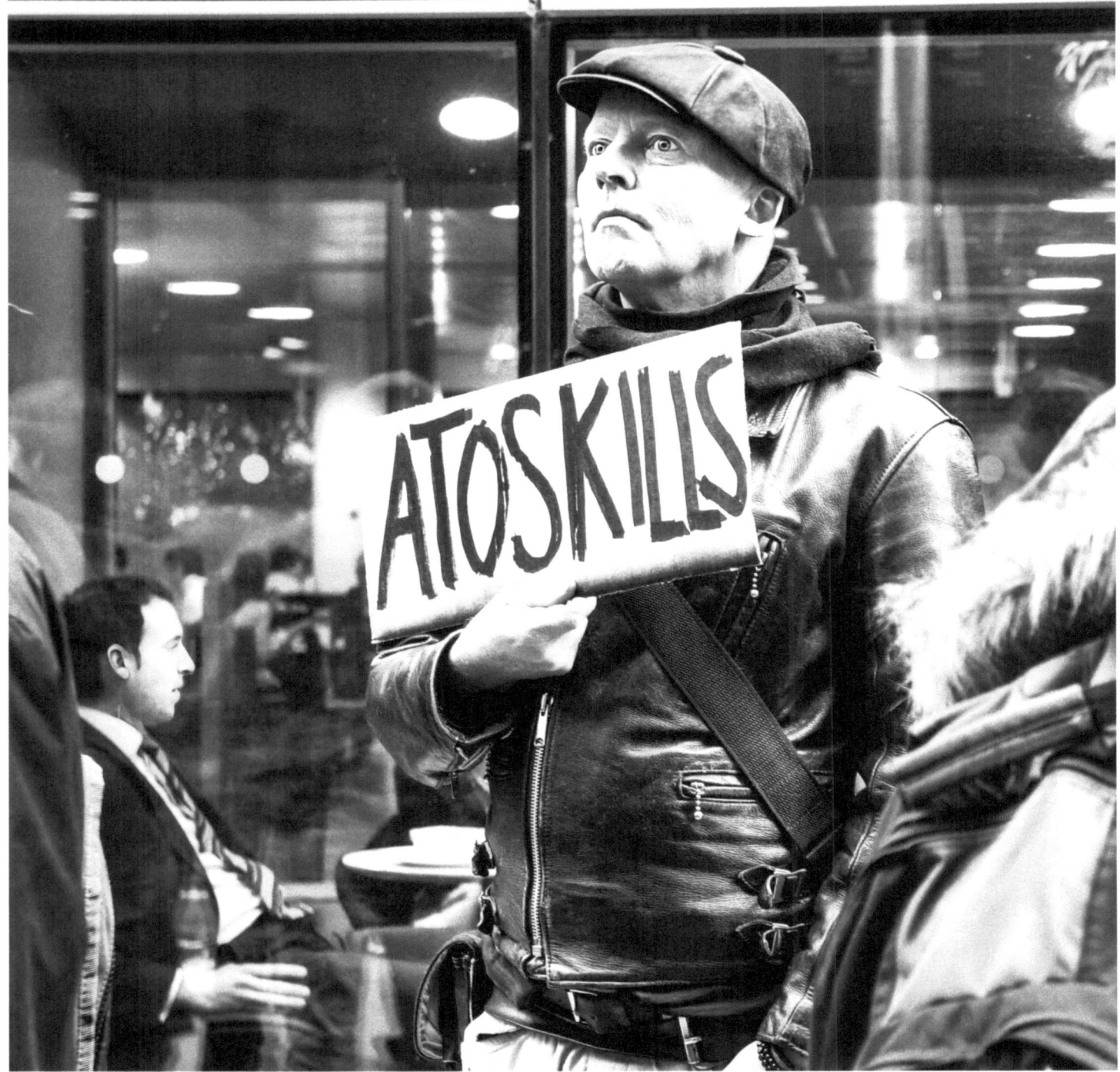

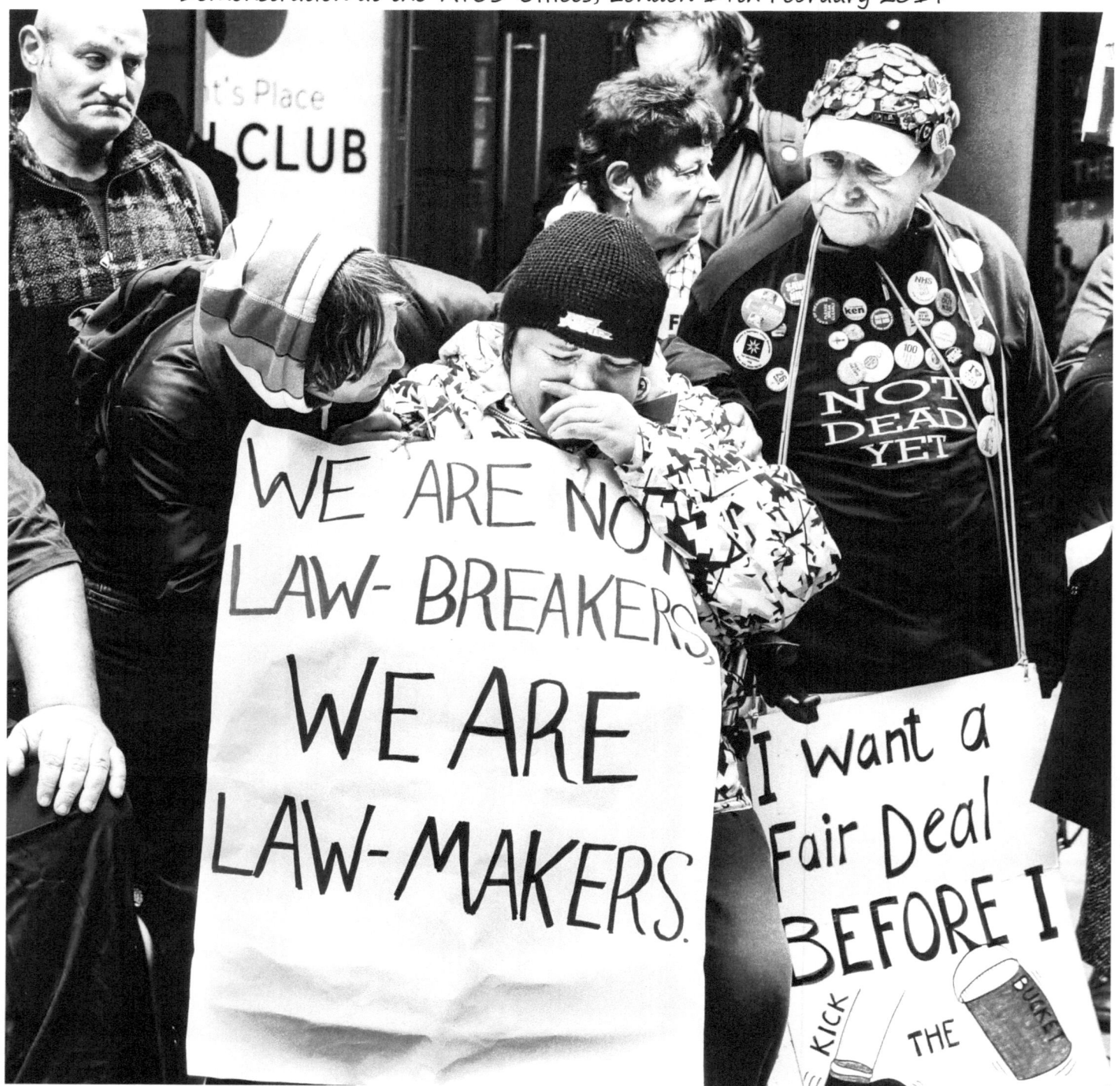

I became a co-founder of 'Disabled People Against Cuts' (DPAC) because it was obvious, from June 2010 onwards, that disabled people's rights were being trashed by the Tories.

We were determined to make our many protests visible and to give a voice to disabled people who were often excluded from having their say.

For this particular event I wanted to do something to show how much I detested the Conservatives and travelled down to London with Jae, who made her notable 'Fuck the Tories' poster on the train, to encourage by me.

Afterwards, going back to the station to get the train home, I got on the bus but then instead of the driver putting the ramp out for Jae and her wheelchair, the driver simply drove off leaving Jae stranded.

This is the sort of appalling treatment disabled people still have to put up with in the 21st century and which we will keep fighting to change.

This wasn't just an inconvenience; it was a stark reminder of the everyday barriers that disabled people still face in the 21st century. Simple acts of inclusion, like deploying a ramp, become hurdles, tests of patience, and sometimes, dignity.

But this incident, like countless others, only strengthens our resolve. We will keep fighting for a world where accessibility isn't a privilege, but a right.

A world where the rumble of a departing bus signifies not just the end of a journey, but the start of a future where everyone, regardless of ability, can move freely through life.

Linda Burnip

'Disabled People Against Cuts' (DPAC)

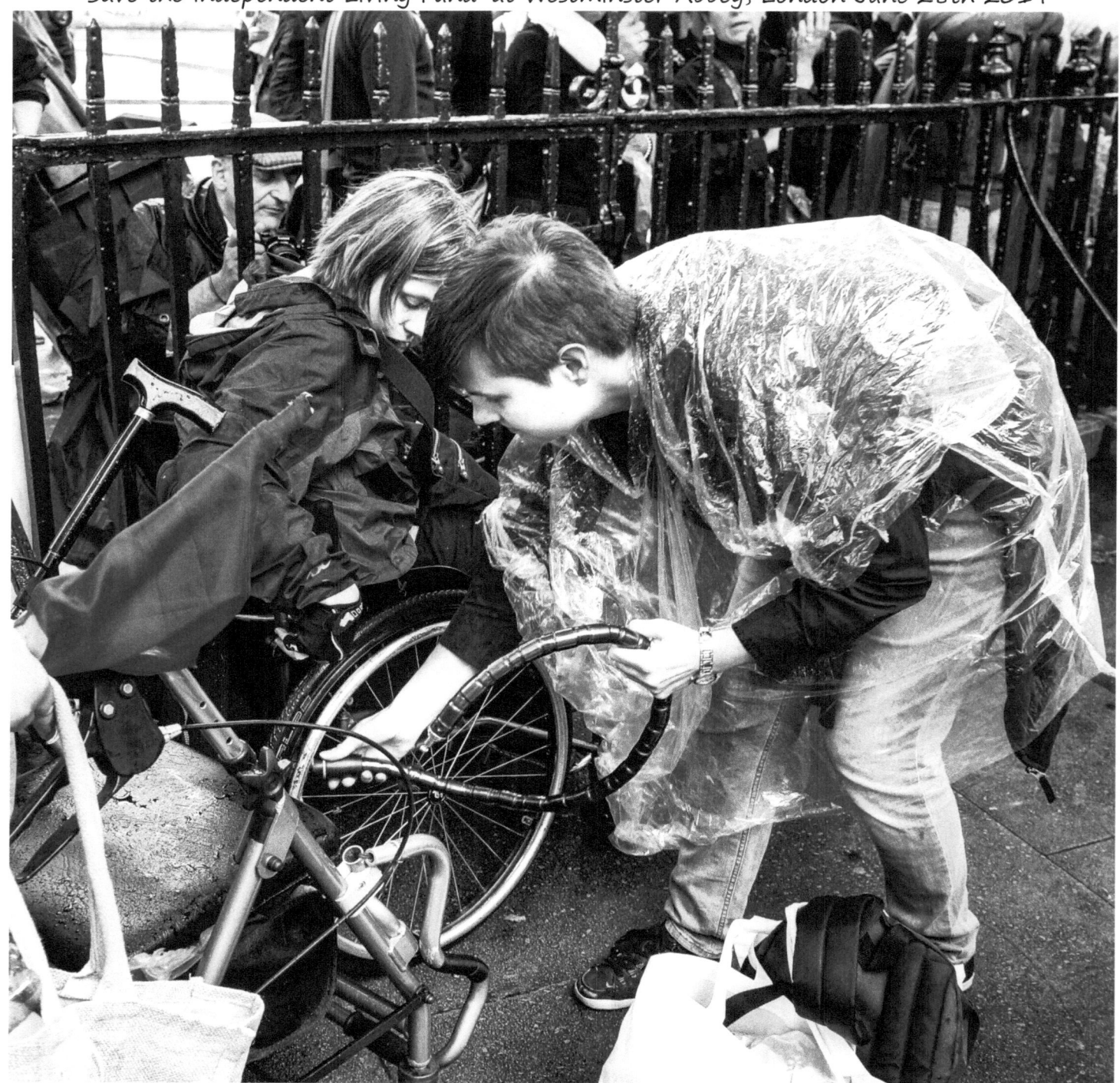

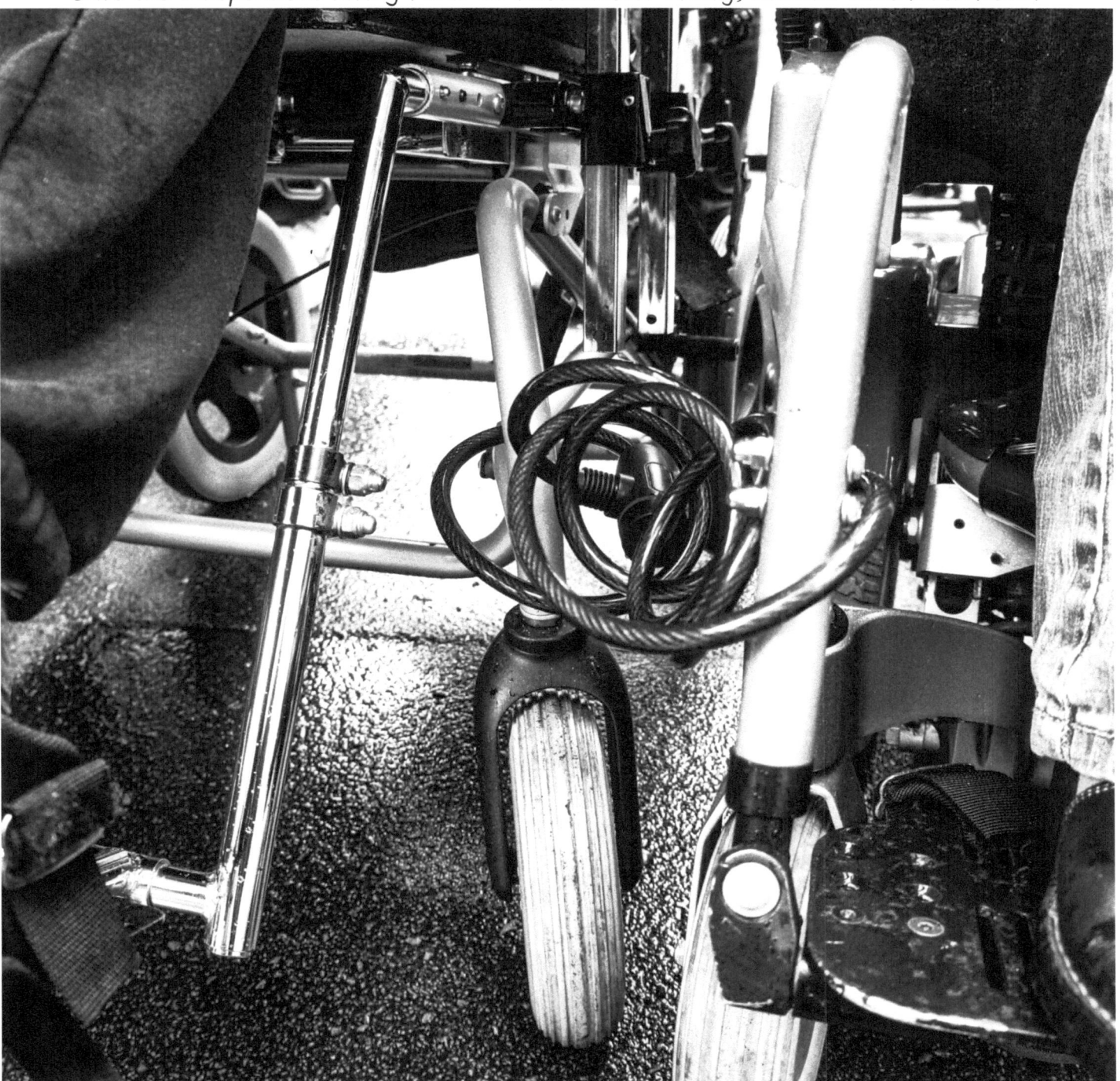

'Save the Independent Living Fund' at Westminster Abbey, London June 28th 2014

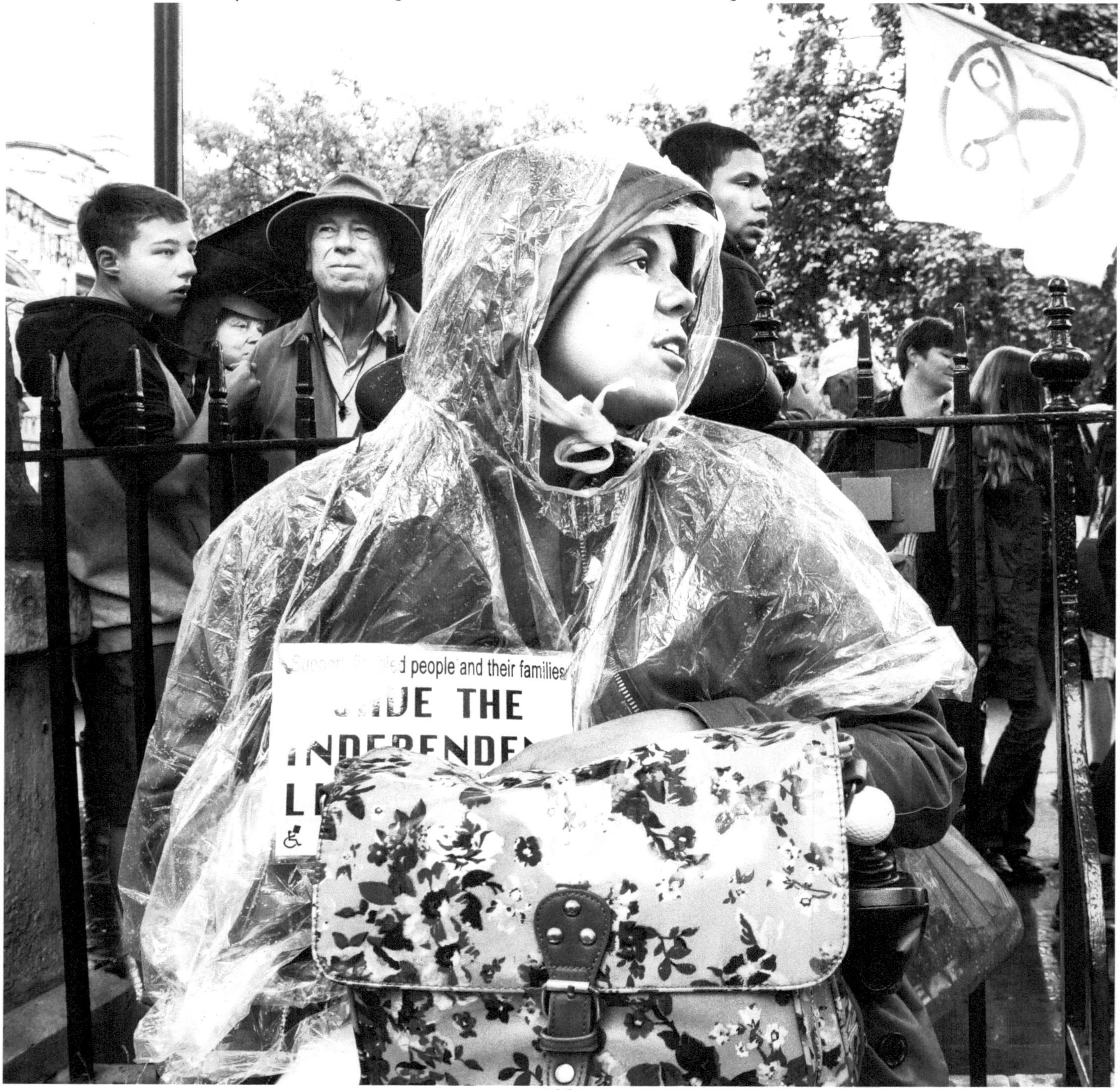

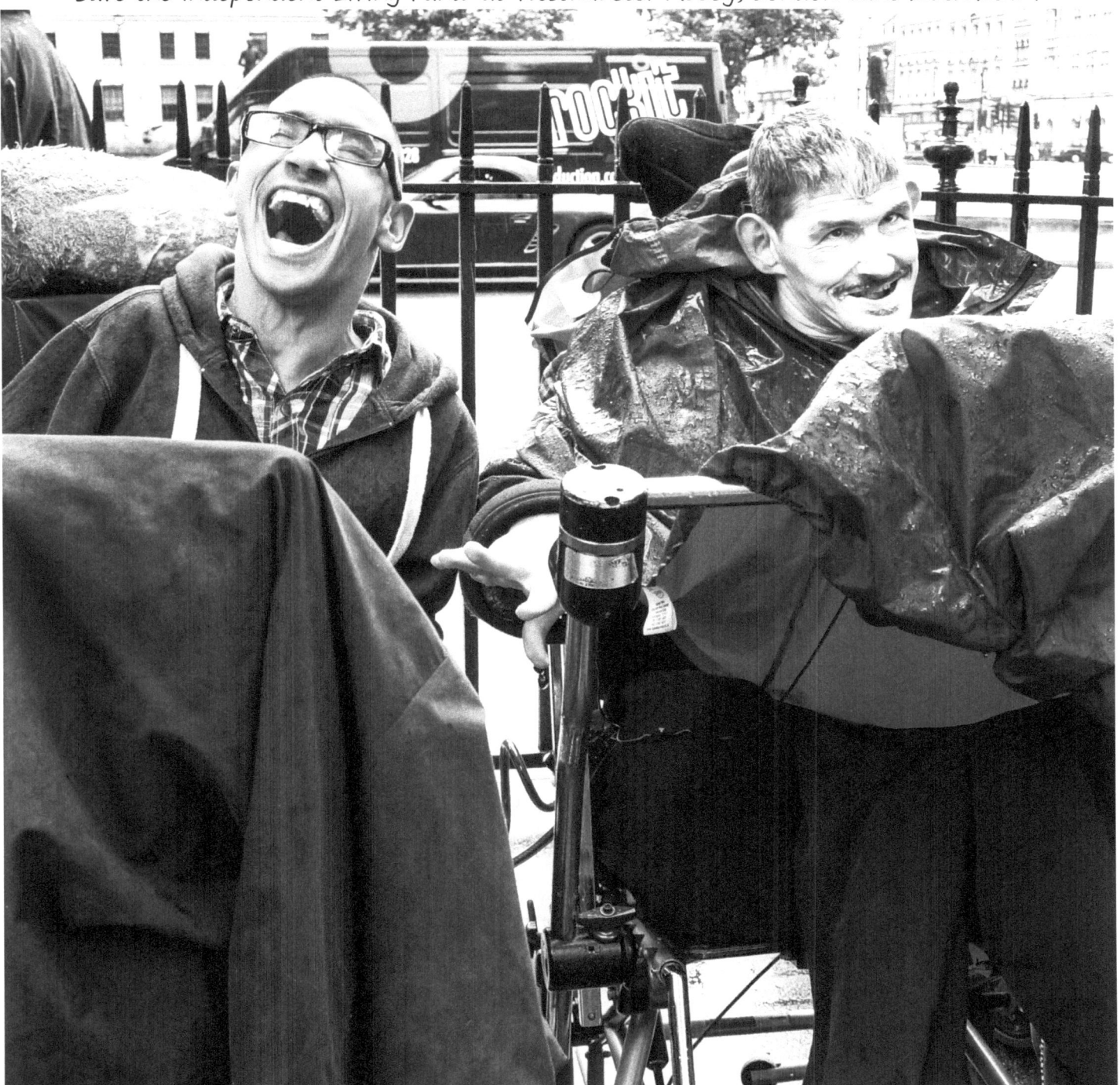

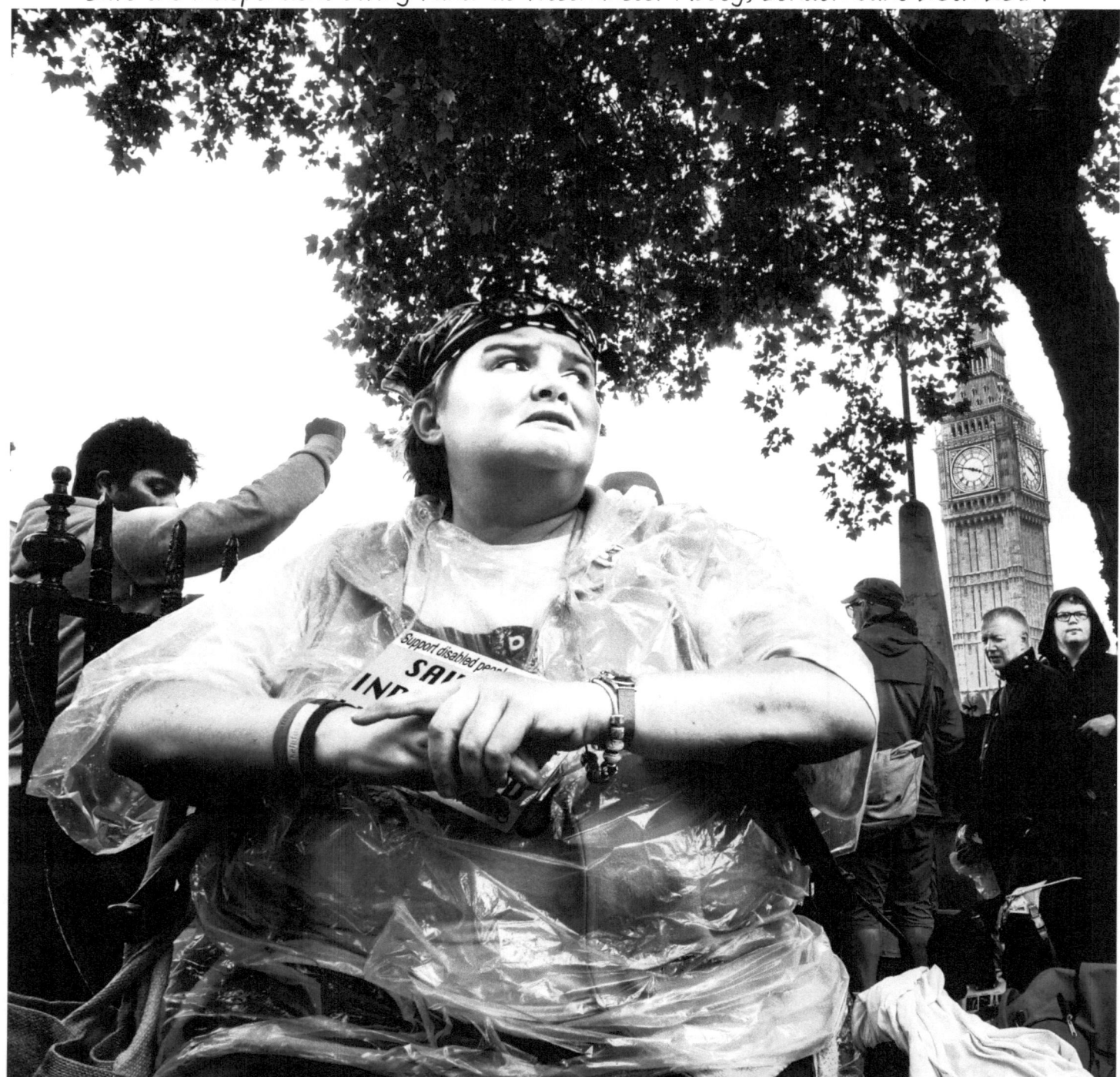

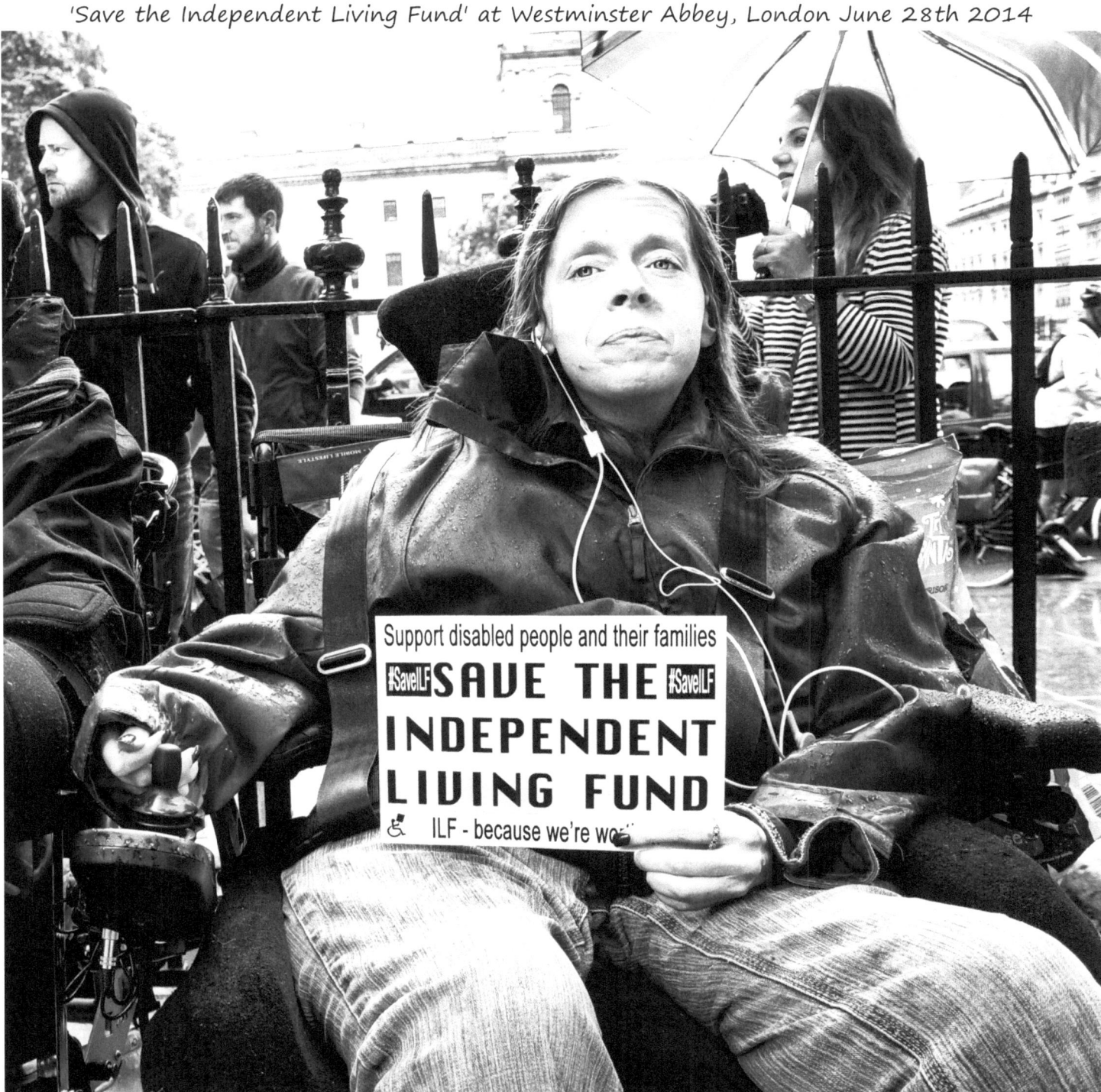

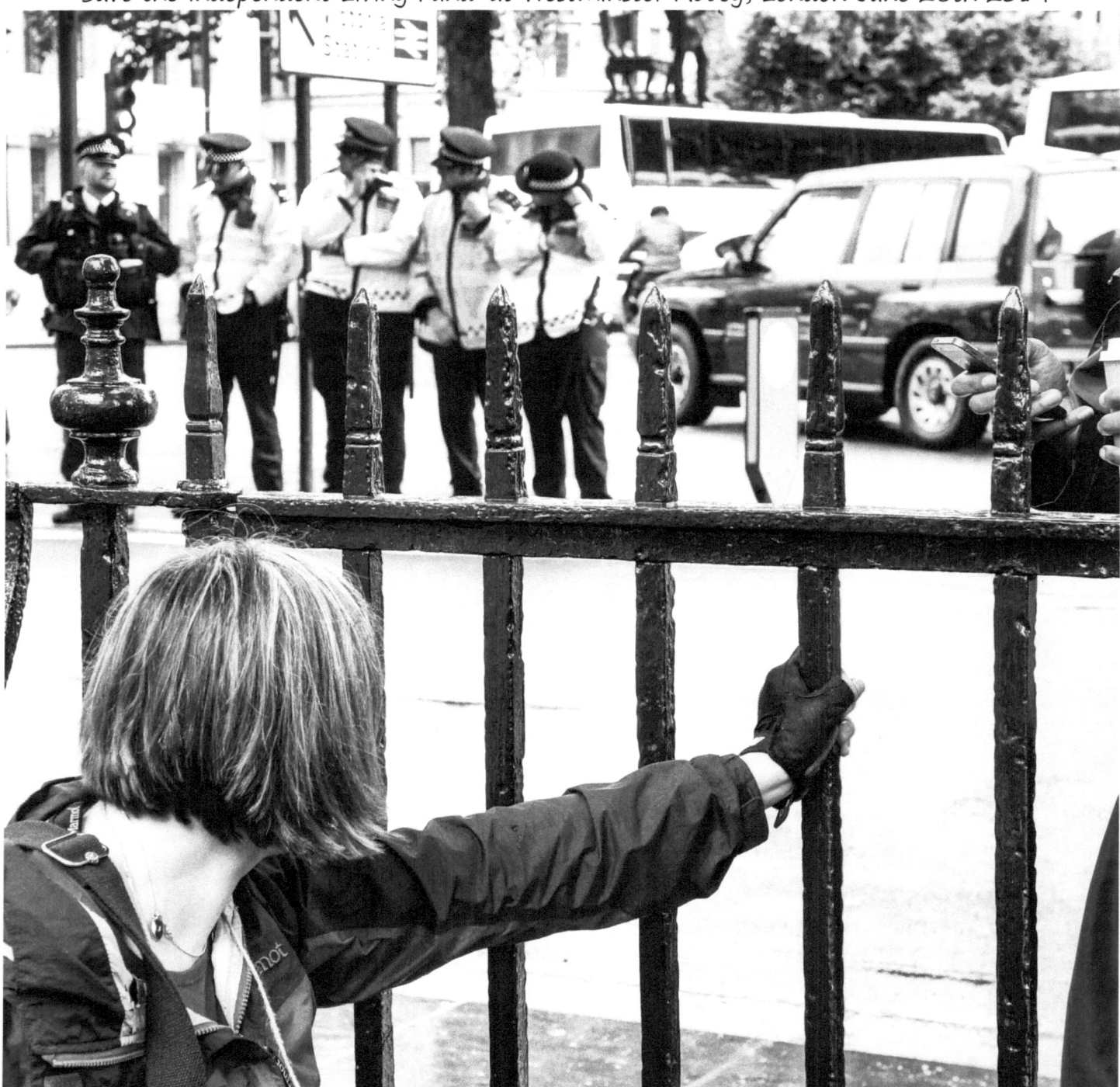

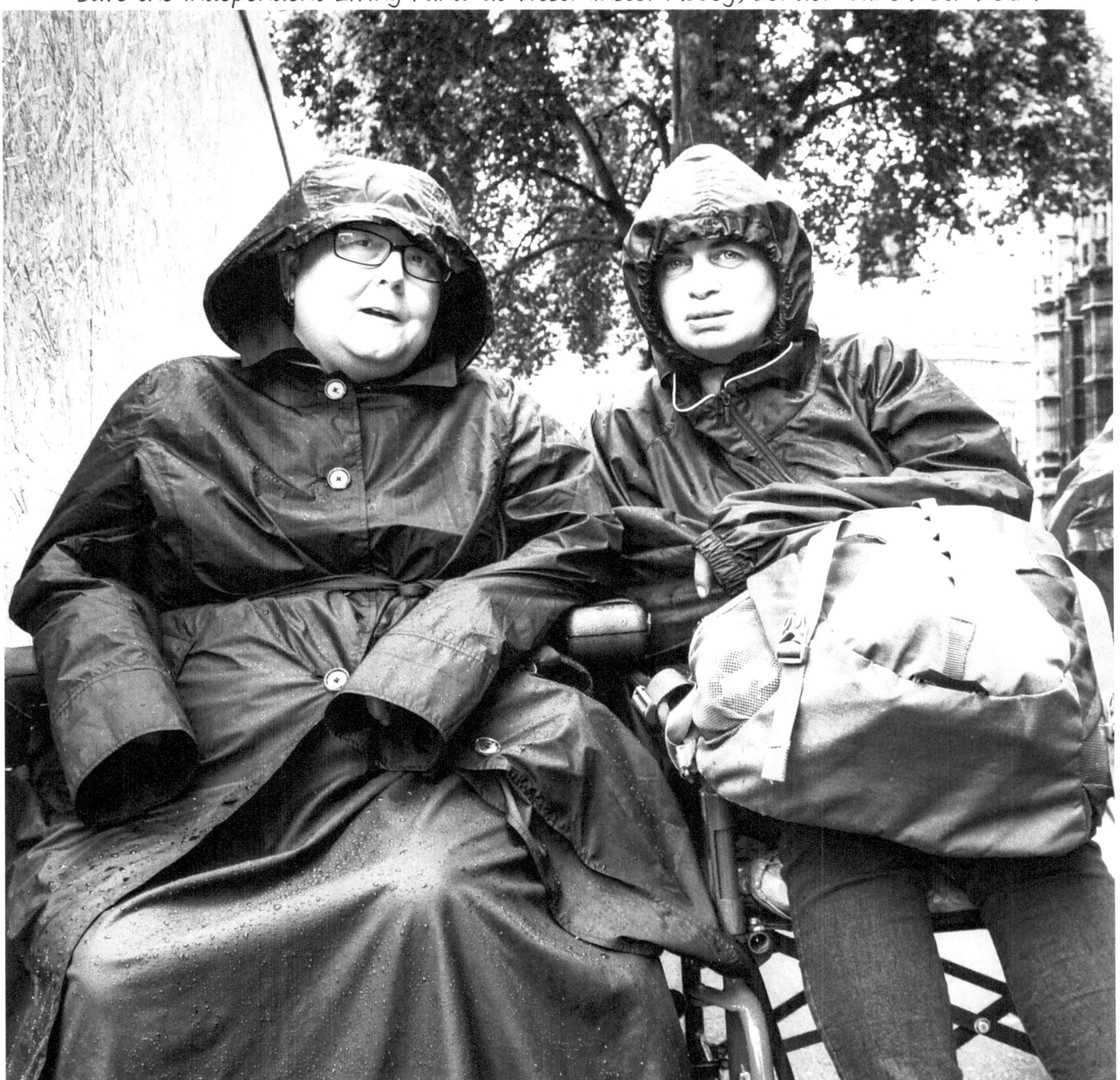

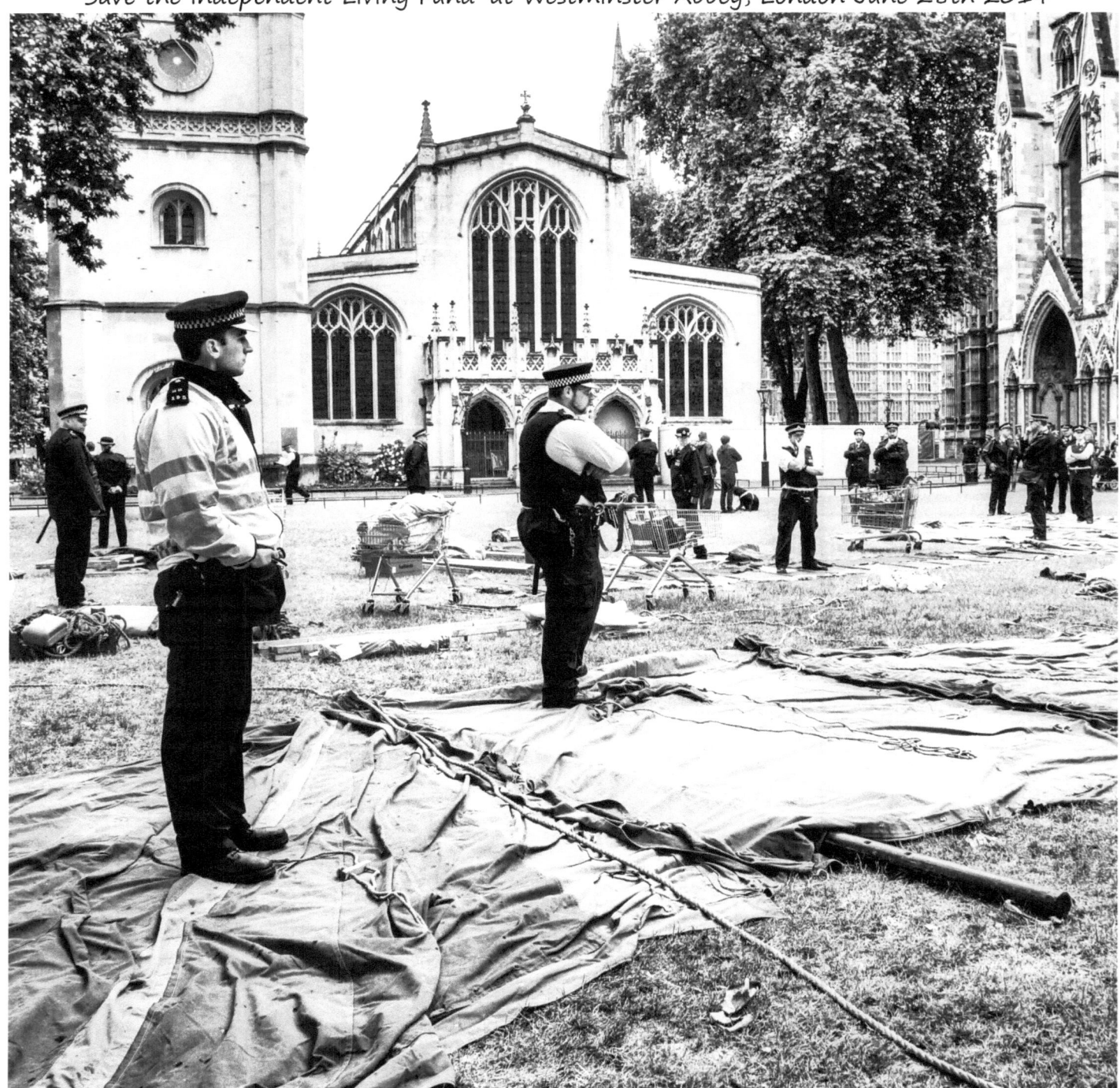

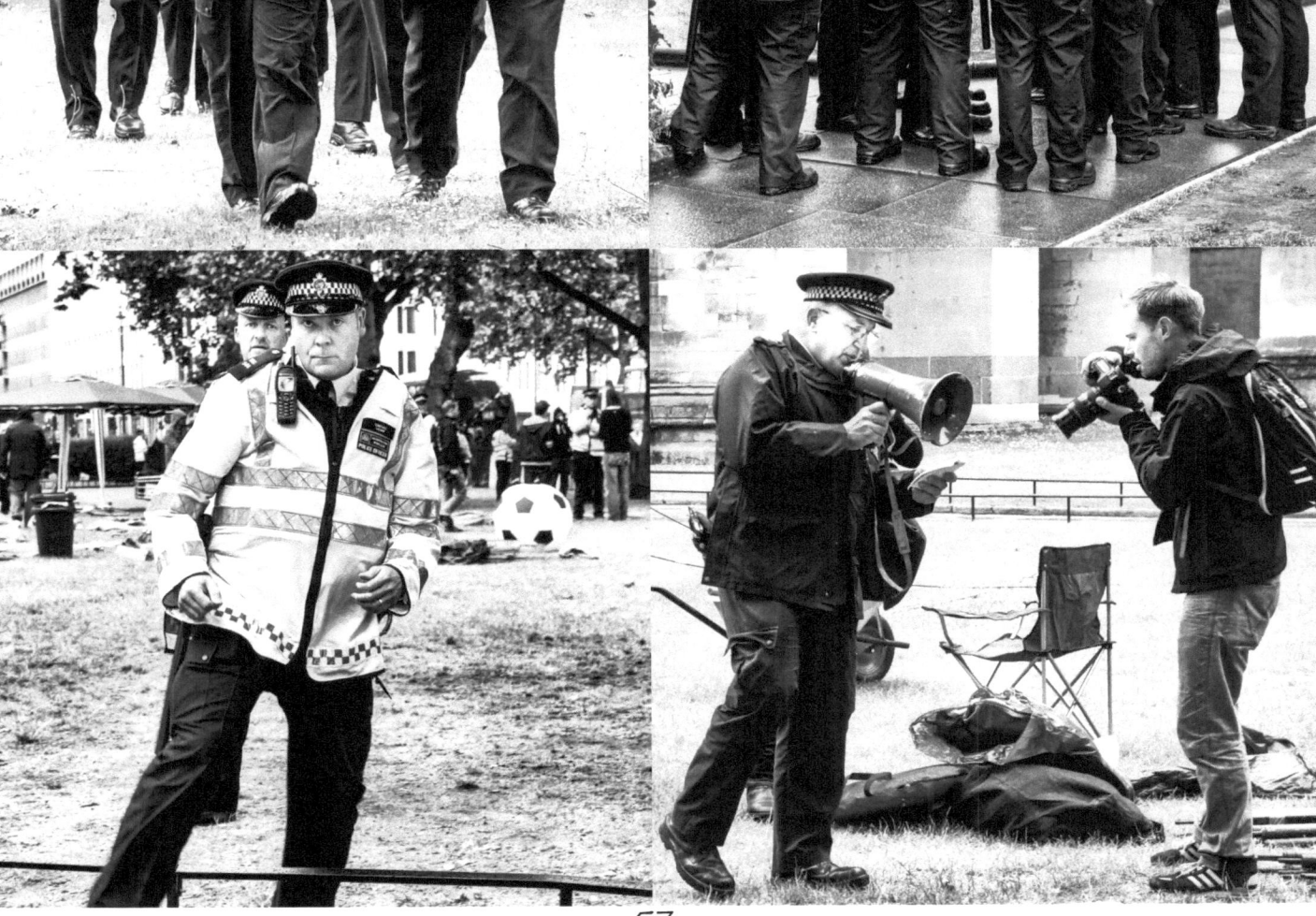

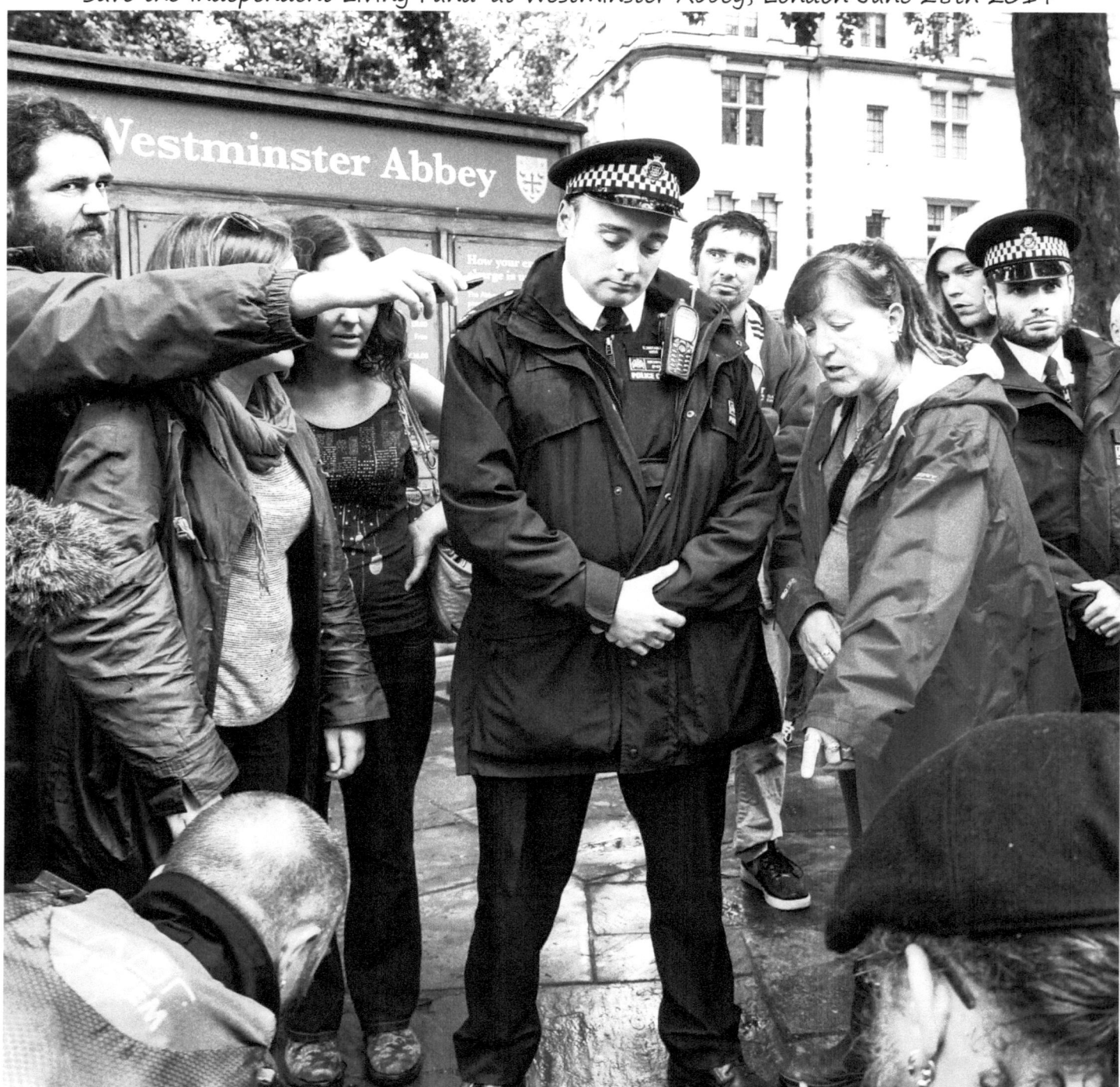

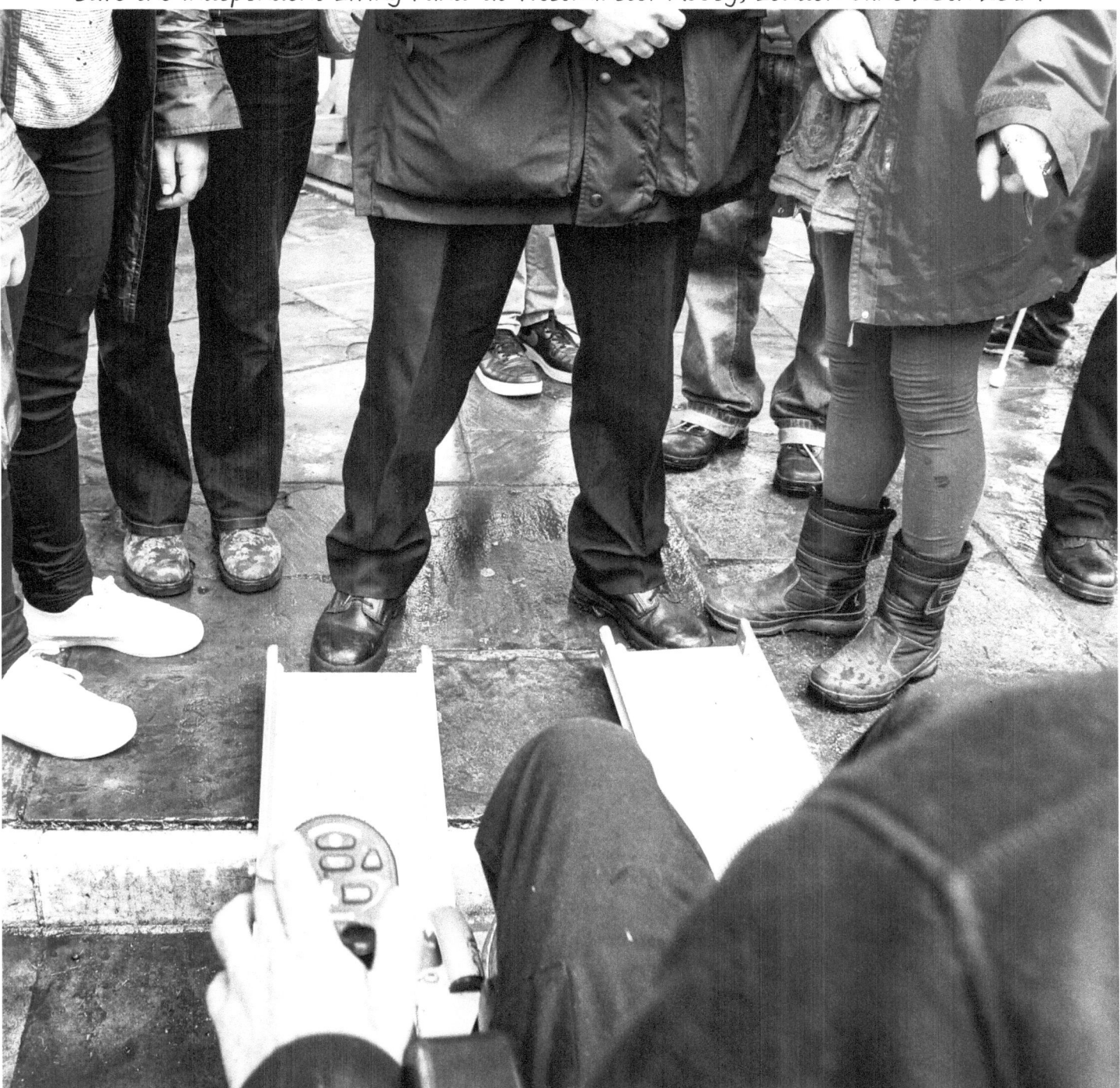

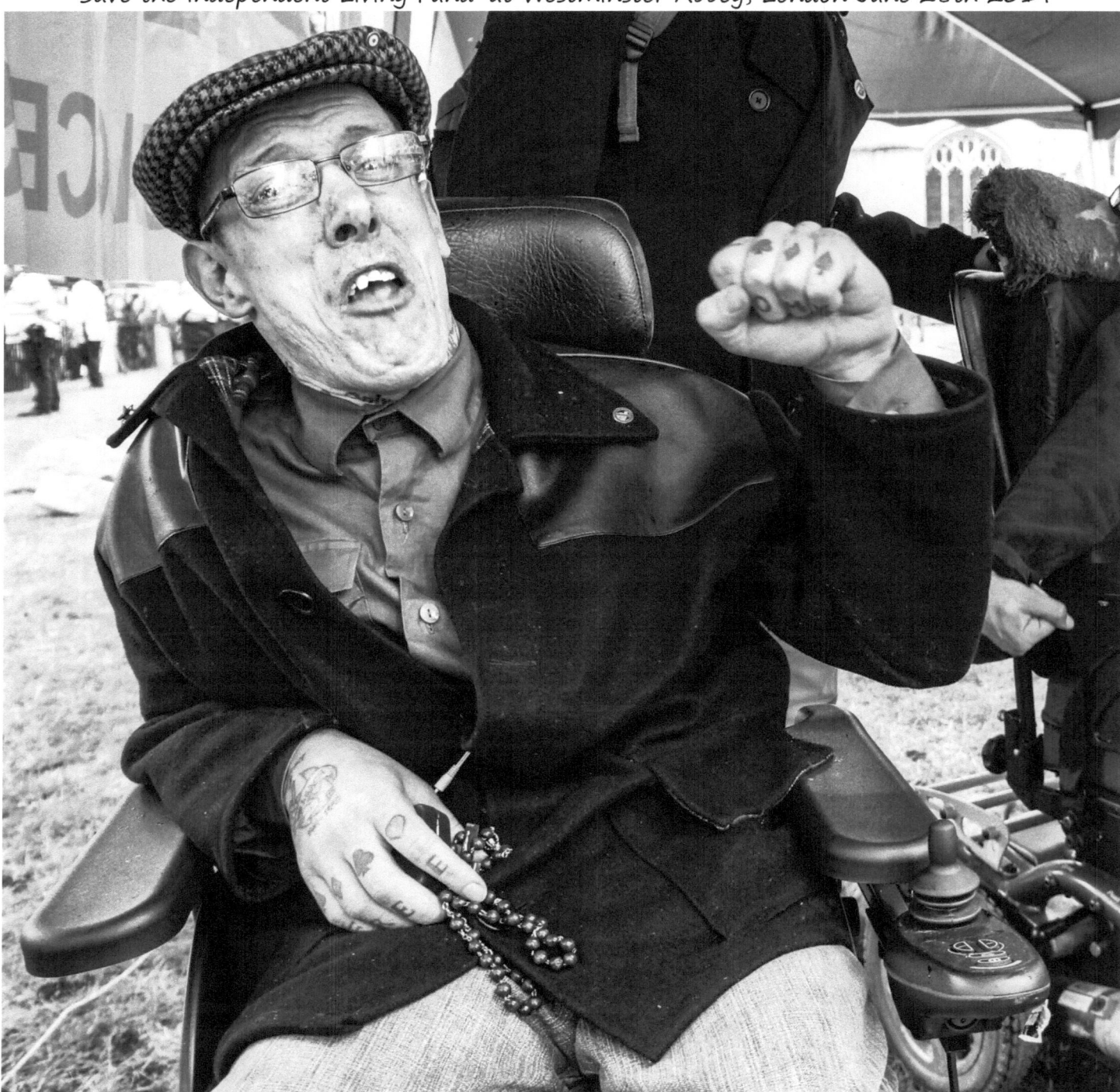

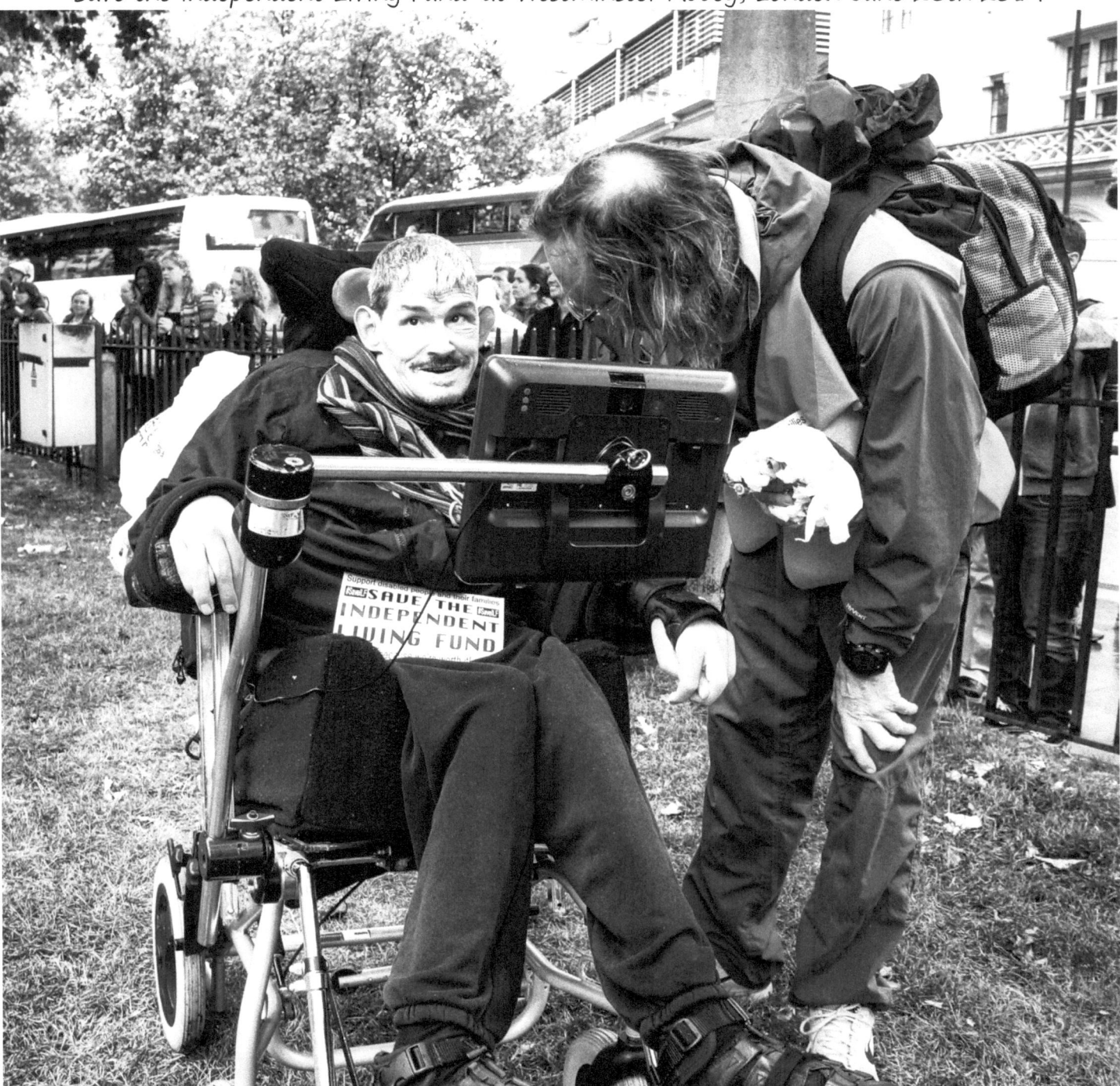

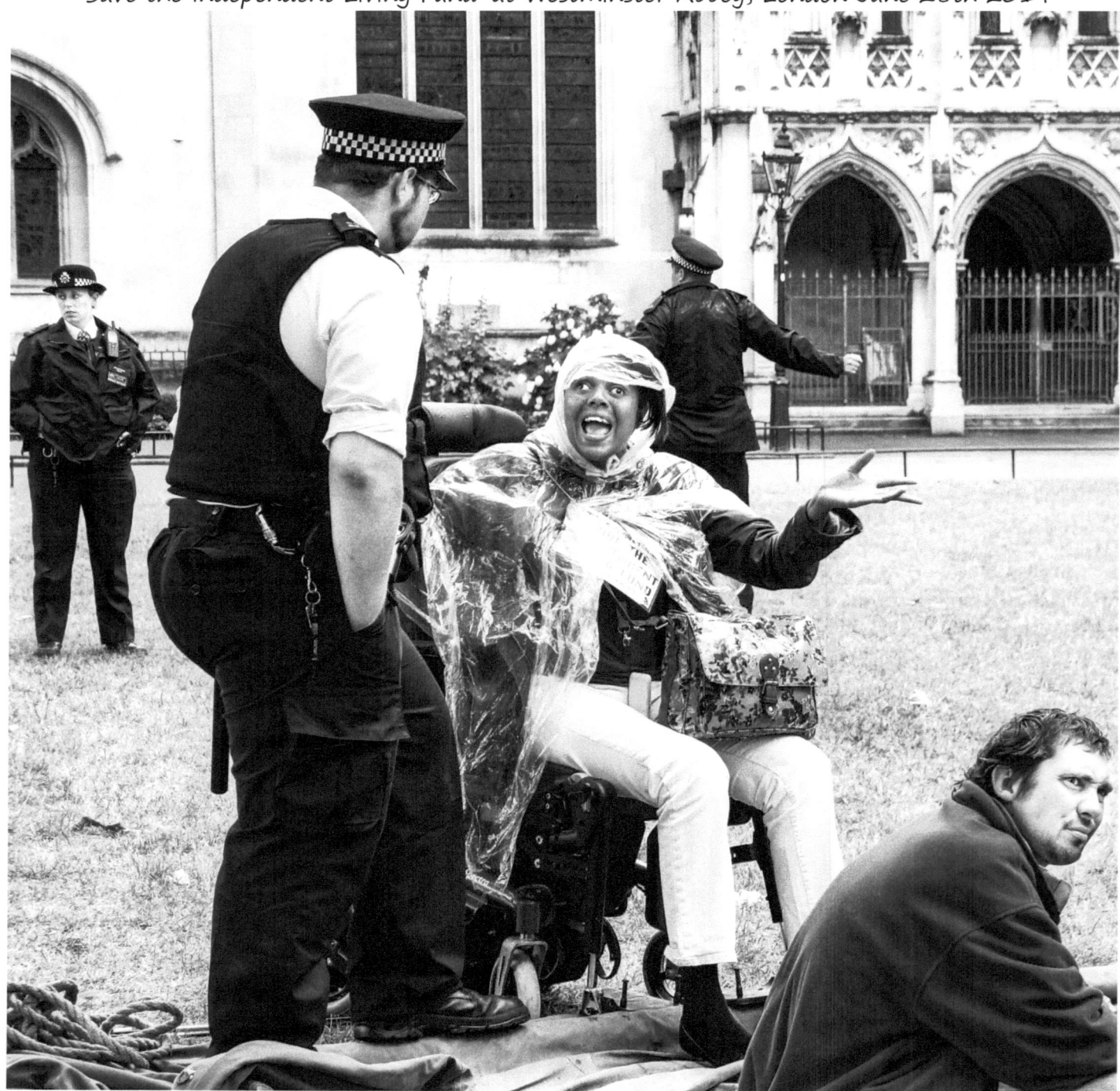

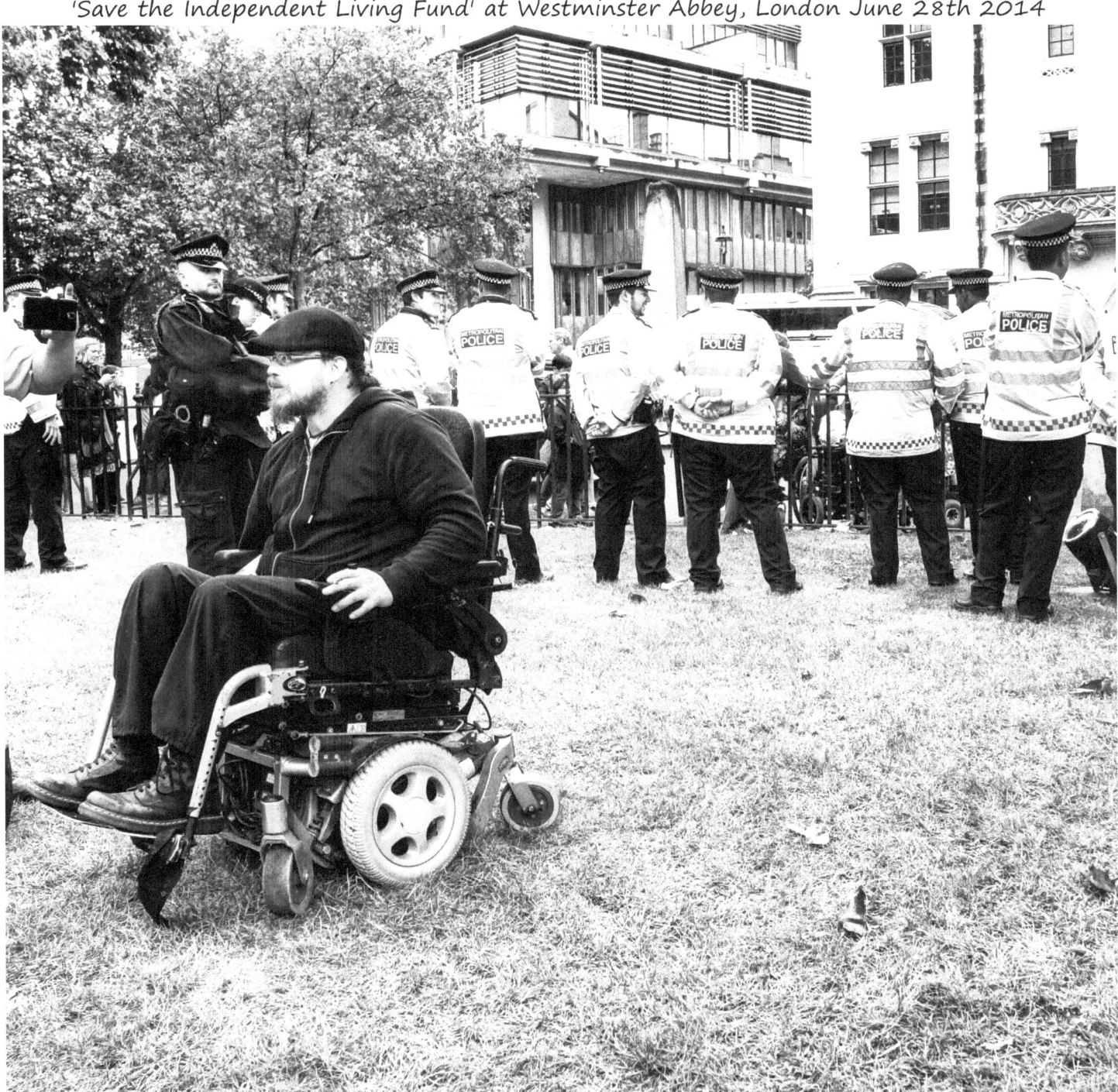

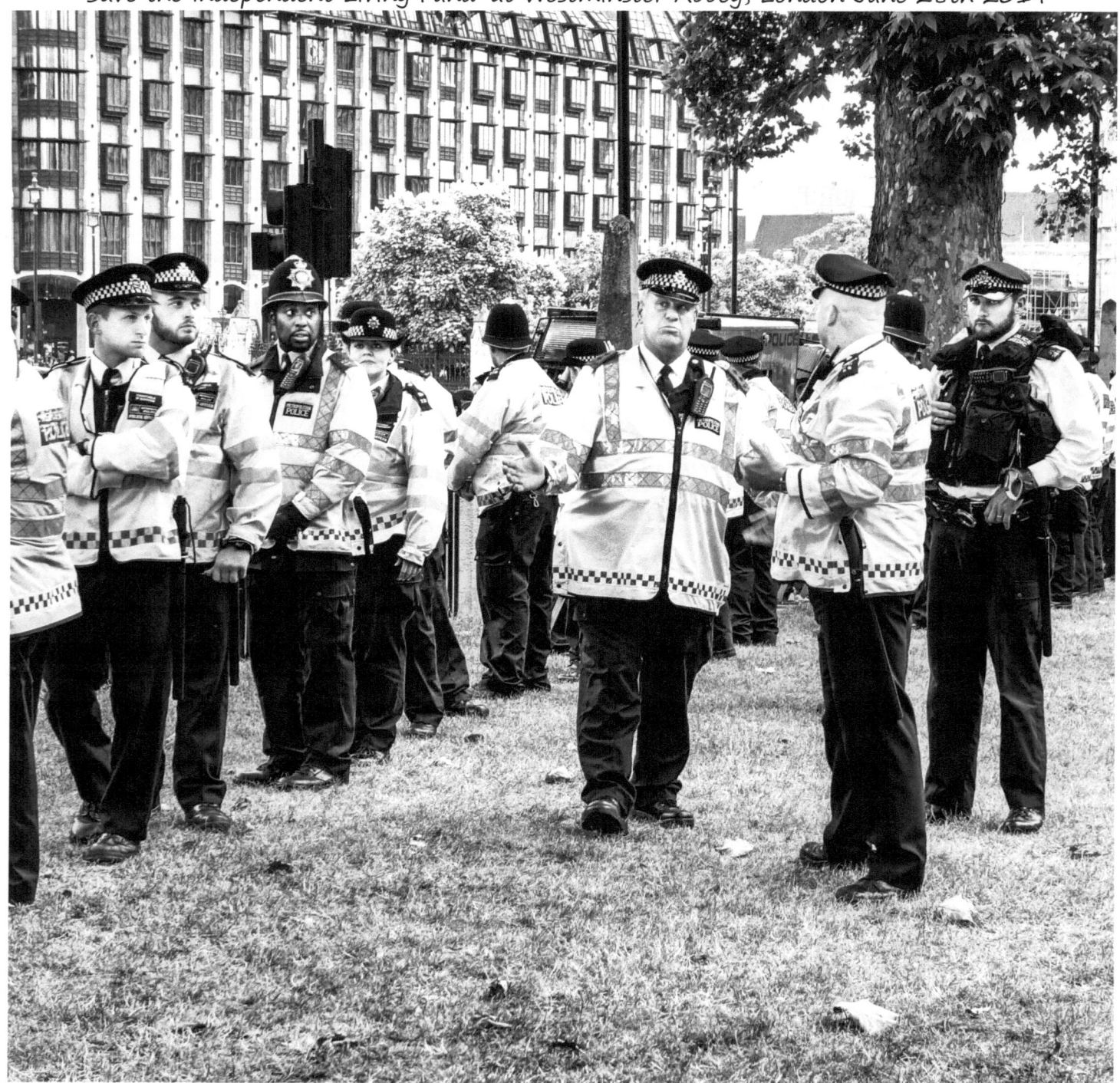

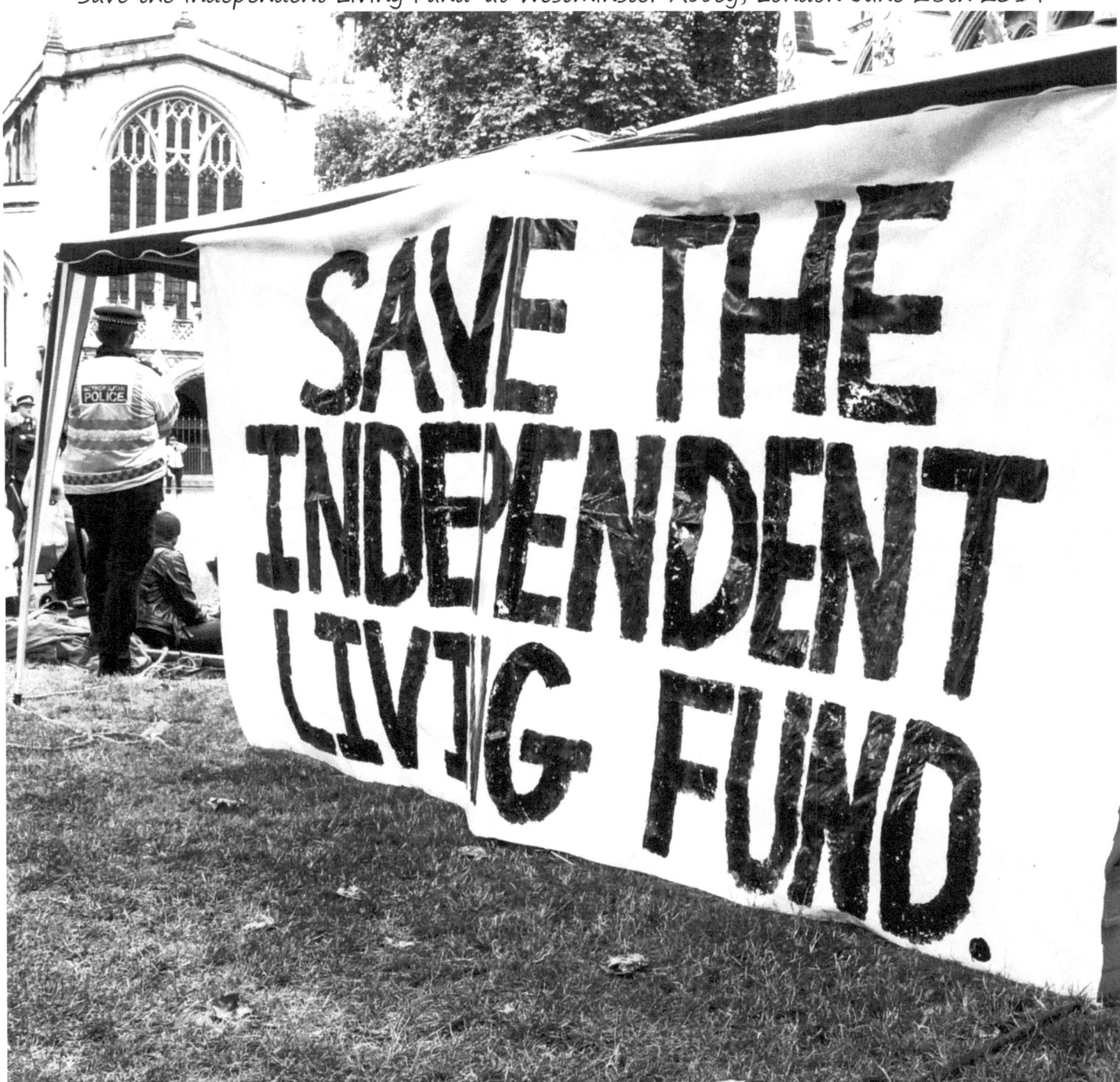

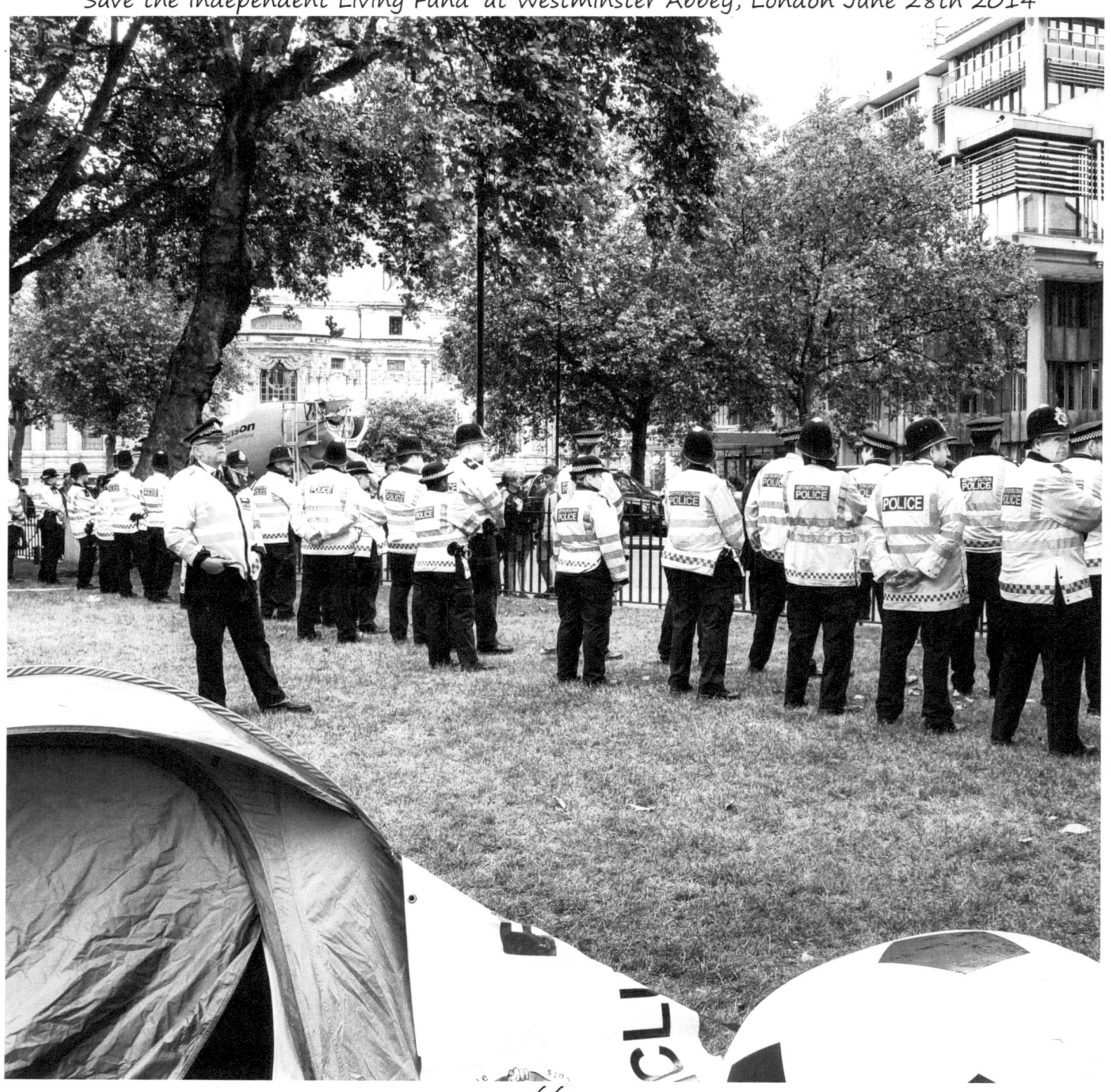

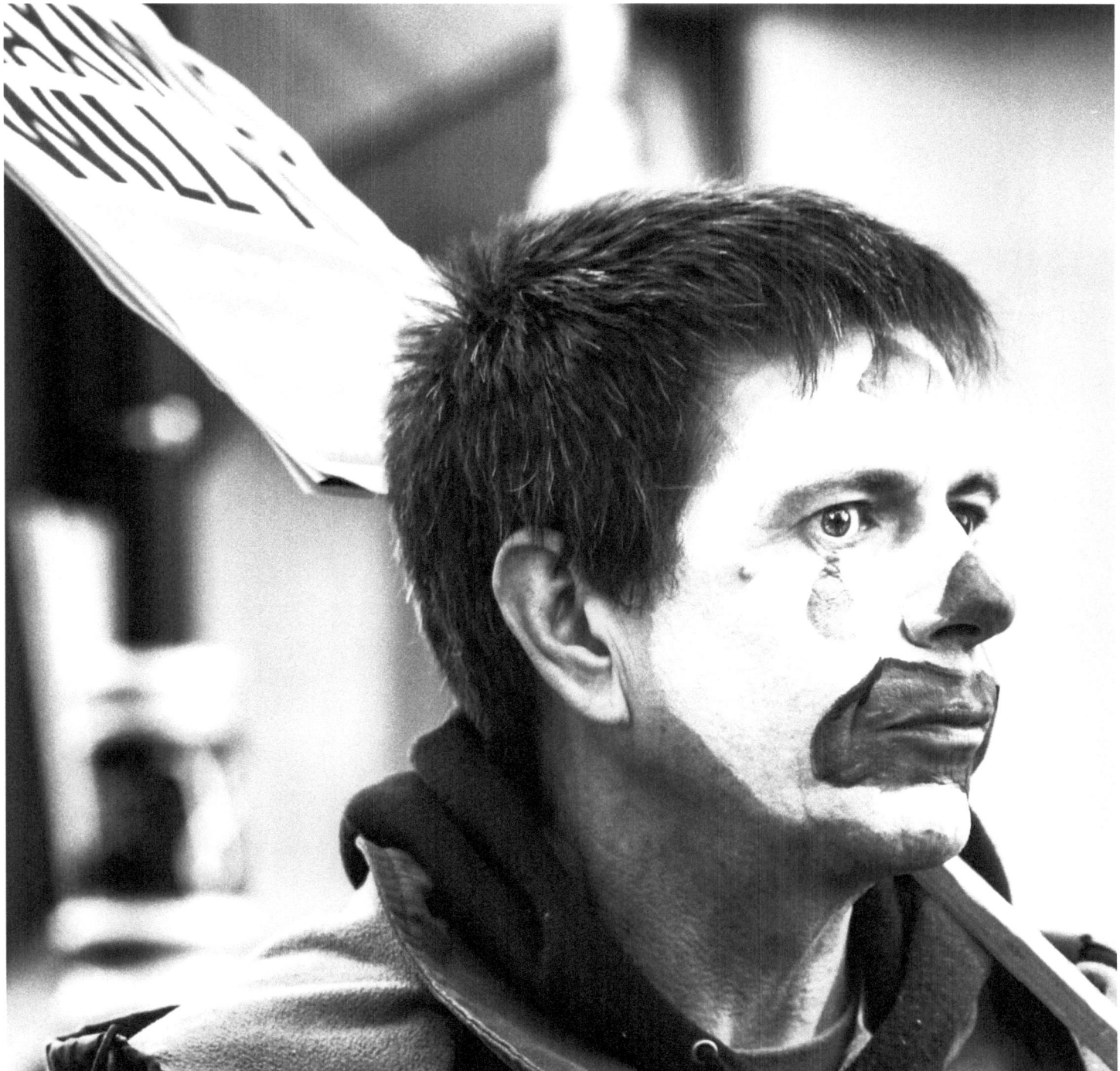

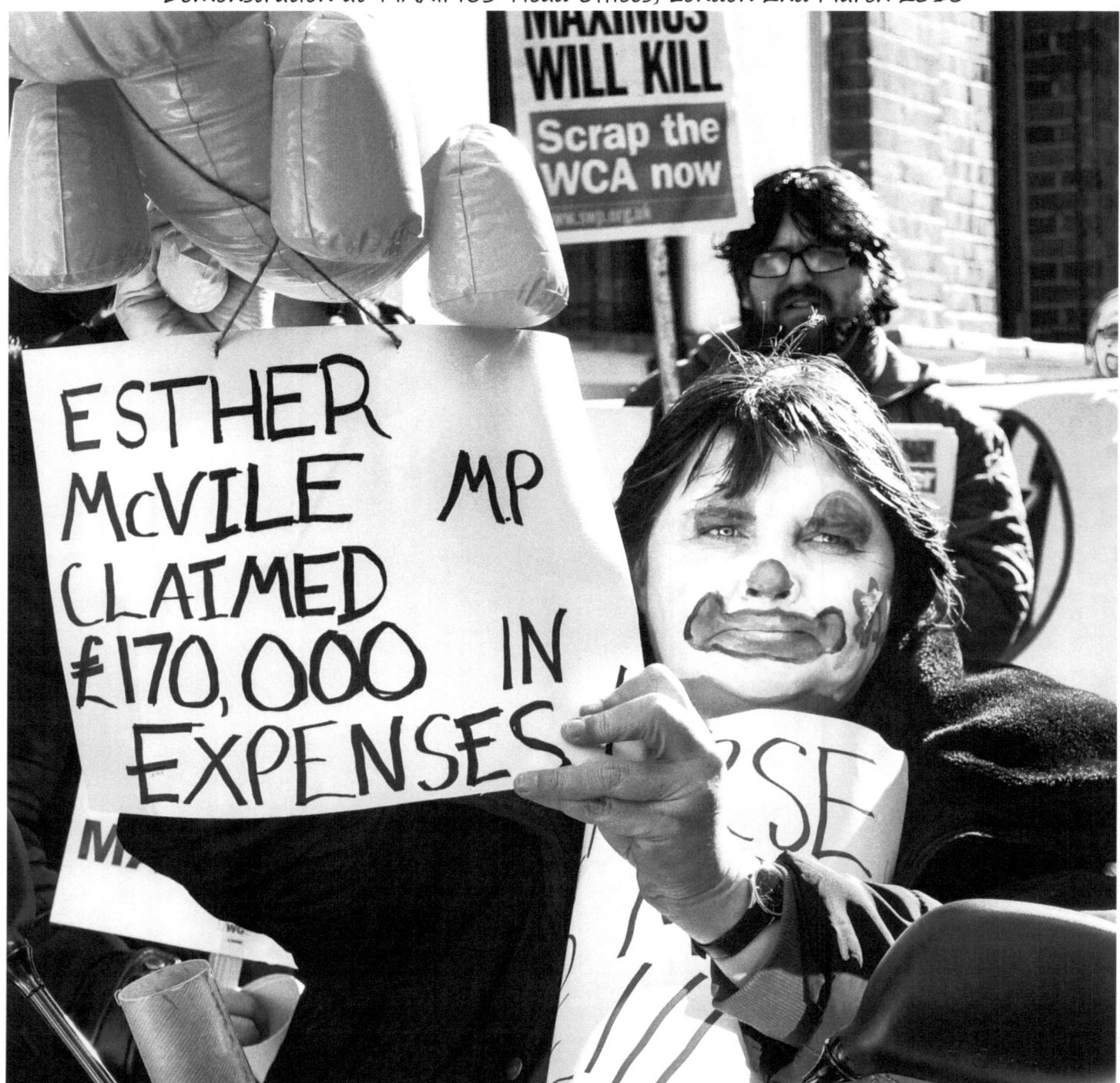

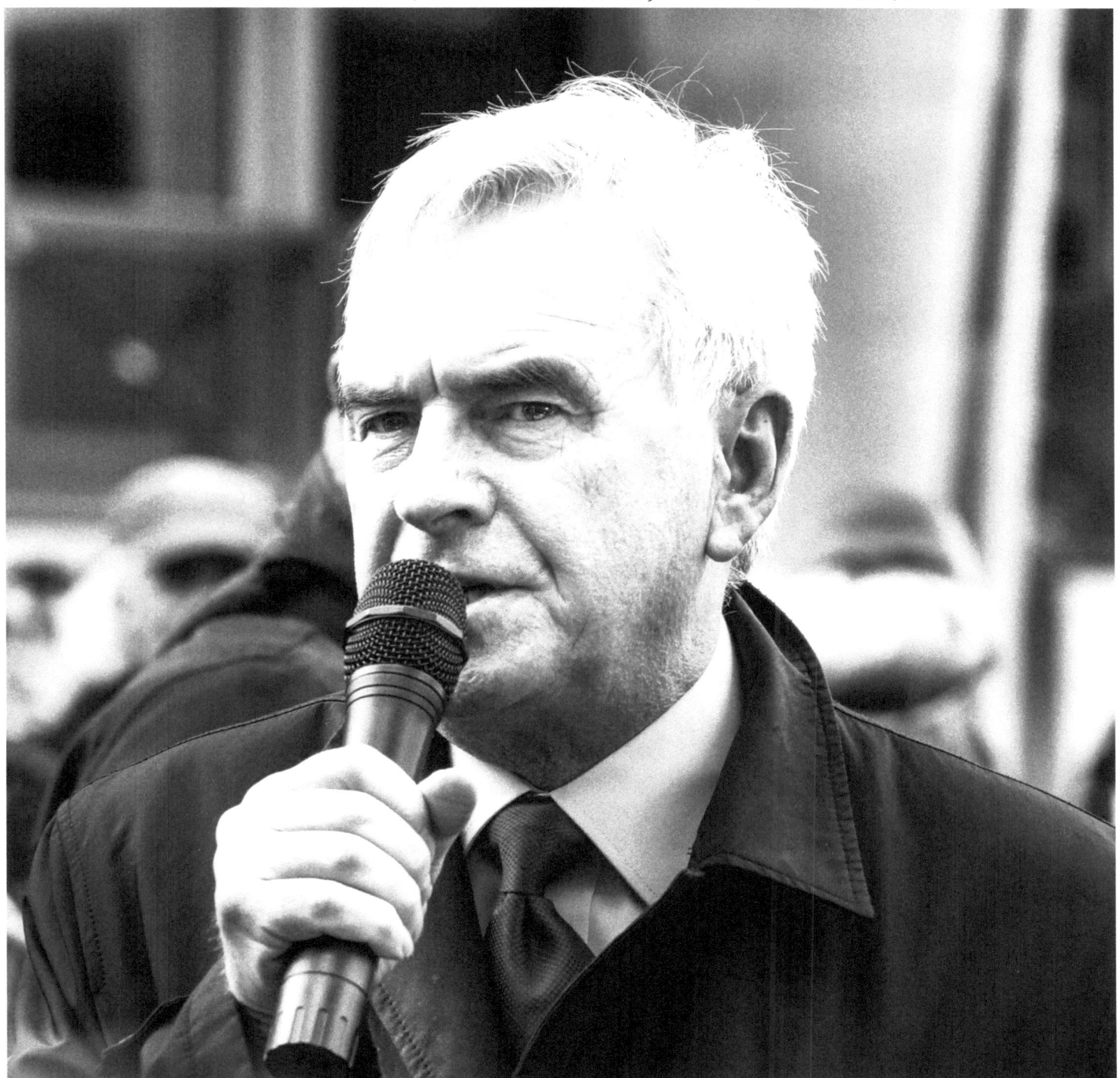

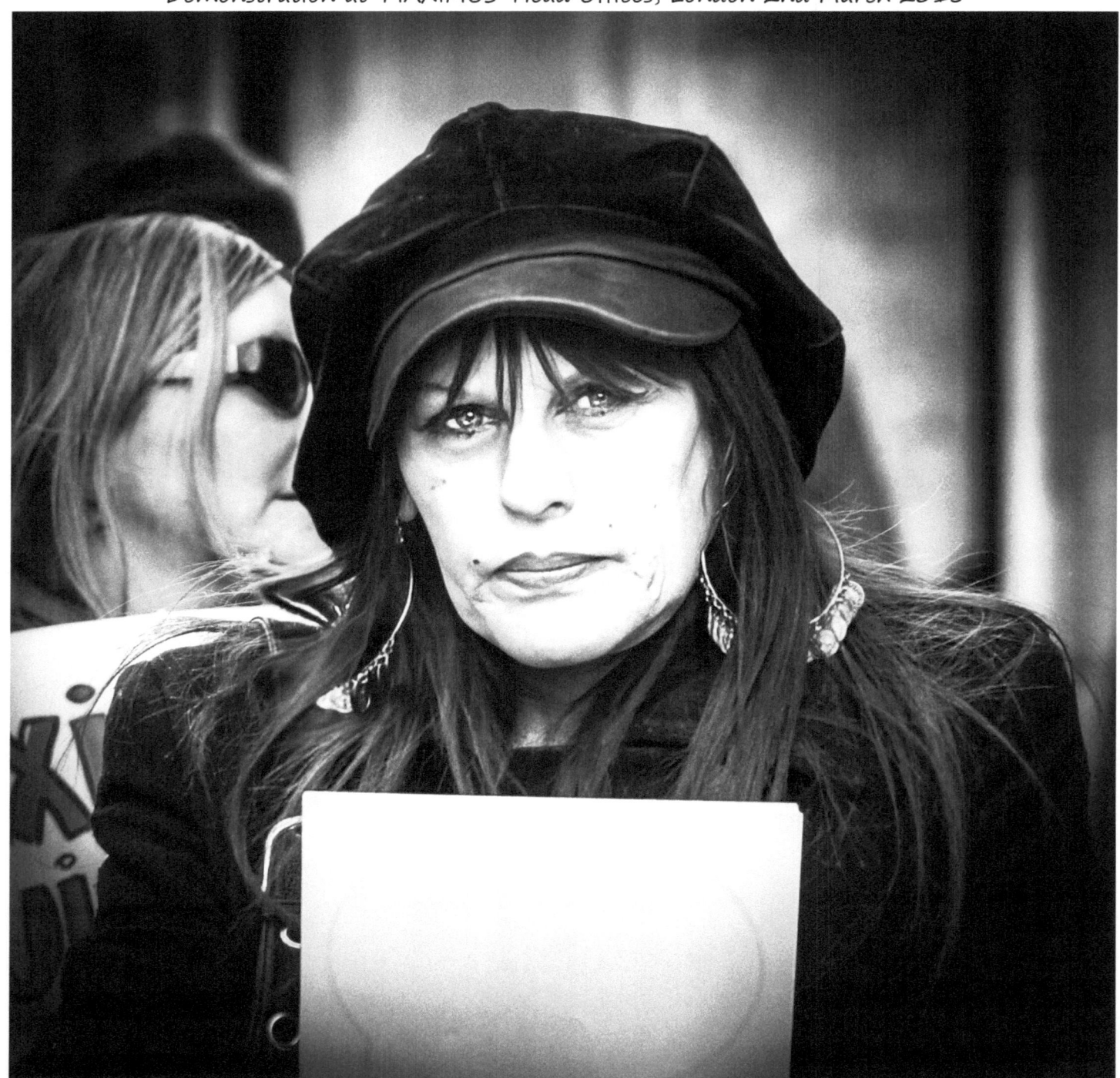

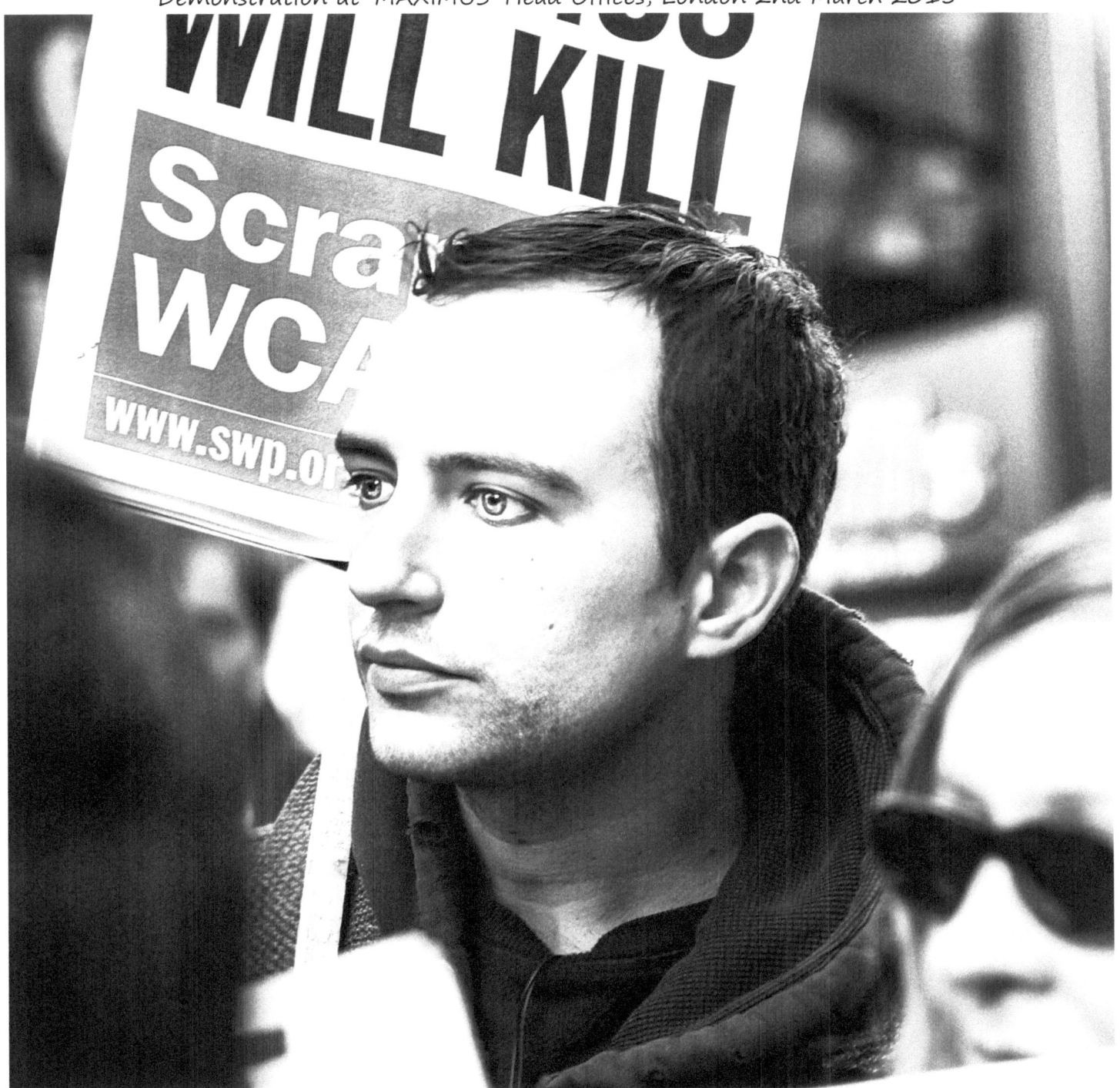

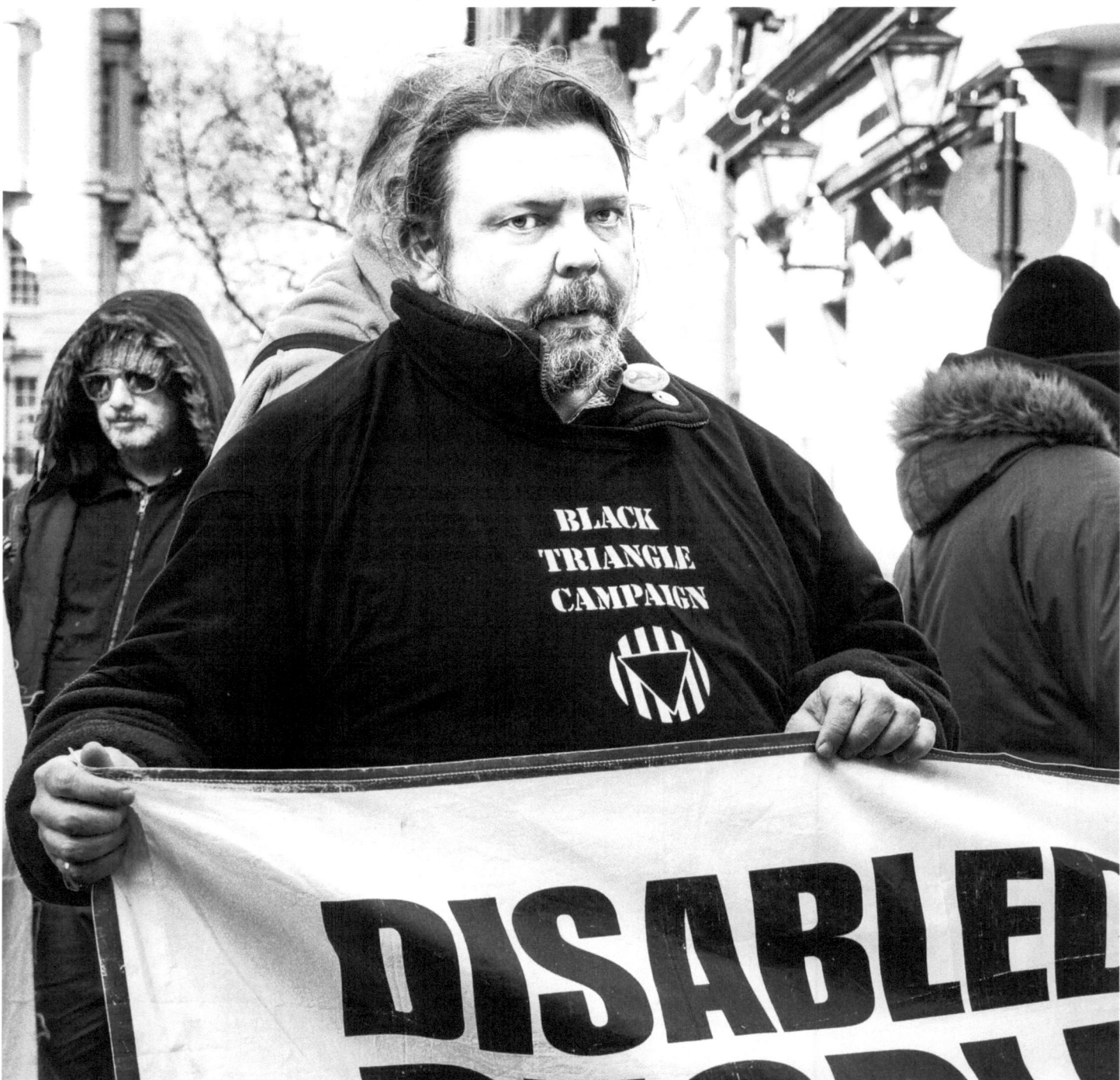

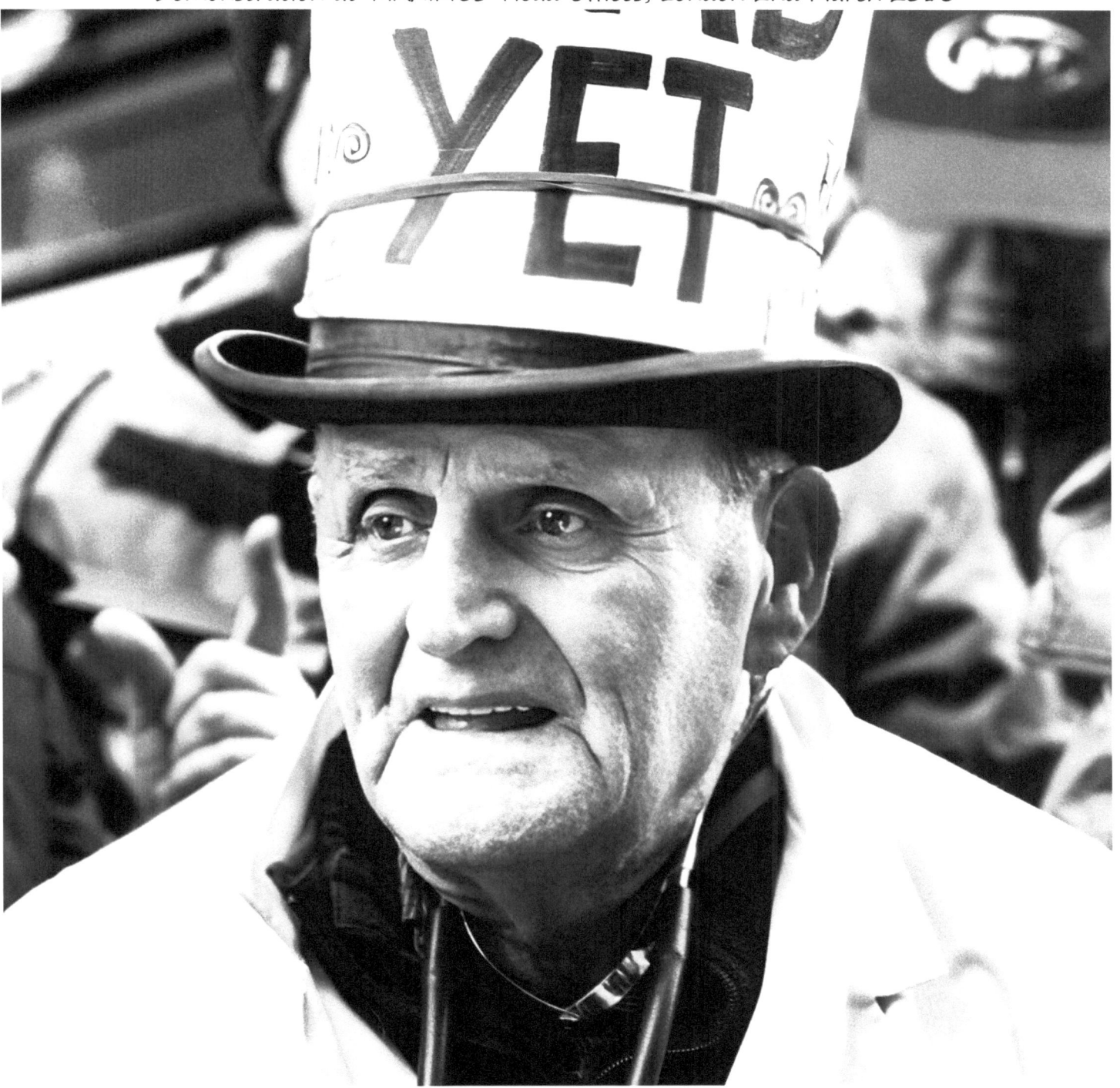

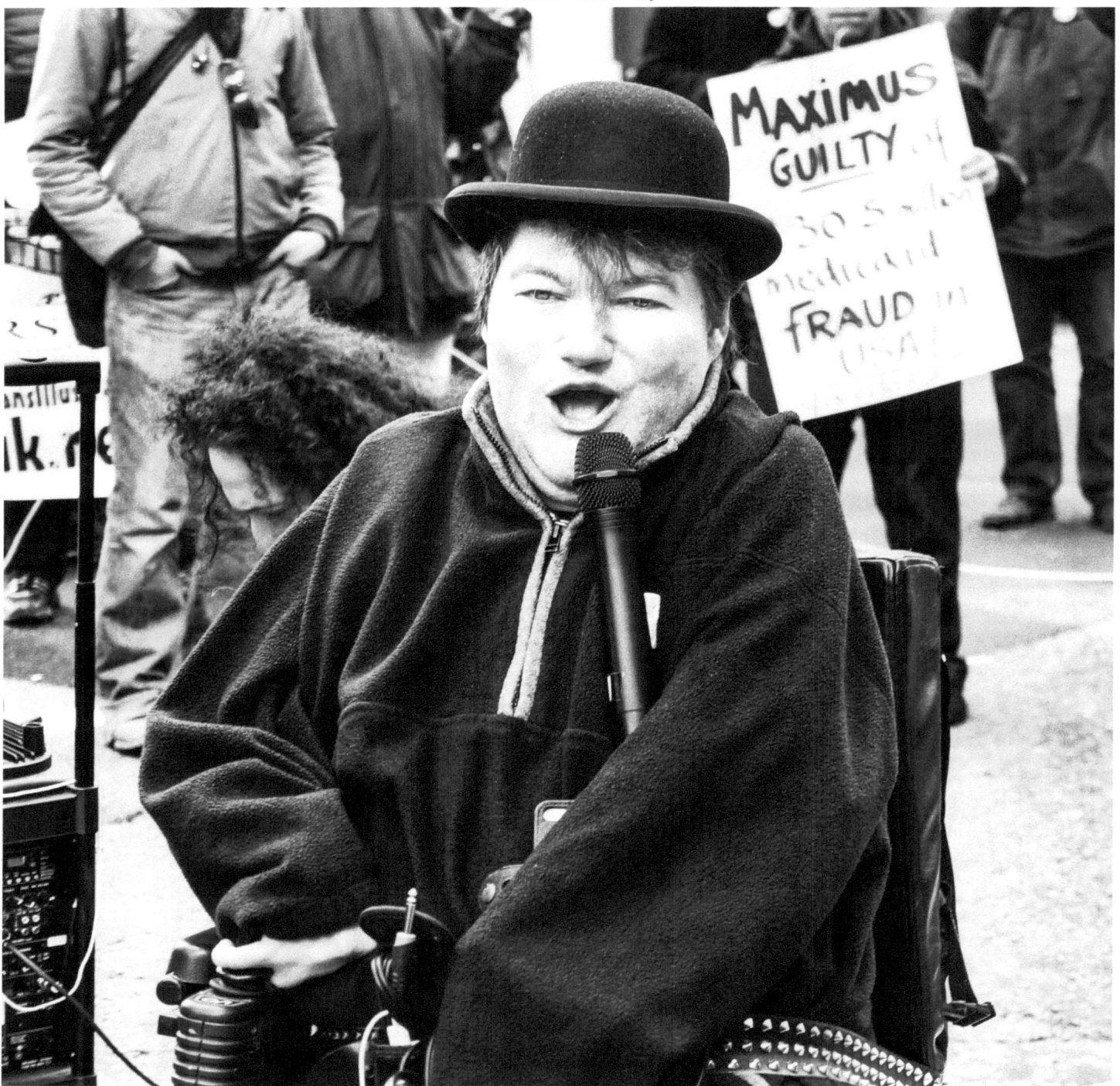

Demonstration at 'MAXIMUS' Head Offices, London 2nd March 2015

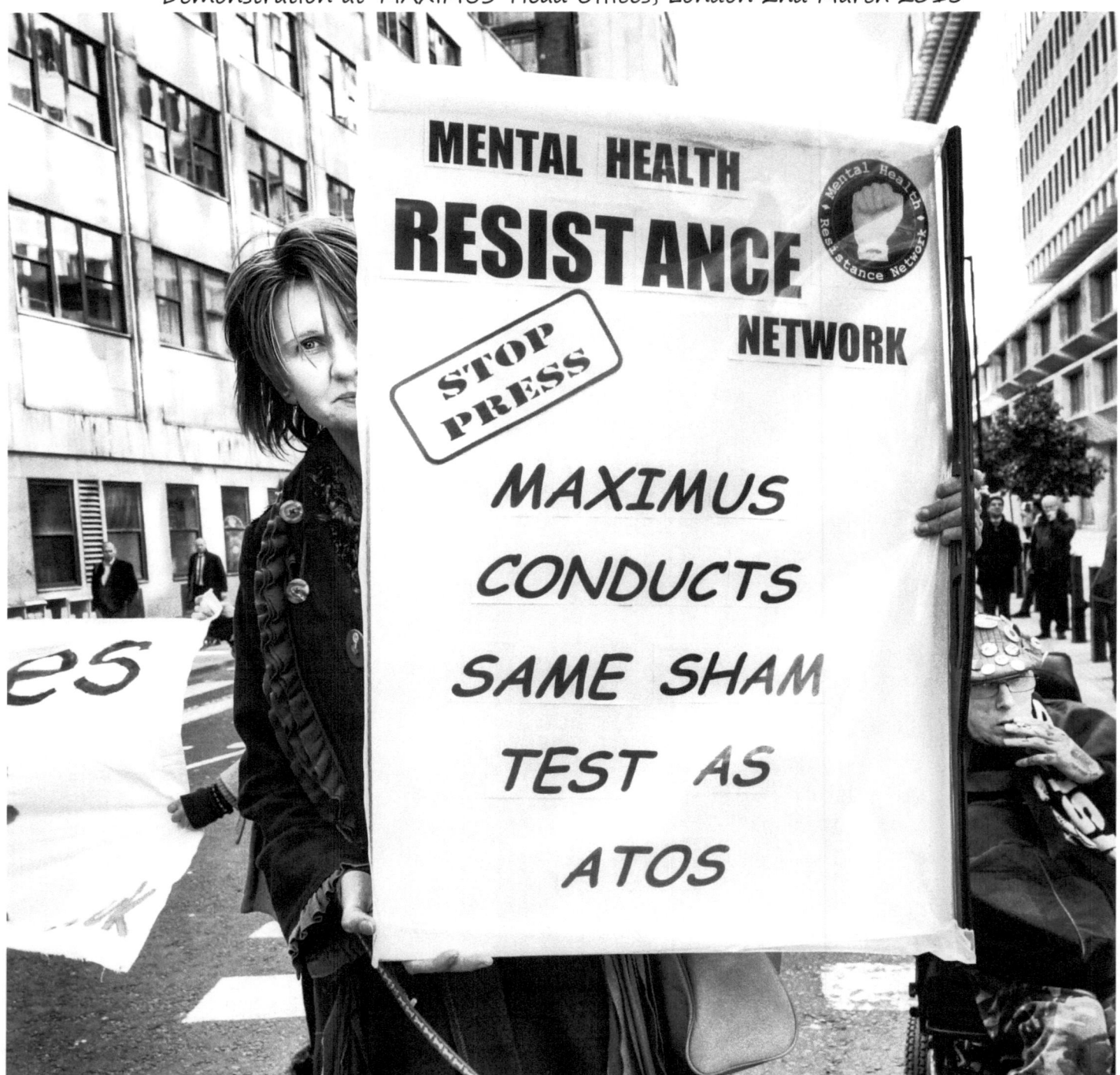

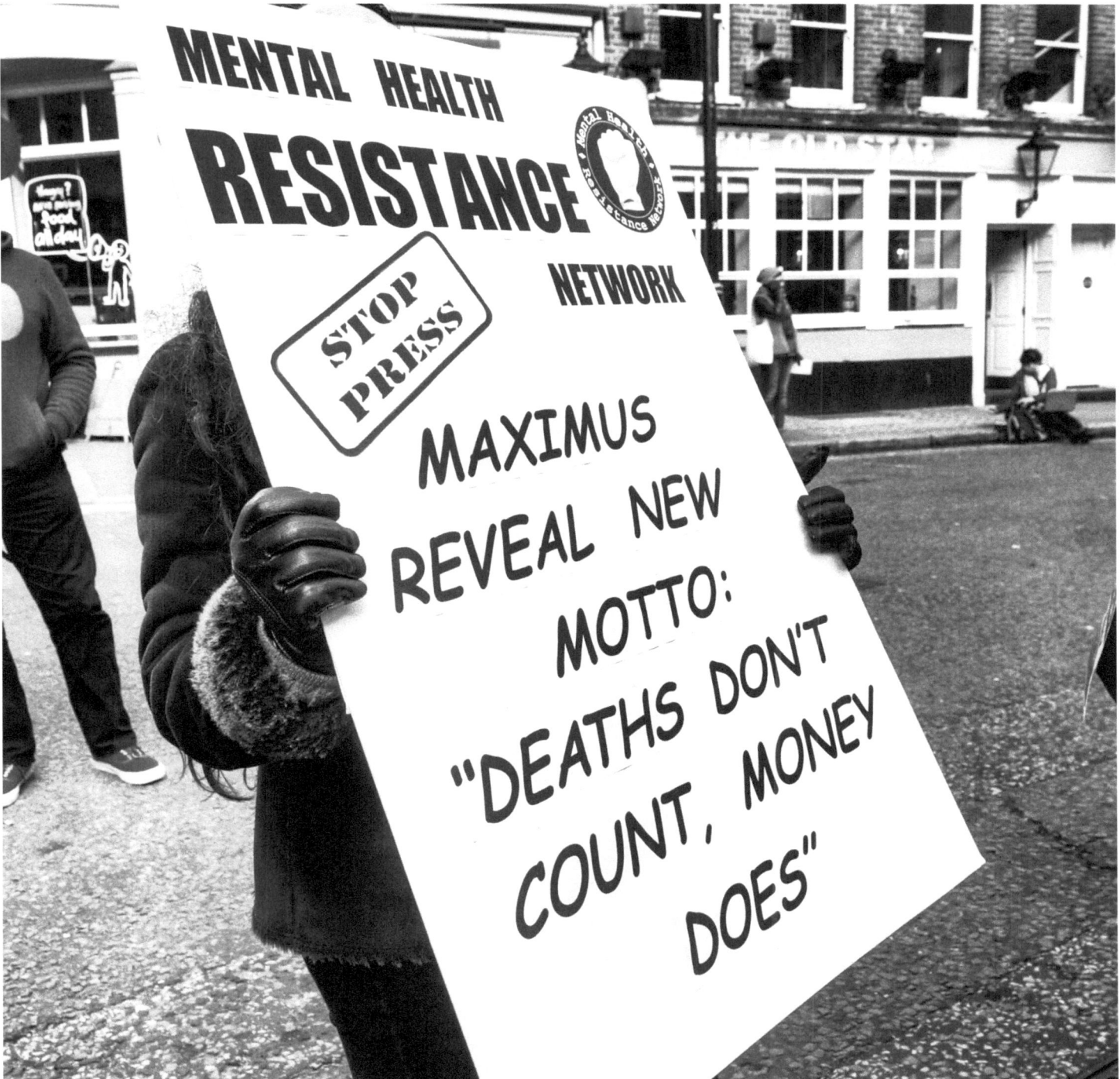

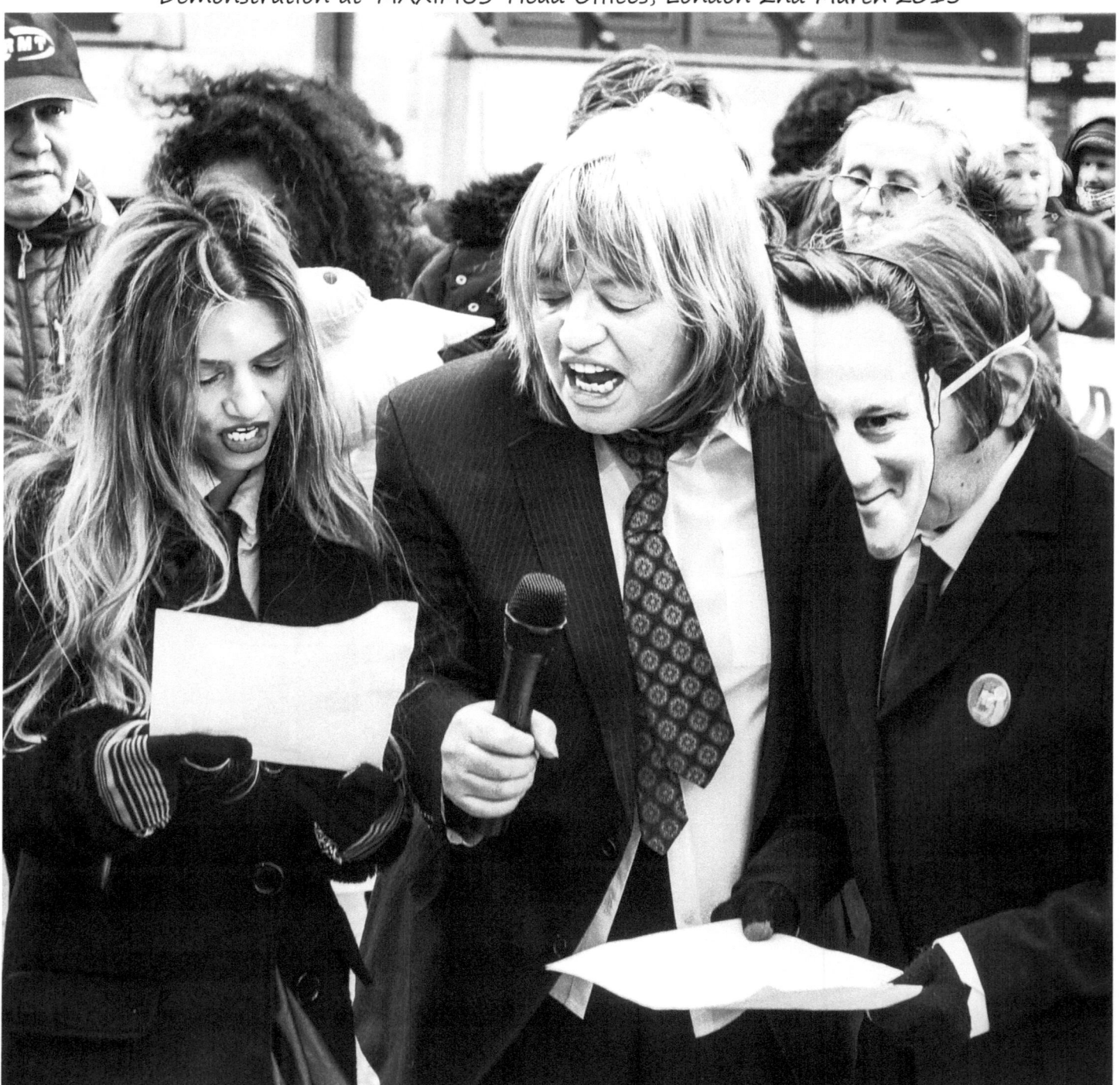

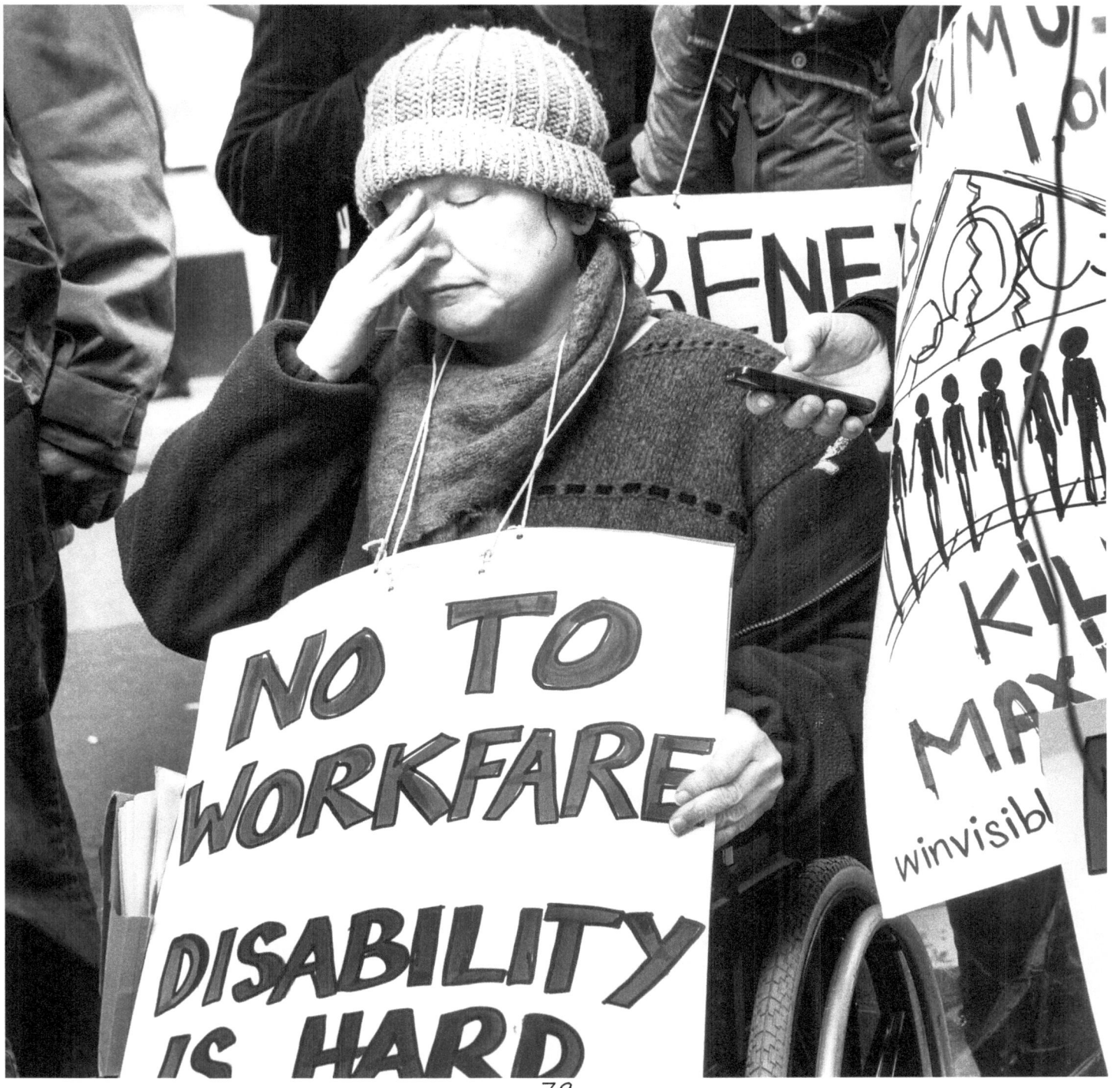

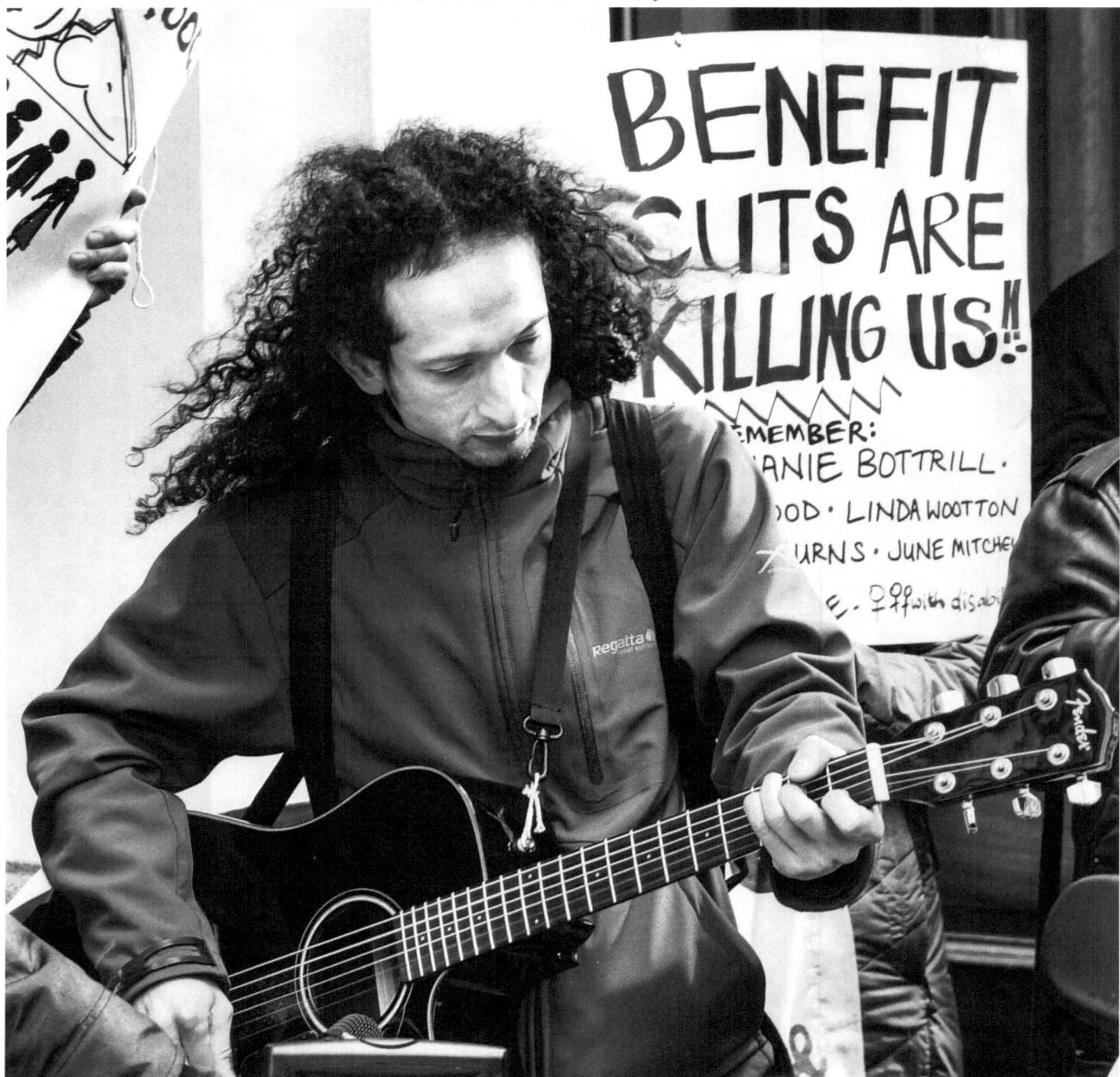

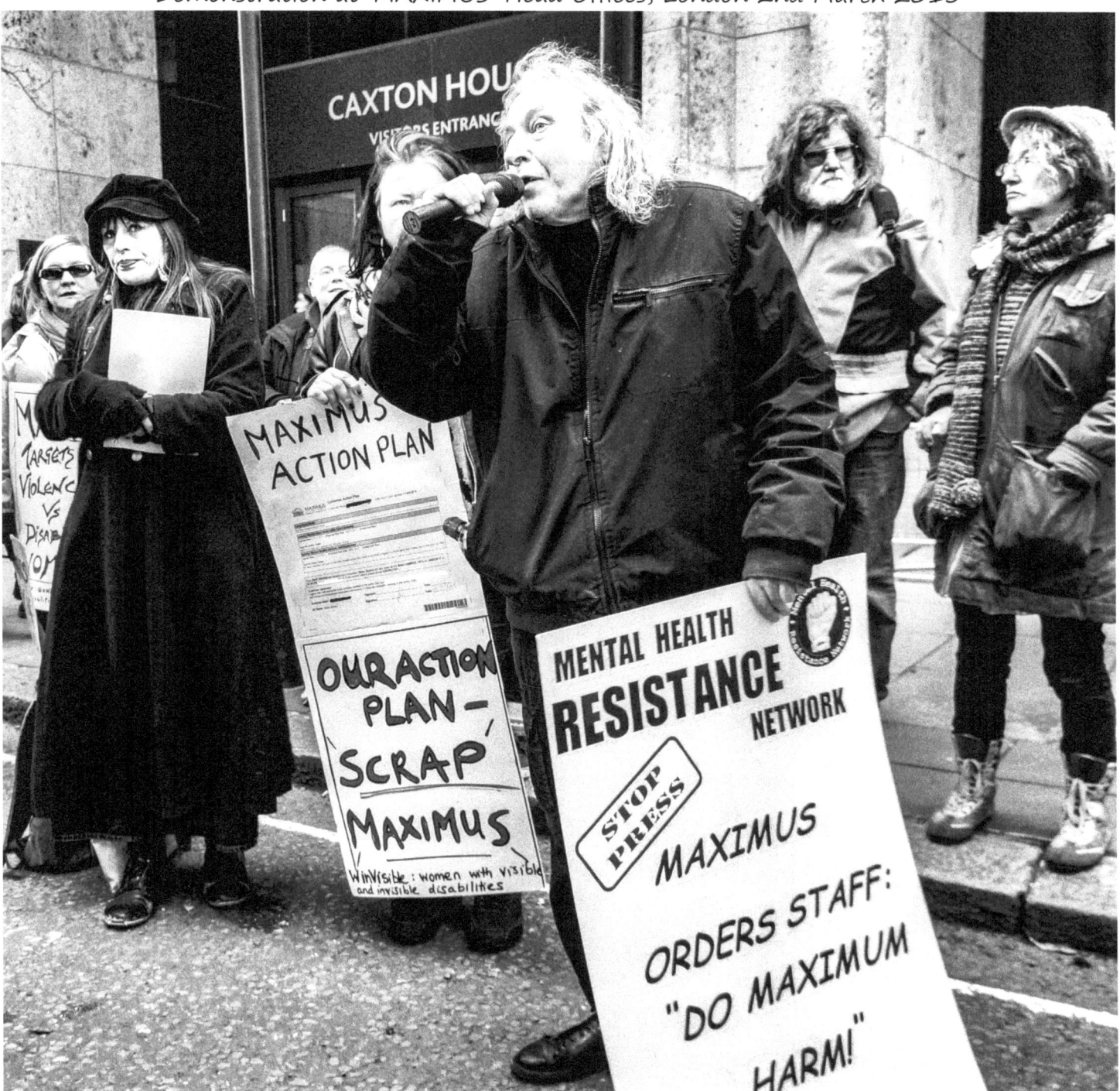

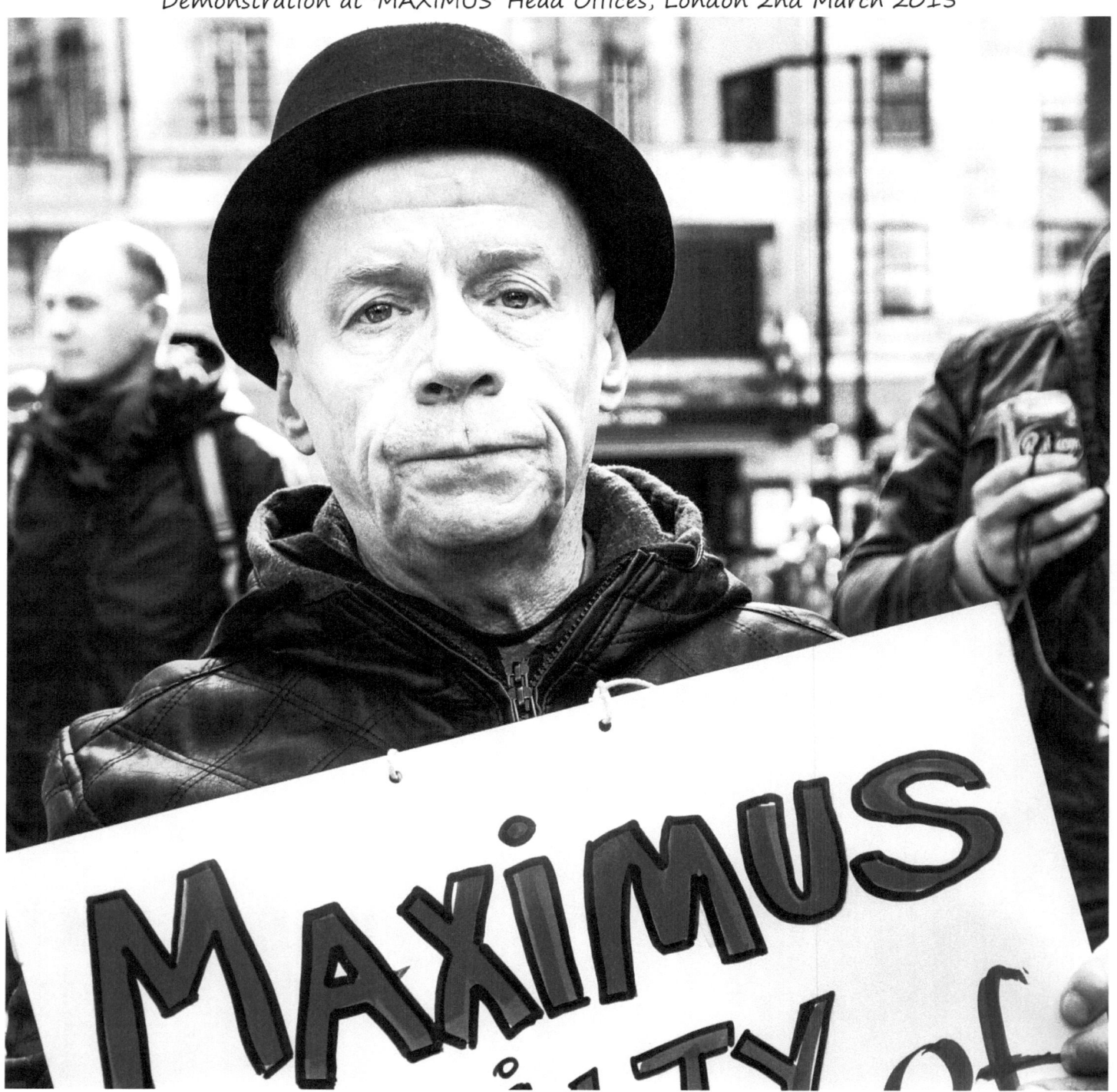

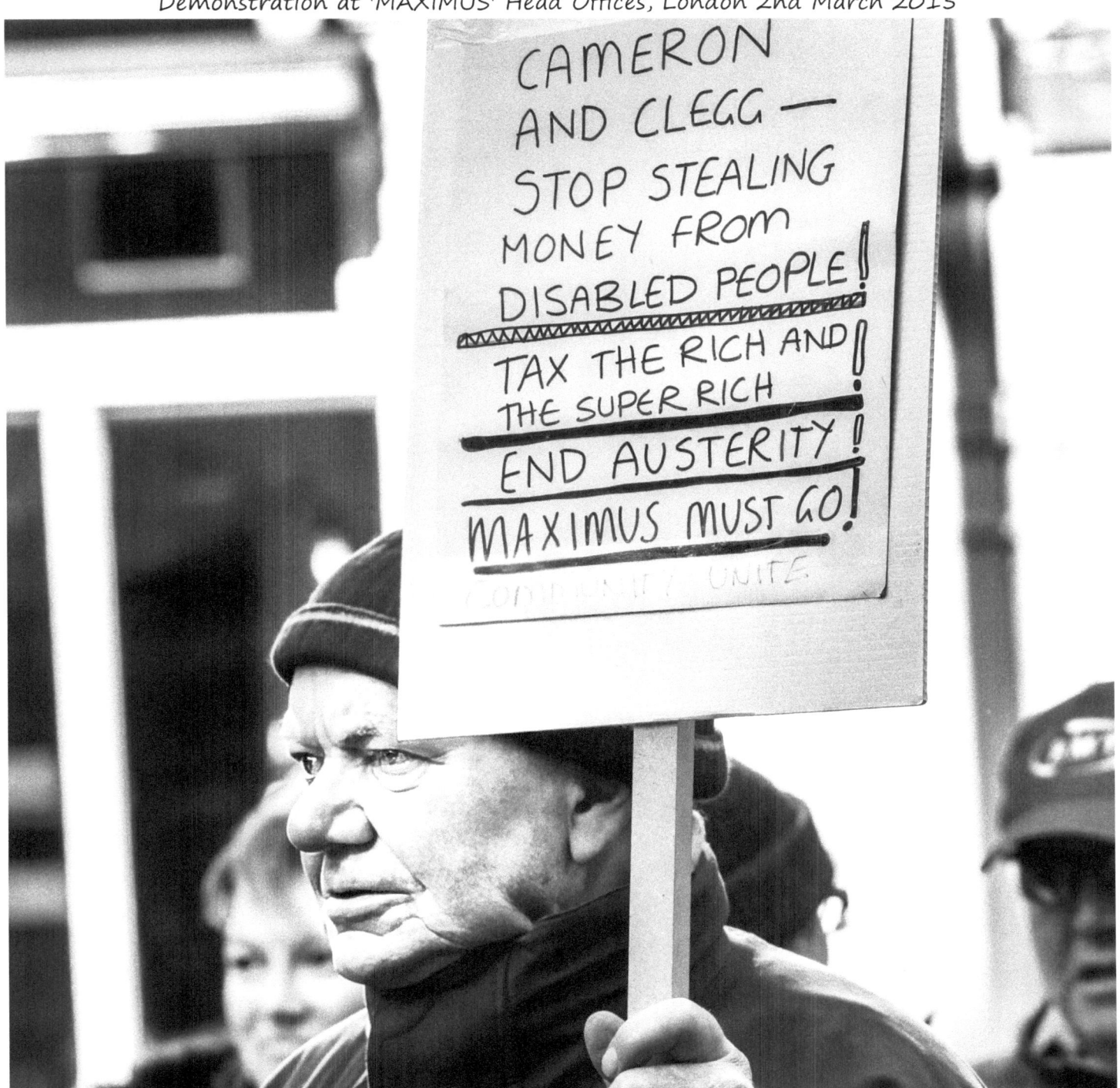

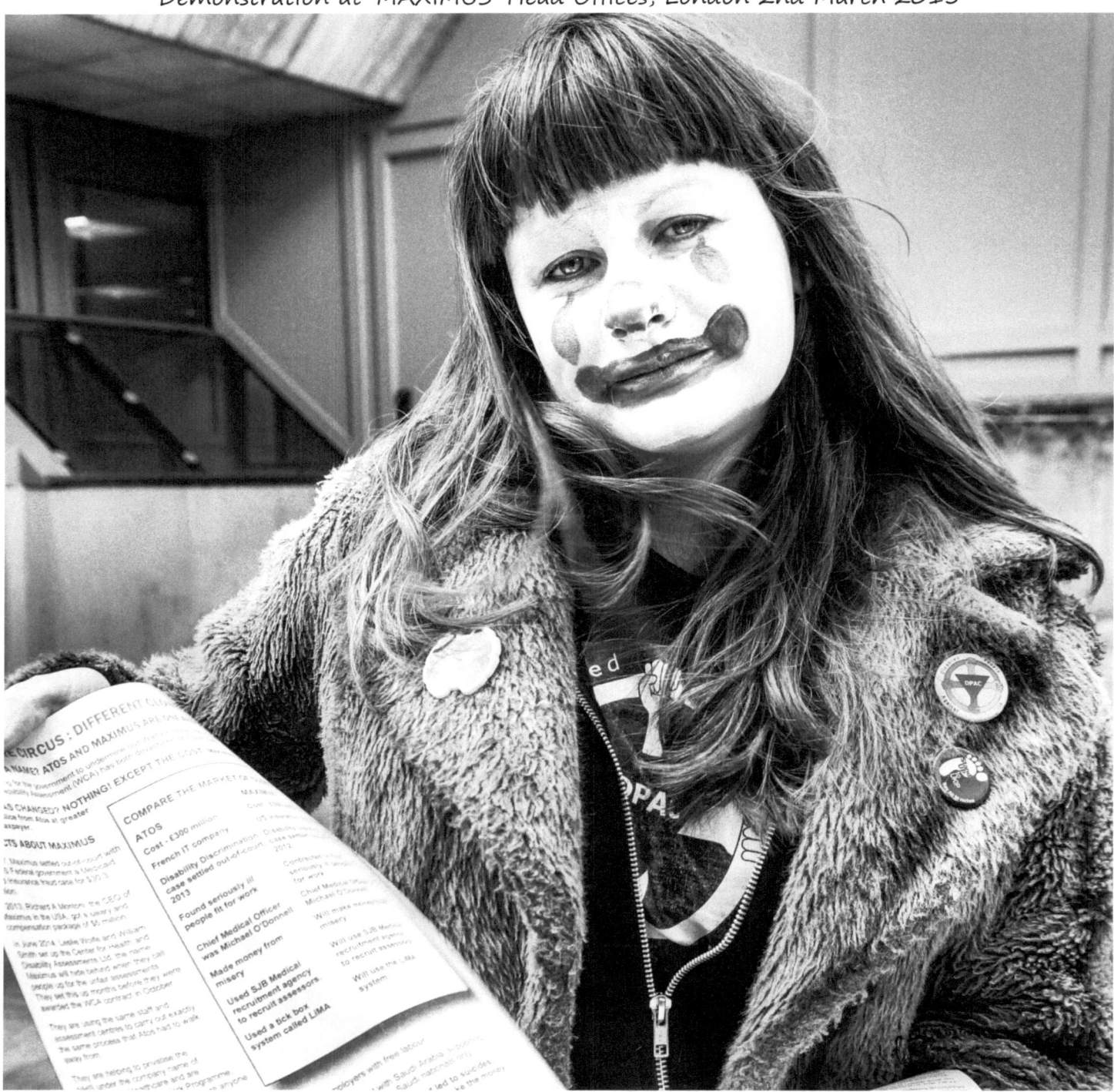

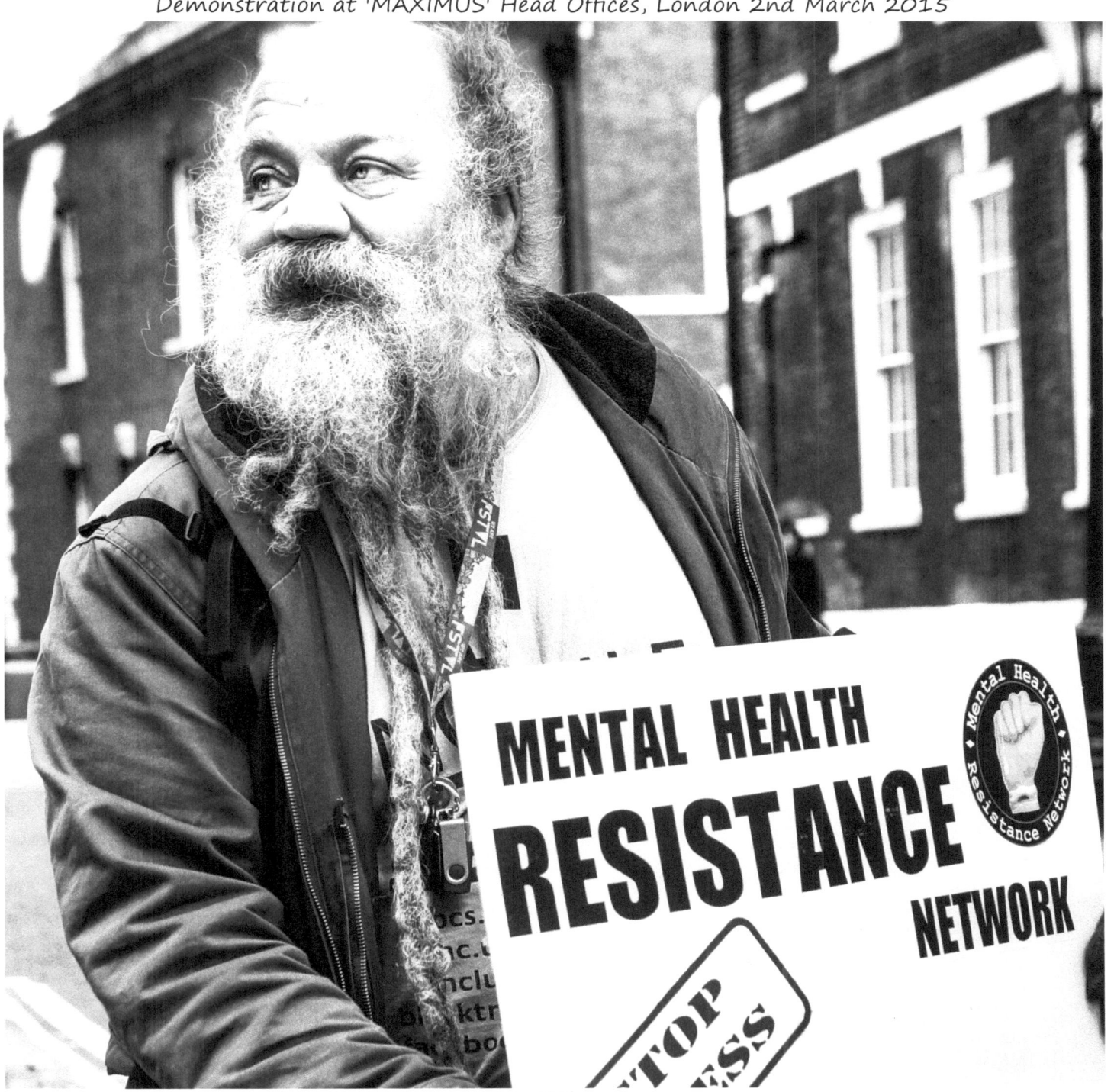

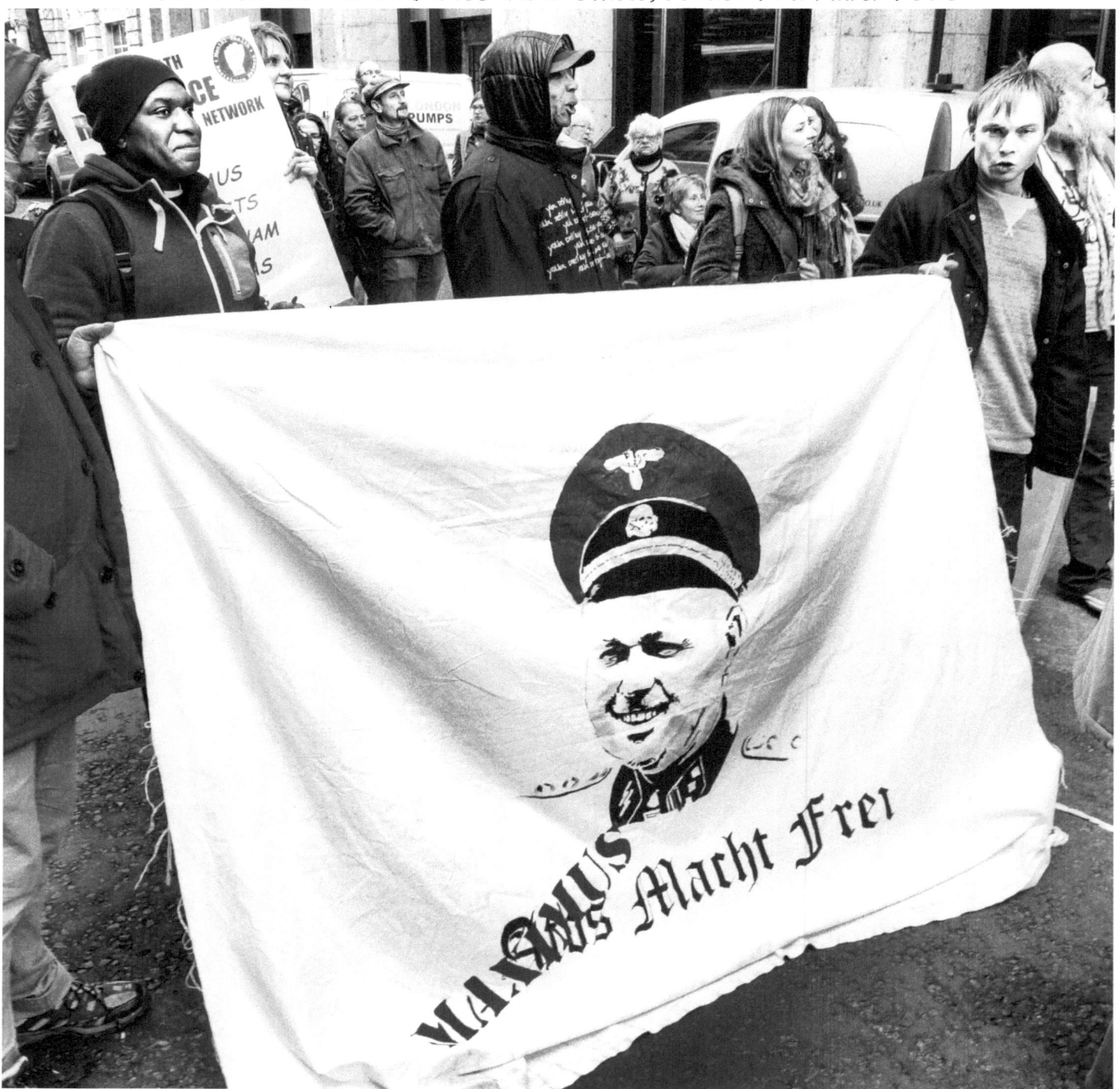

SCREWING THE DISABLED FOR MONEY-

MAXIMUS

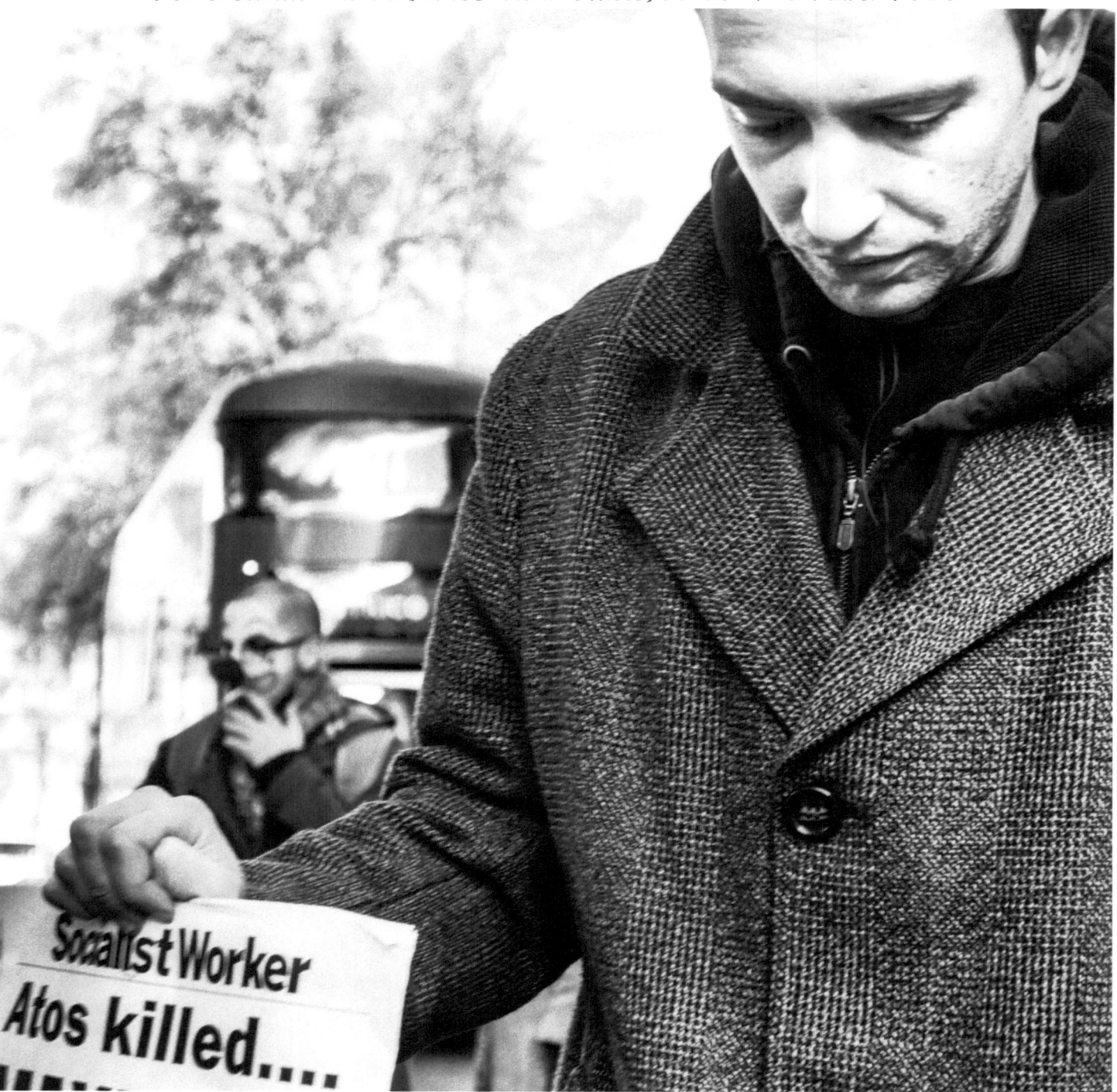

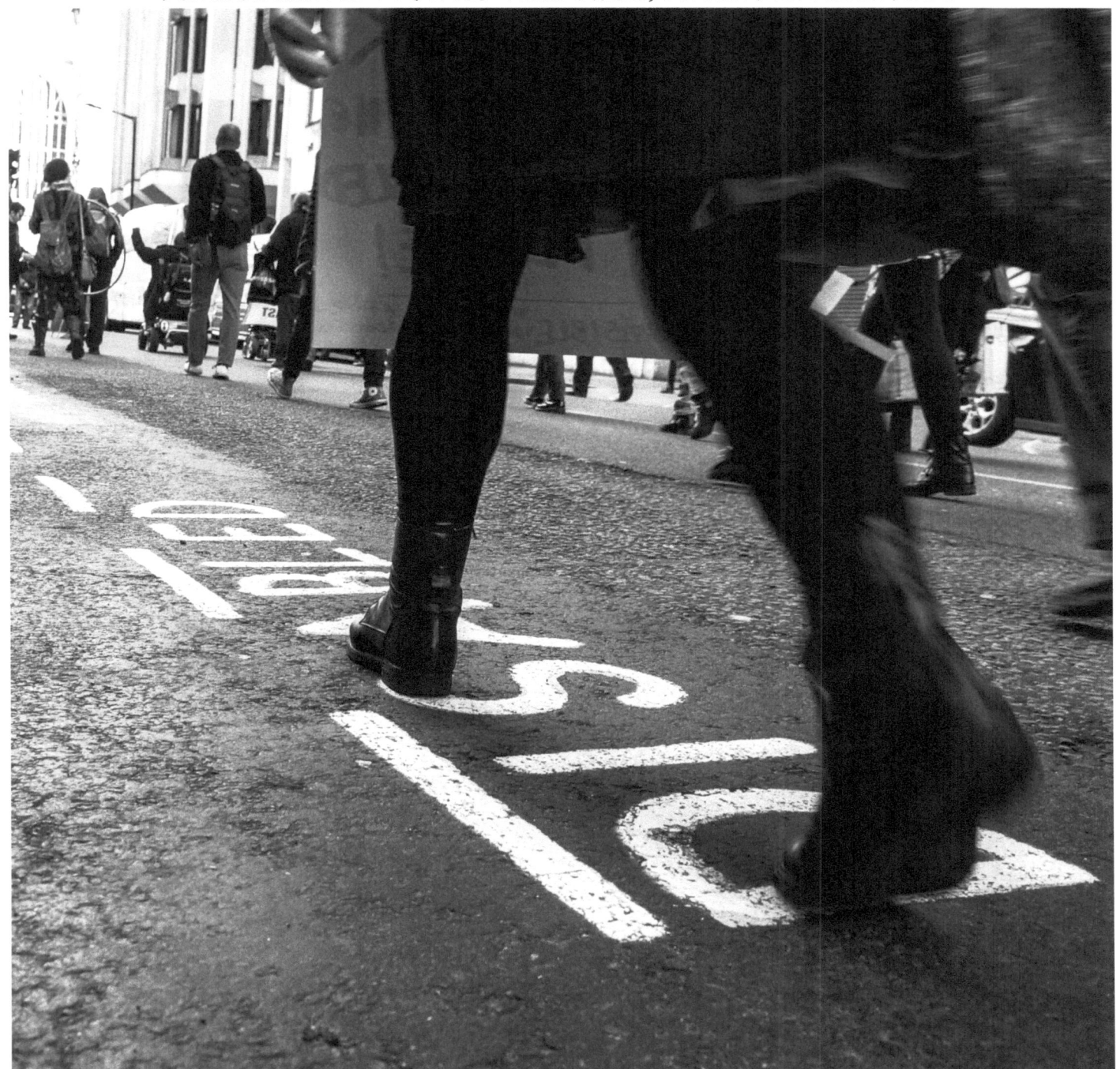

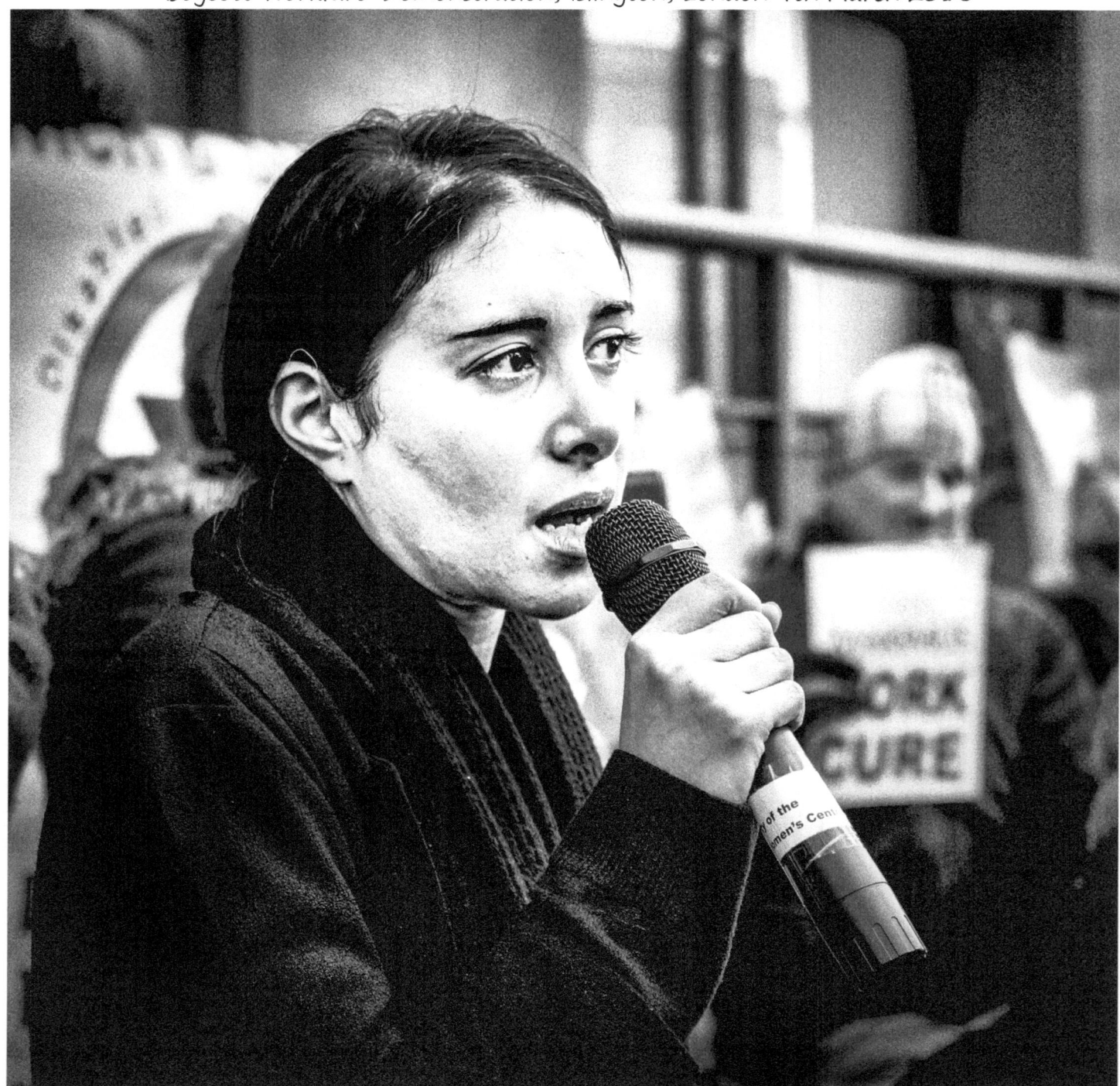

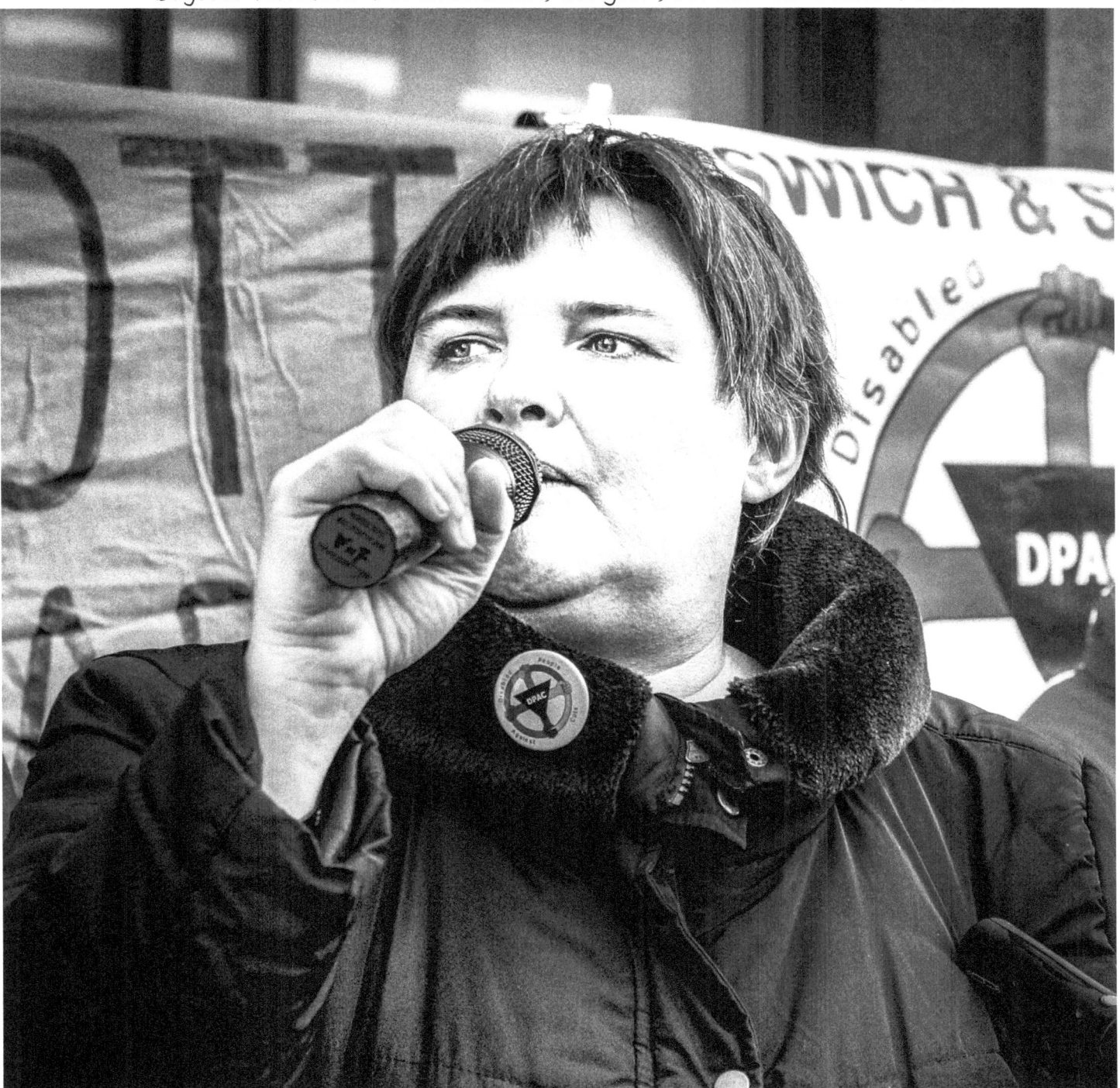

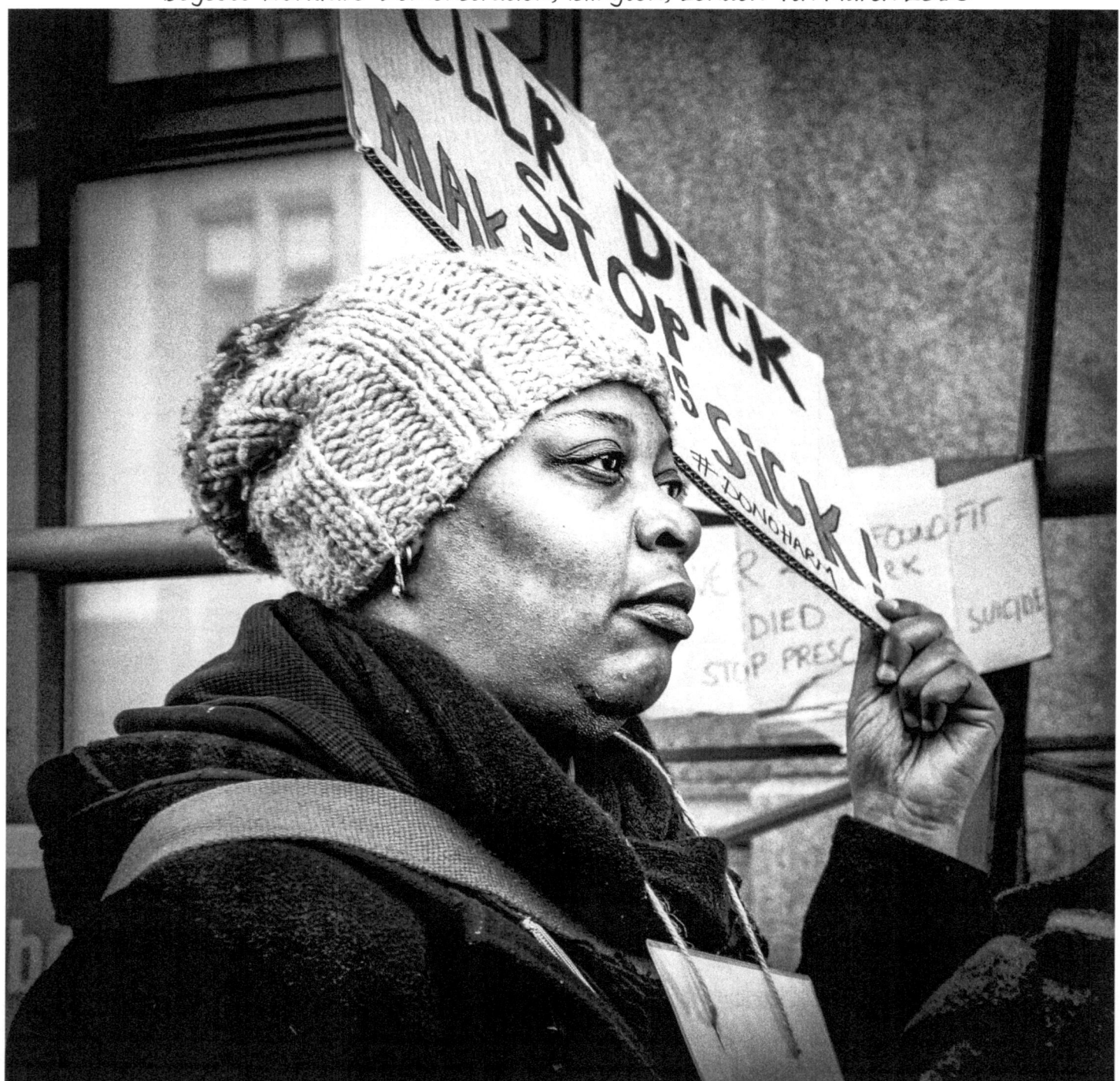

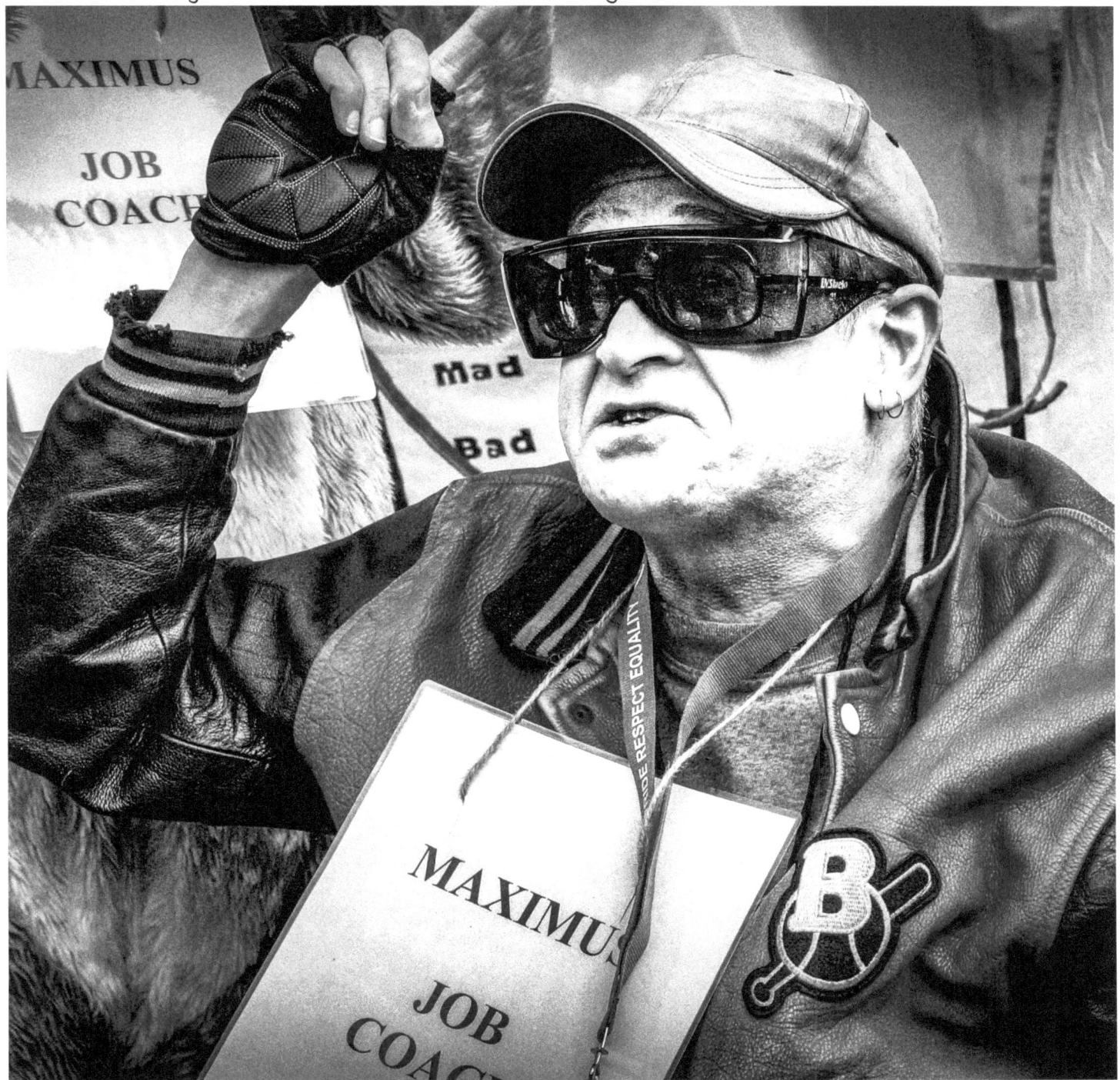

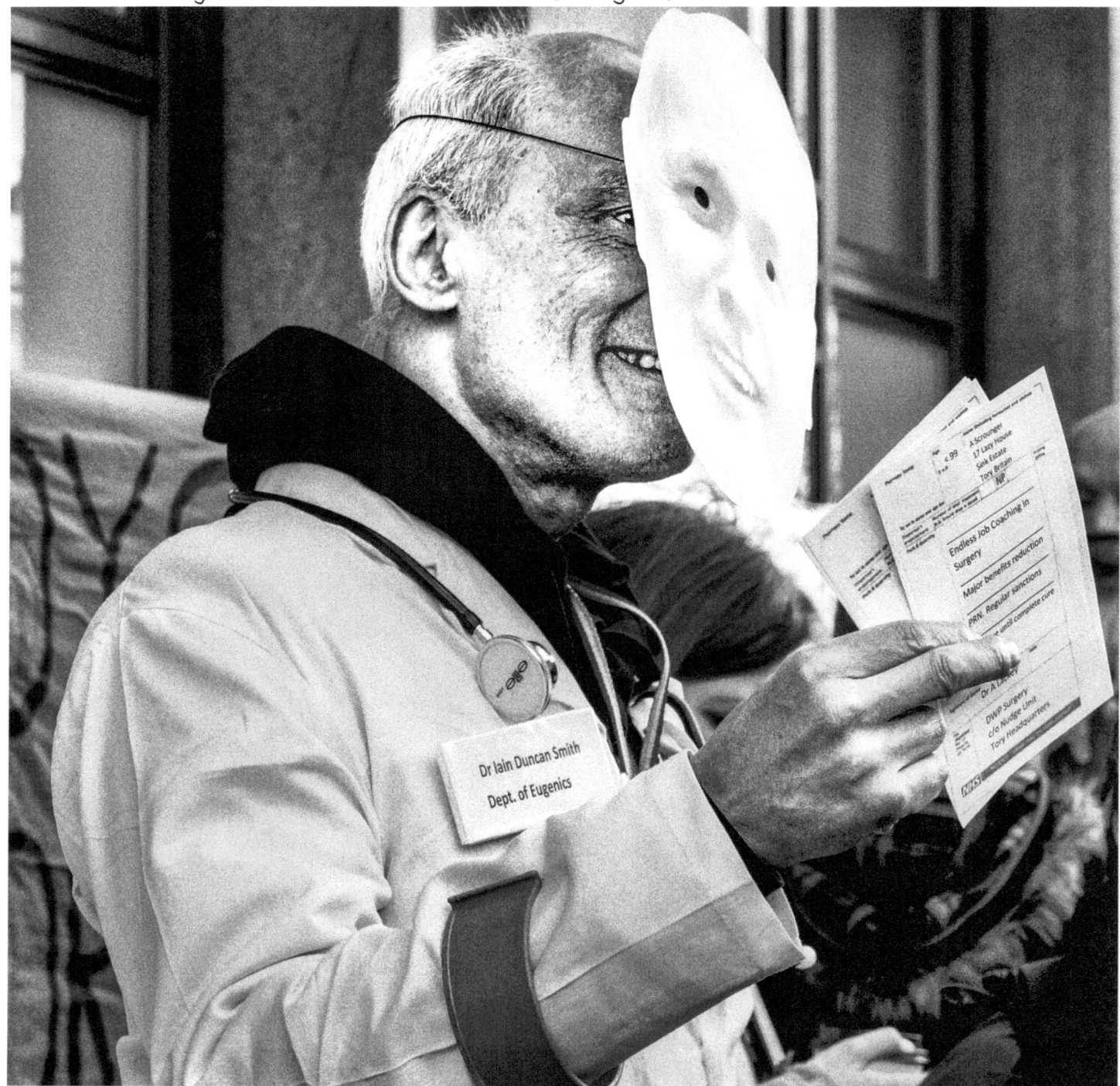

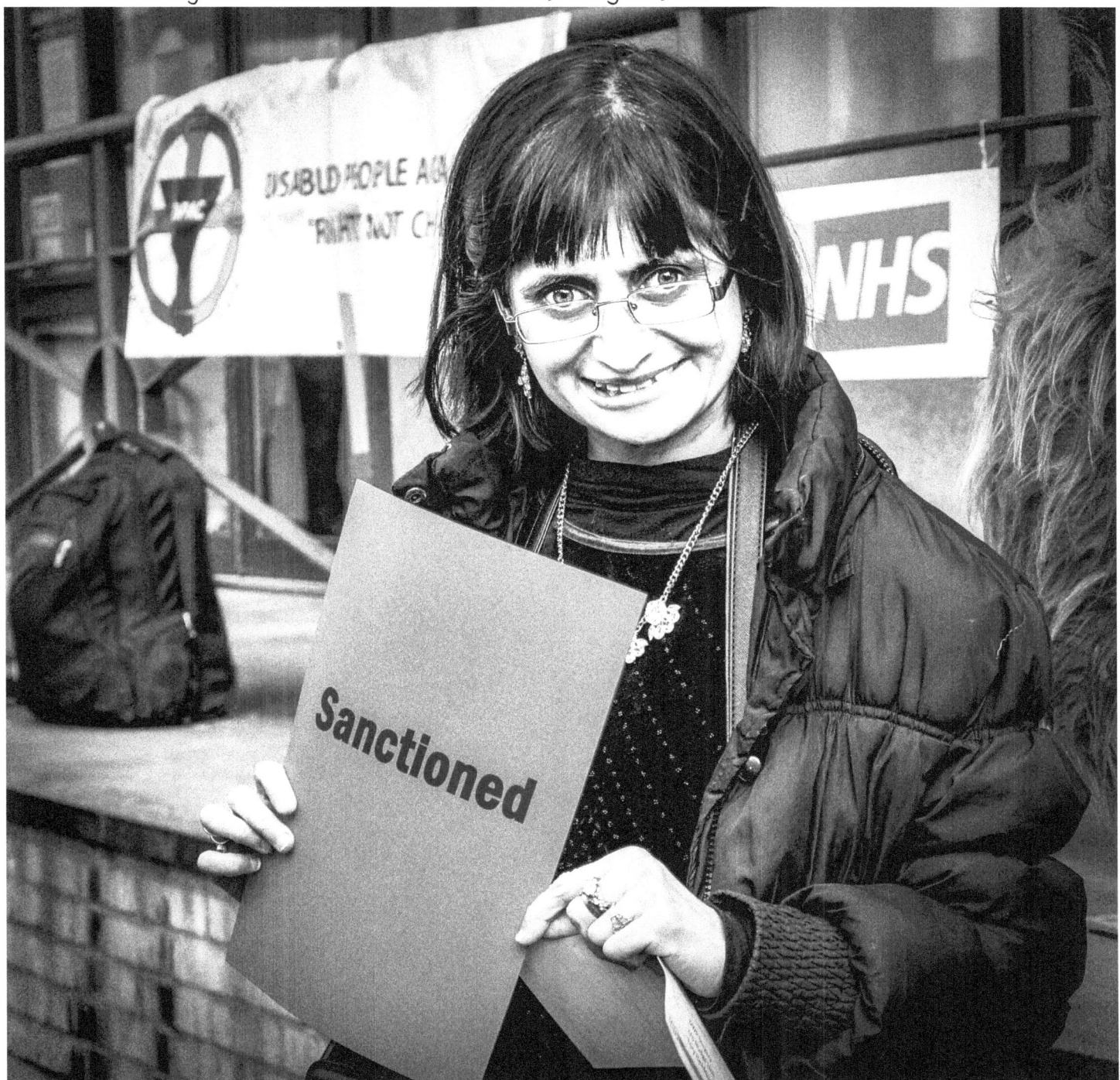

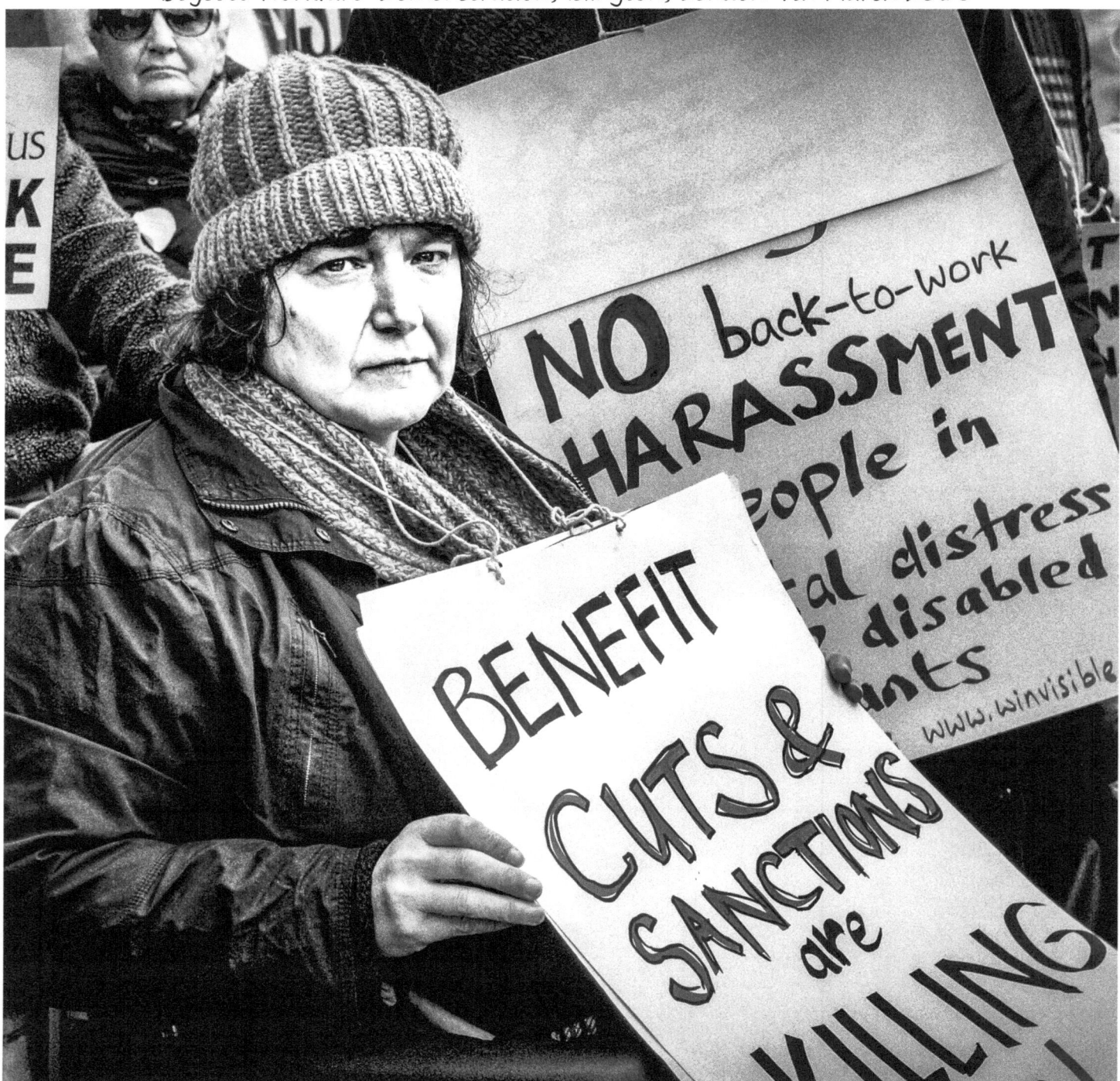

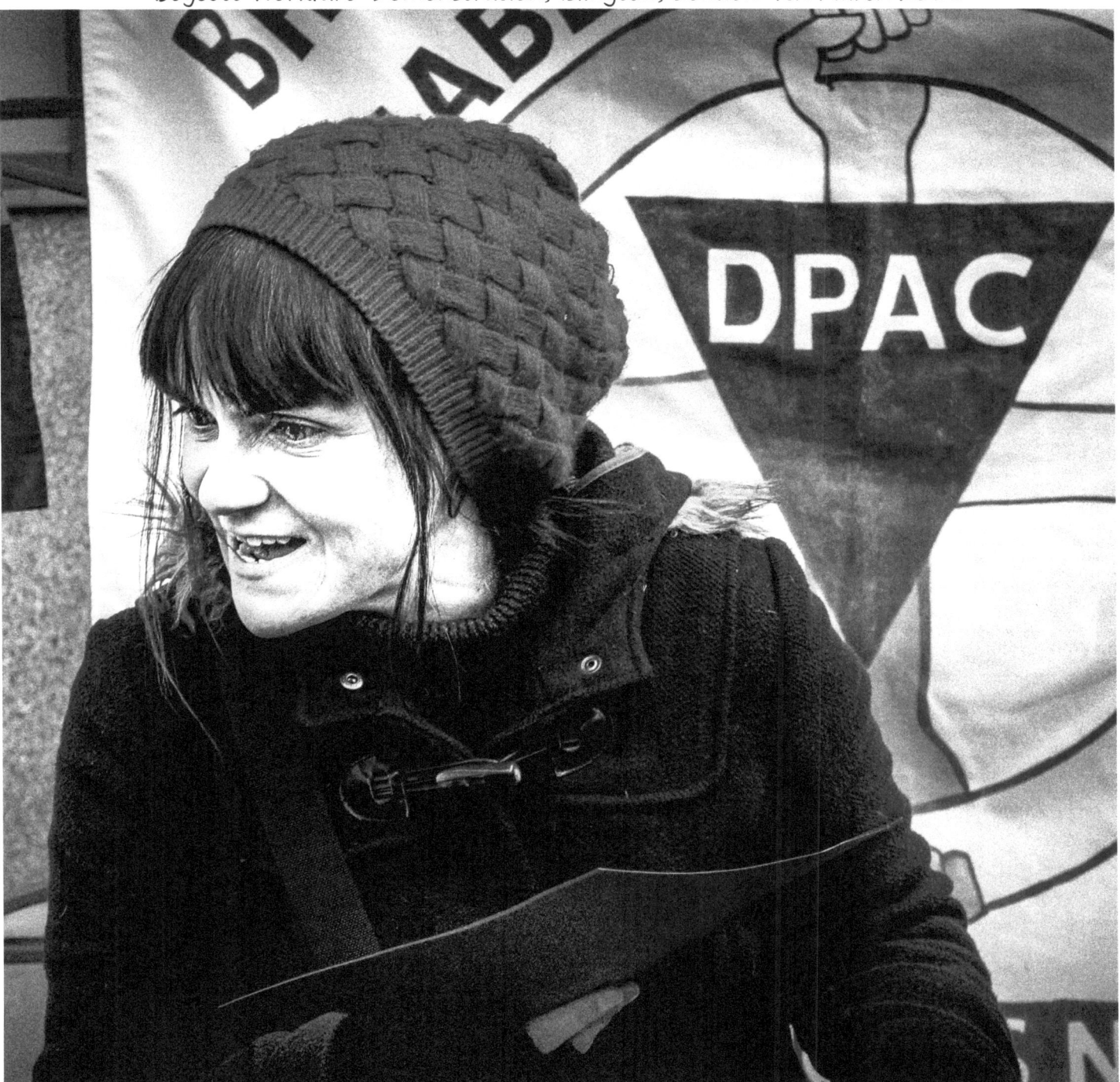

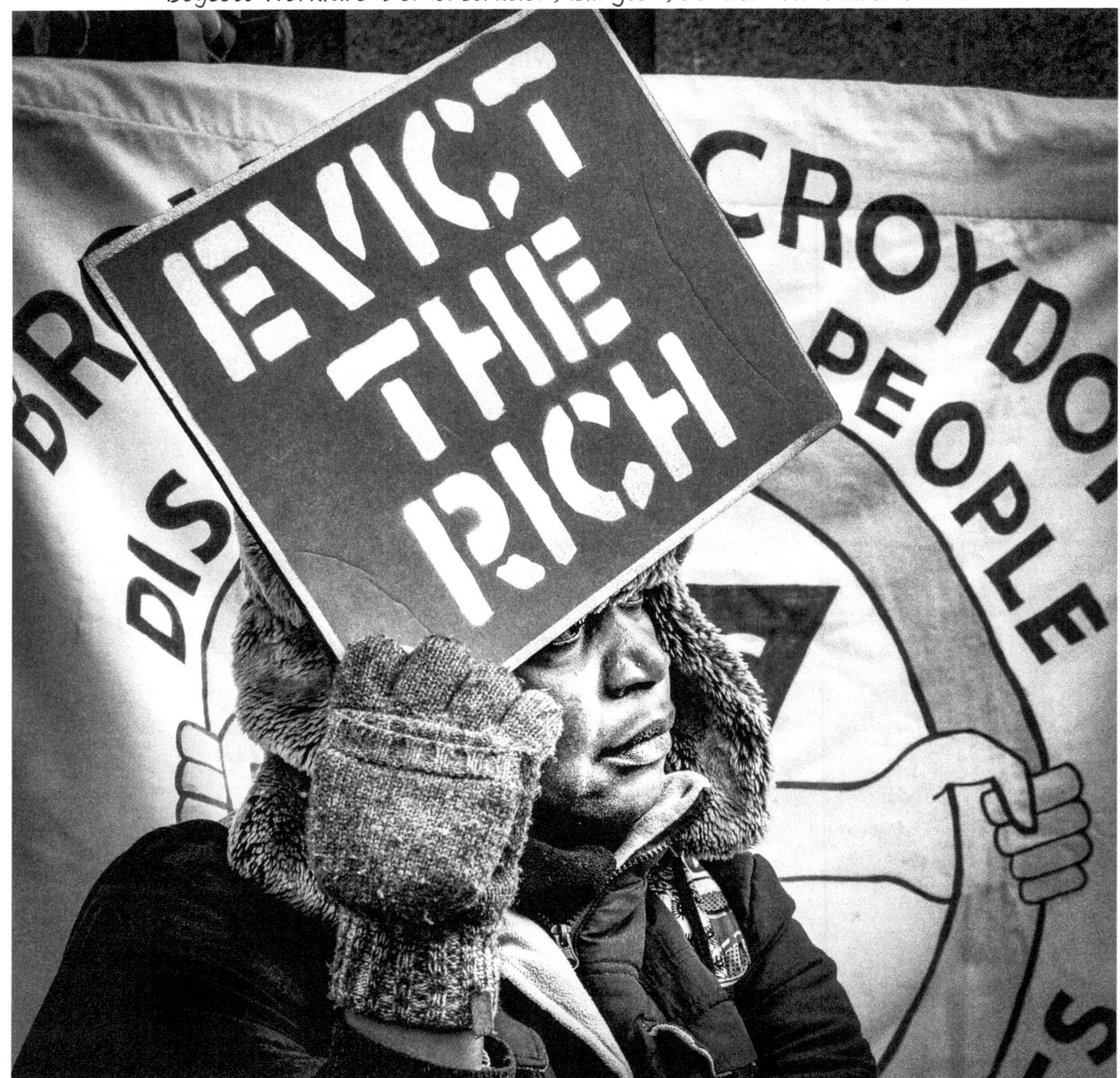

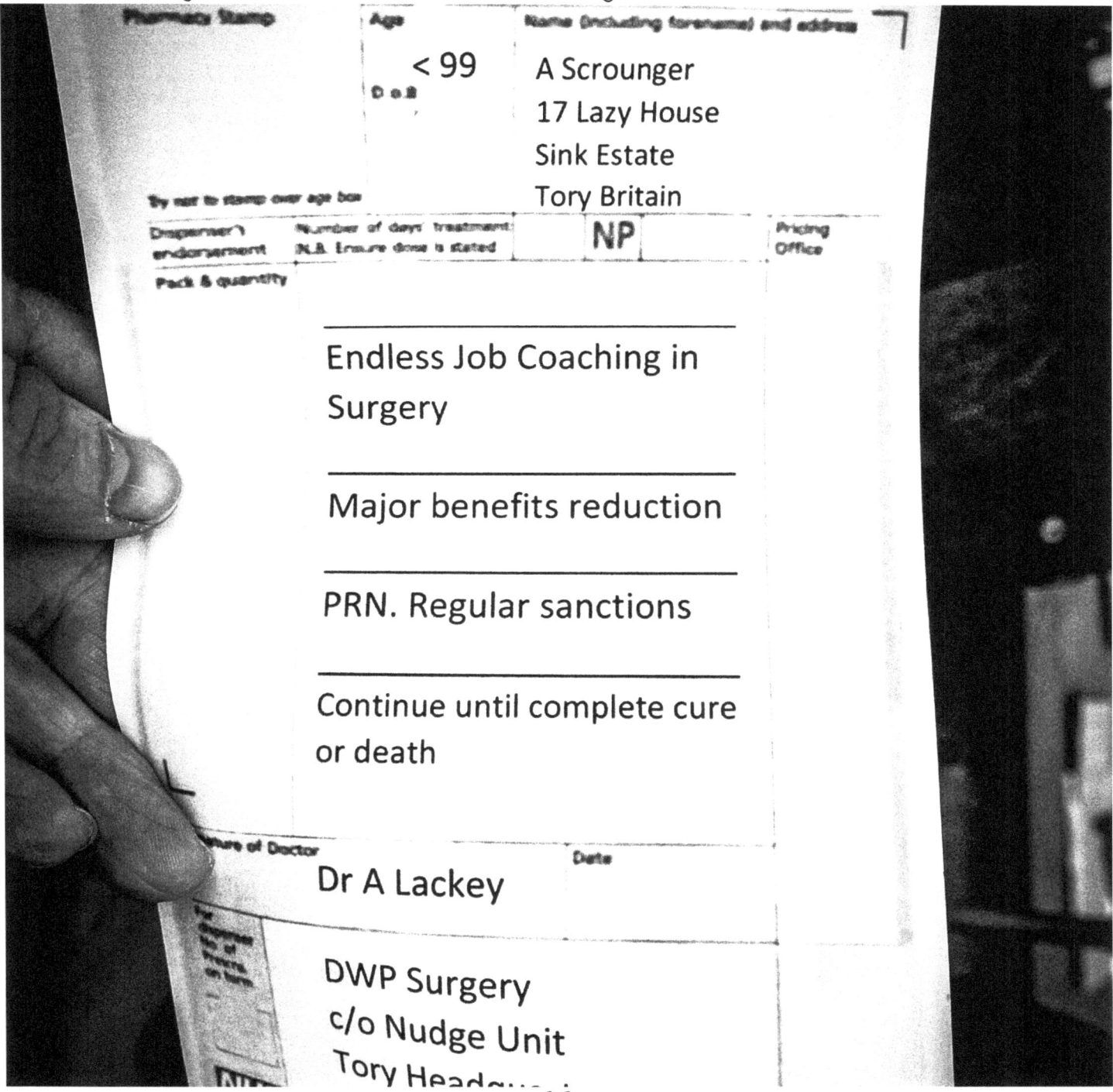

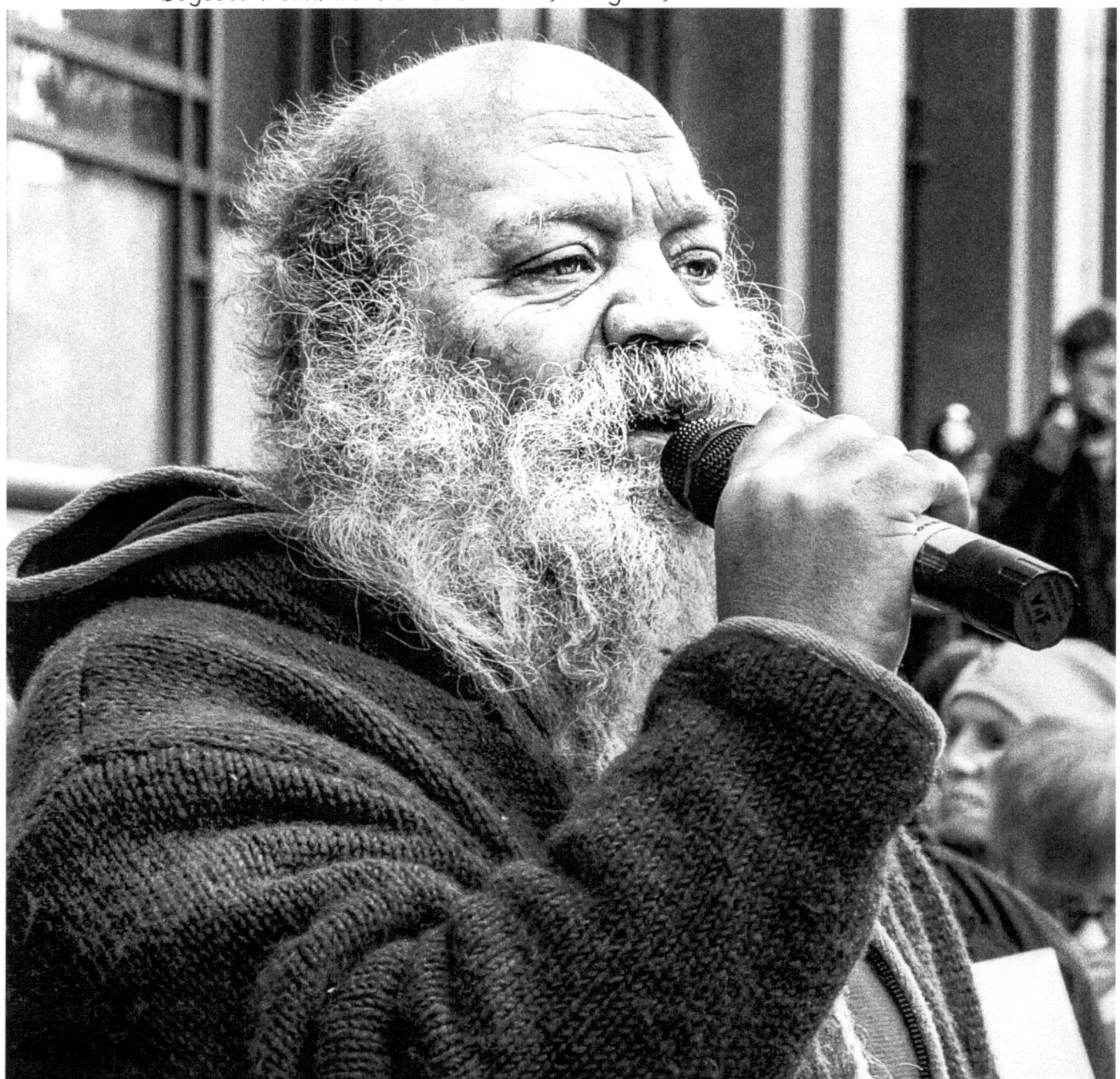

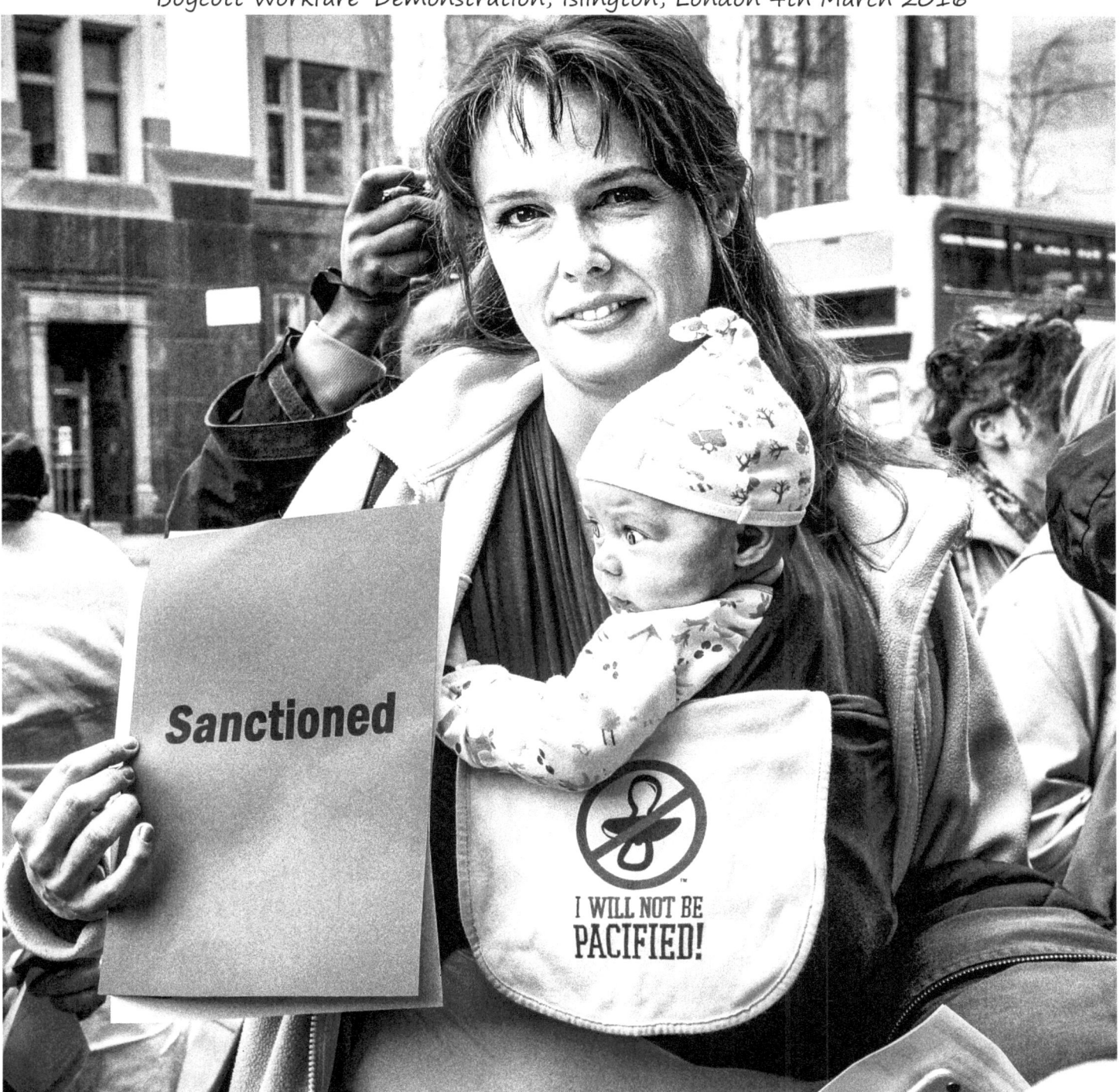

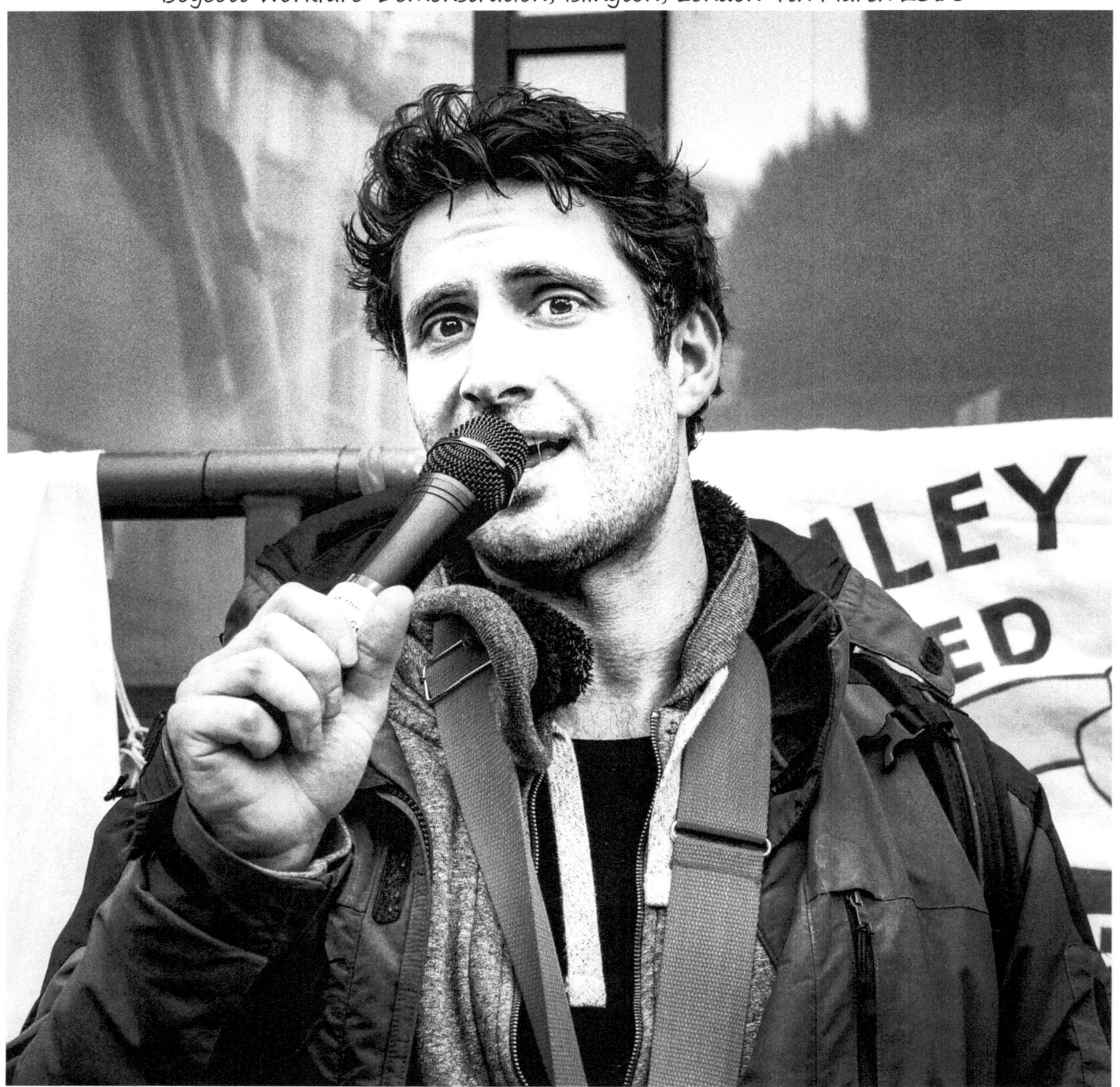

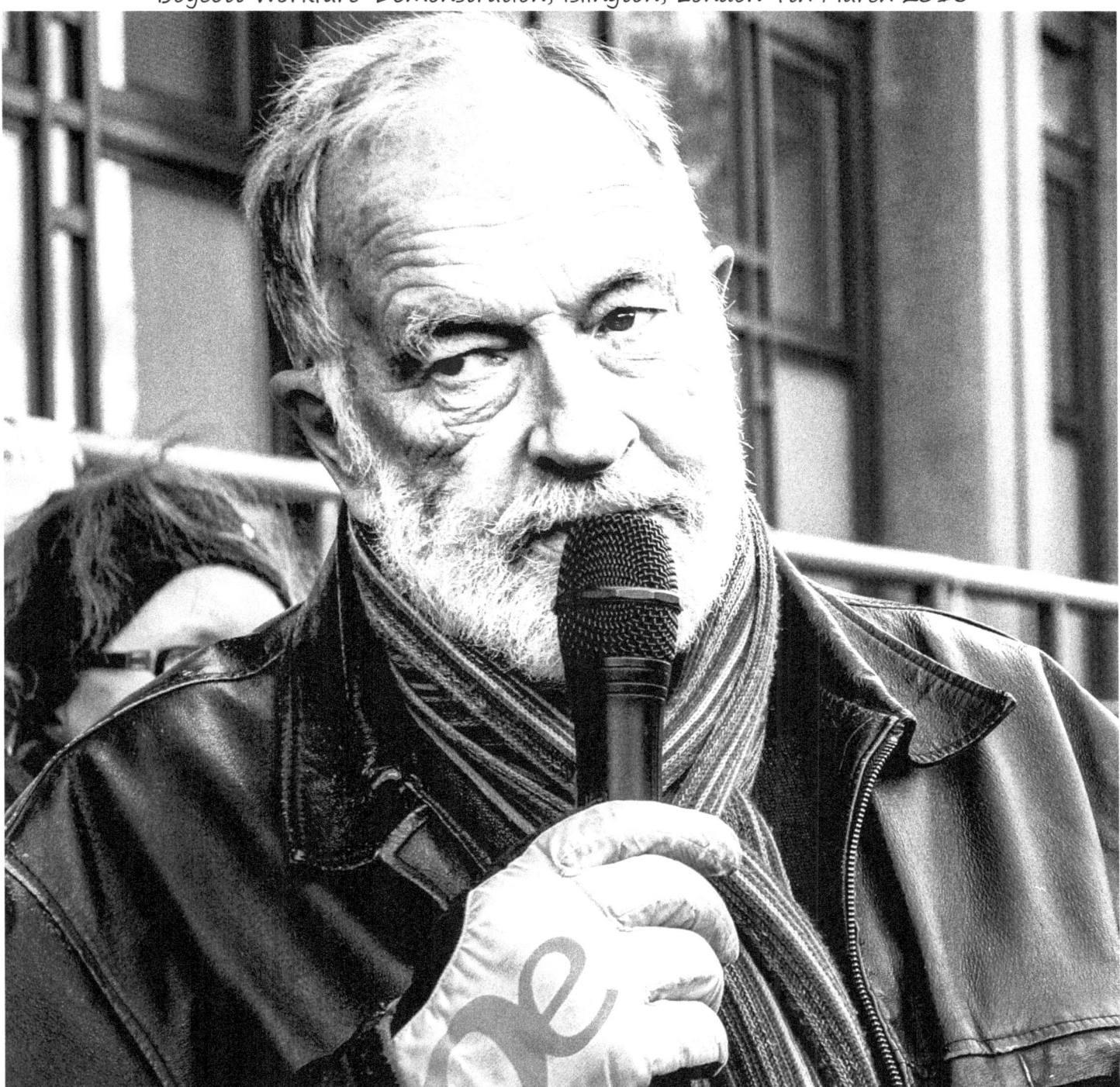

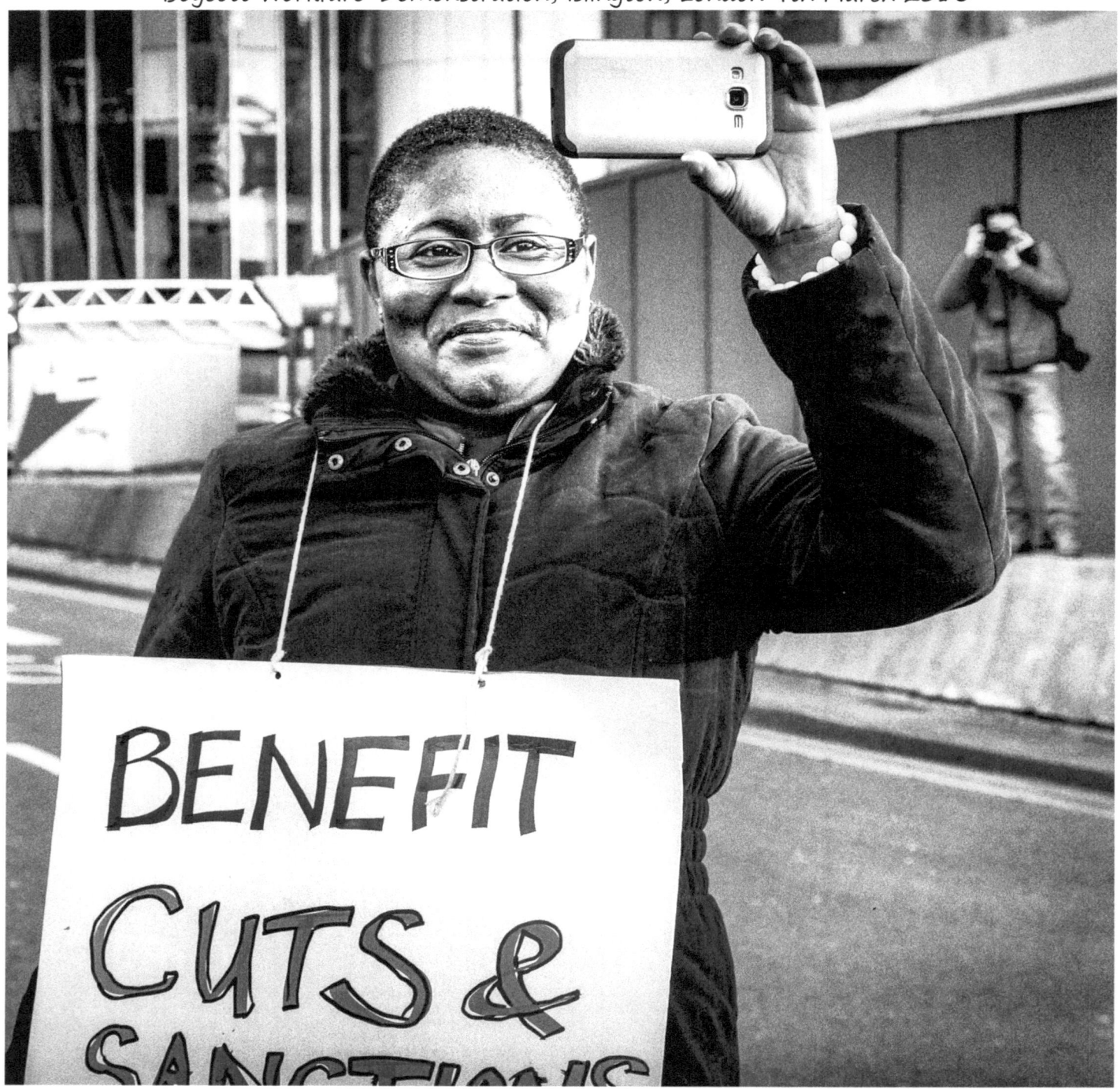

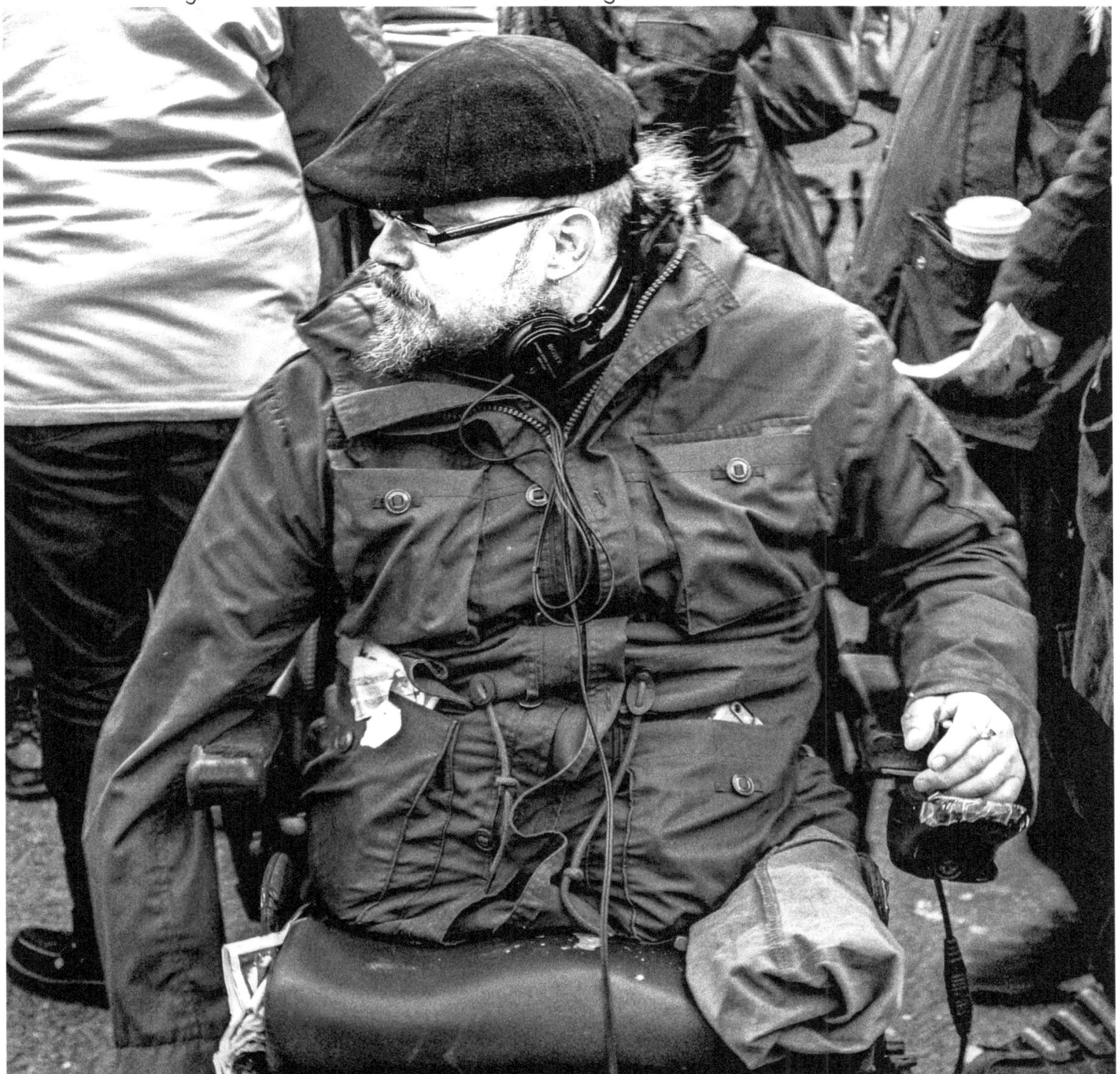

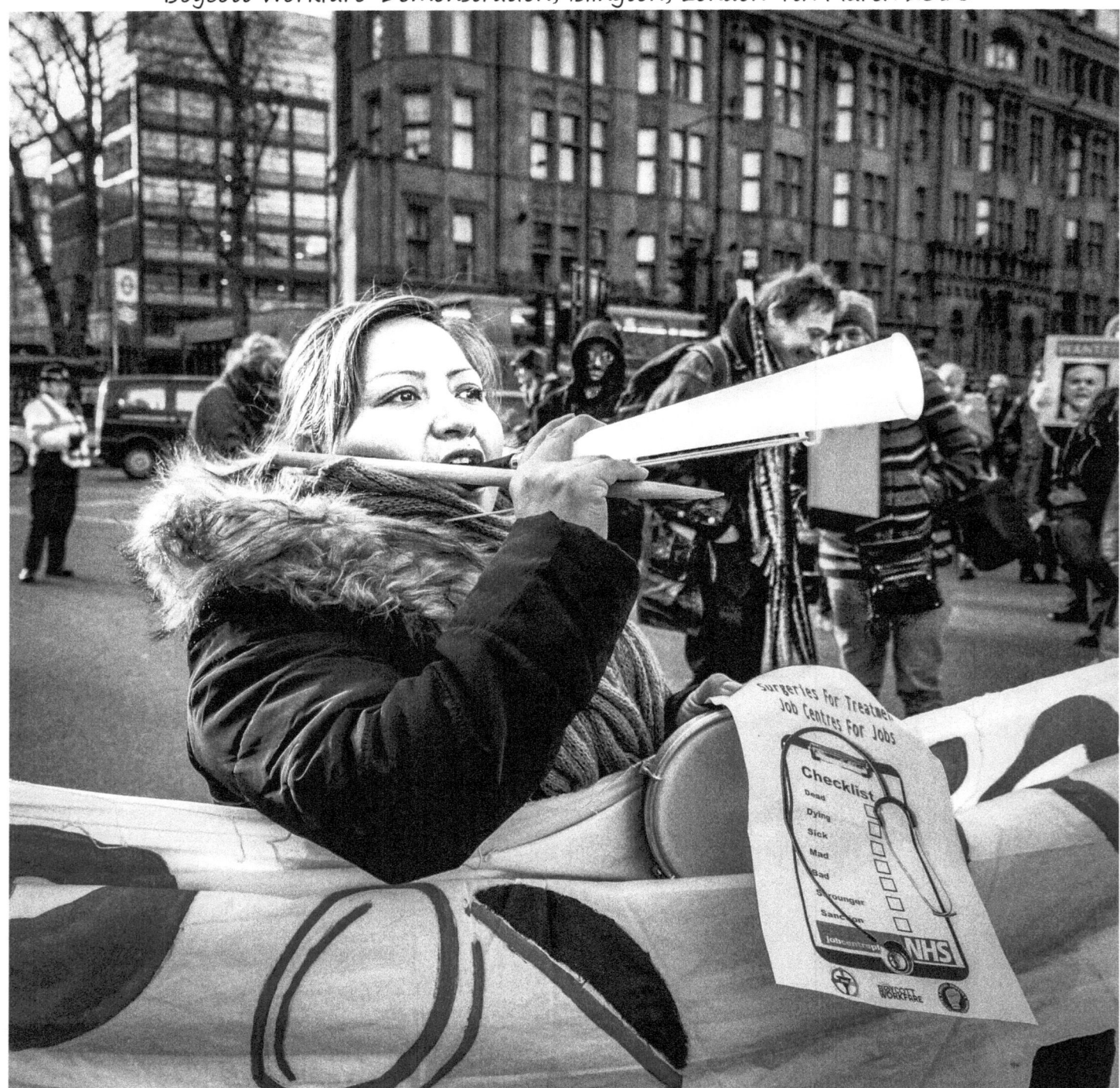

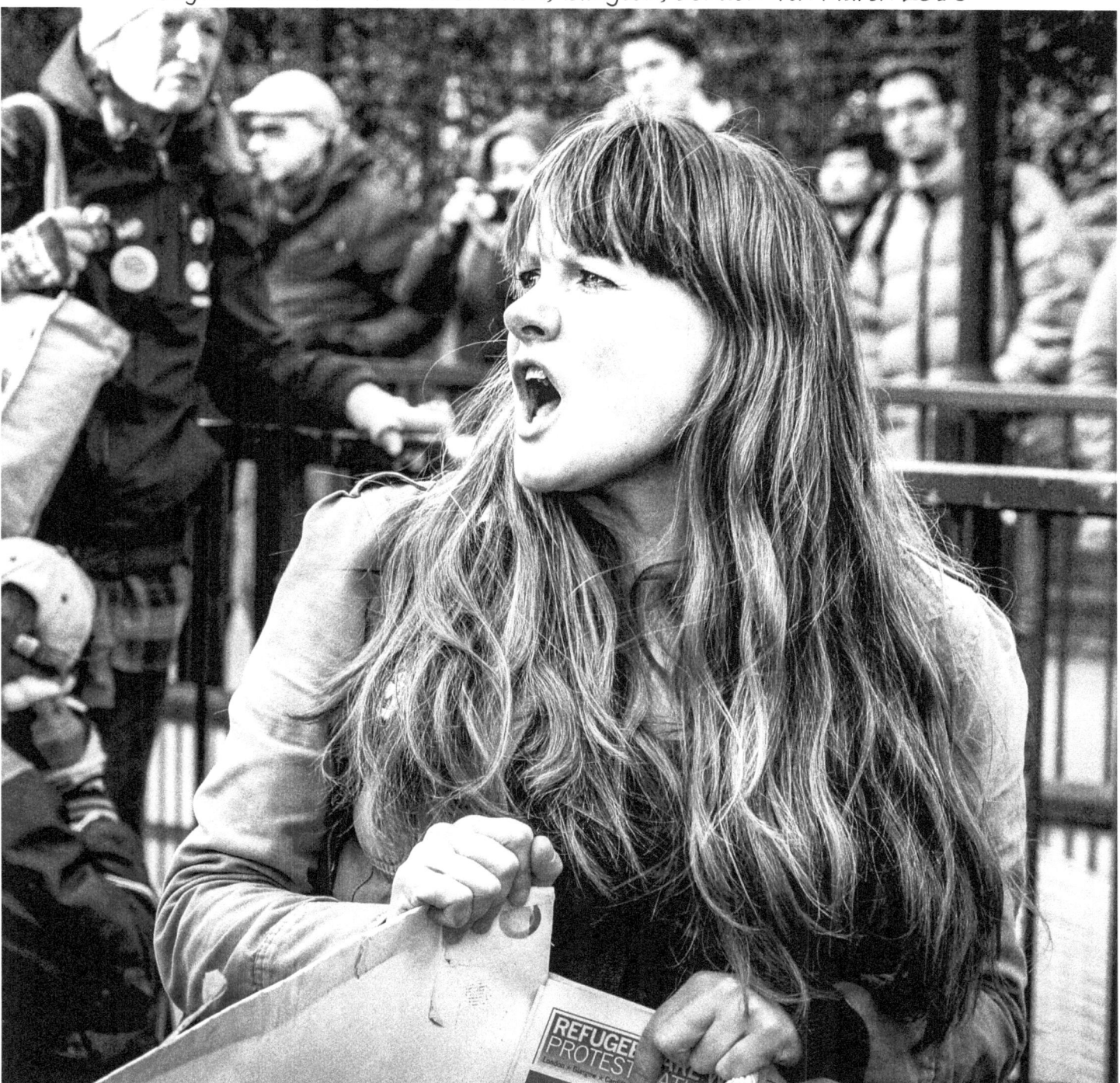

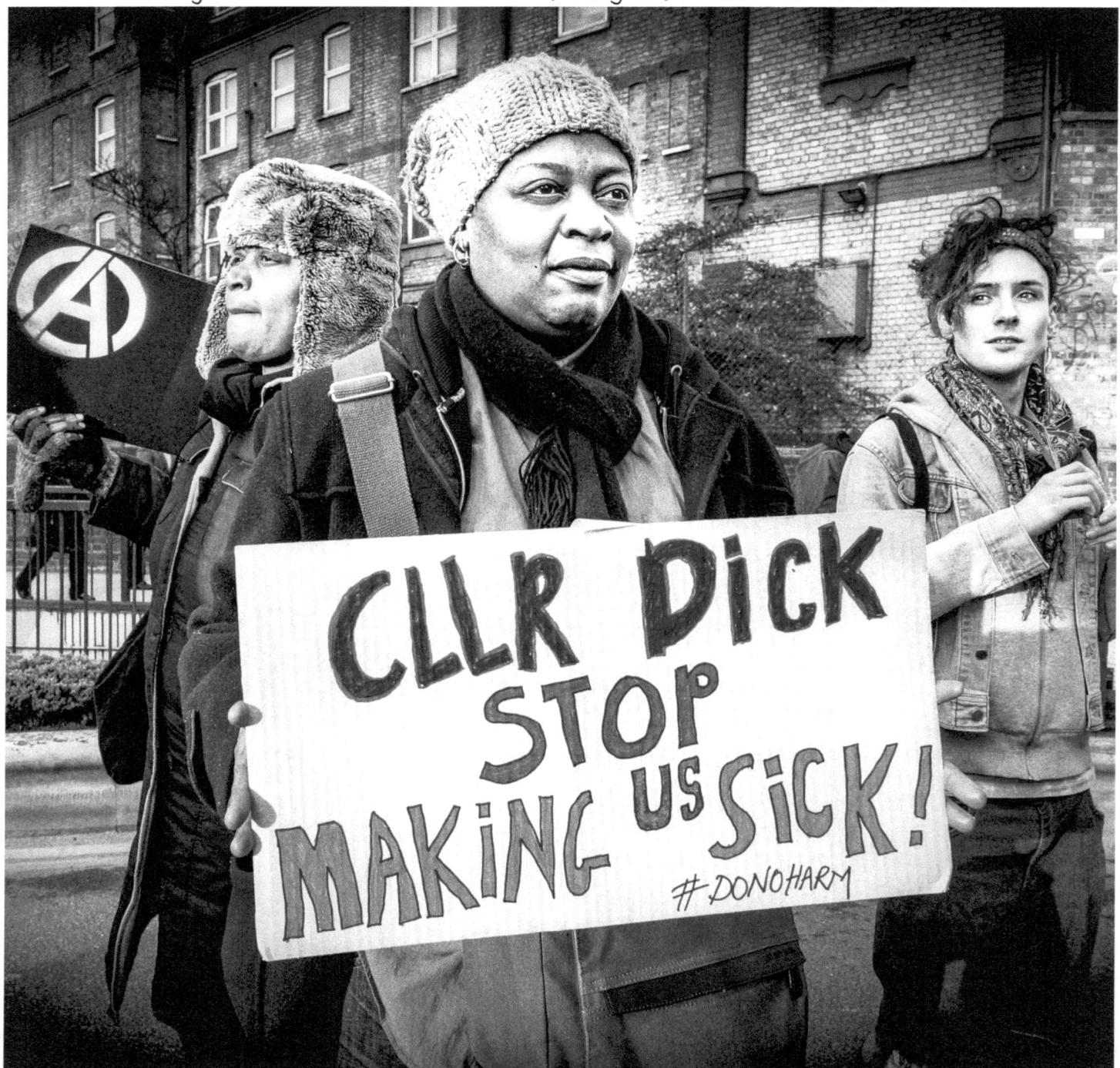

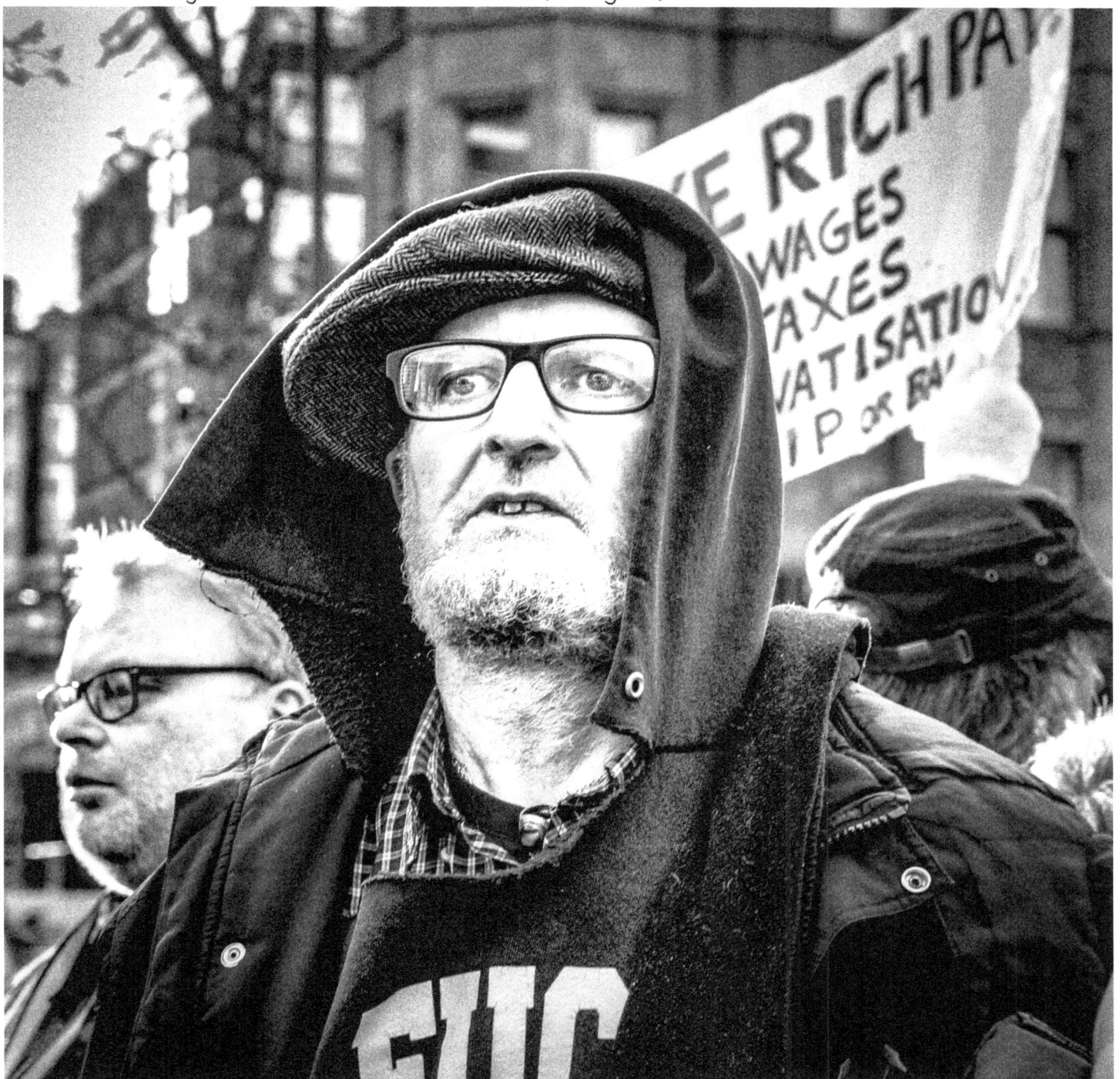

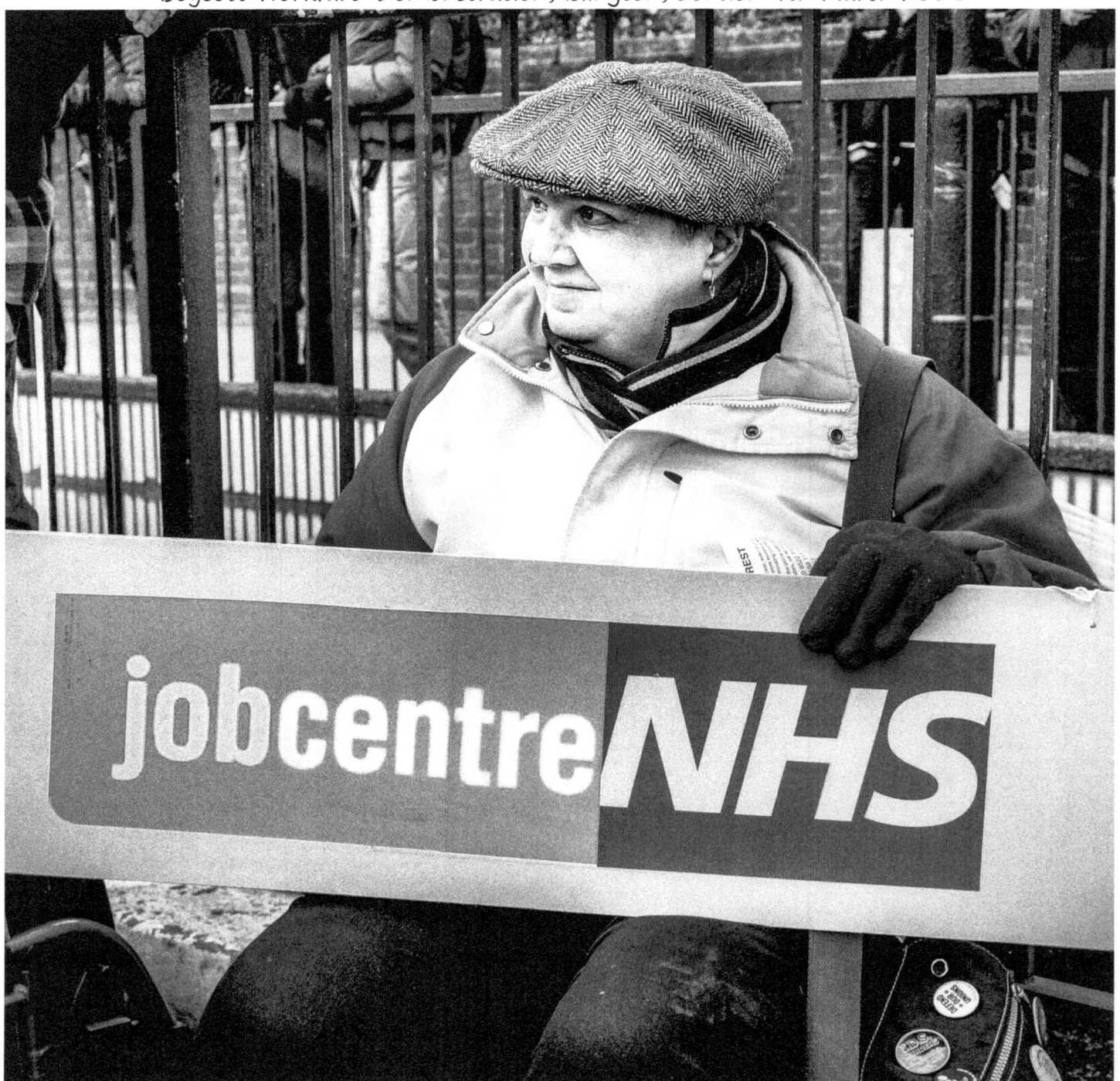

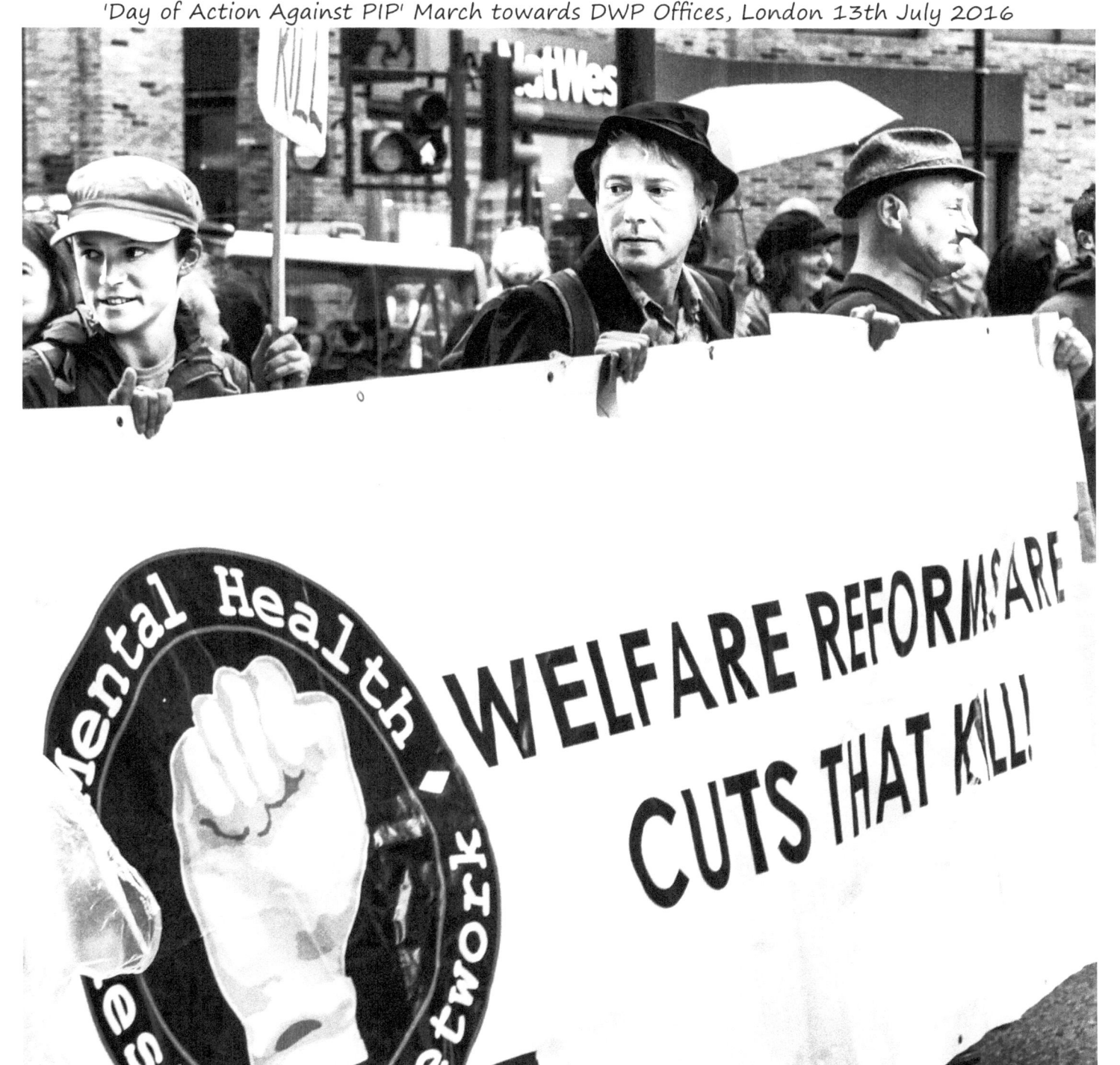

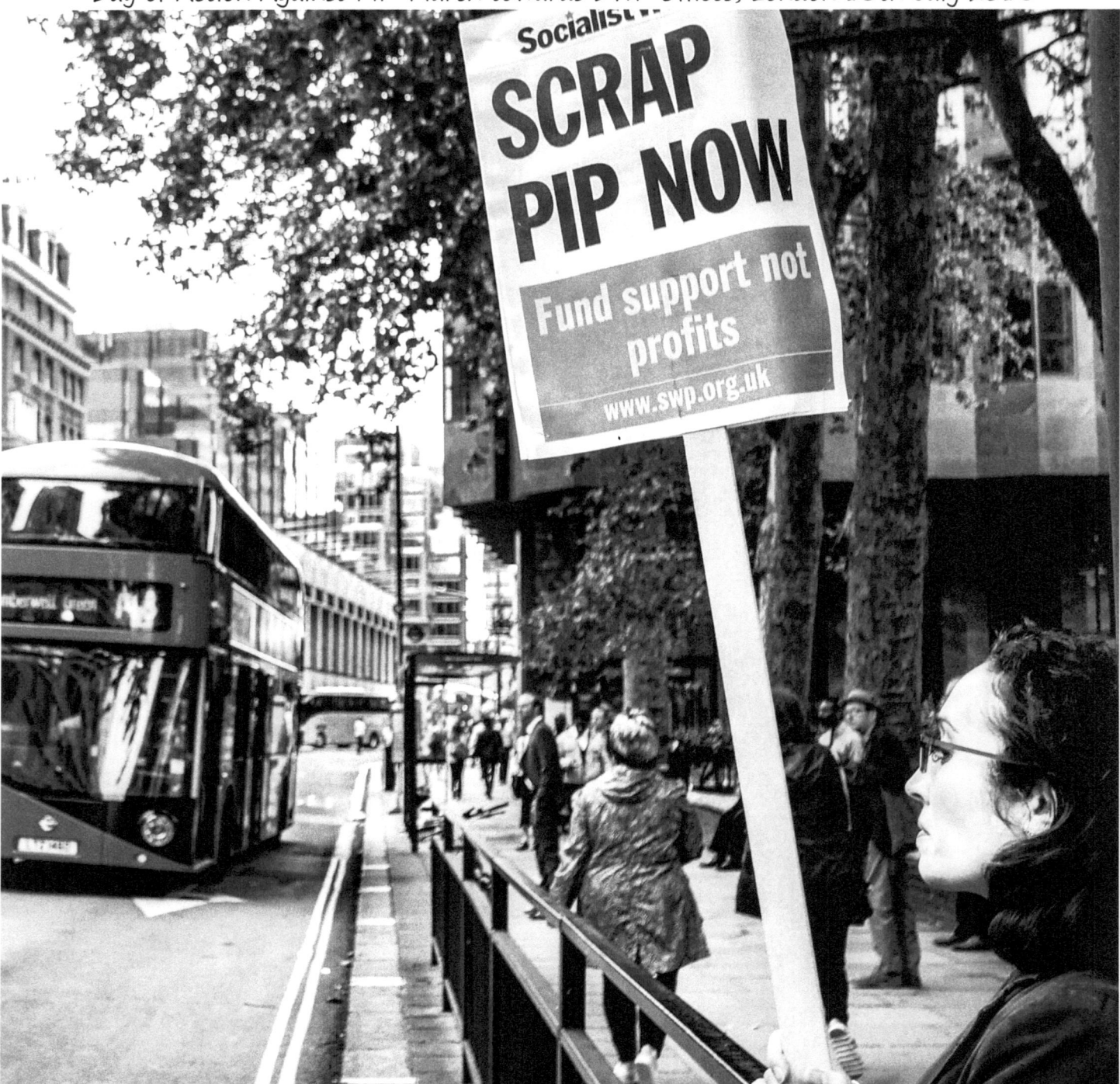

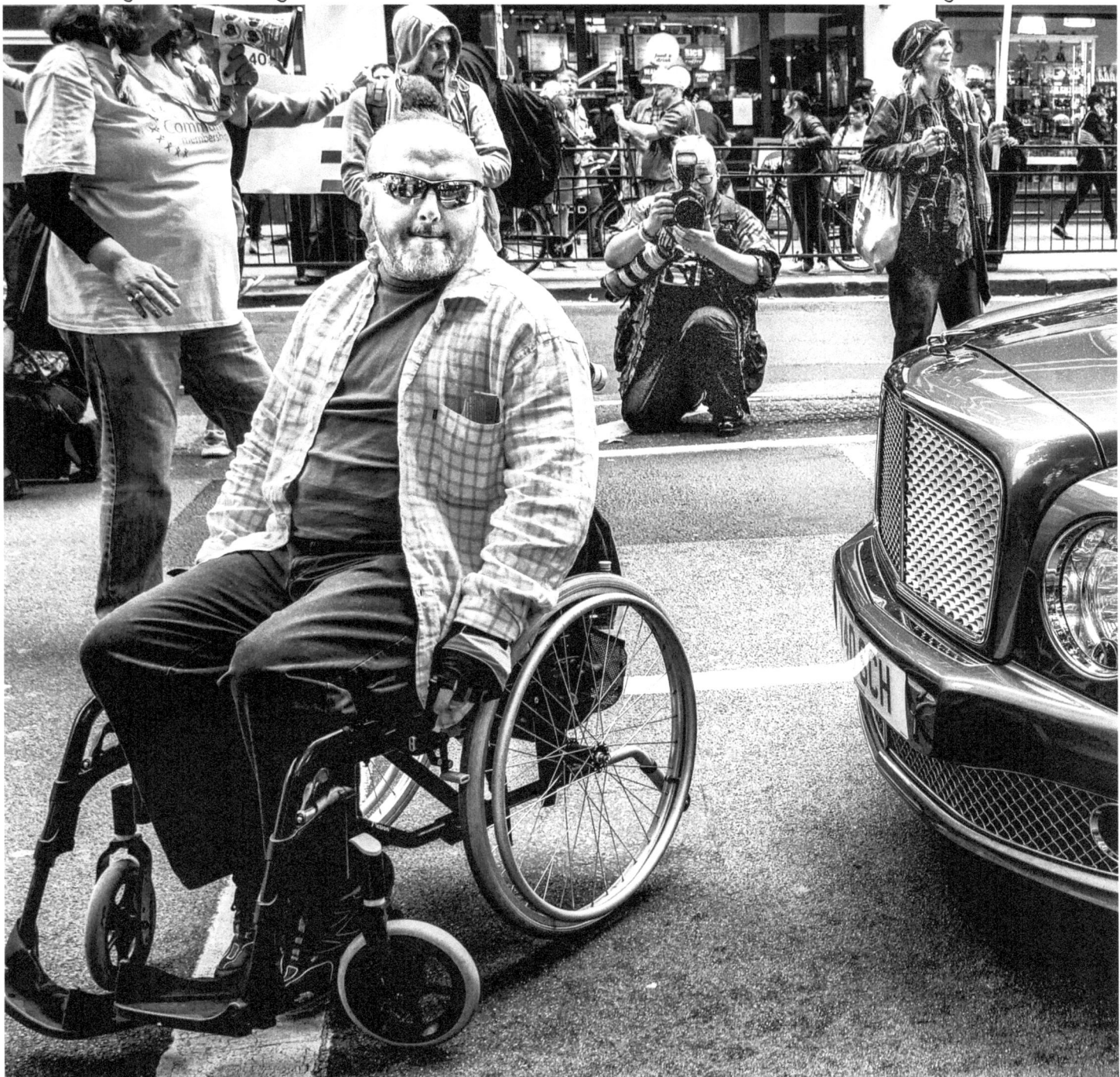

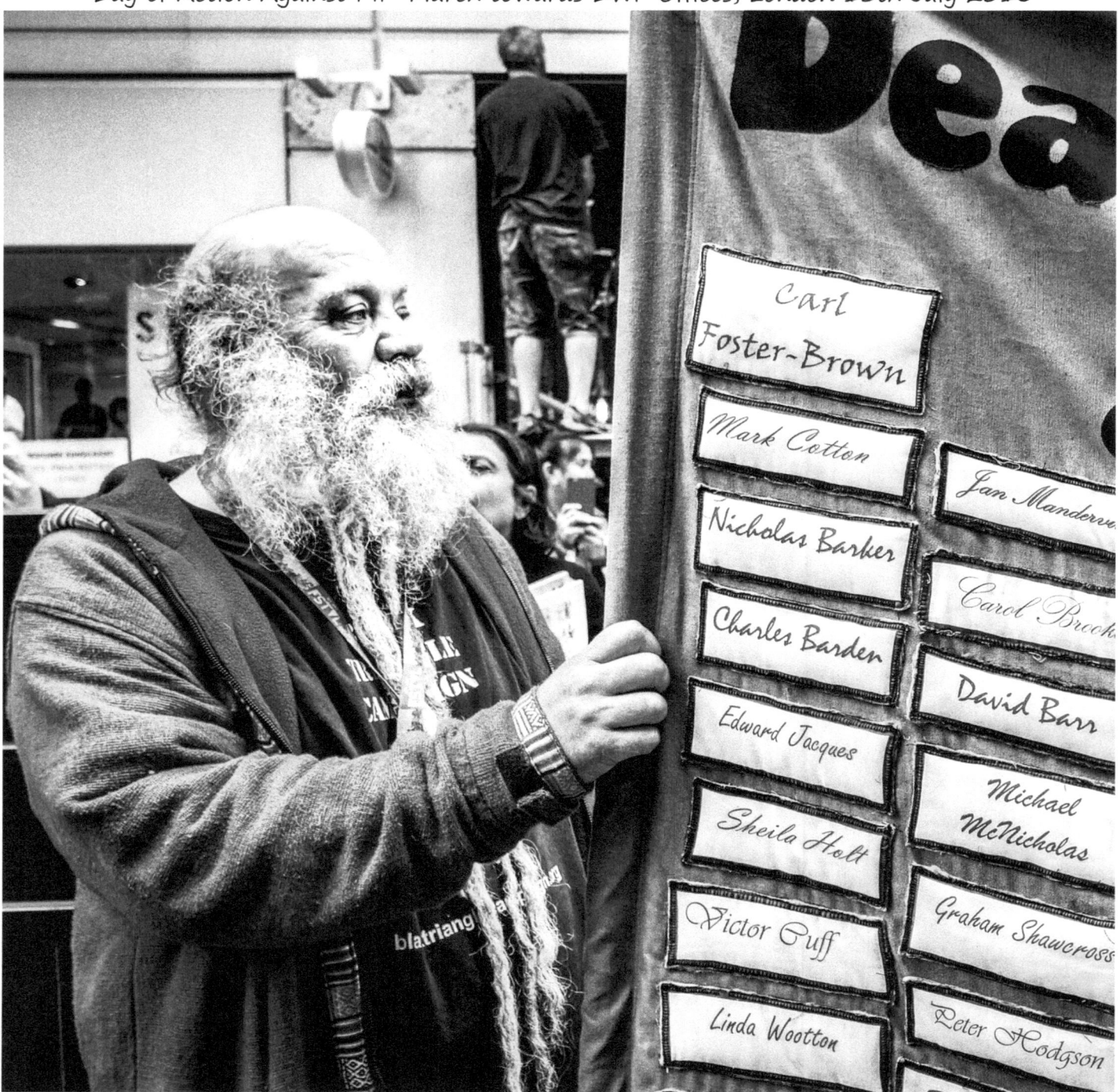

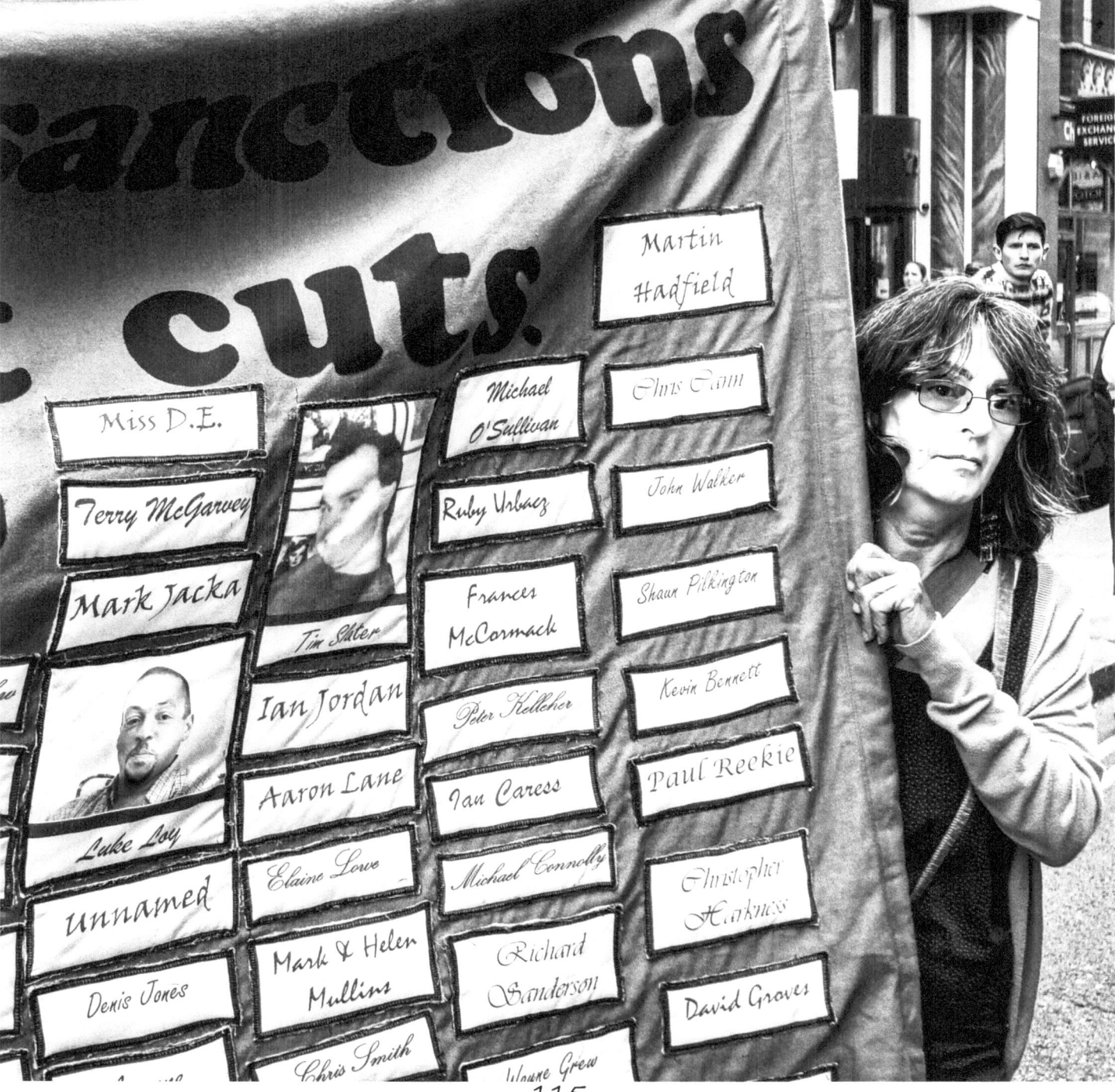

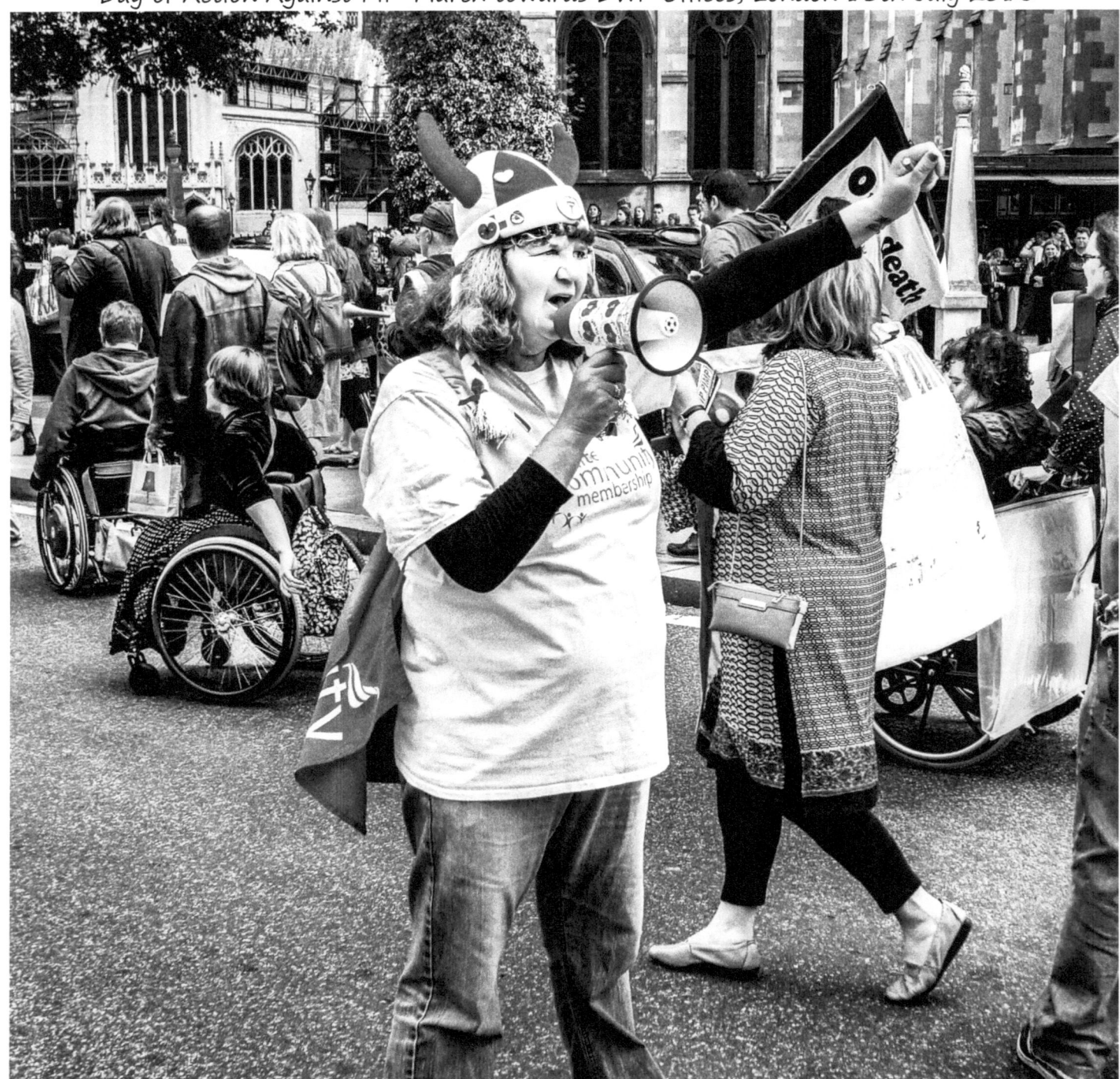

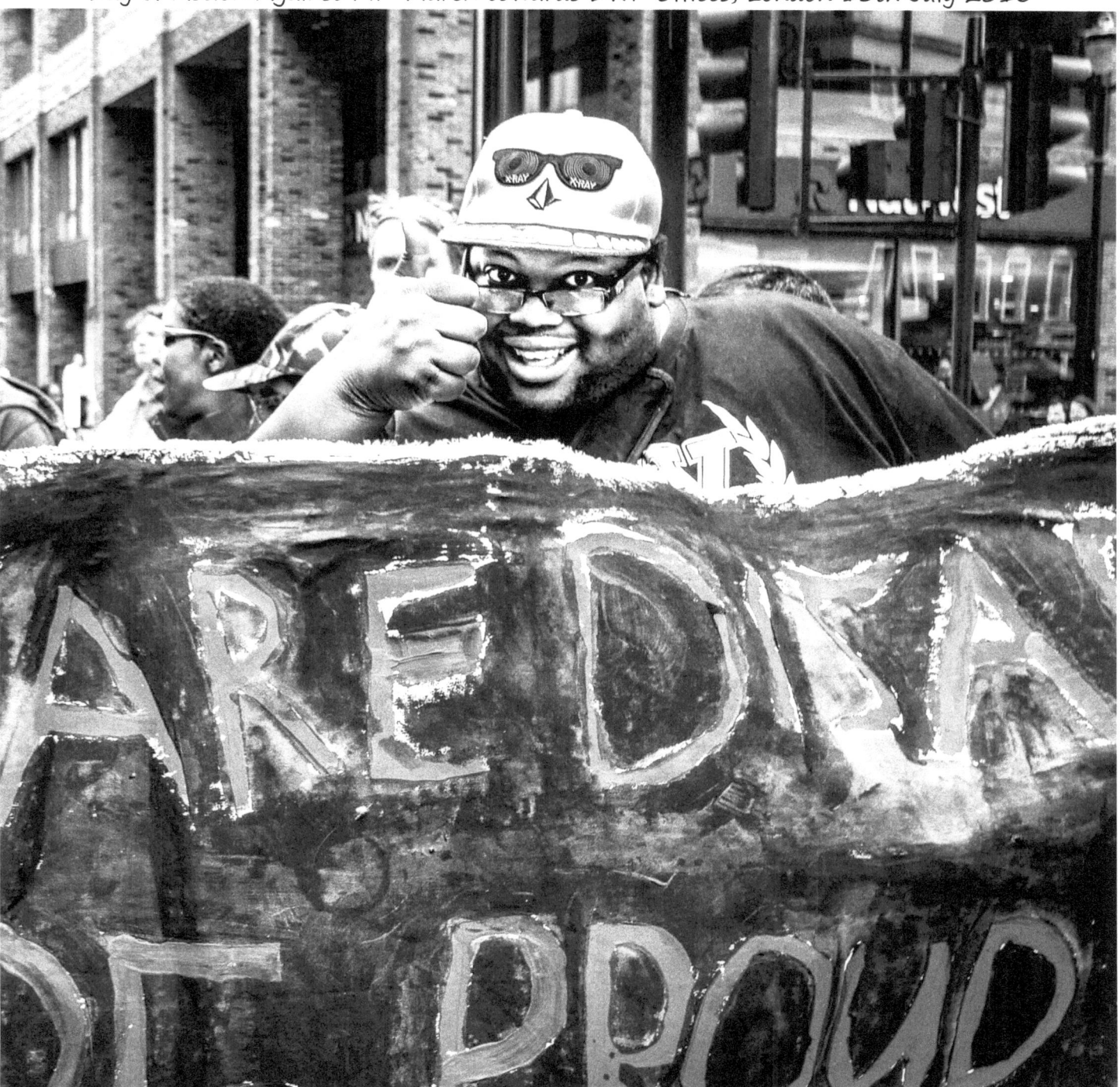

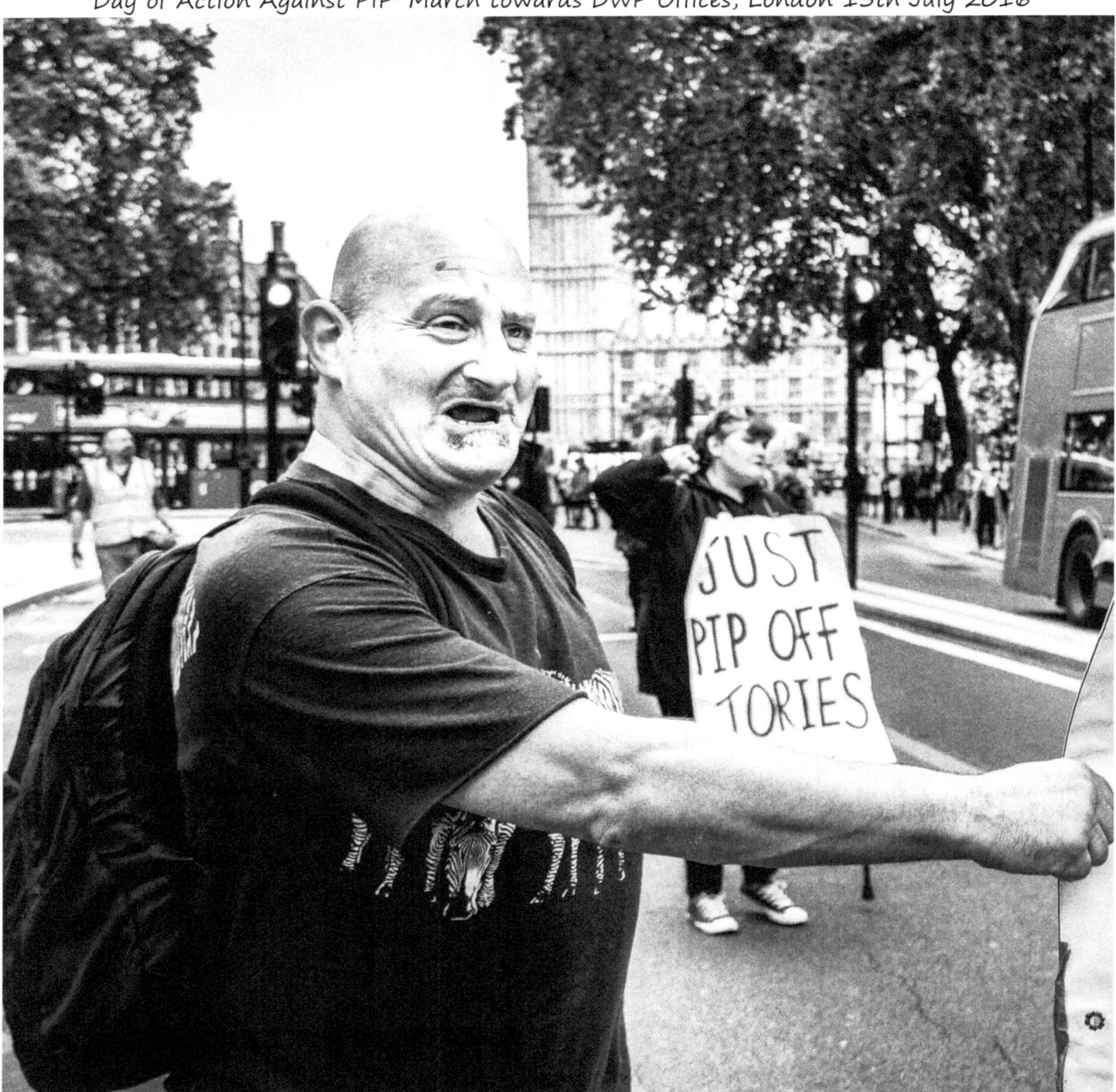

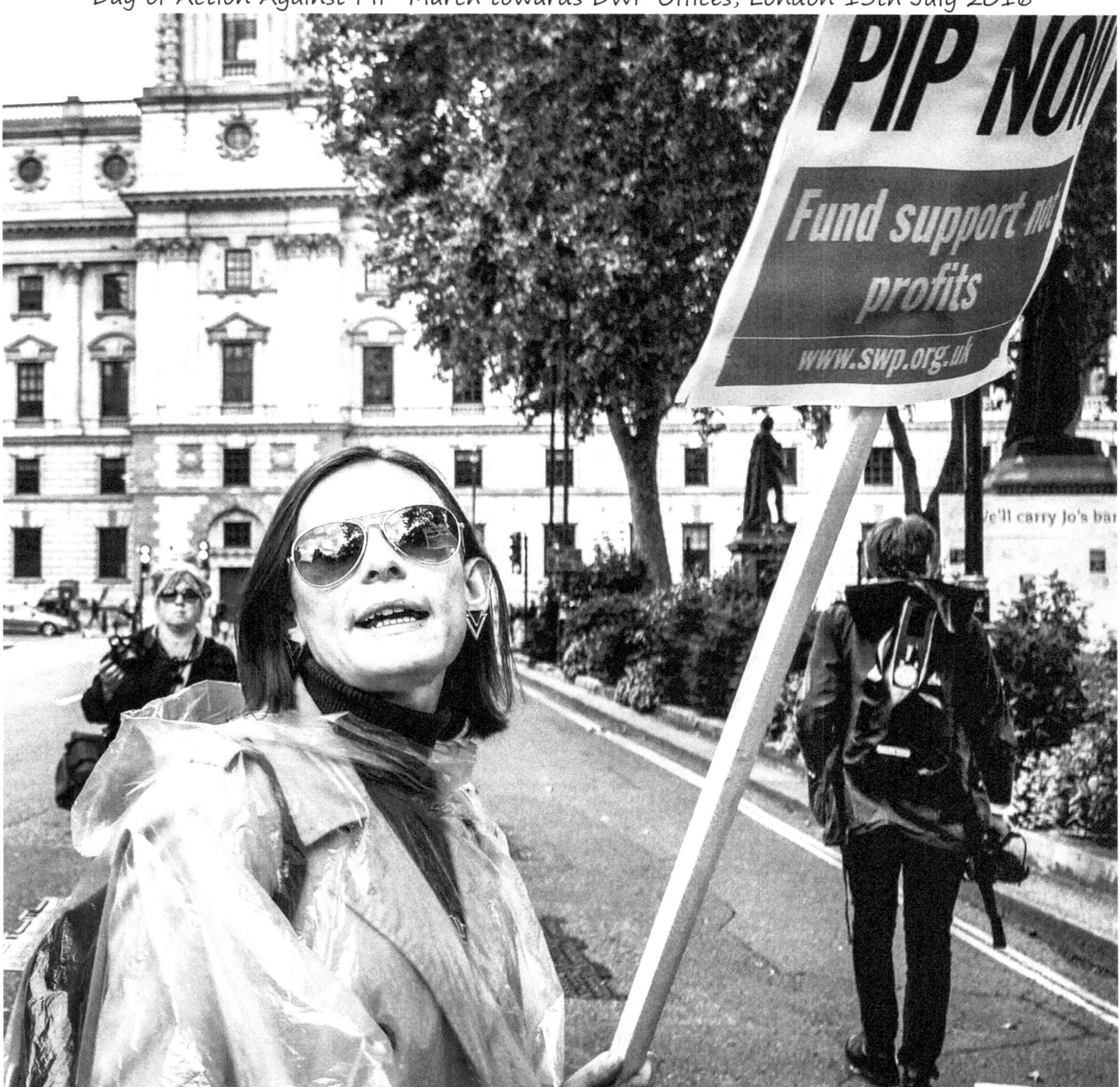

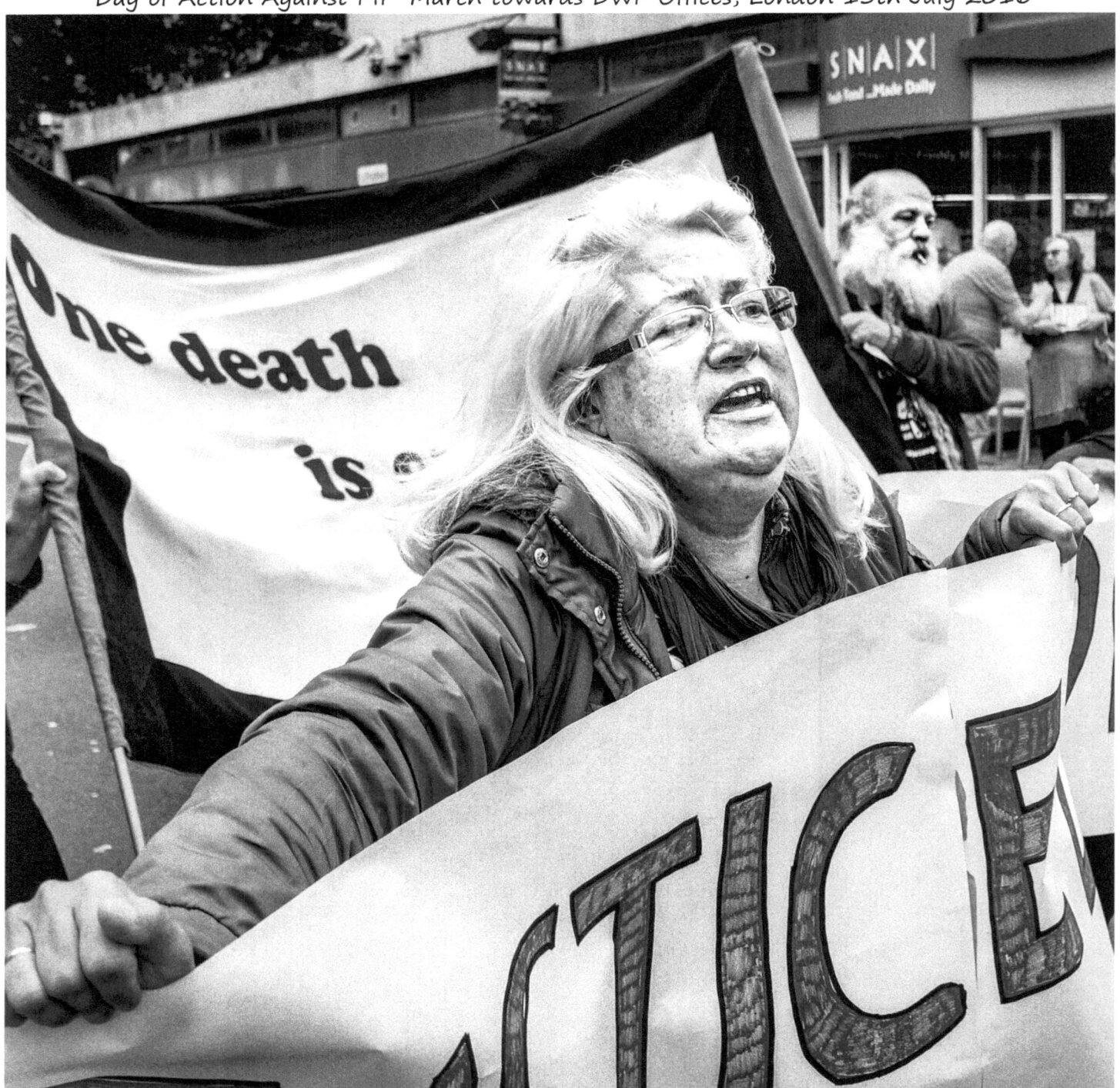

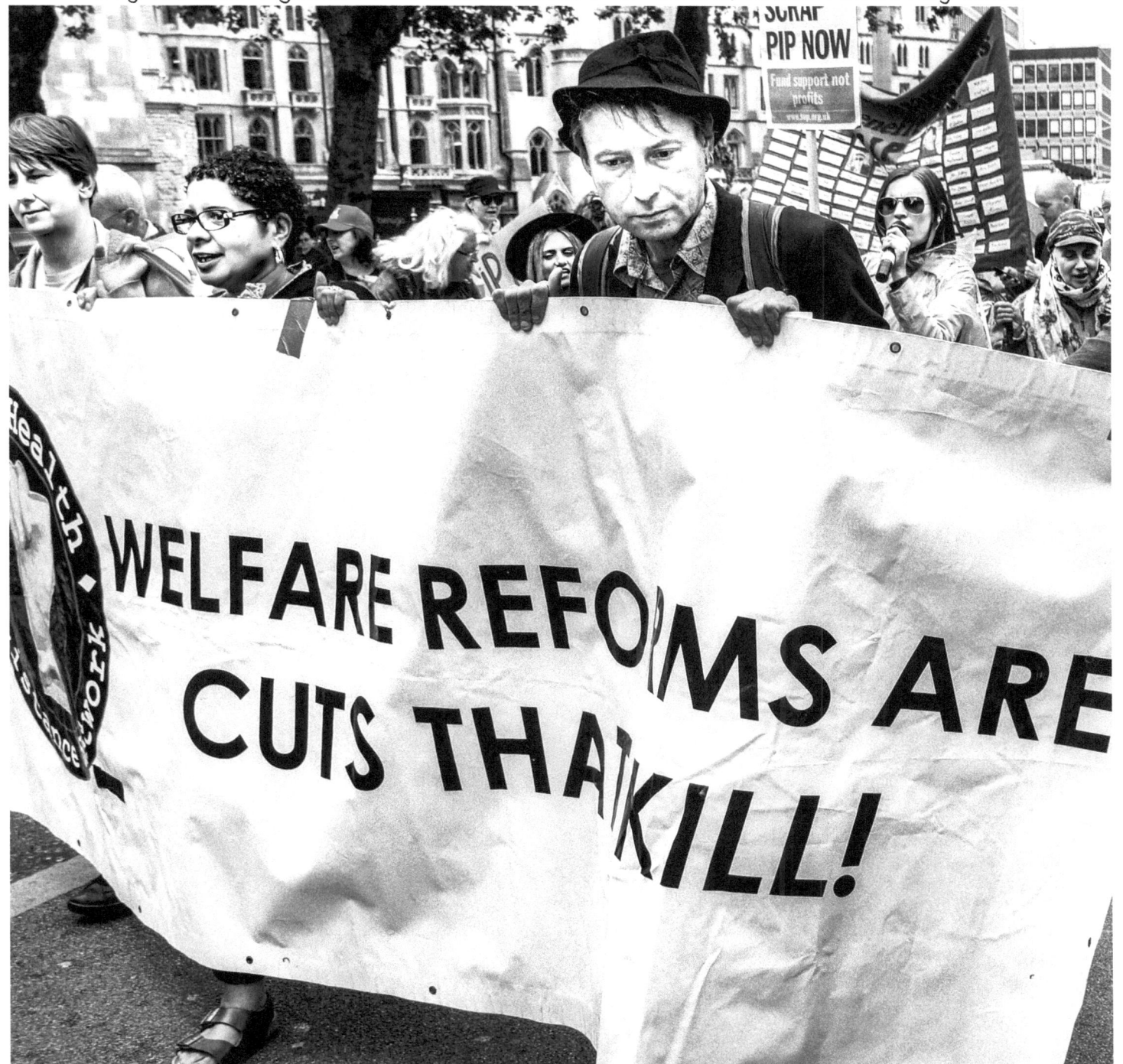

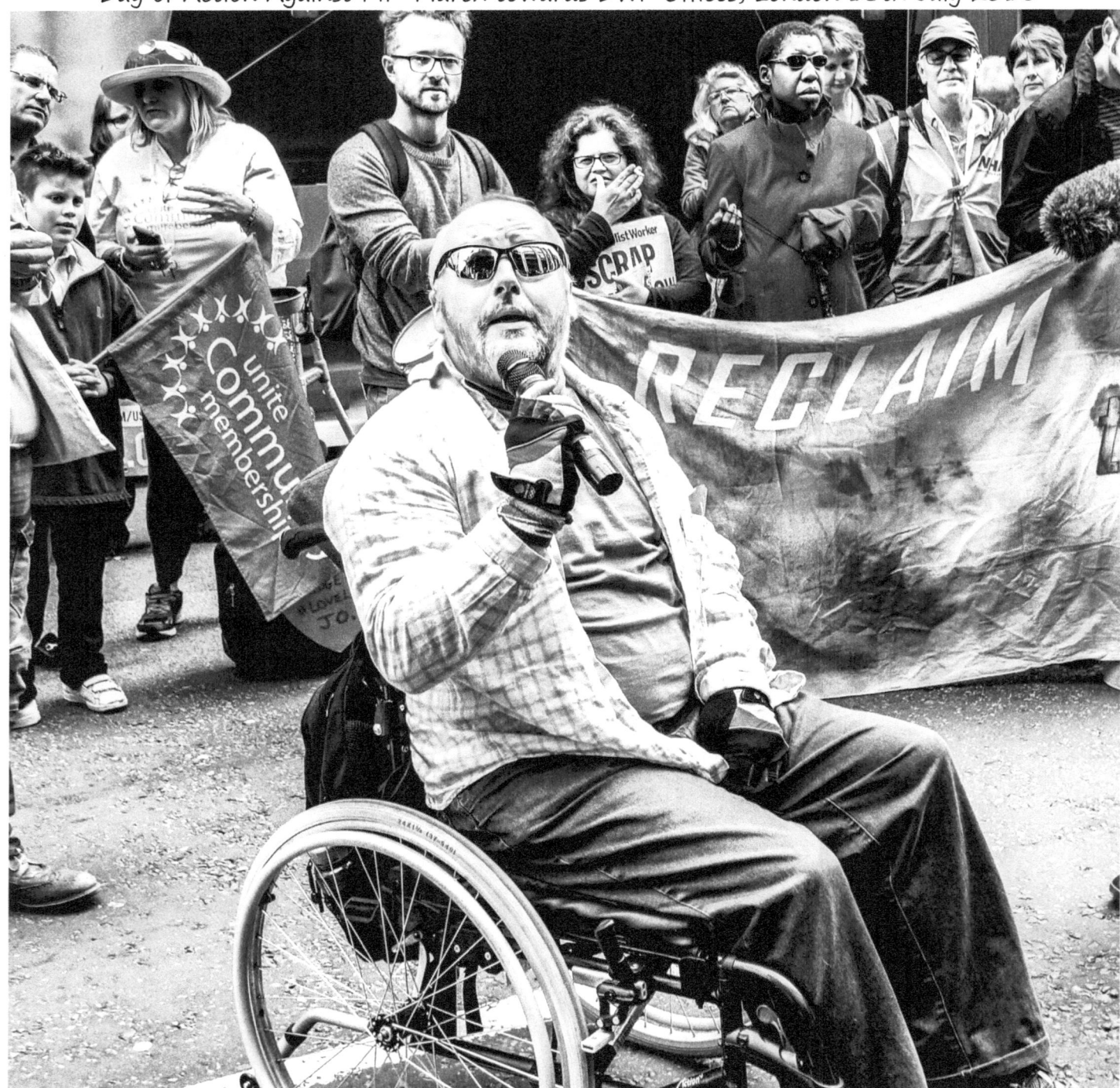

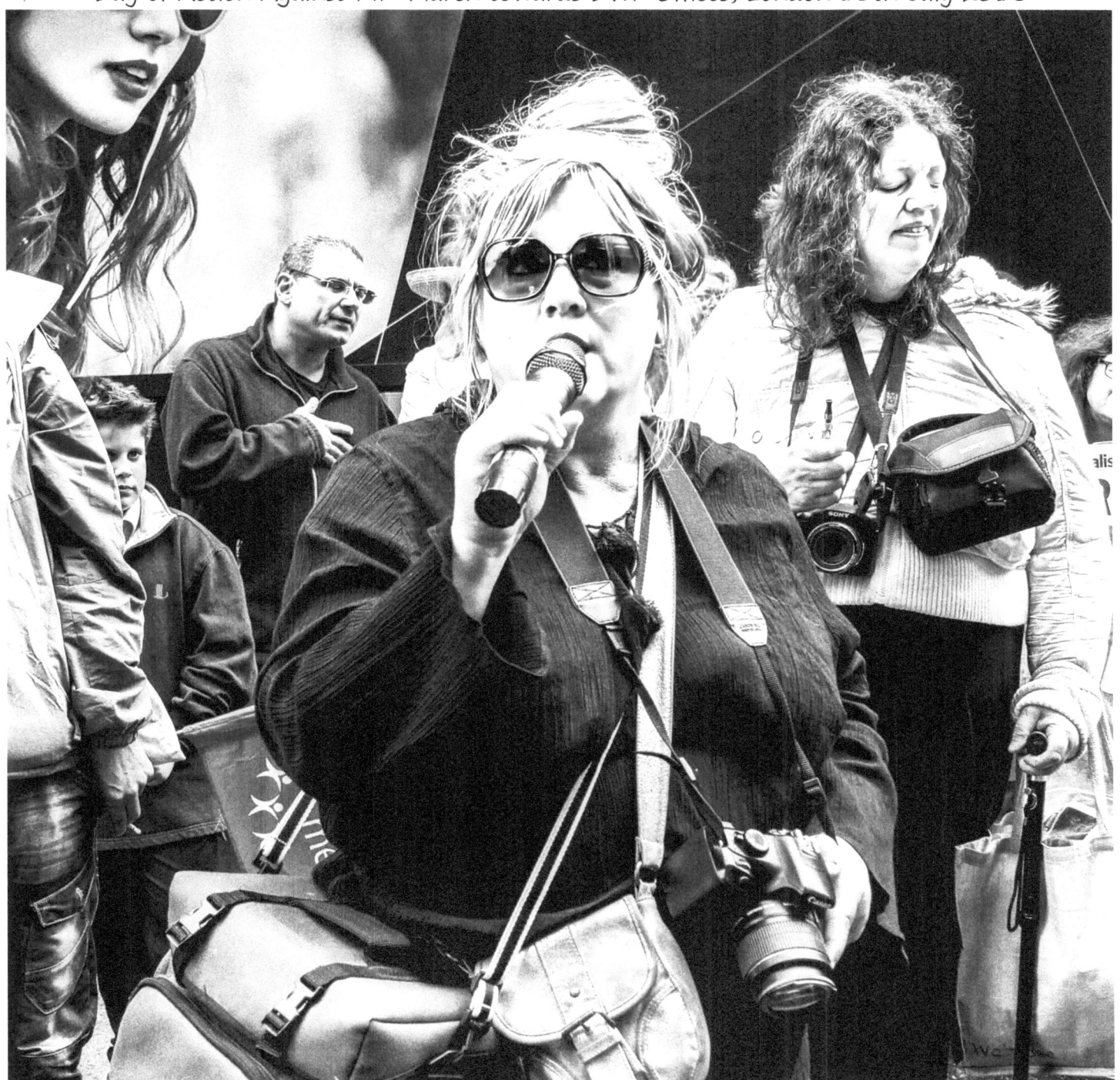

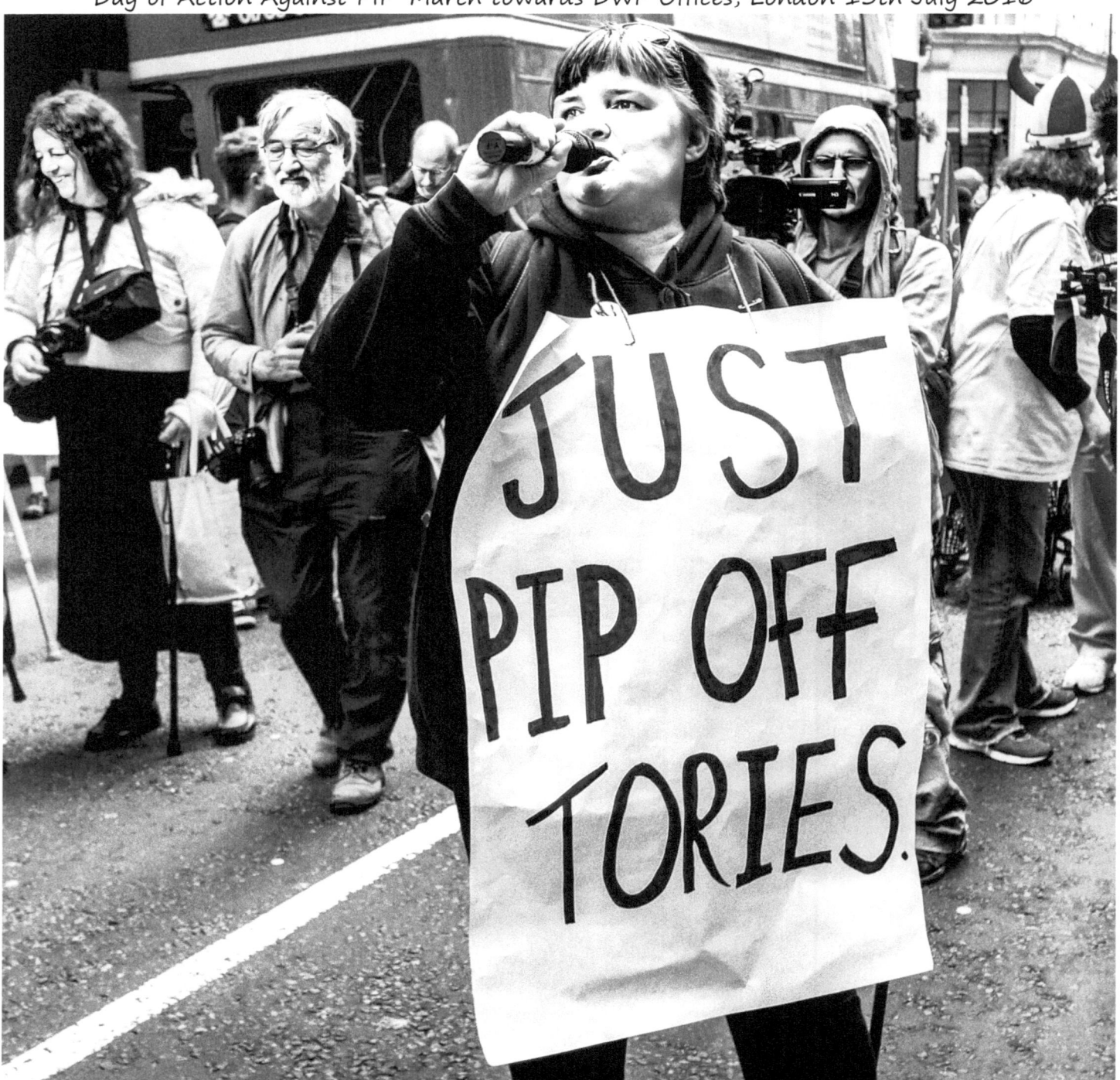

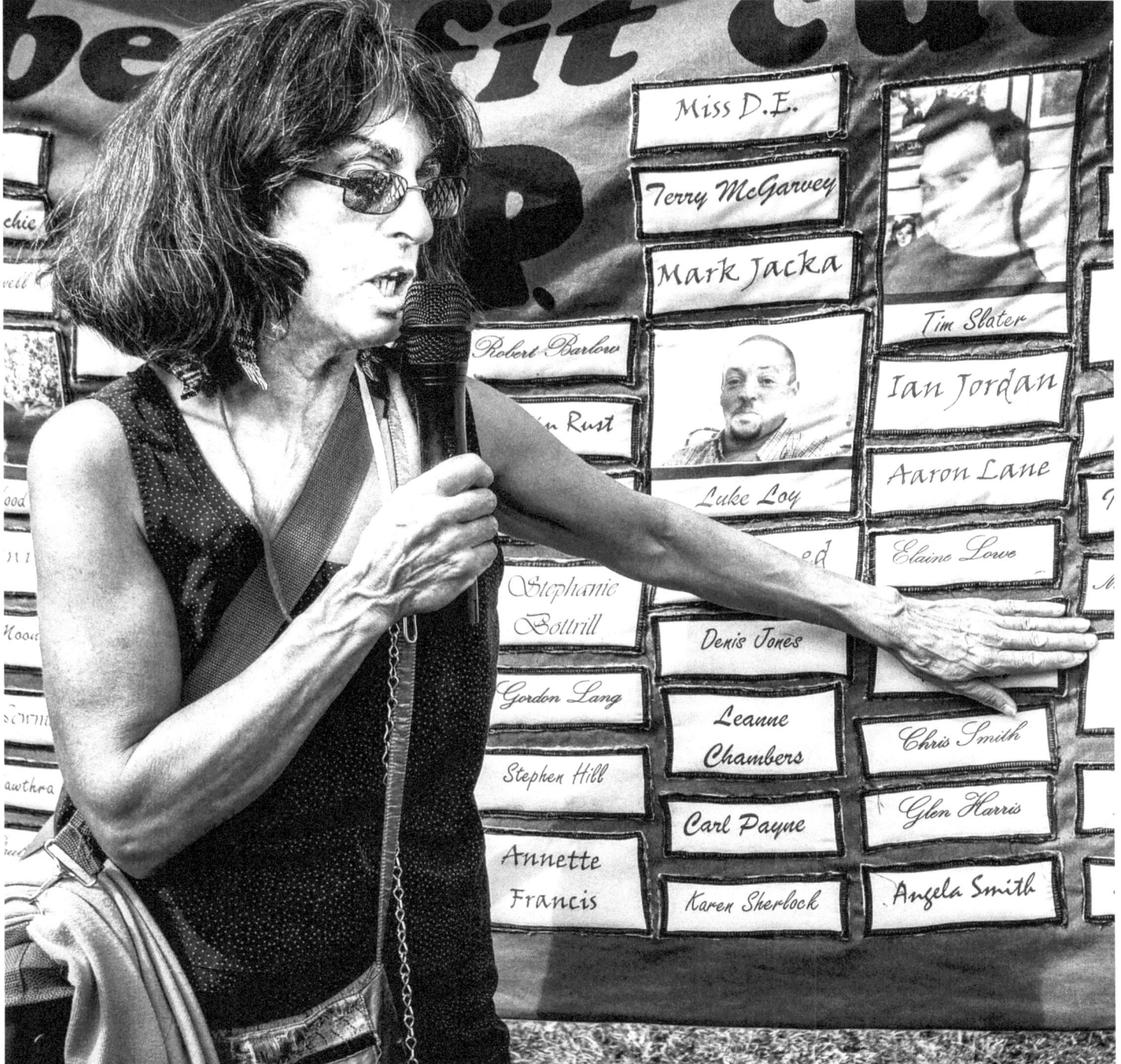

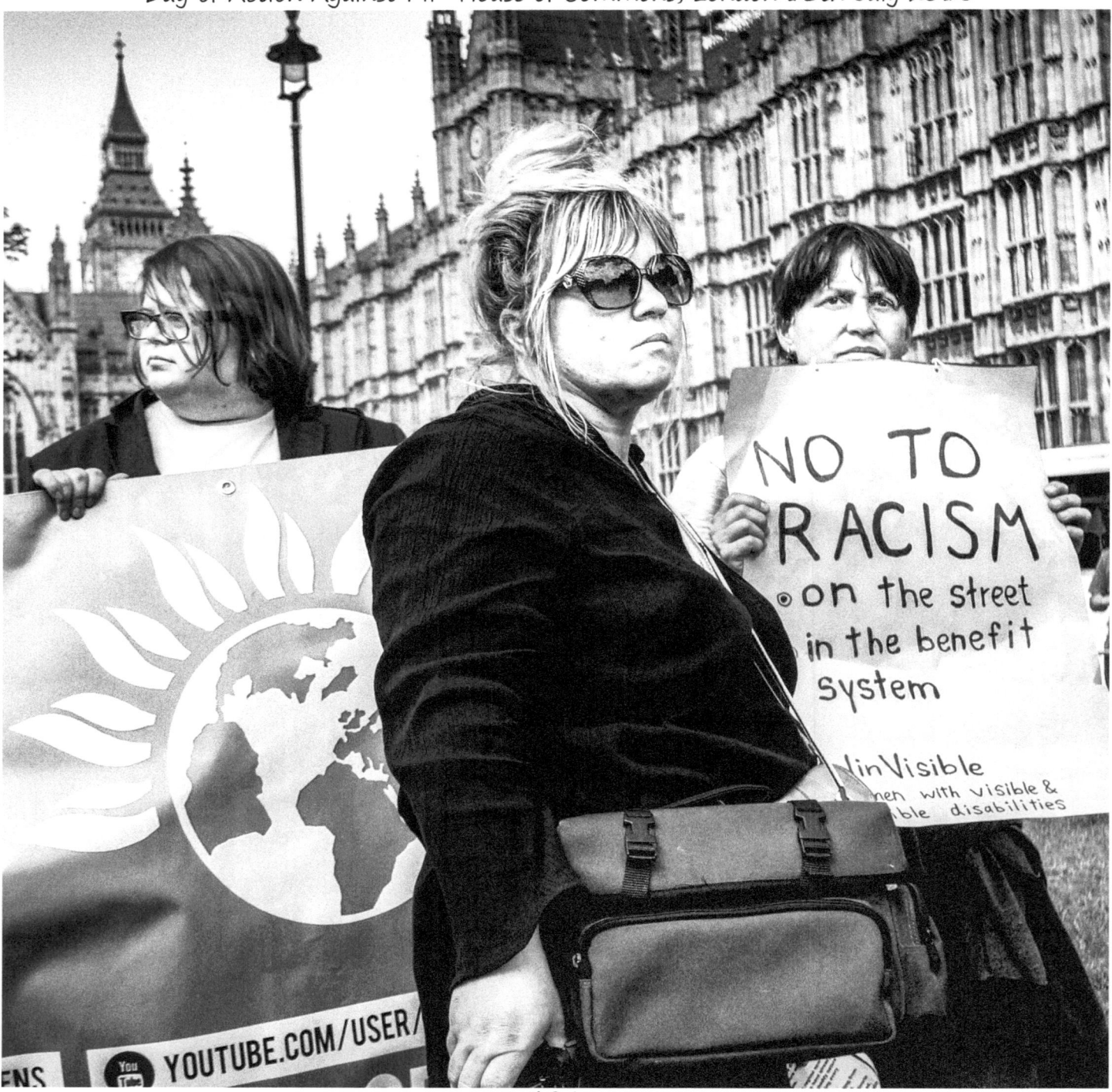

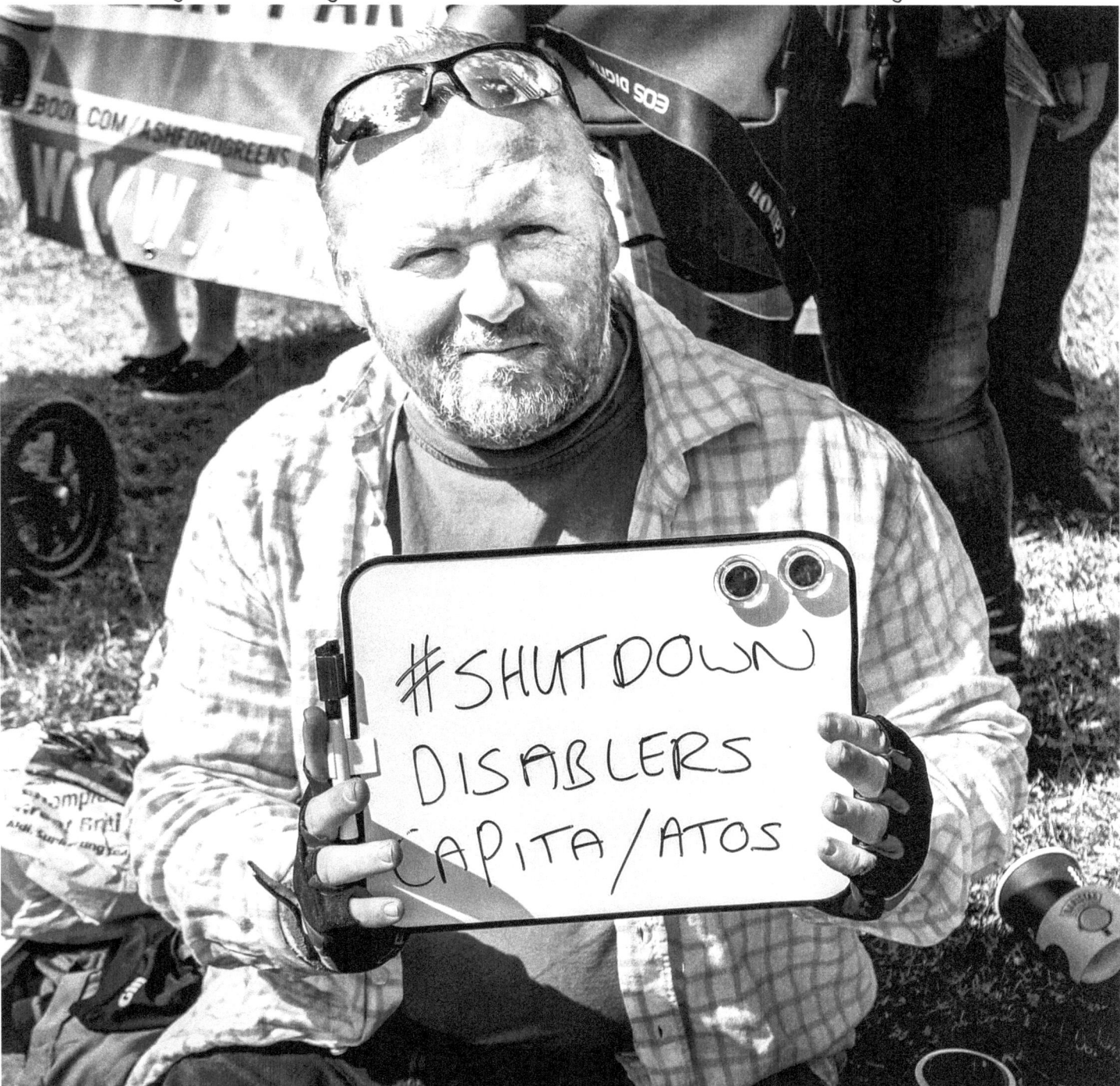

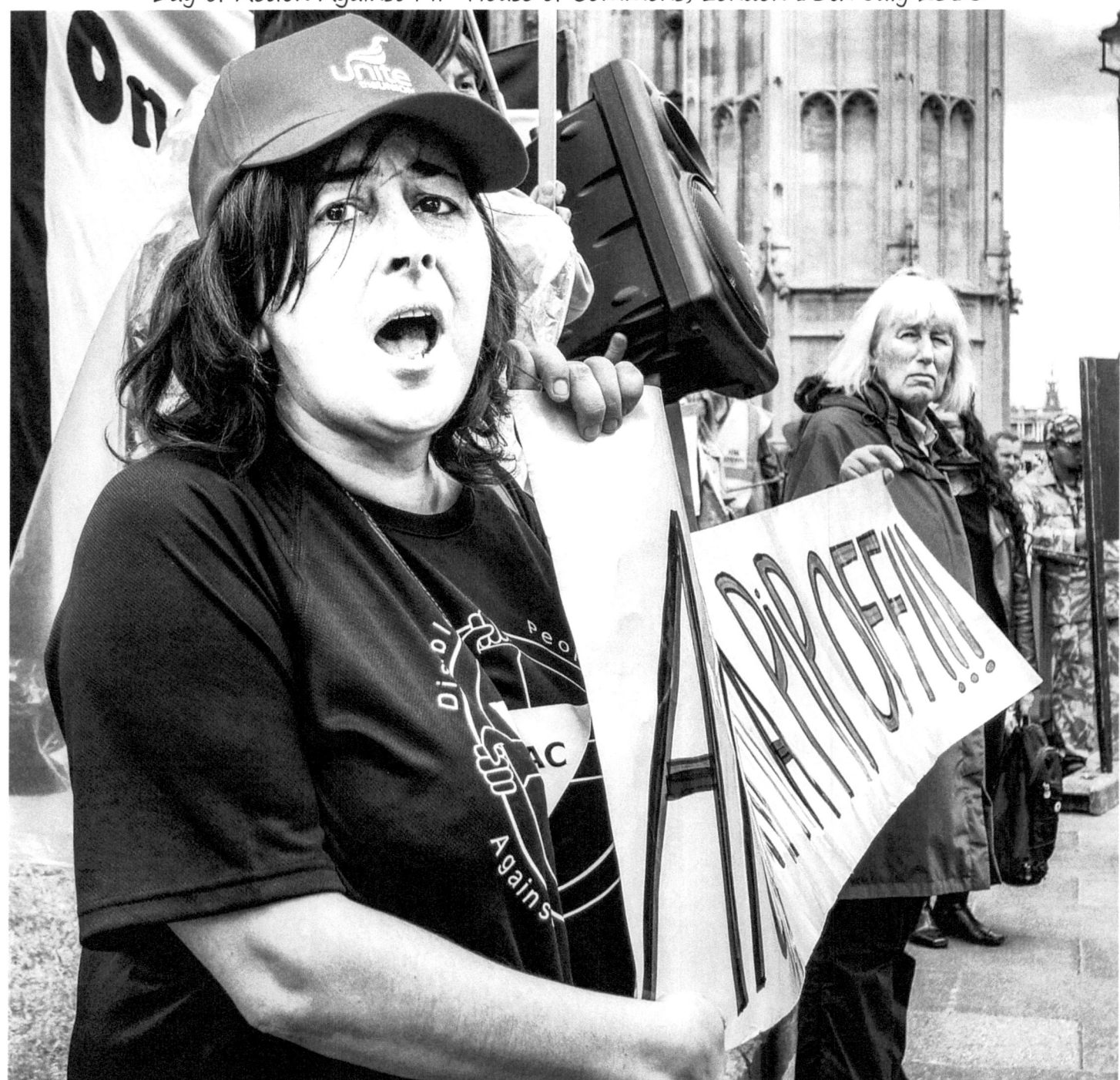

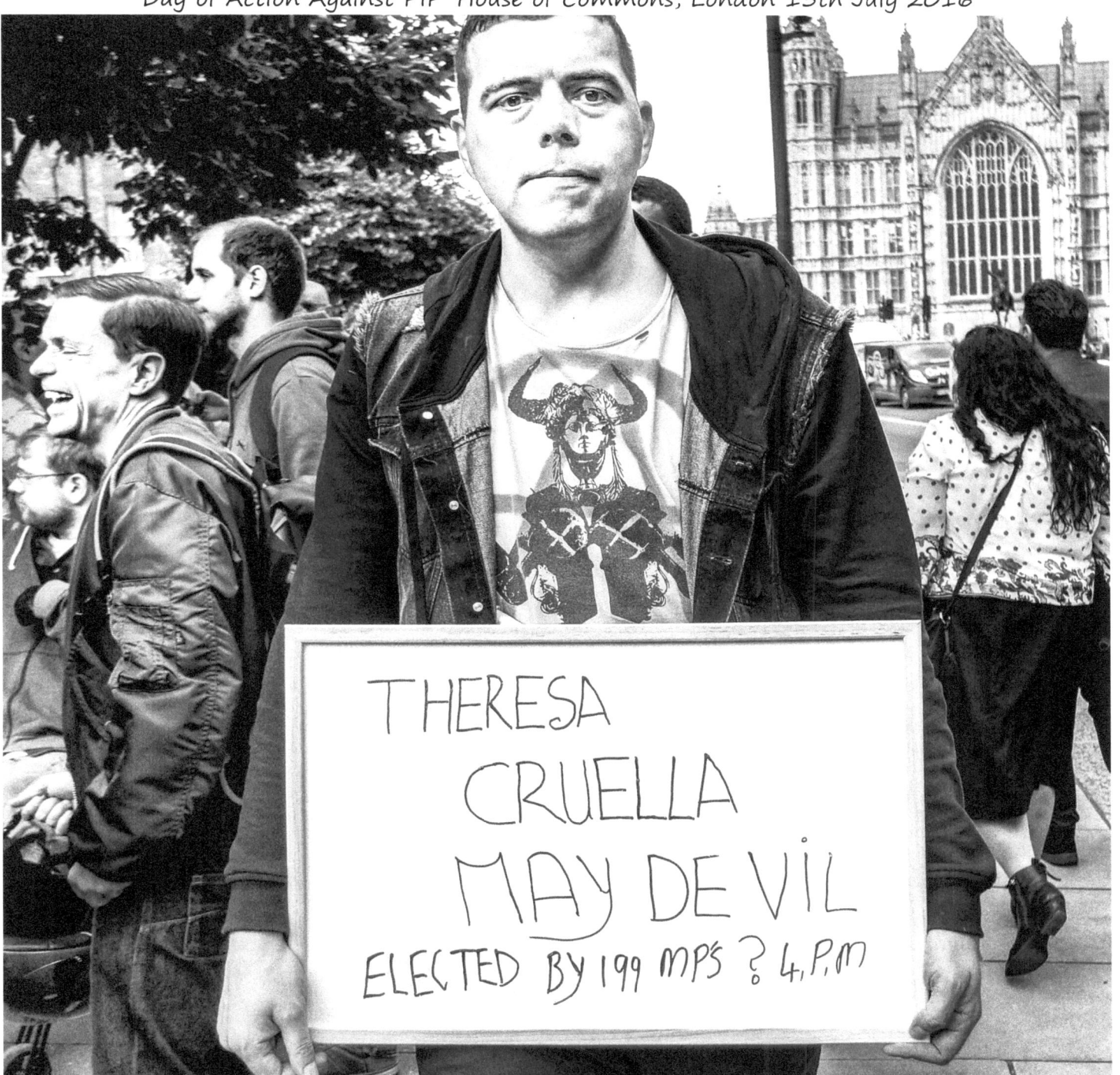

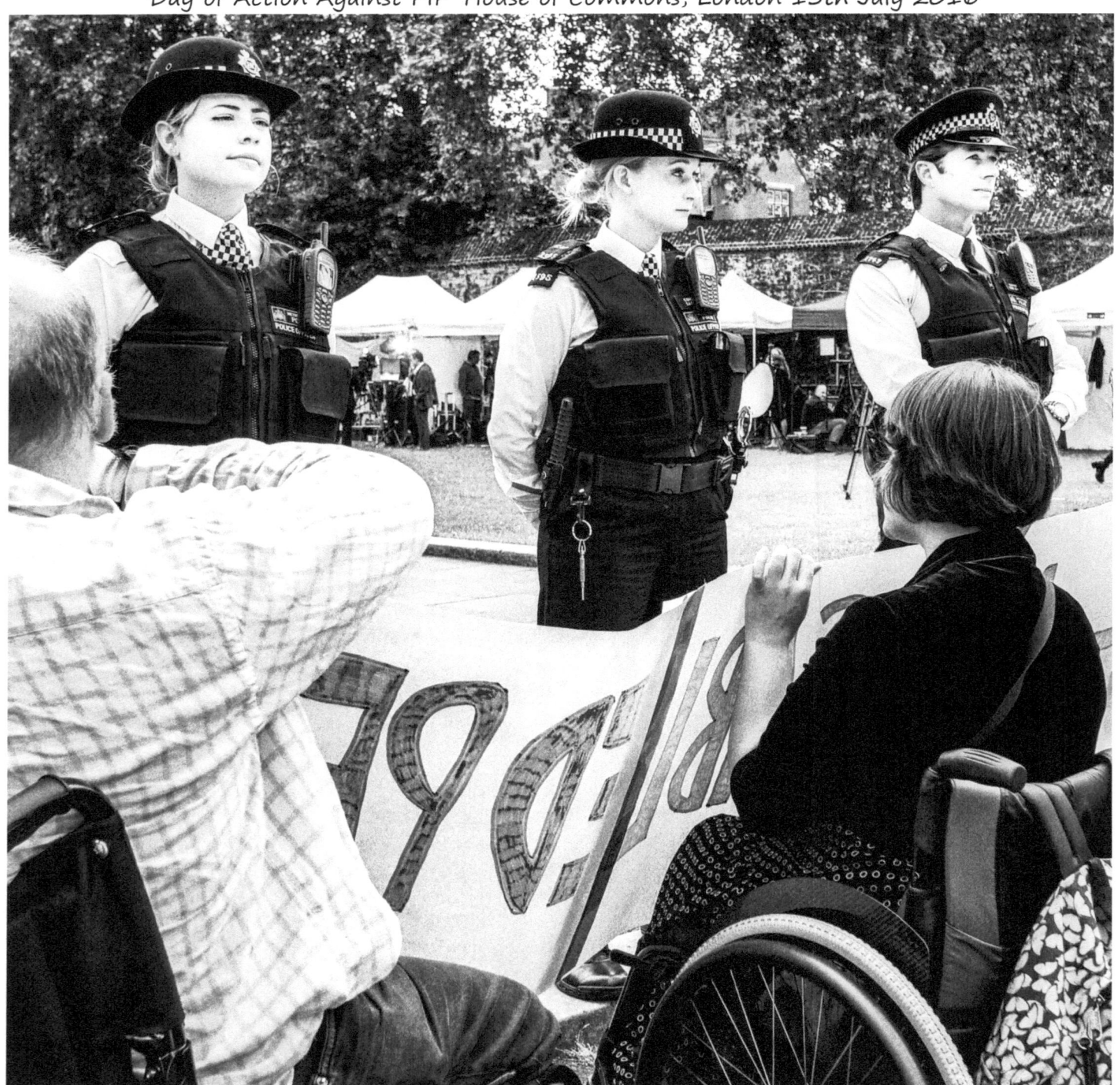

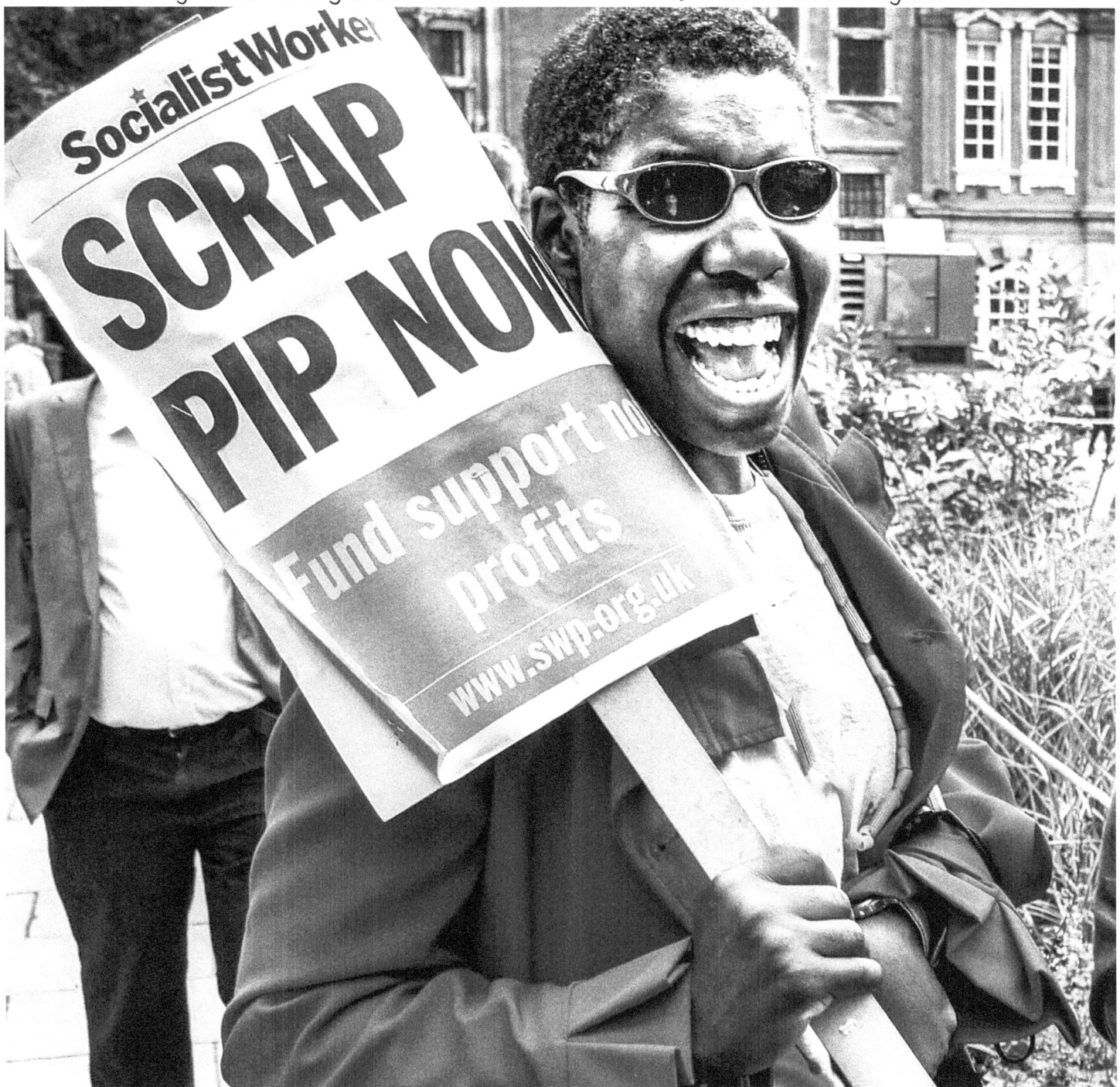

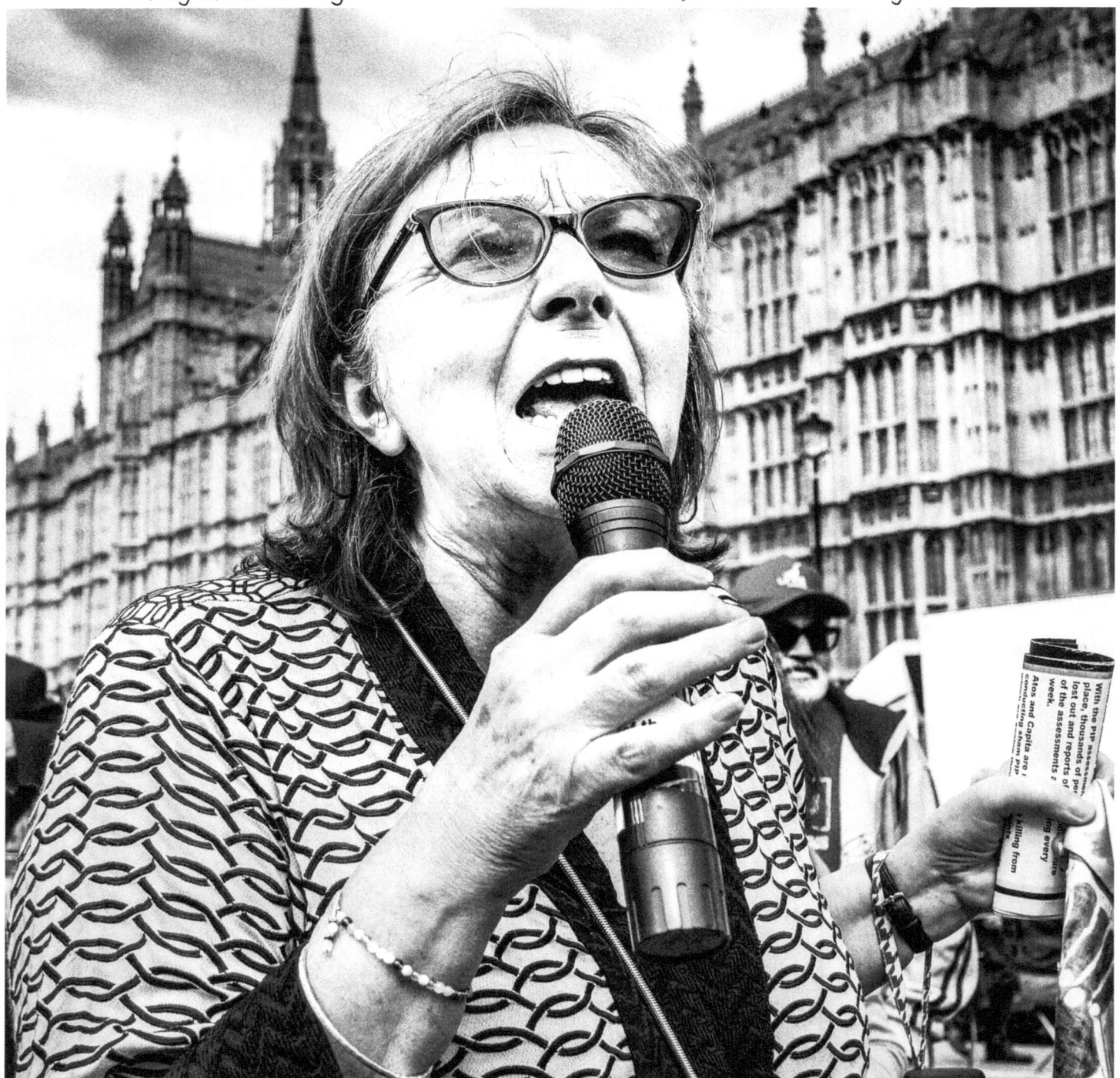

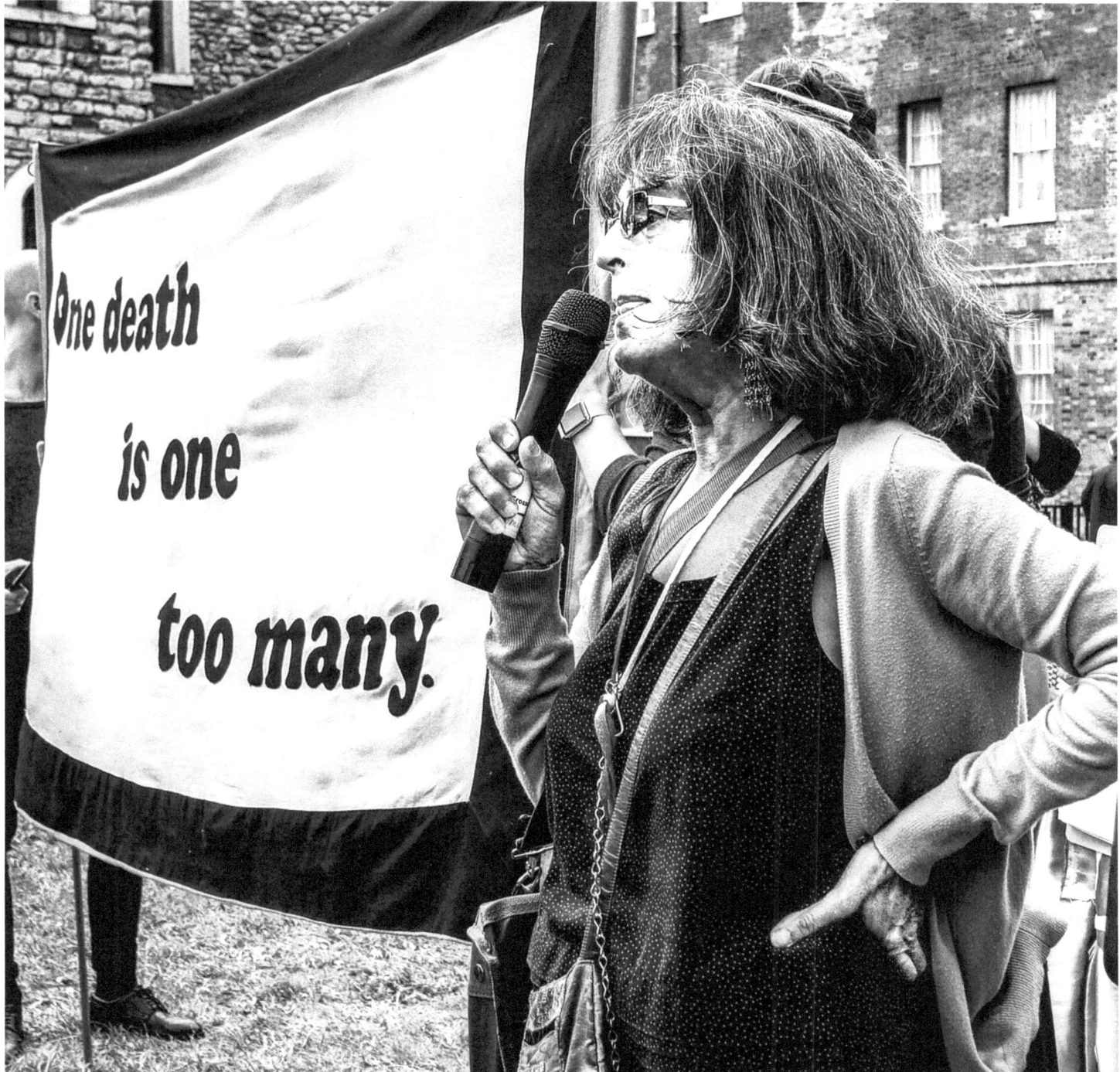

One death
is one
too many.

SCRAP
PIP NOW

'Rights Not Games' A Week Of Action In London September 4th-10th 2016

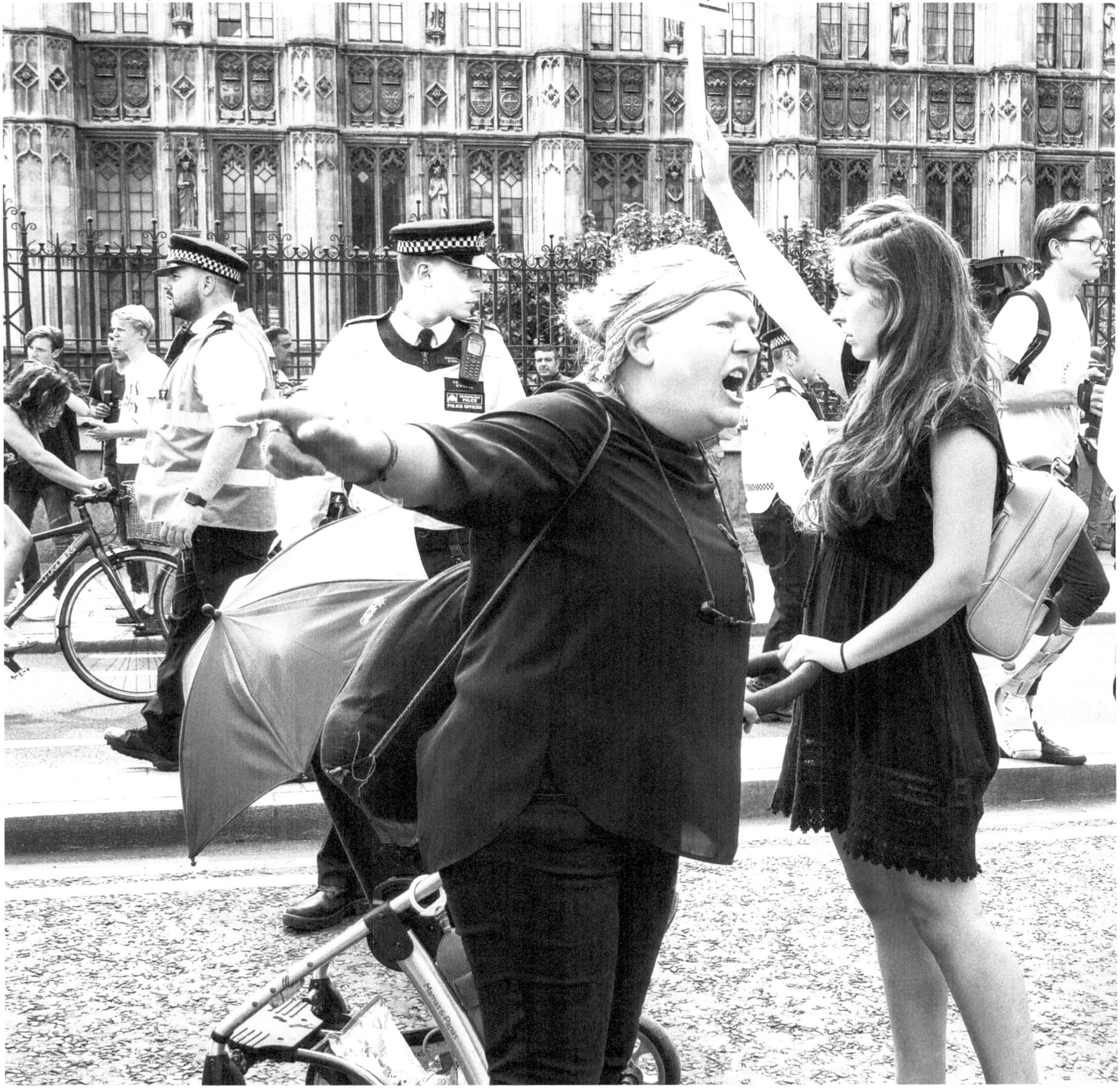

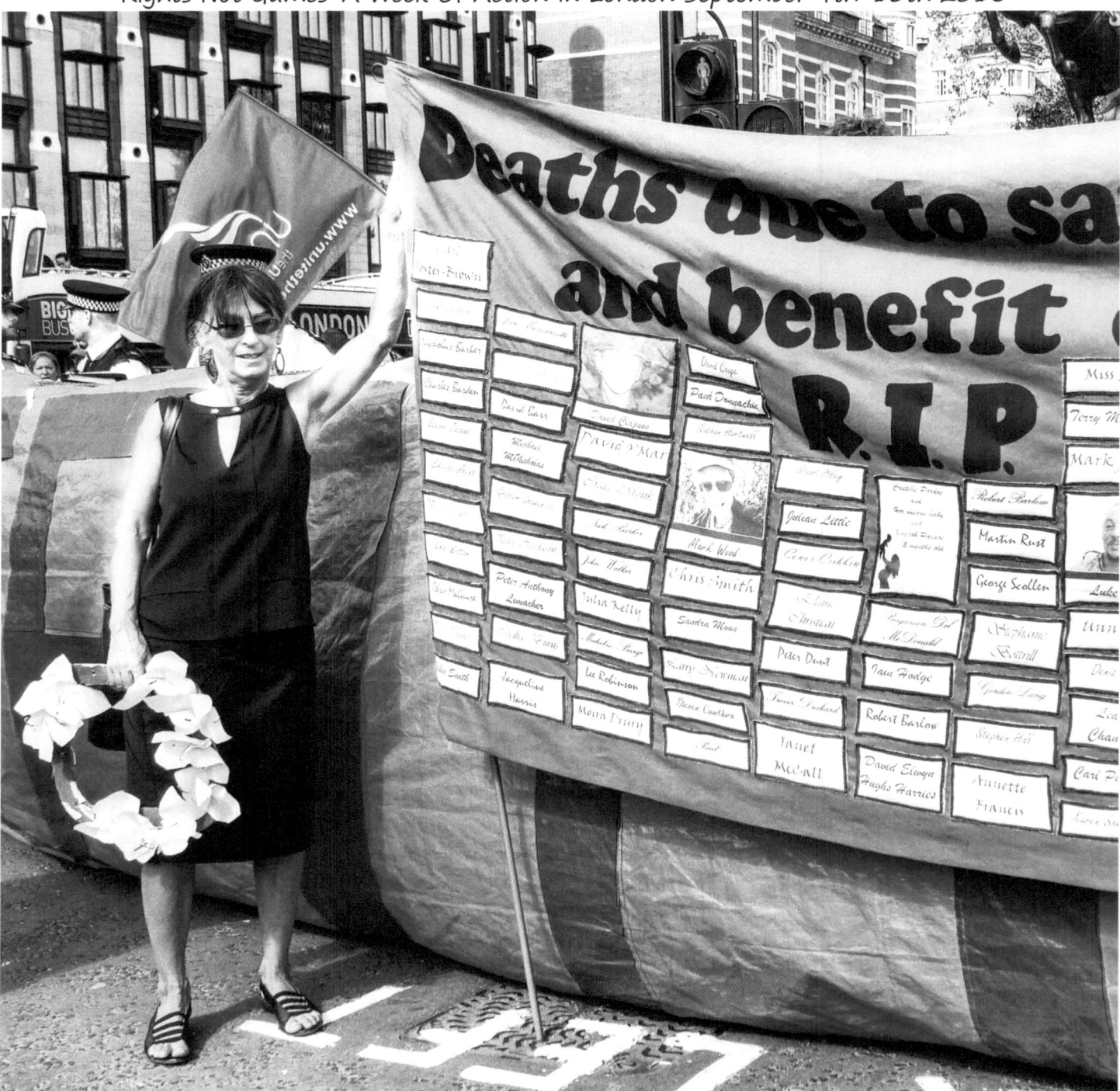

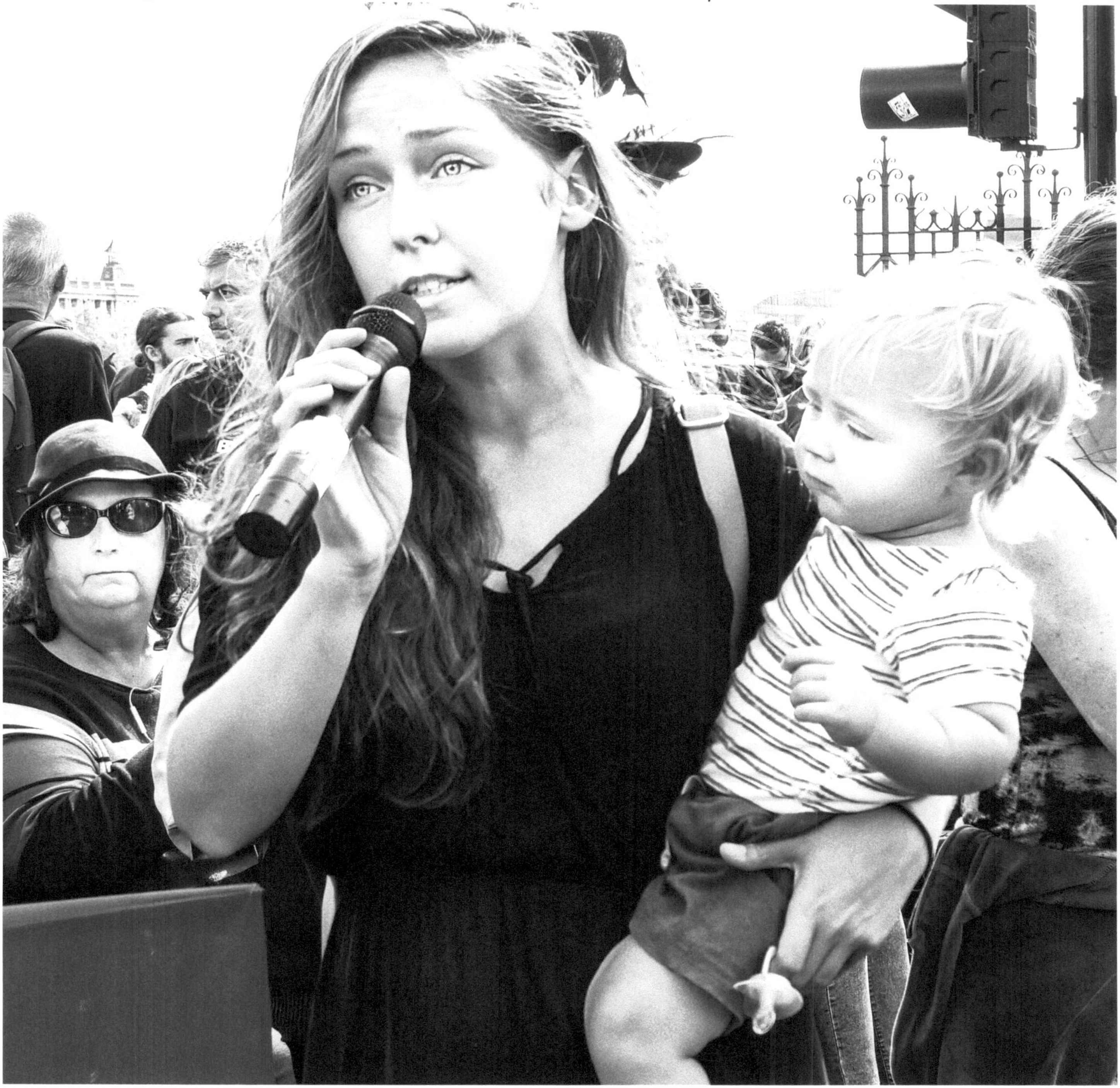

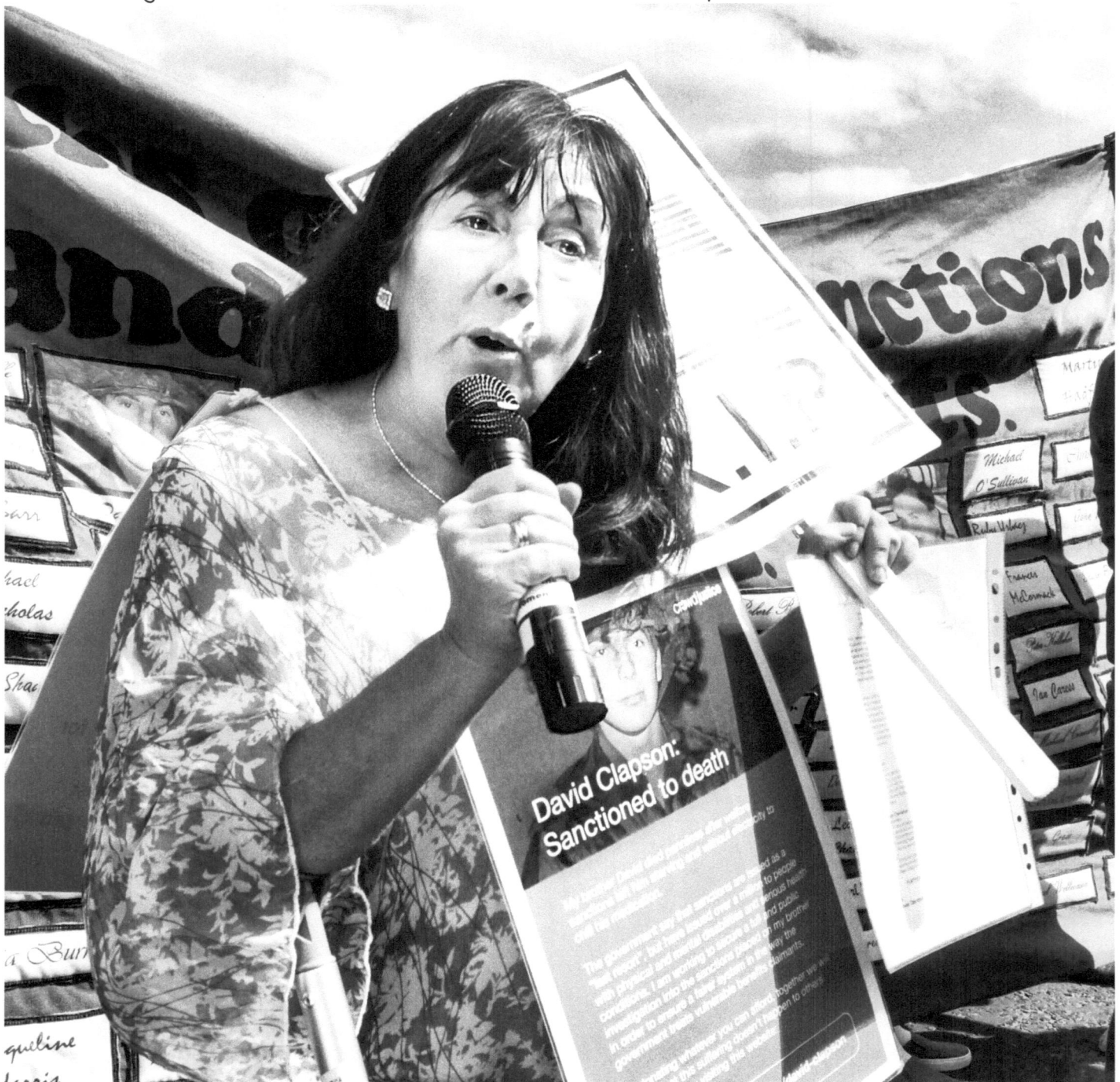

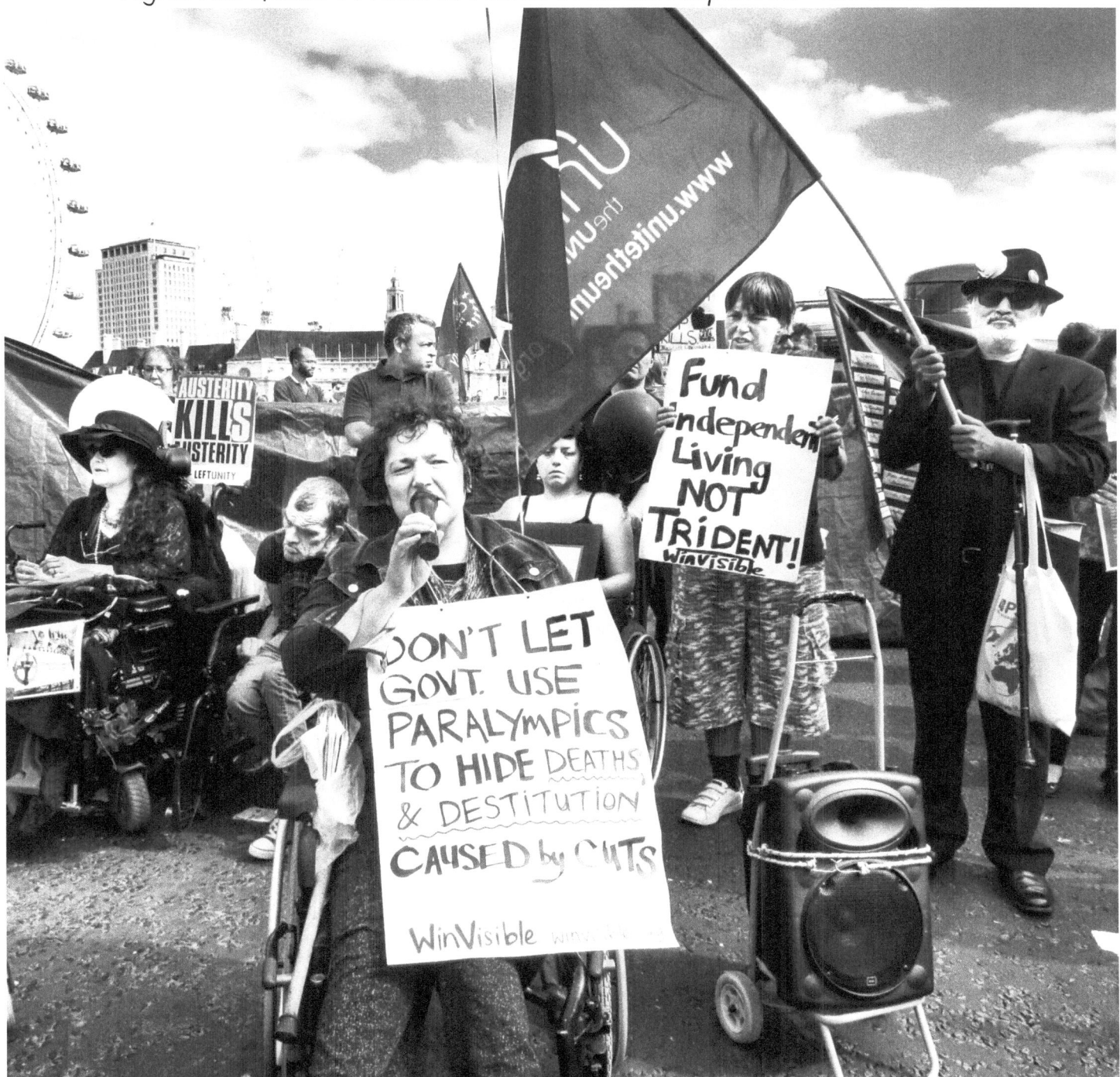

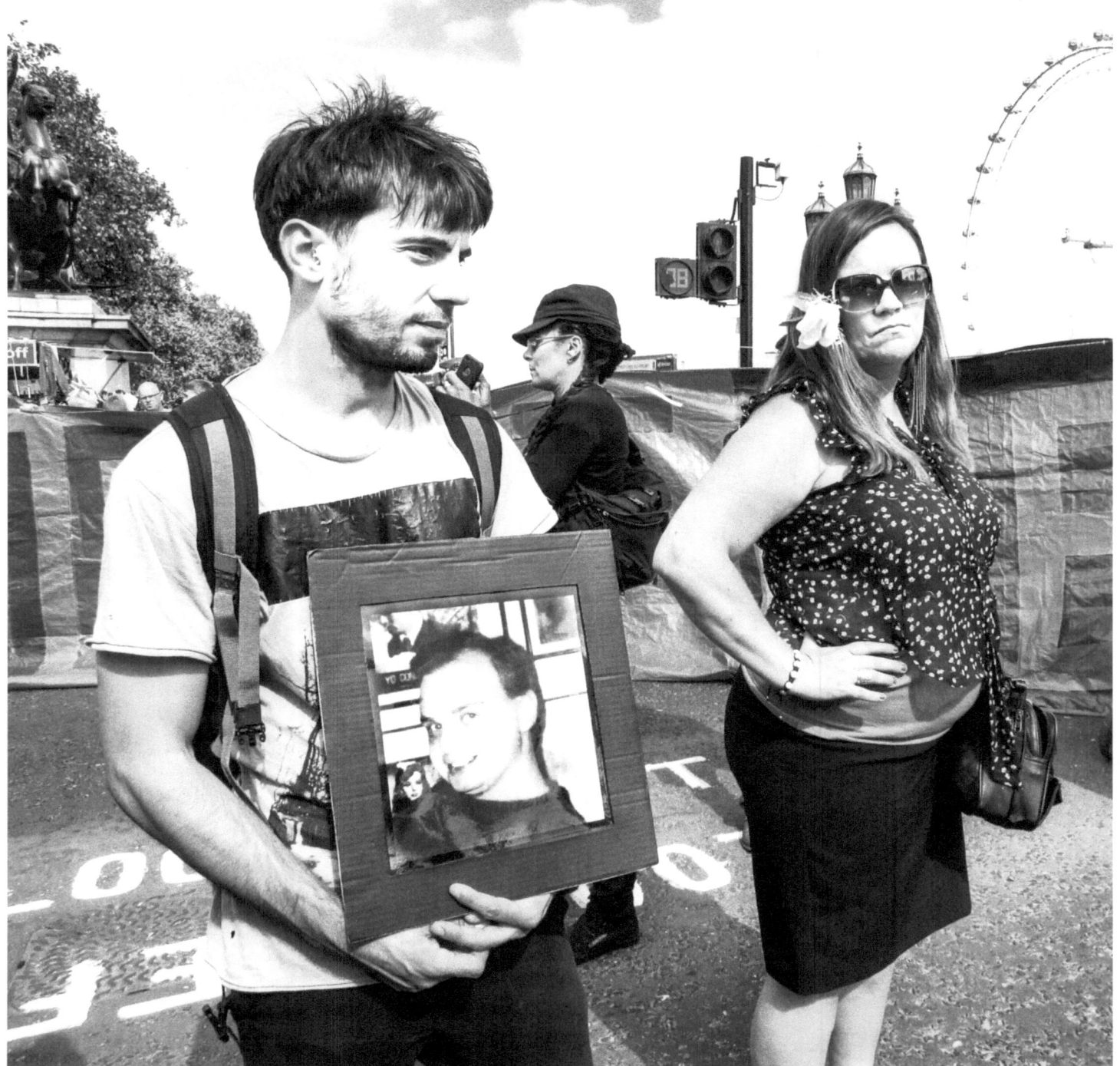

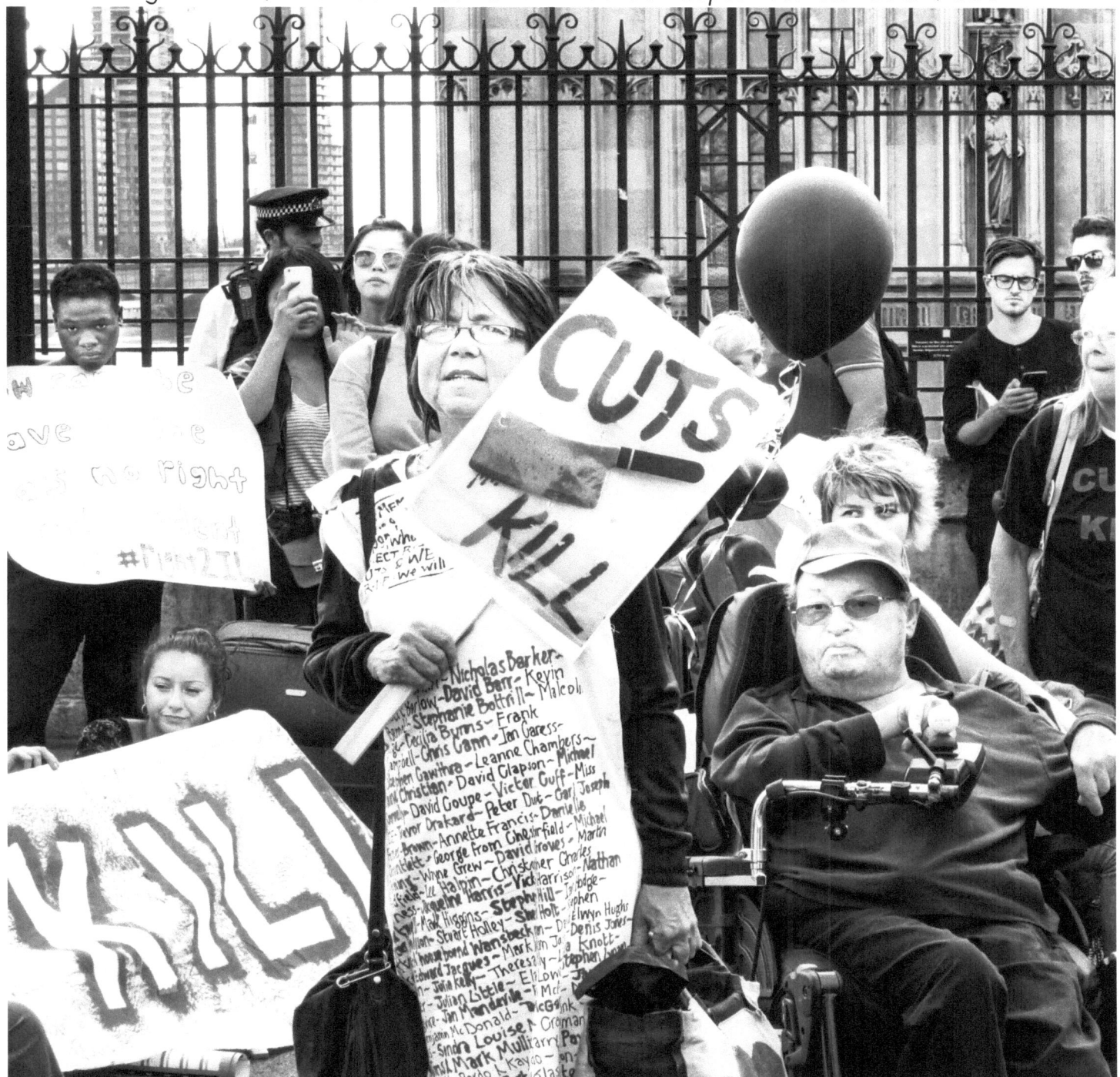

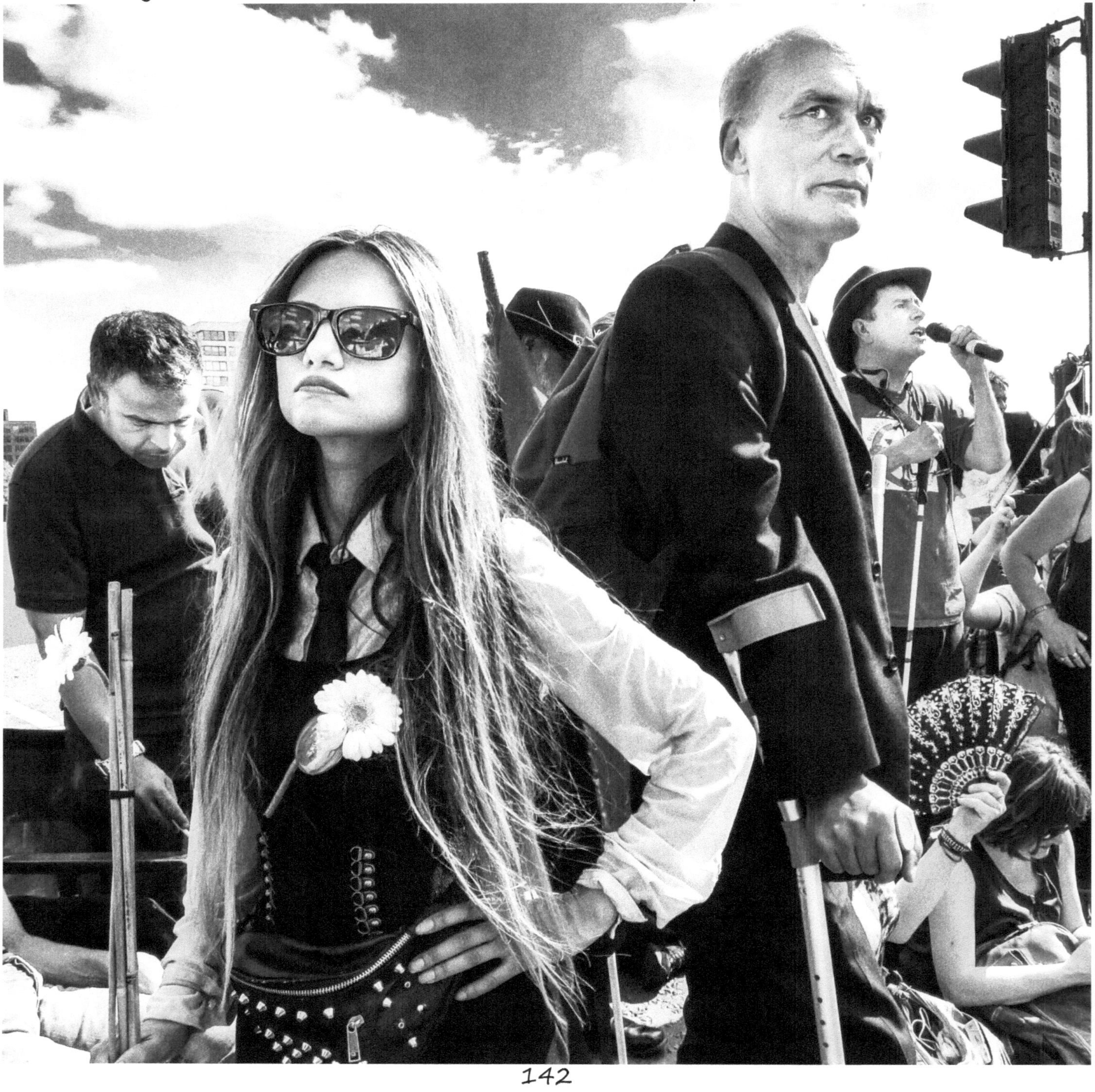

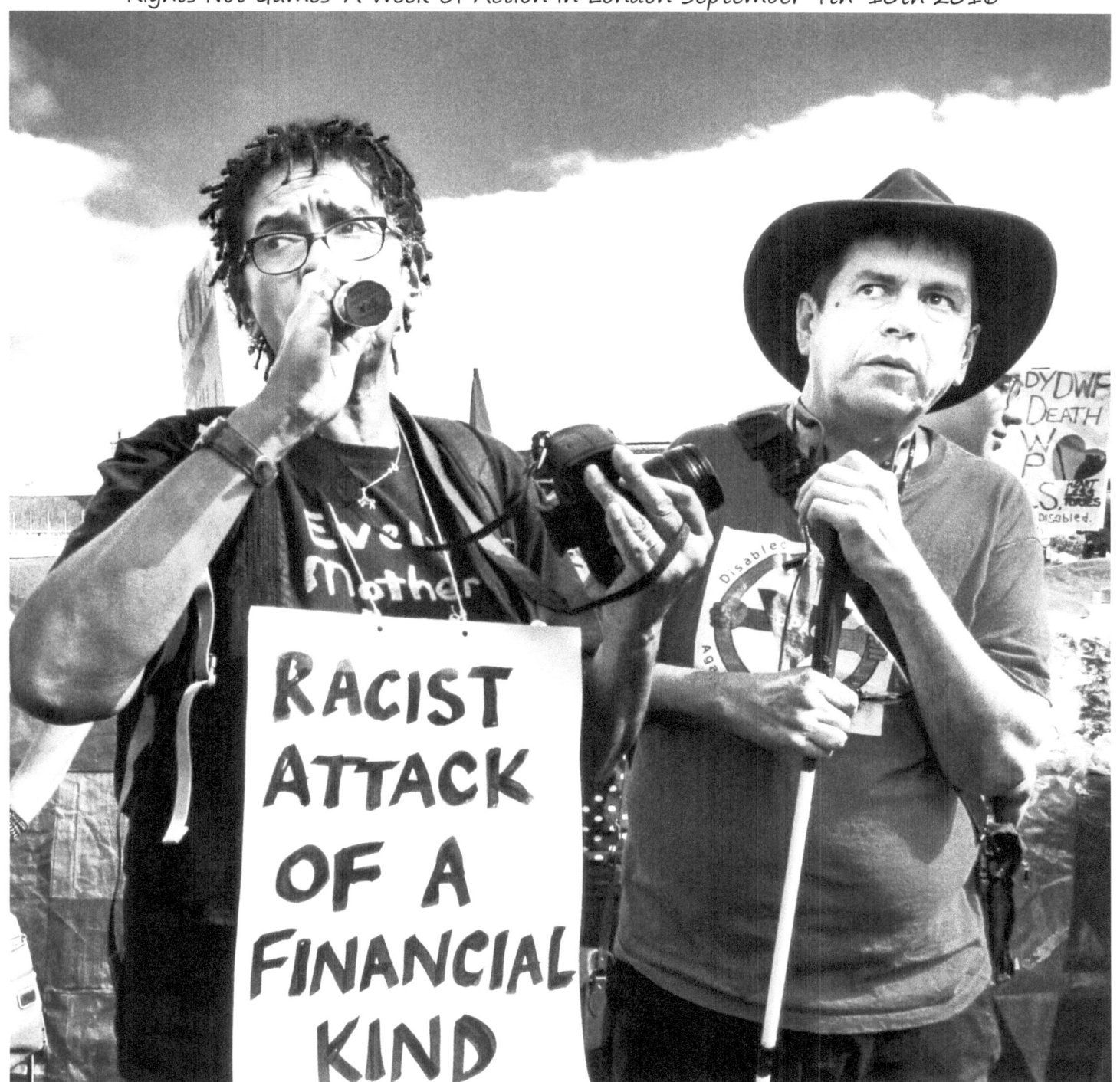

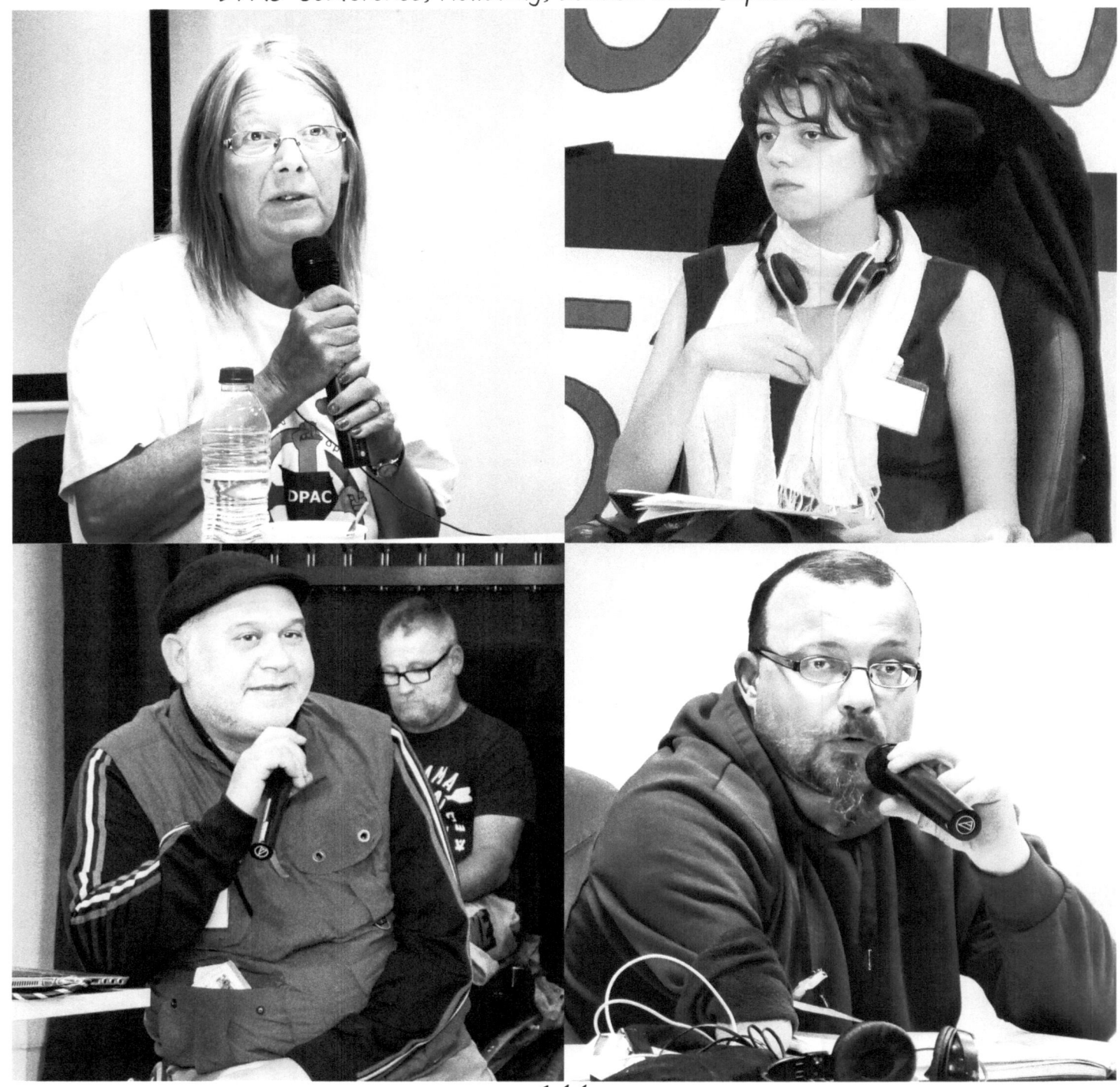

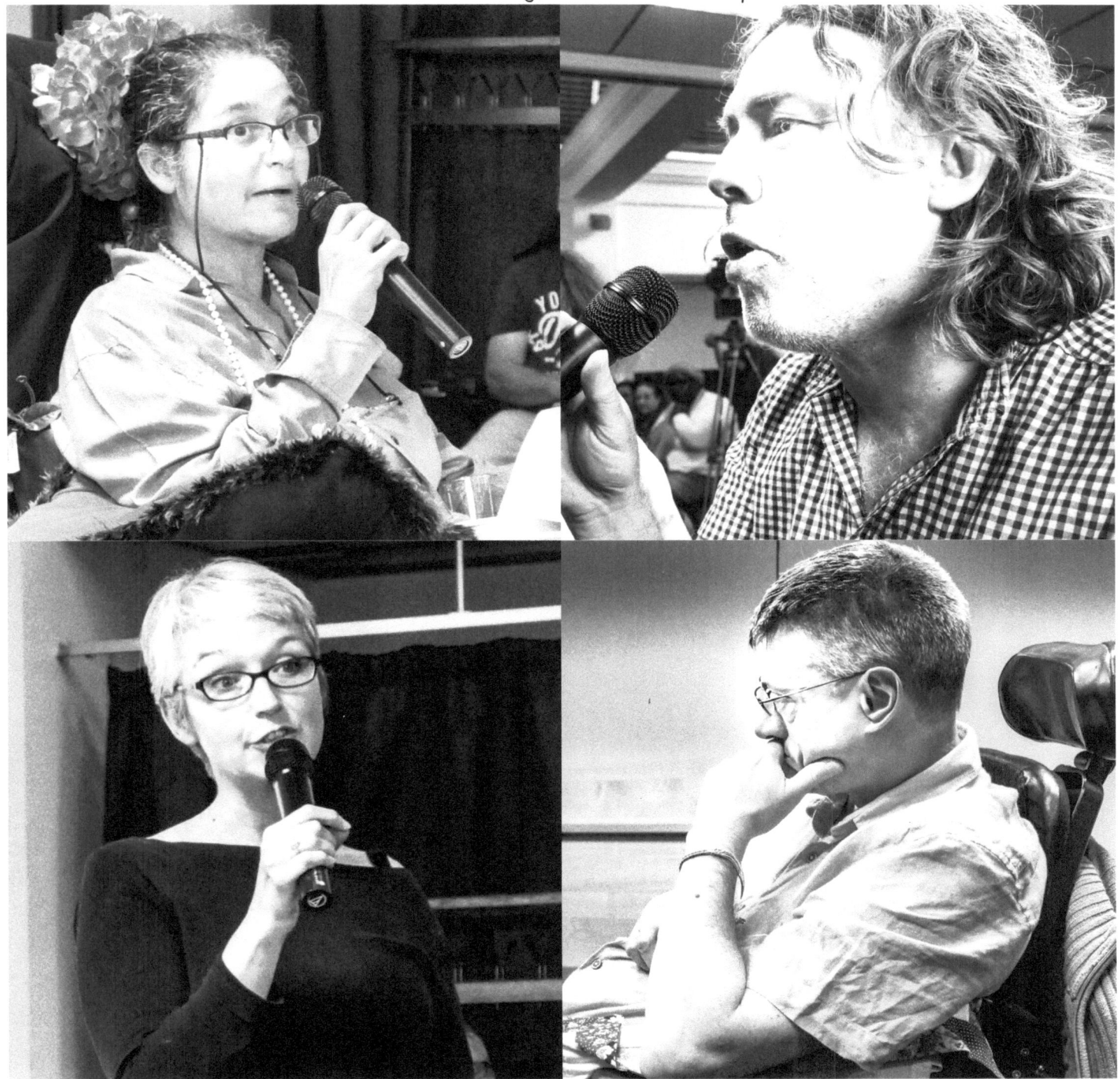

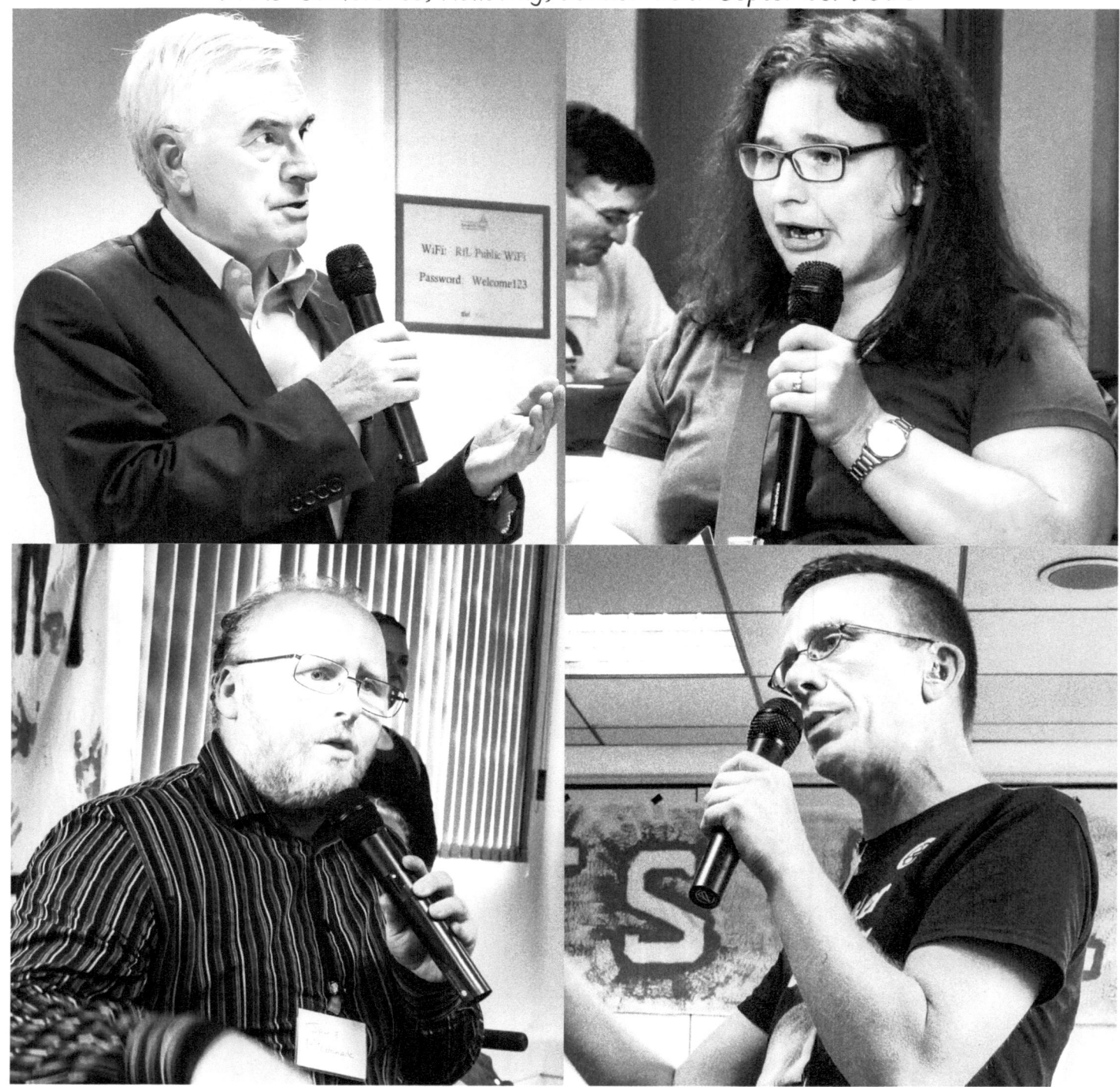

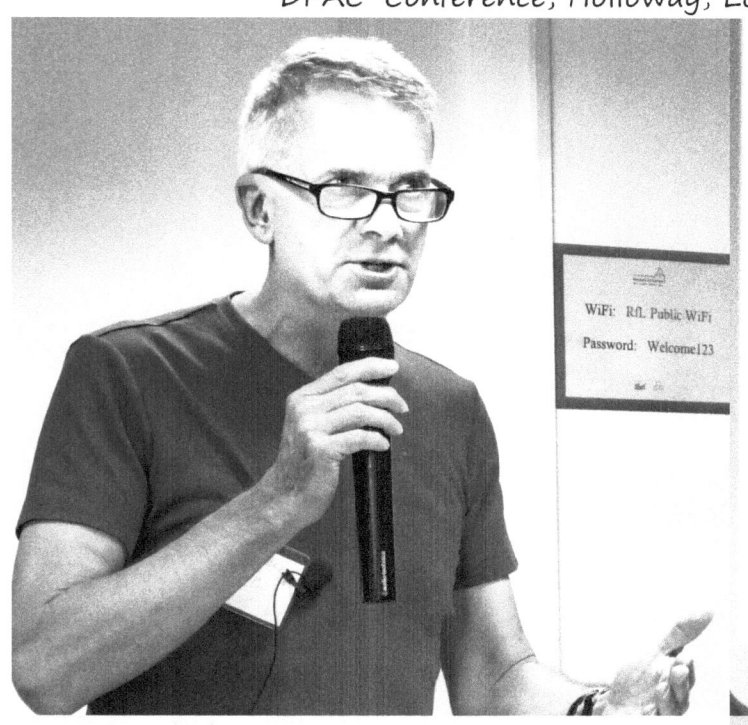

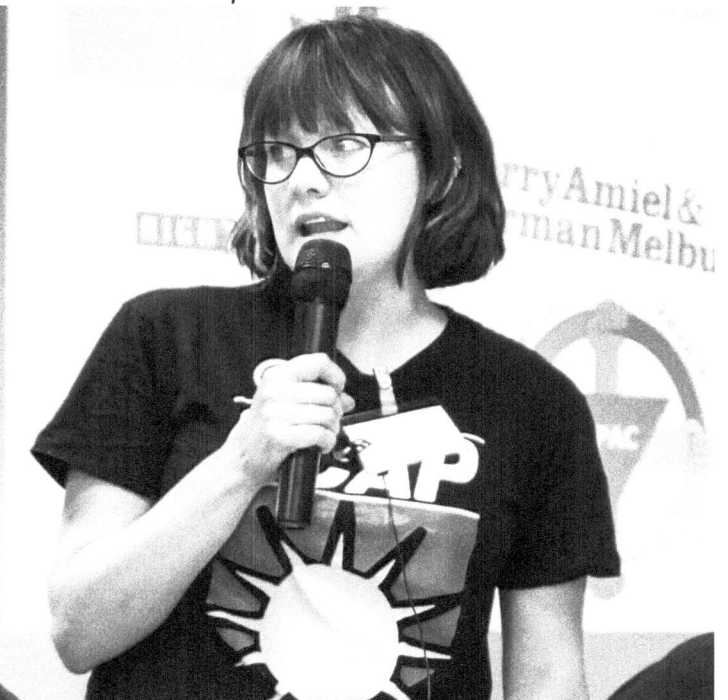

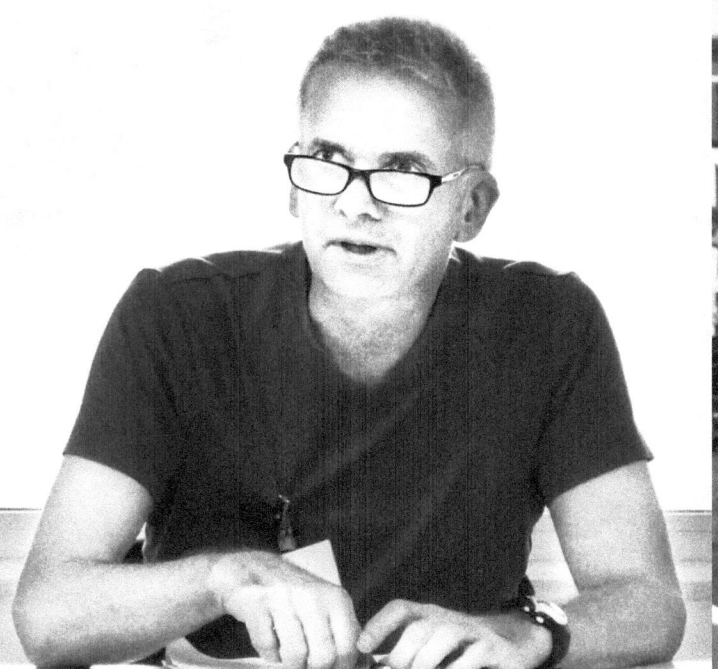

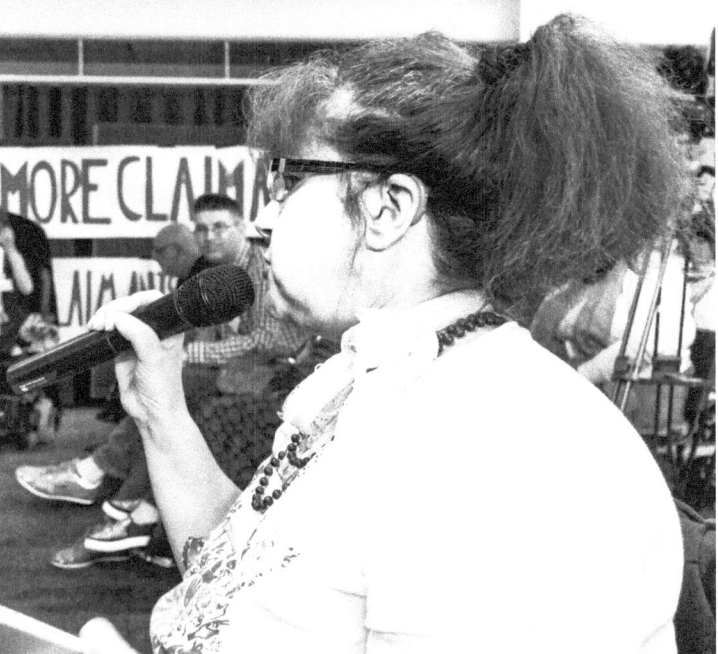

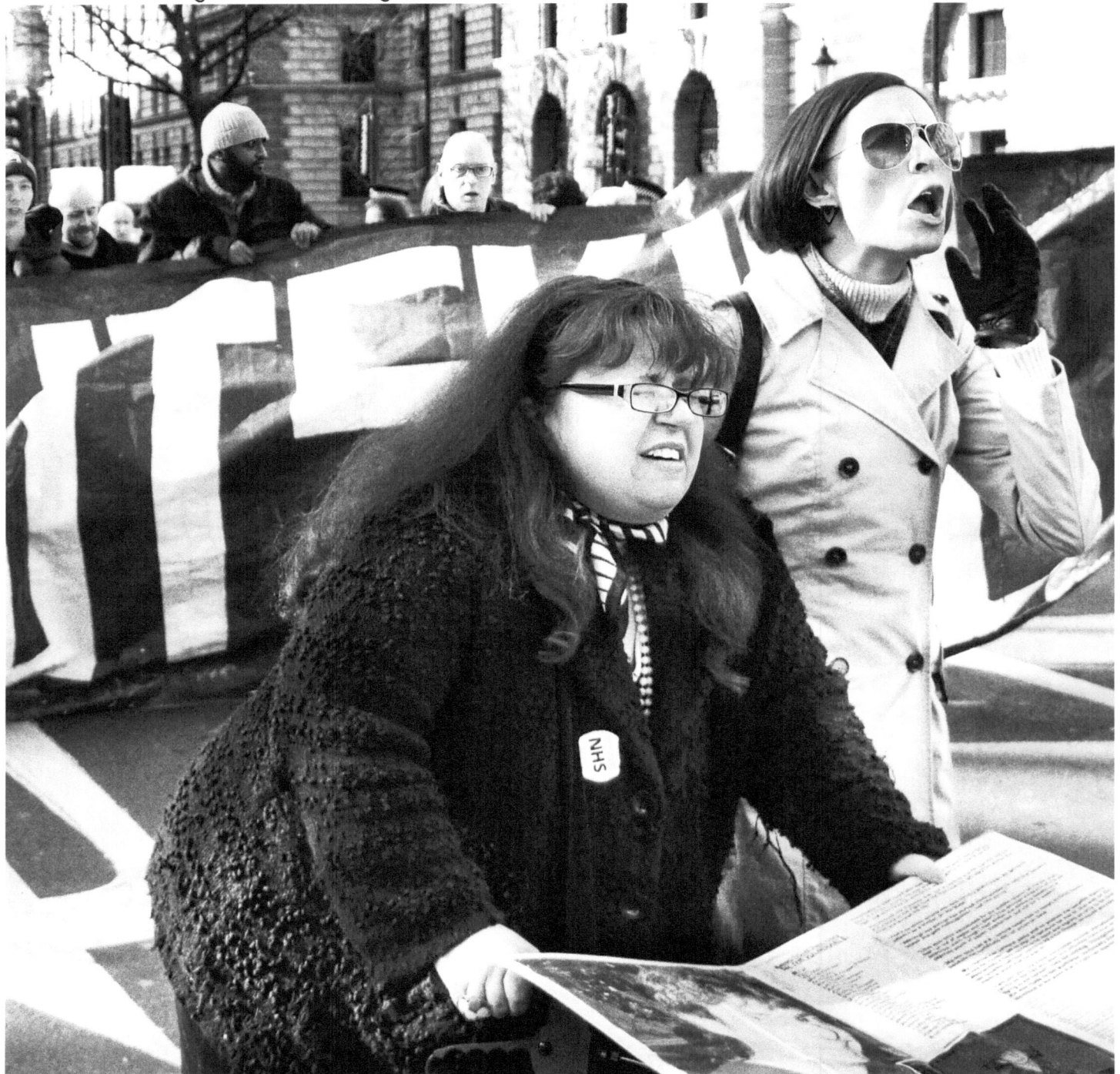

'Protest Against The Changes To PIP' House of Commons, London 7th March 2017

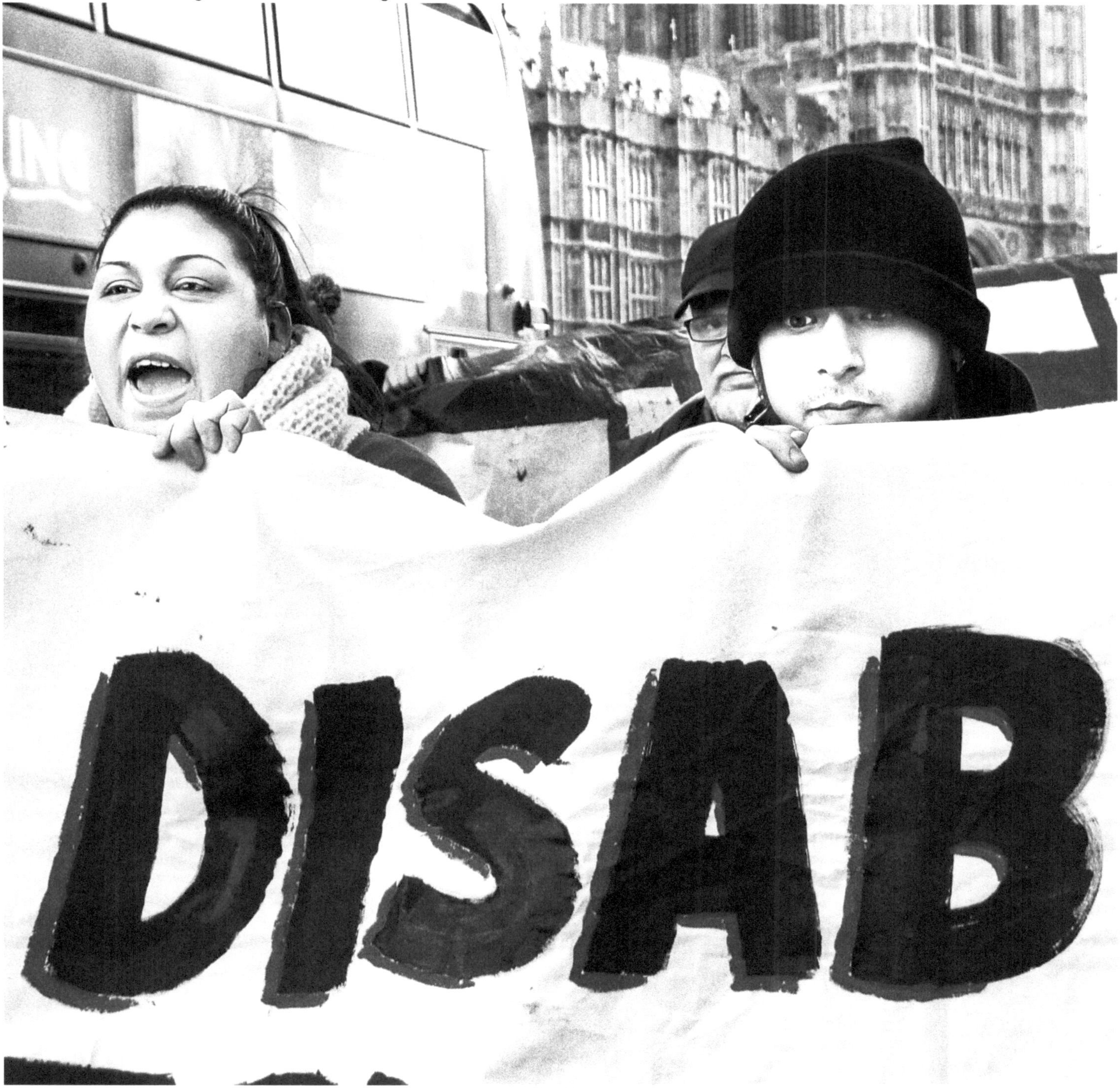

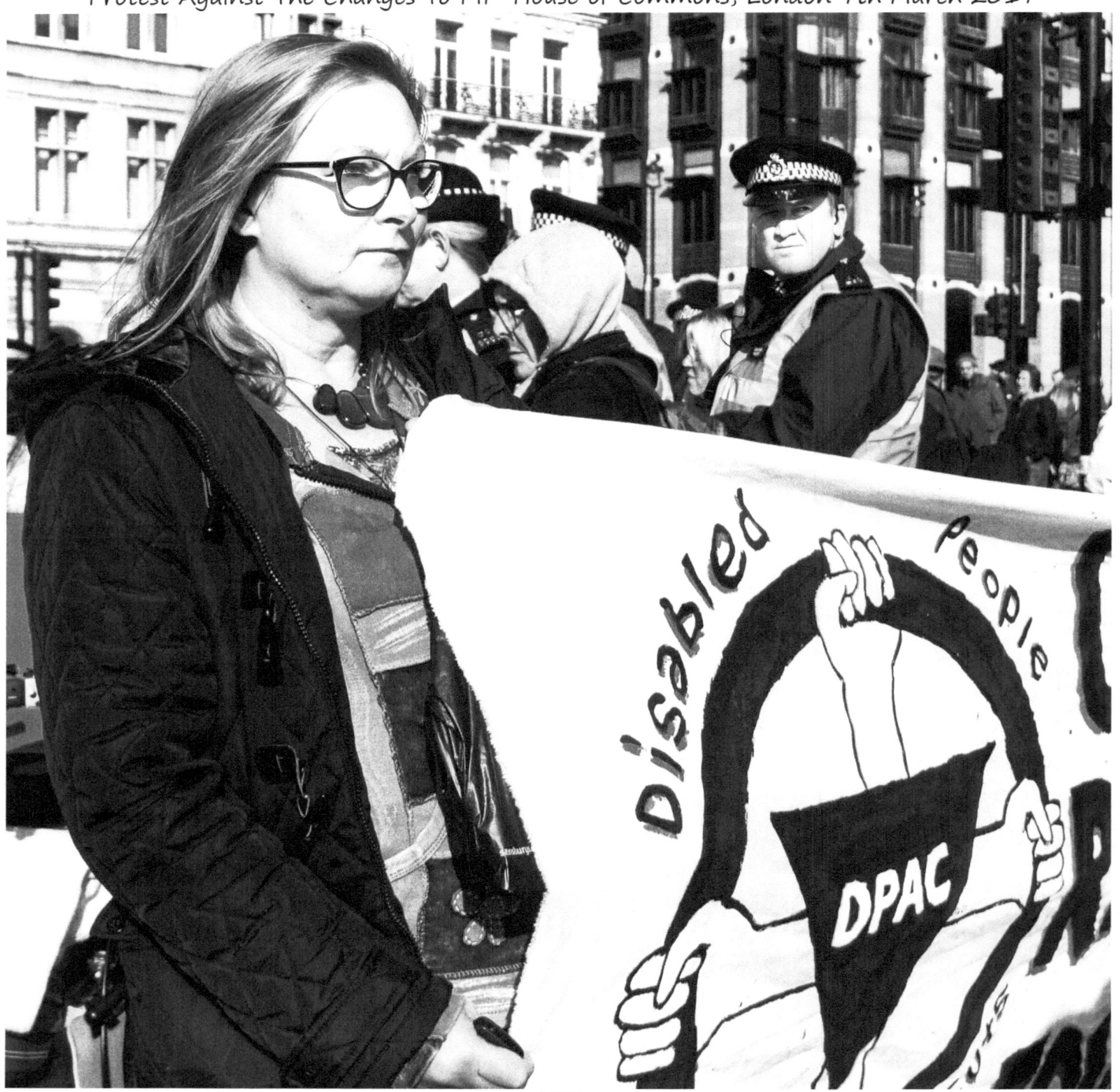

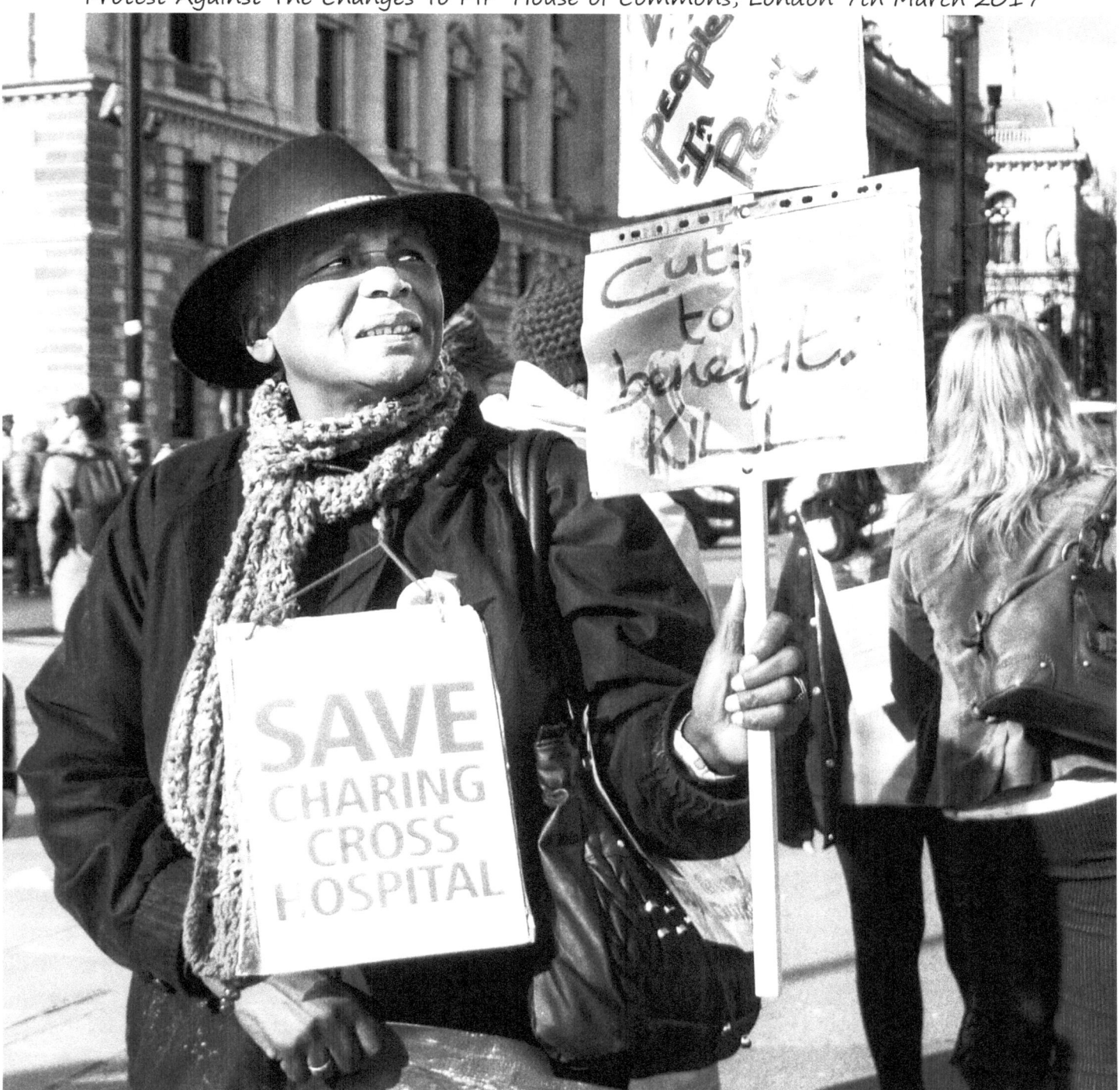

'Protest Against The Changes To PIP' House of Commons, London 7th March 2017

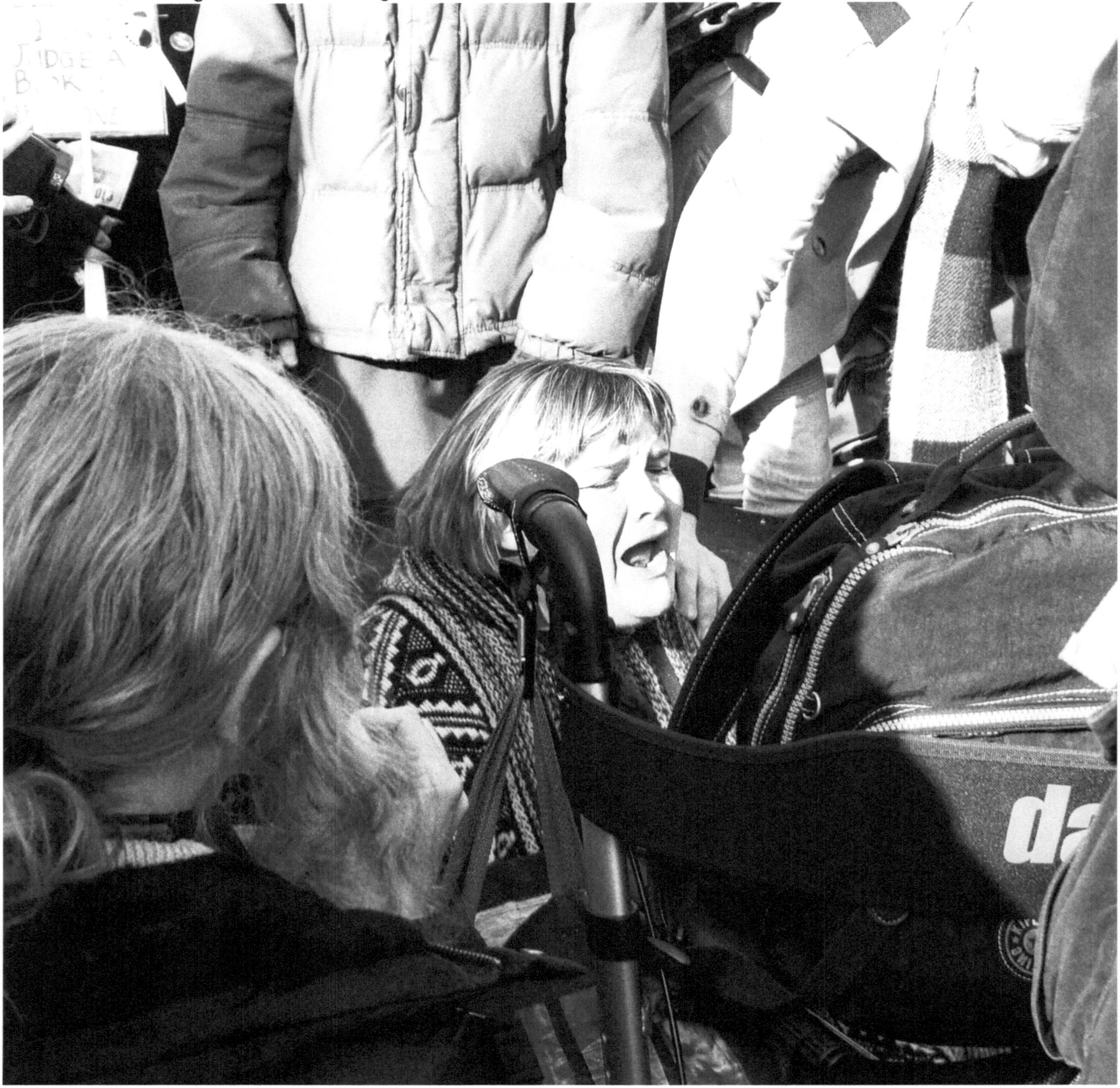

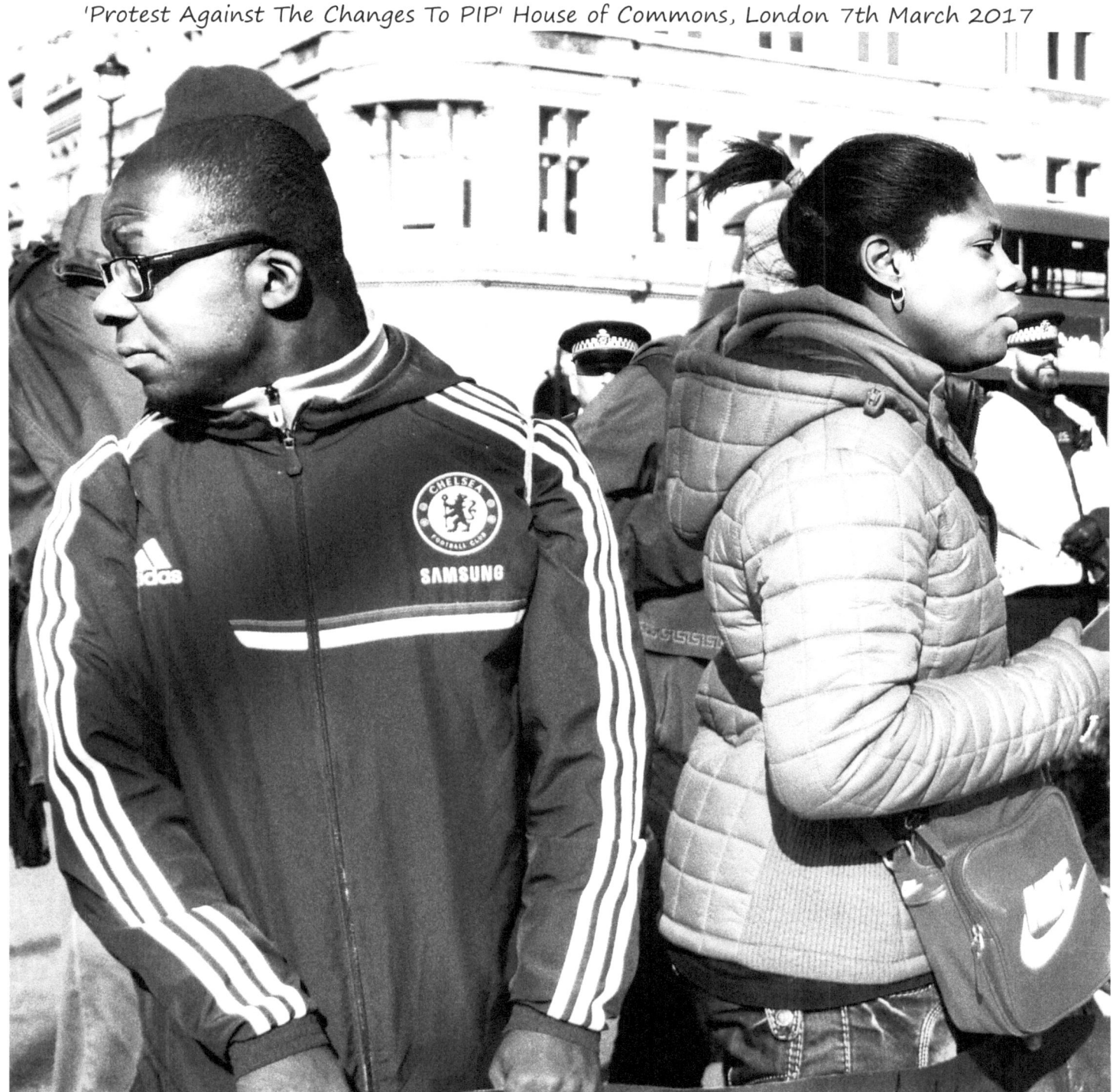

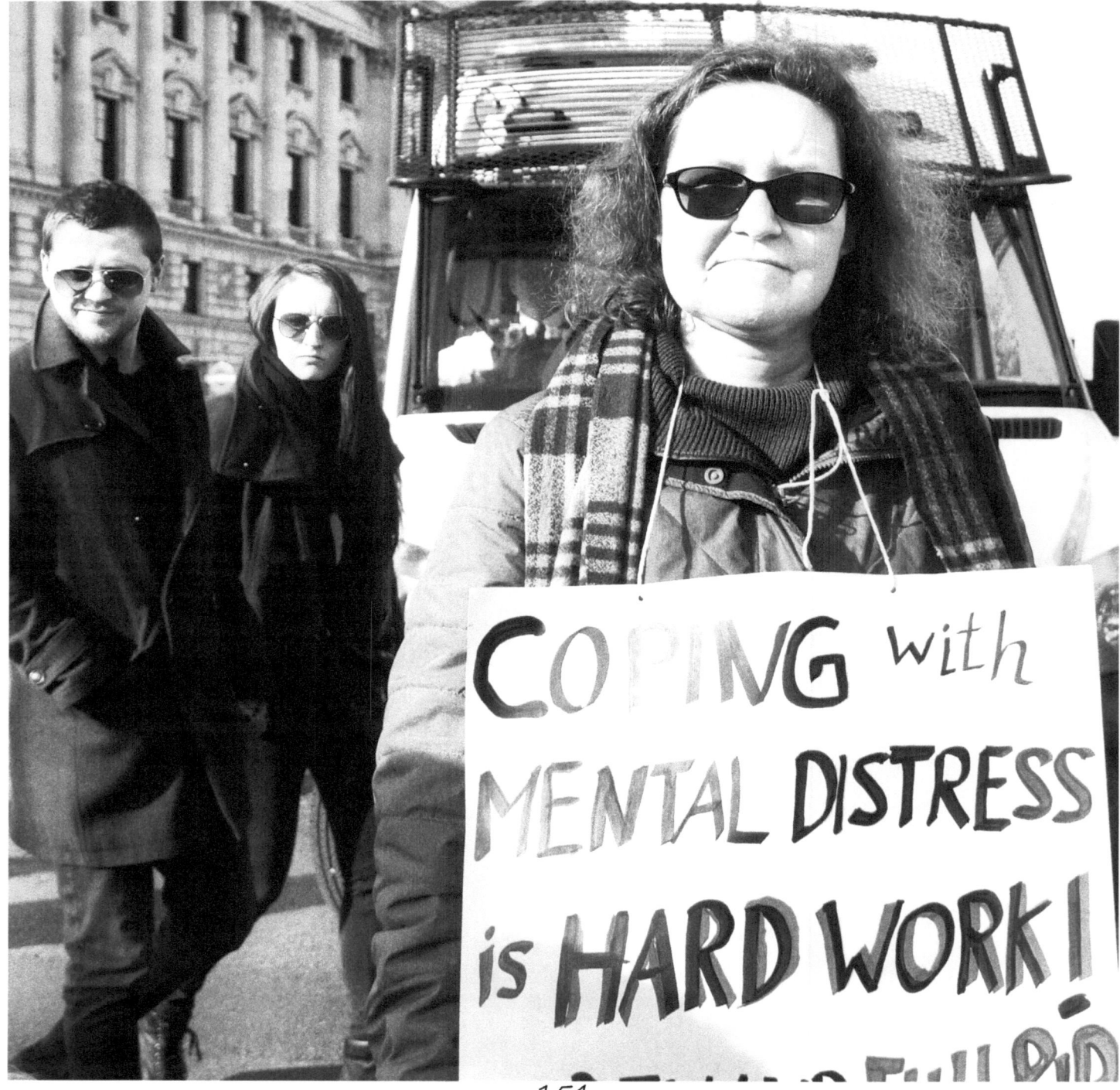

UN declares UK's austerity policies in breach of international human rights

The UN are "seriously concerned" by the state of inequality in the UK.

... citing the absence of due process and access to justice for those affected by the use of sanctions affecting the most vulnerable and disadvantaged groups.

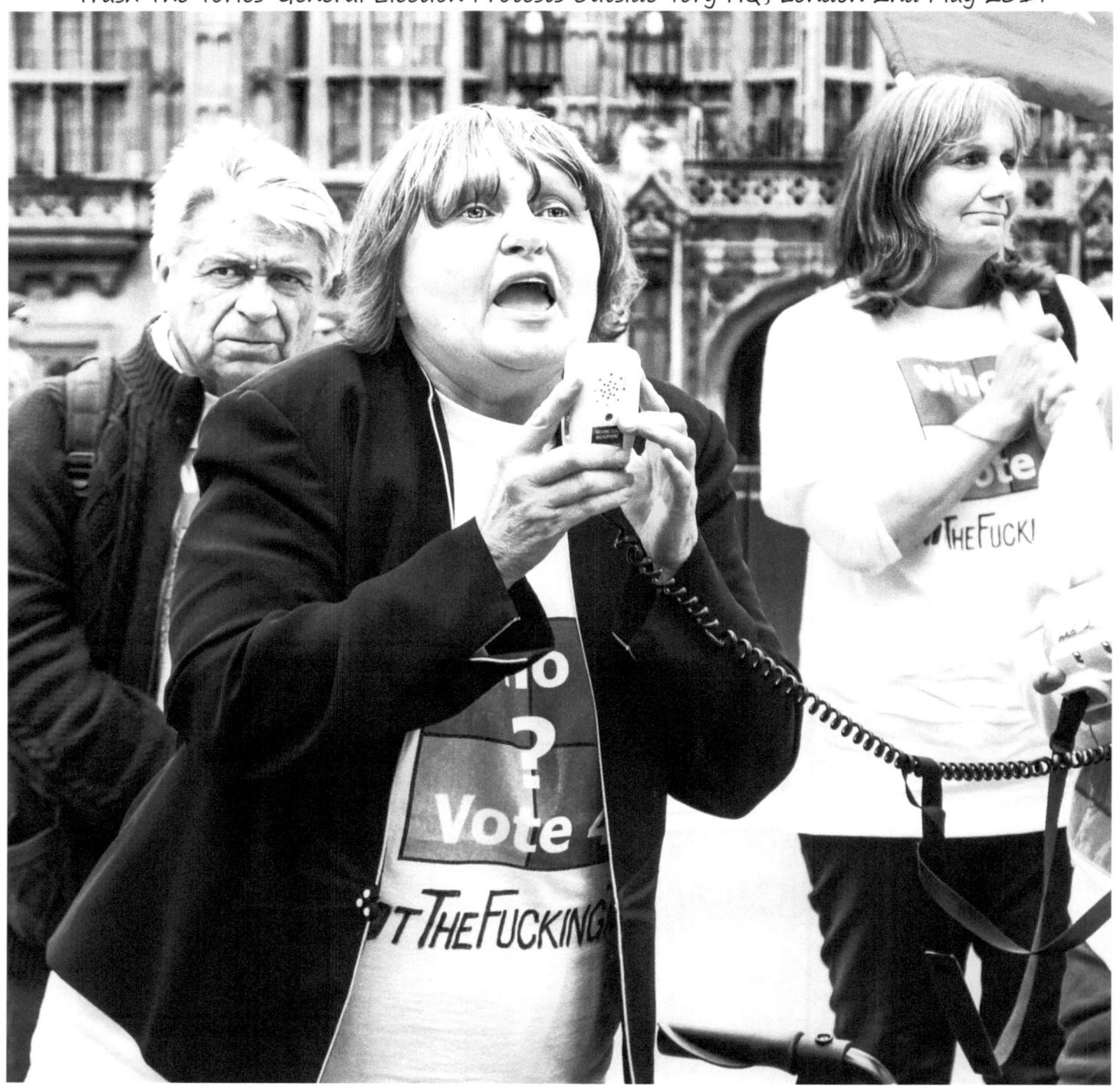

DISABLED PEOPLE AGAINST CUTS
'RIGHTS NOT CHARITY'

have always voted VS benefit cuts

...sioners & disabled people
...GED for people CAR...
...ERS GE...
...PIL...

Disabled People Against Cut

DPAC

We all
lose out when
Human Rights are wronged
An injustice to one is an injustice to us all

Art installation by - Mary-Ellen
Please join and add your support for DPAC www.dpac.net

Who 2?

KÖSCHALL

Spectra

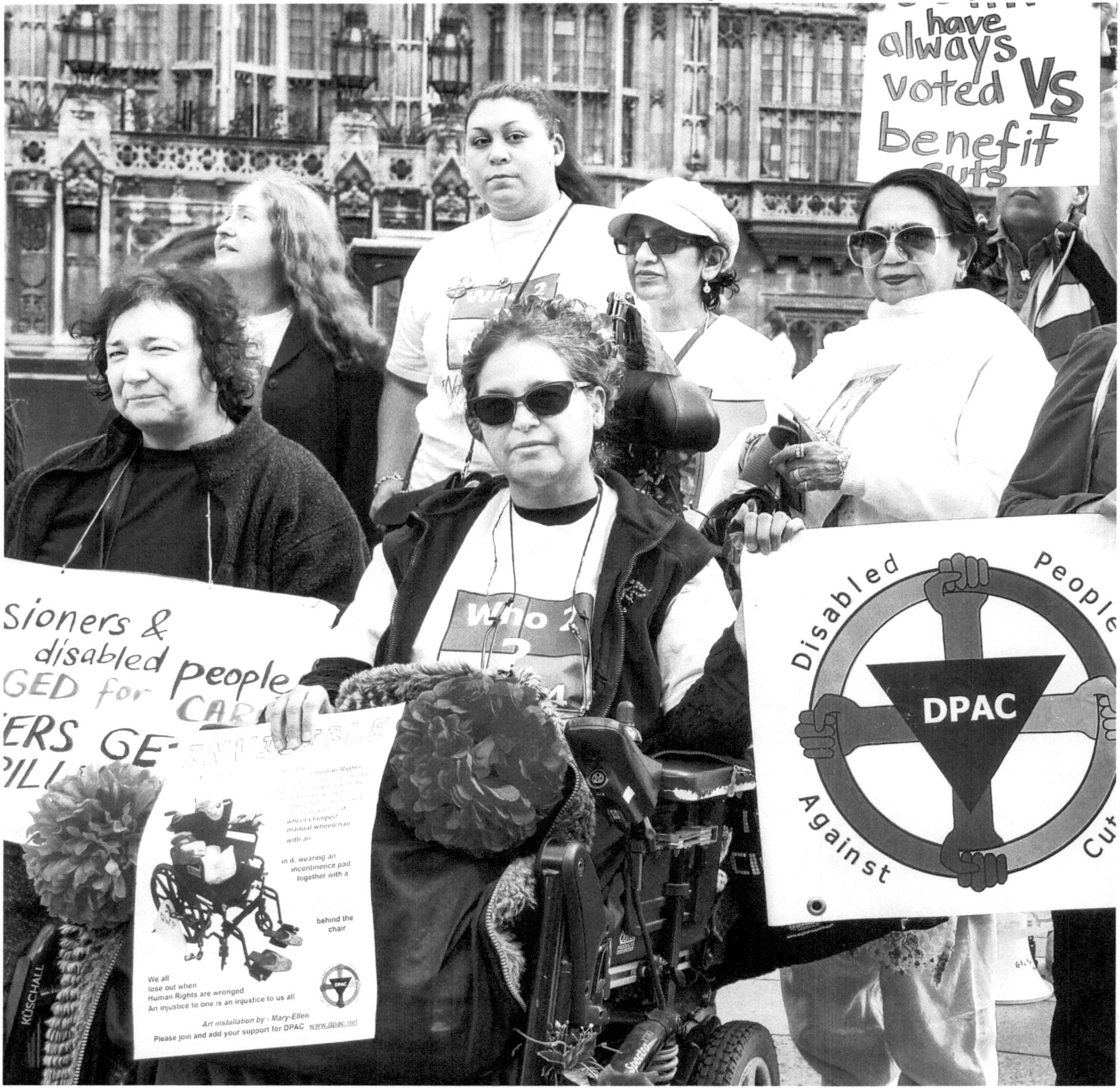

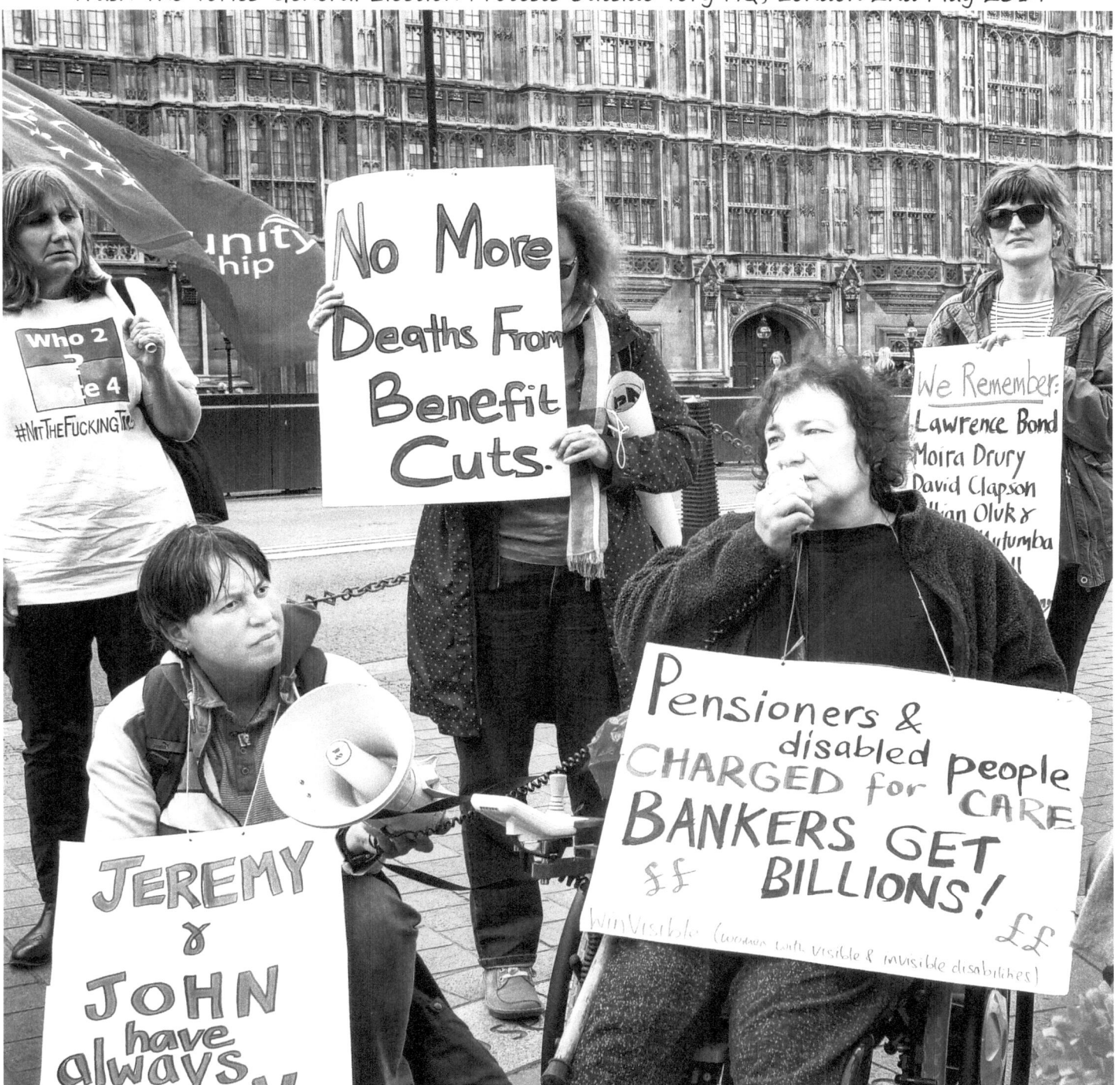

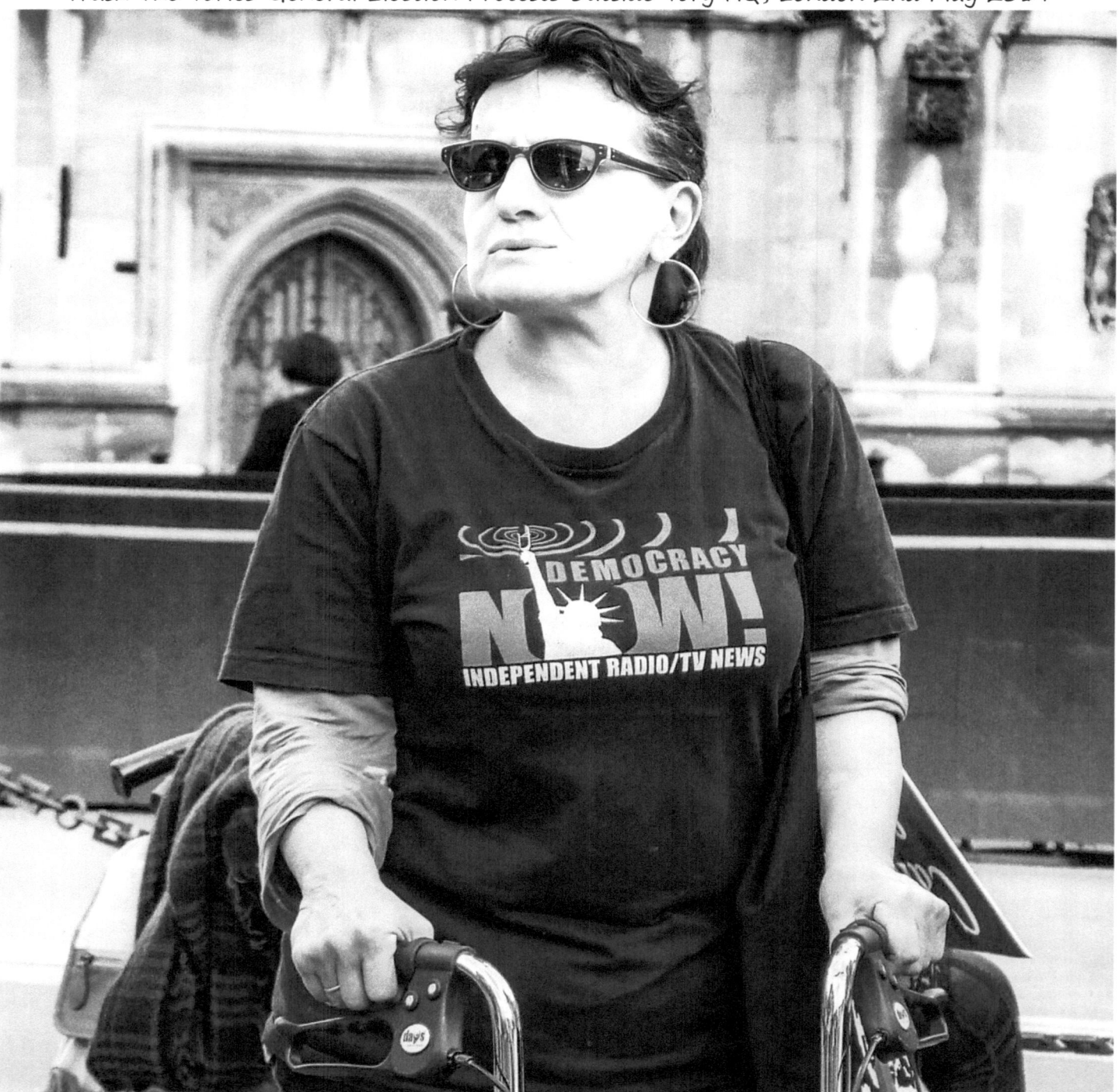

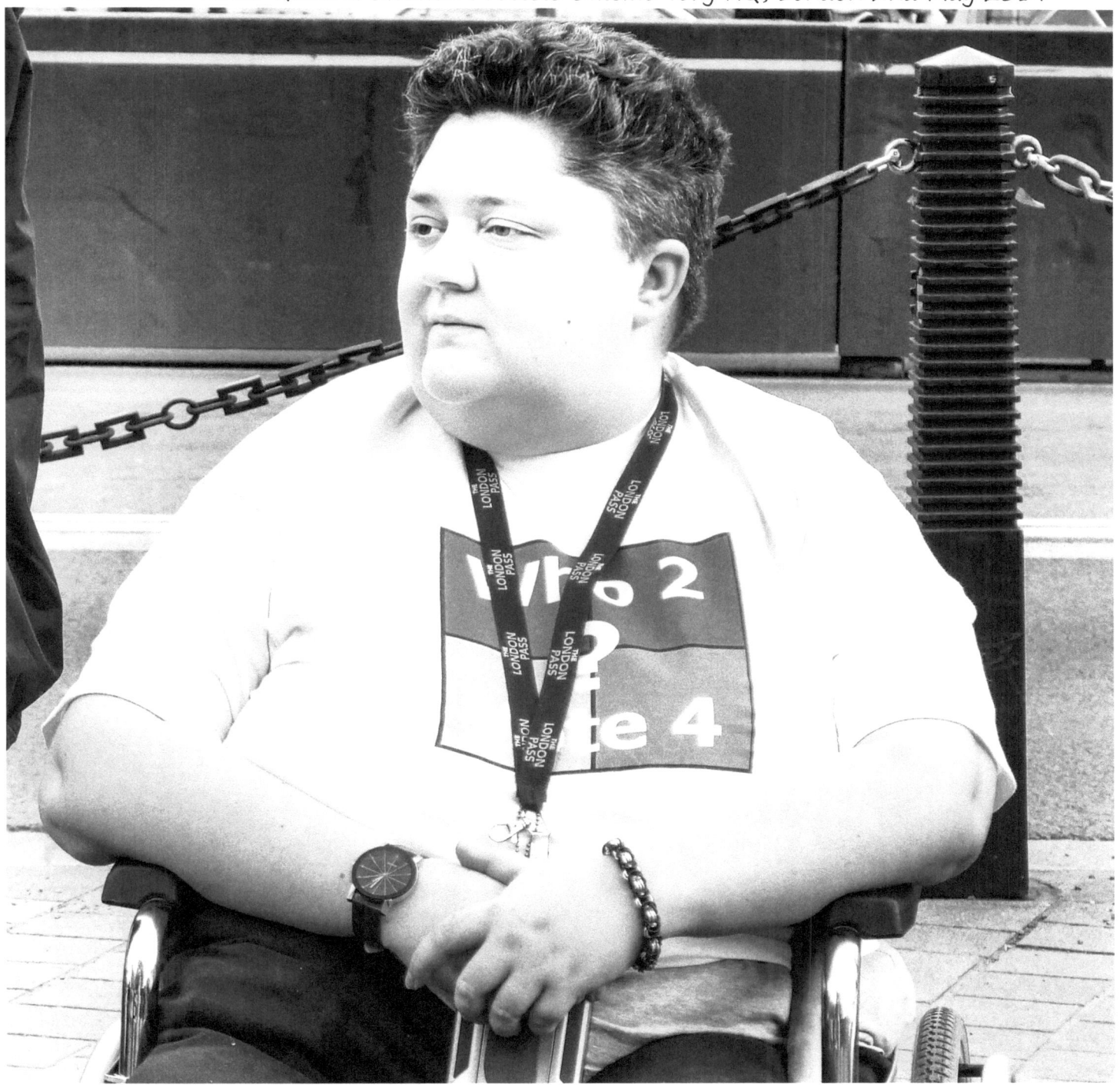

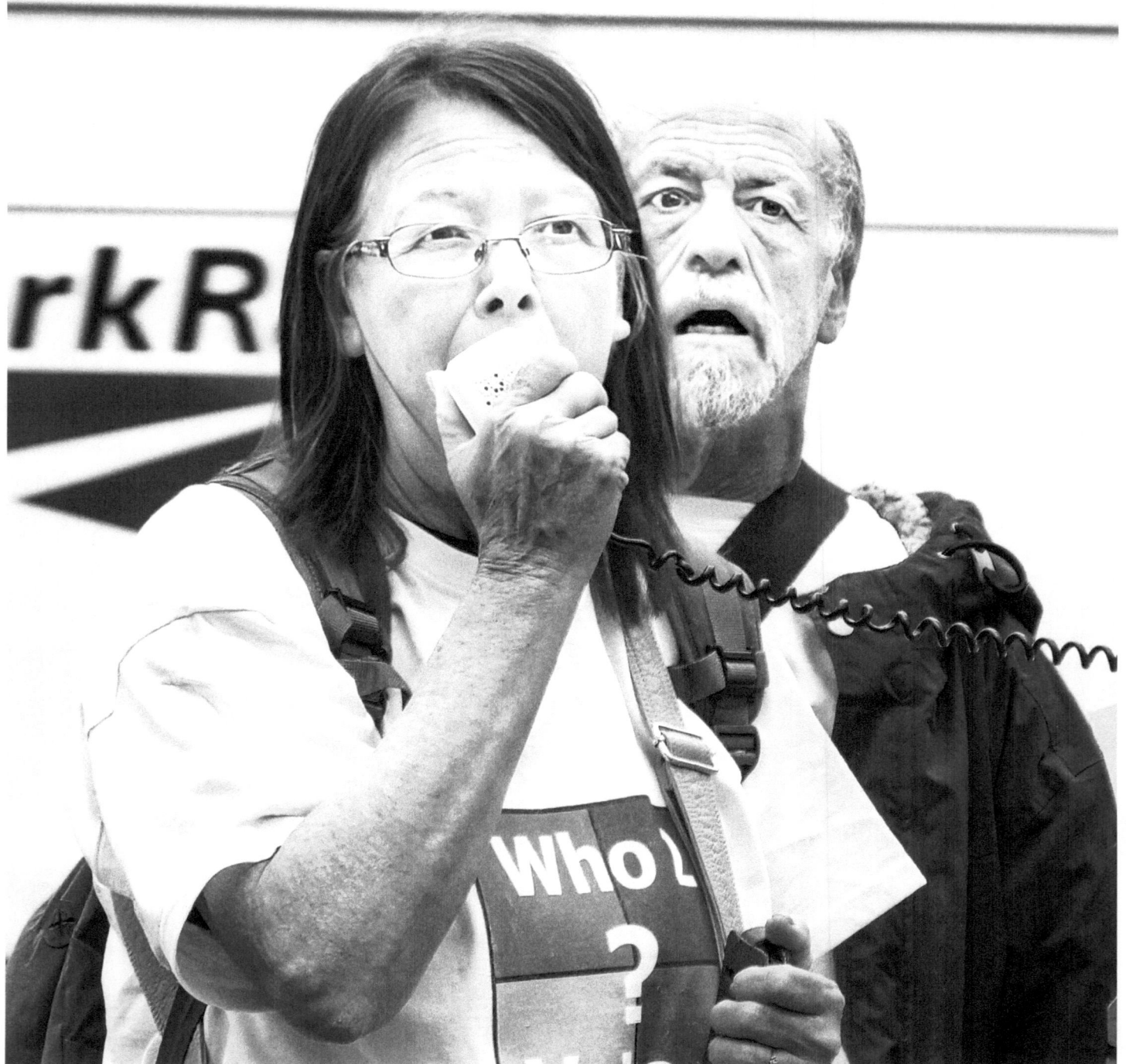

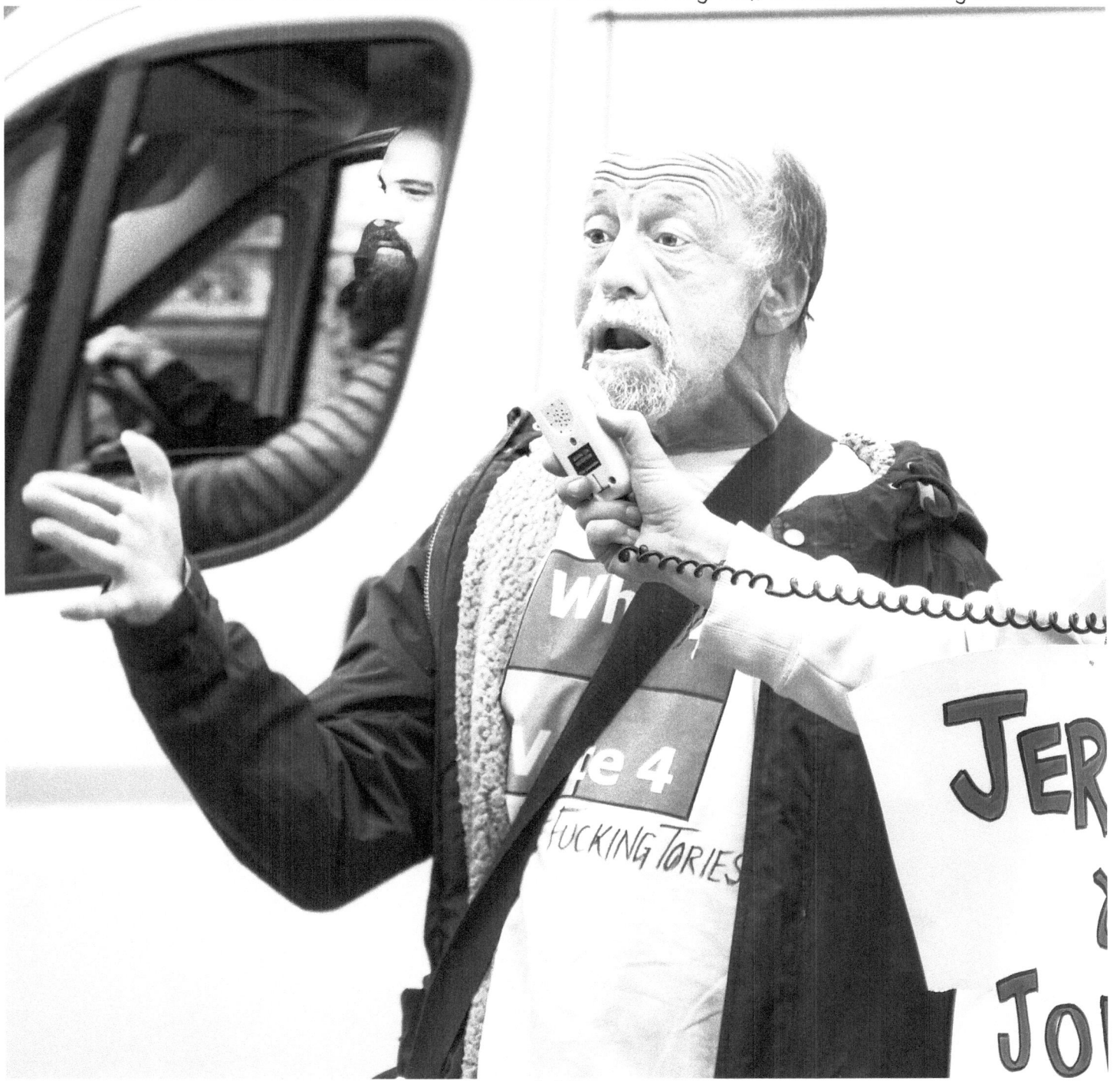

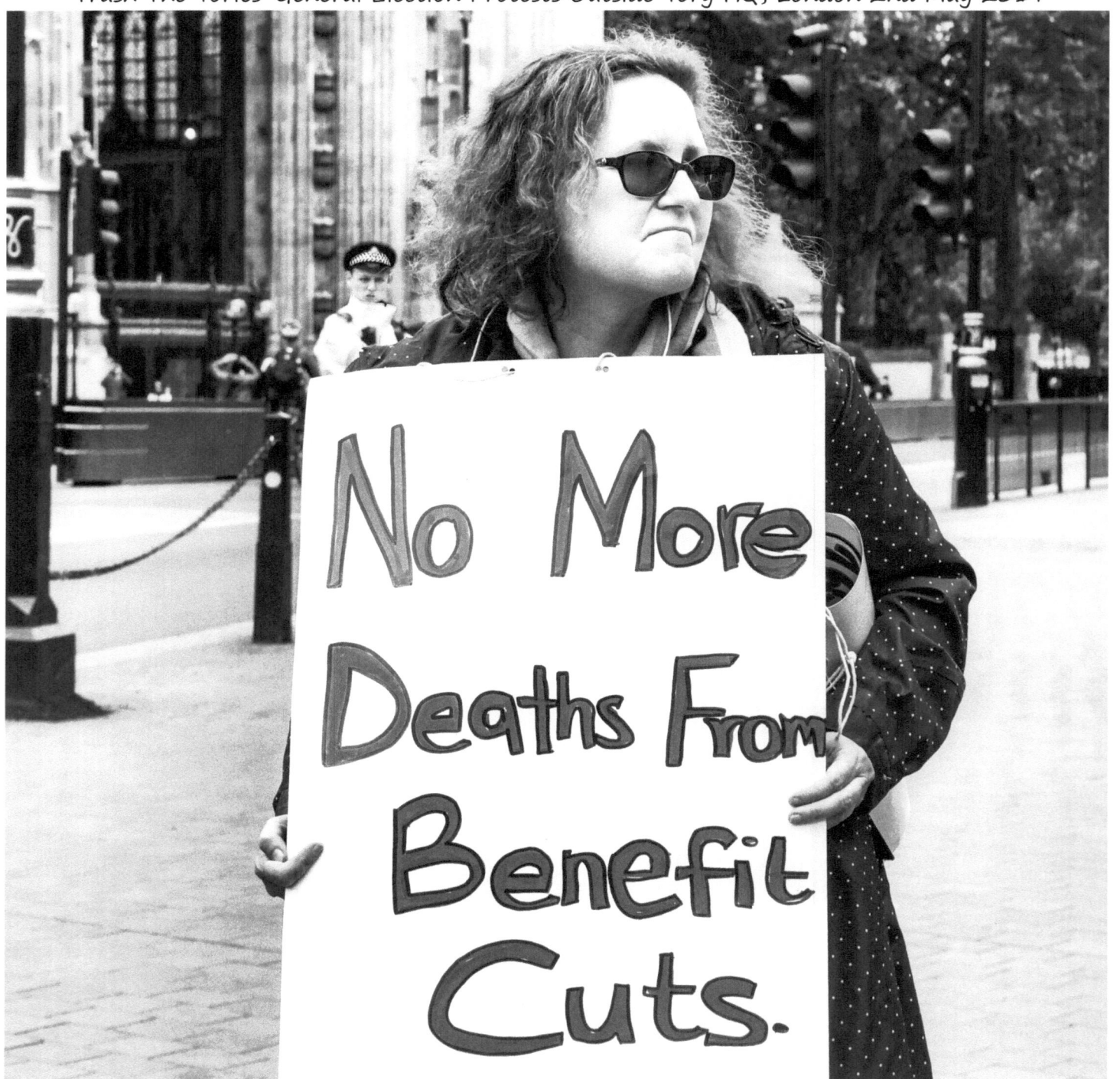

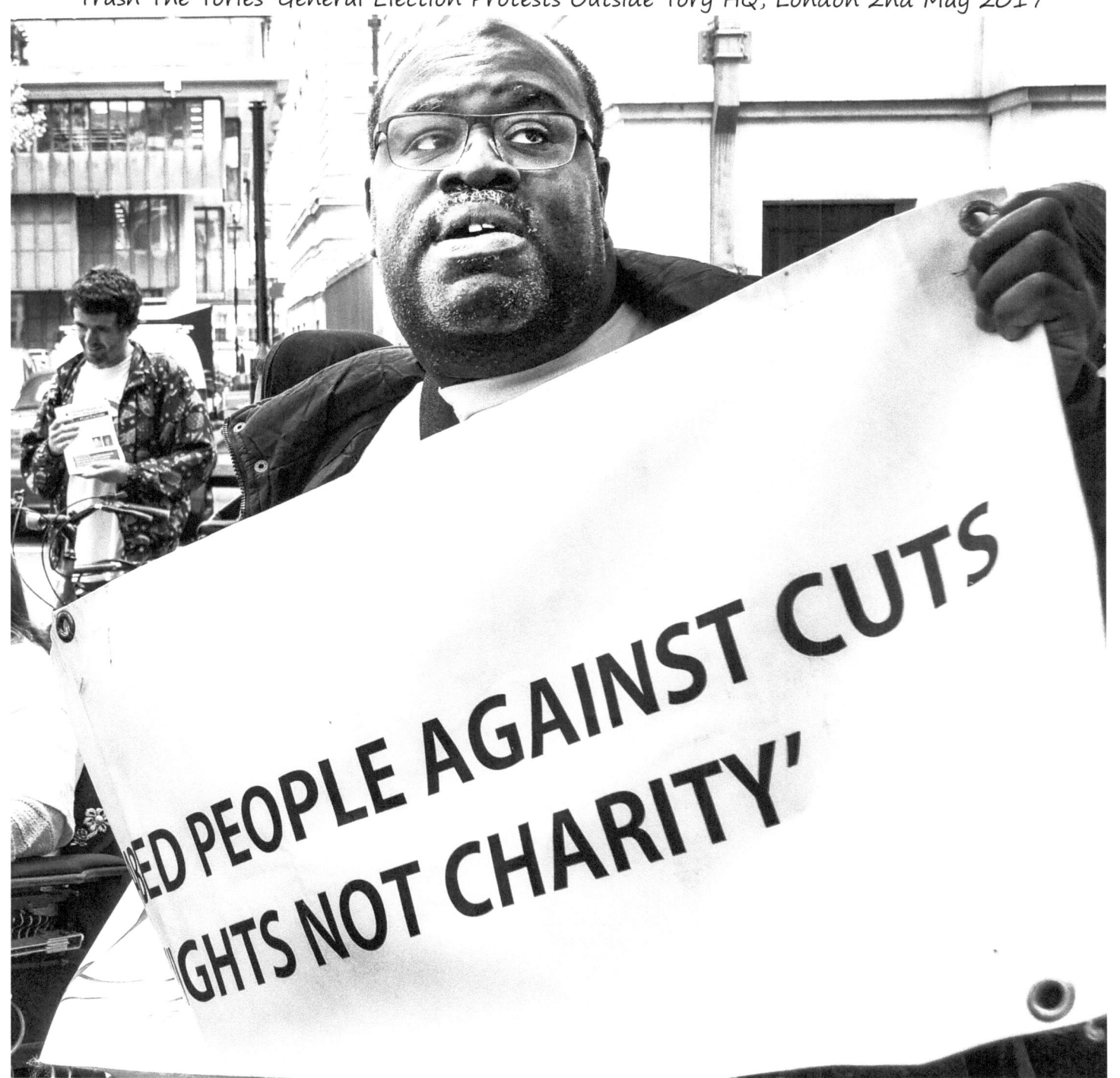

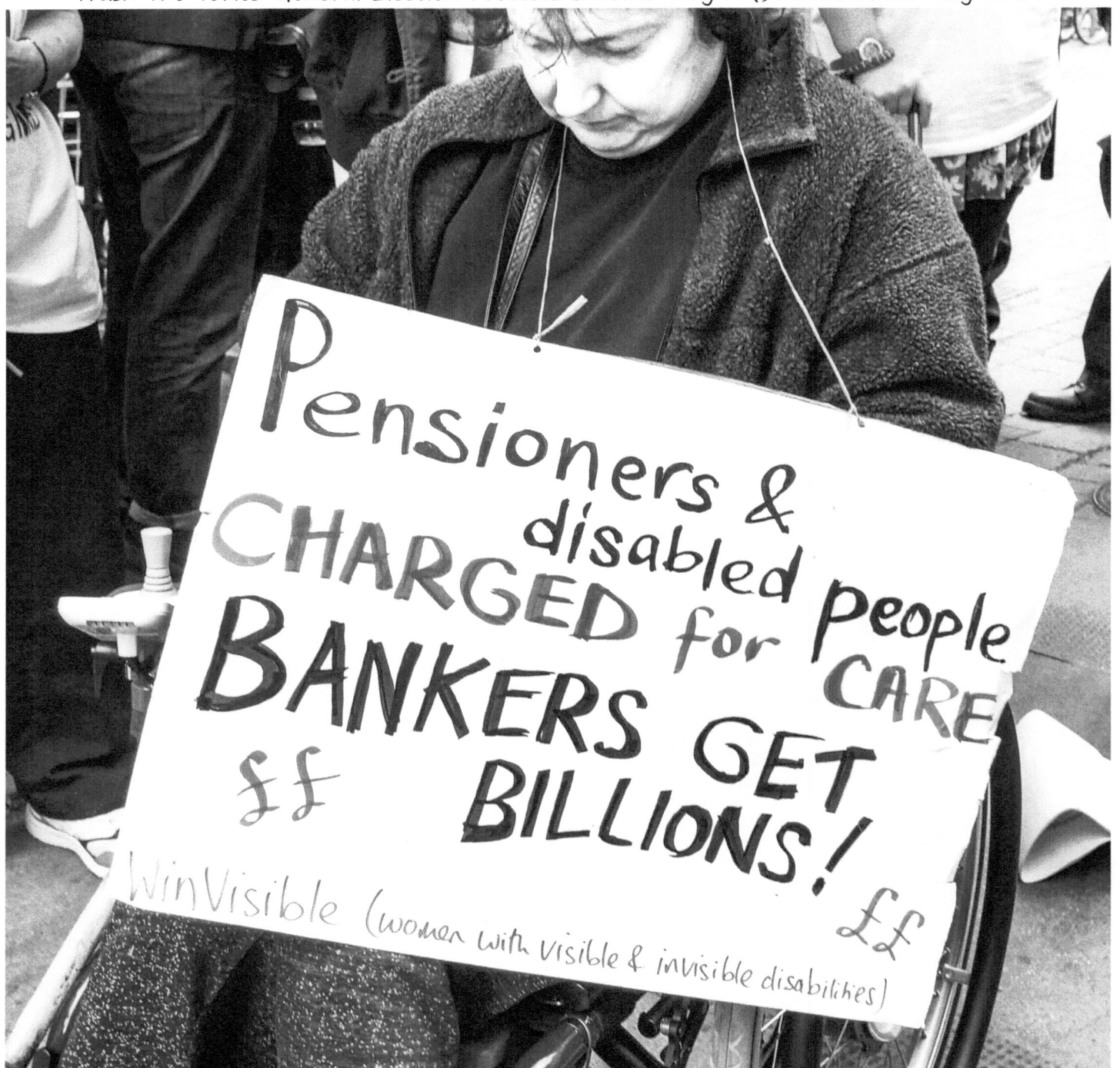

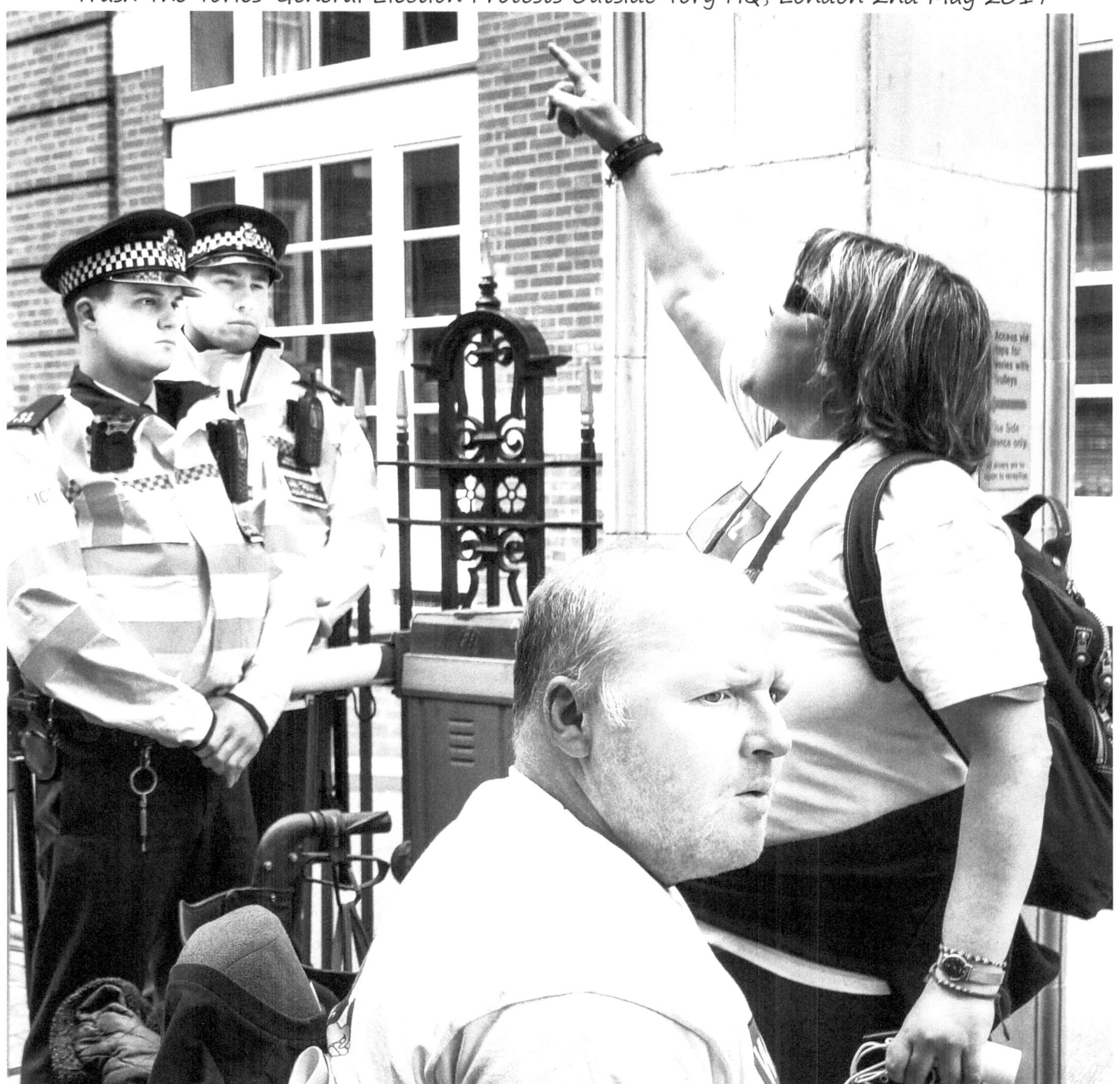

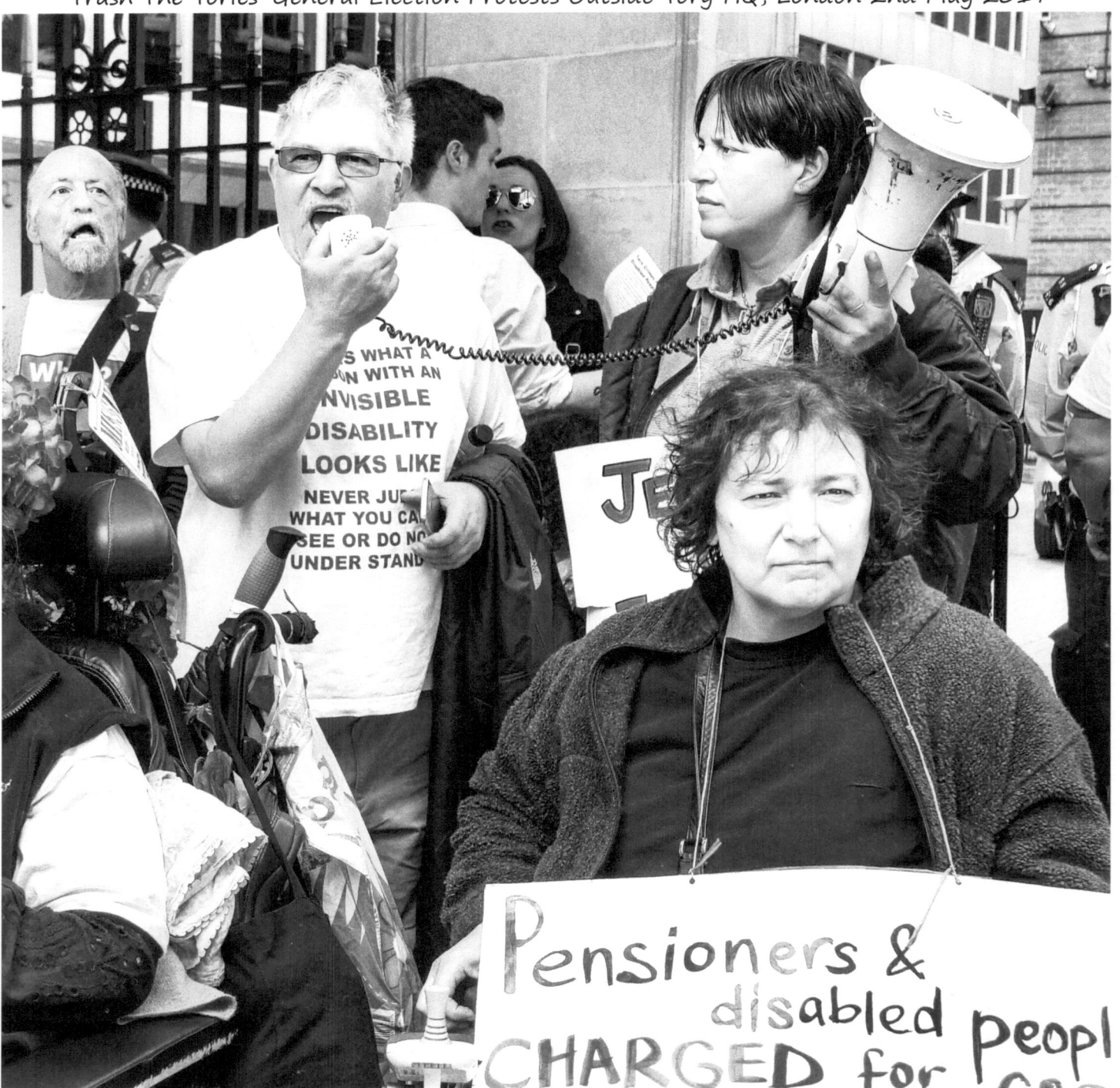

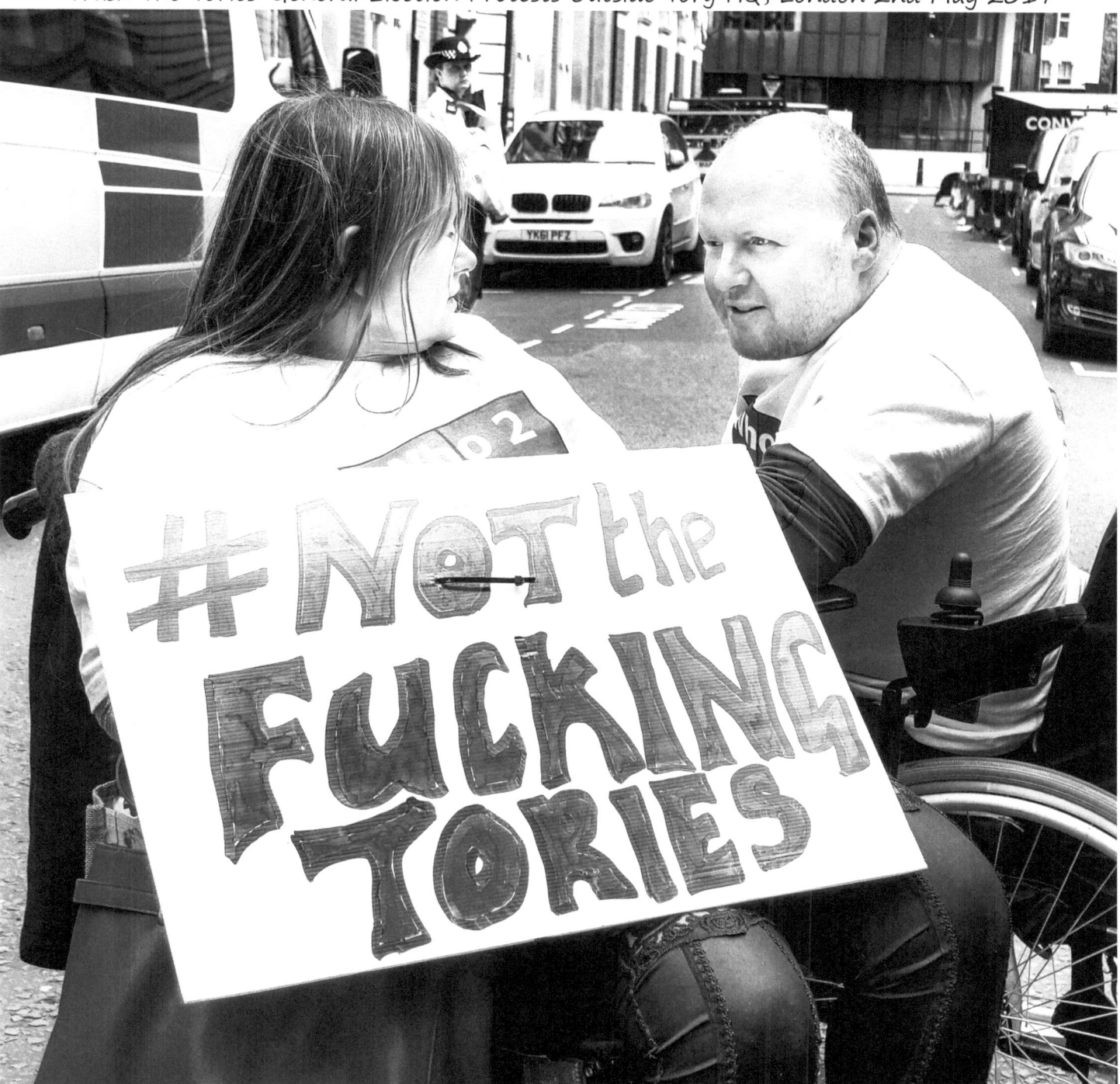

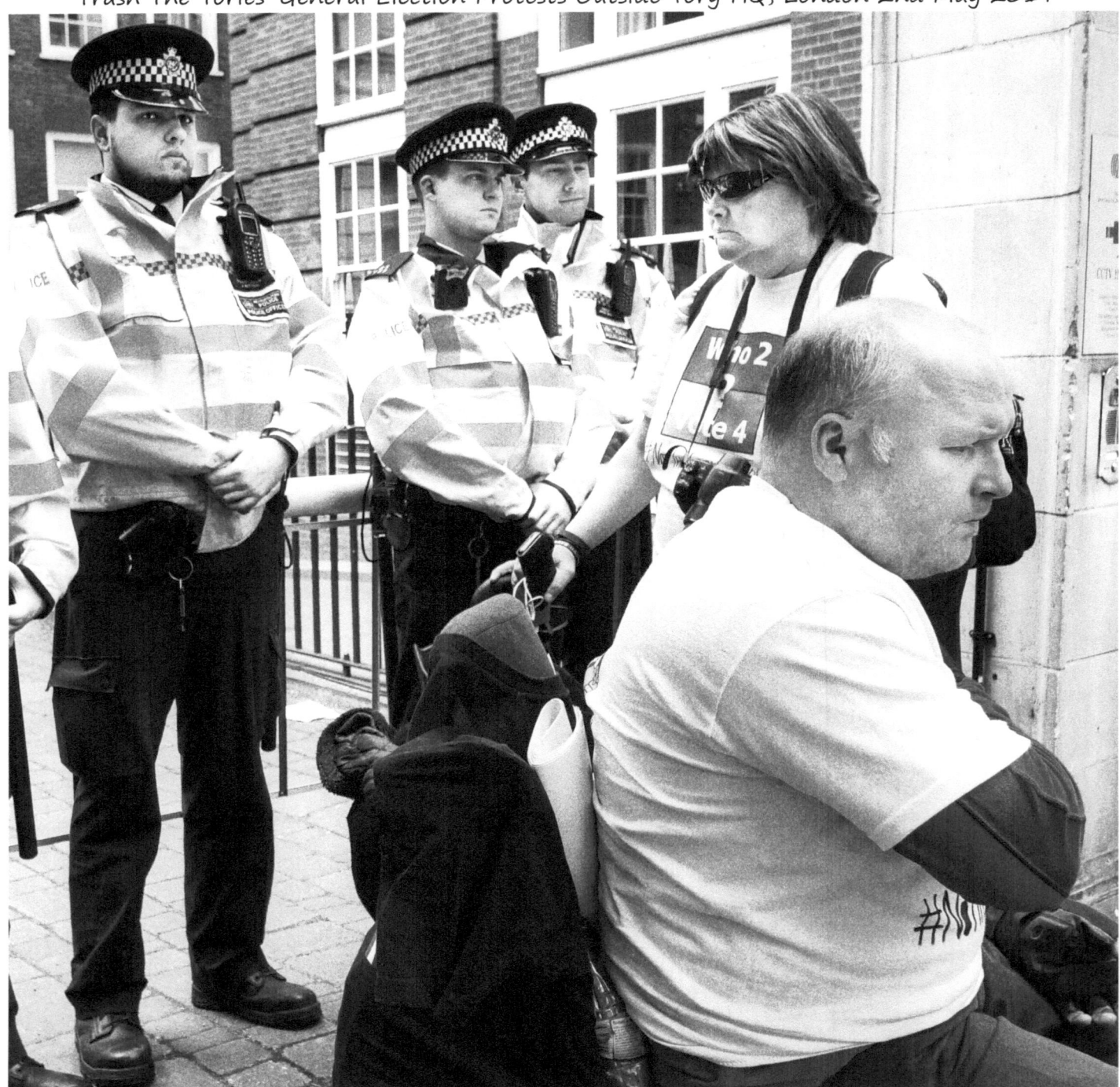

I first met Chris at a demonstration in London, and subsequently would often see him at actions in the Capital when I travelled down from the North. I knew he was an accomplished professional photographer yet I am still stunned, STUNNED!, by this collection of photo reportage of the London actions over the last decade of the disabled people's movement.

Chris has done an extraordinary job of simultaneously reporting, documenting, and creating images of artistic merit. Sometimes when the mainstream is ignoring us you can question the impact and even forget actions you have taken part in, of course that emphasises how important it is for disabled people to also be our own historians. Would that every city had their own Christopher John Ball, creating such a brilliant and essential record of our struggle.

In Manchester we have co-produced with the People's History Museum an exhibition of our movements history, the 'Nothing About Us Without Us' show has closed after a year, but I can guarantee the next iteration of our history will be immeasurably enhanced with the work Chris has collected here.

Yes, this all happened, we would not go quiet into that good night, as the British State embarked on democide of disabled people, we resisted, everywhere, every day, and we still do.

There is one thing I ask of you as you look at these images of resistance- Join Us!

Rick Burgess
Manchester Disabled People Against Cuts
Recovery In The Bin
Greater Manchester Coalition of Disabled People

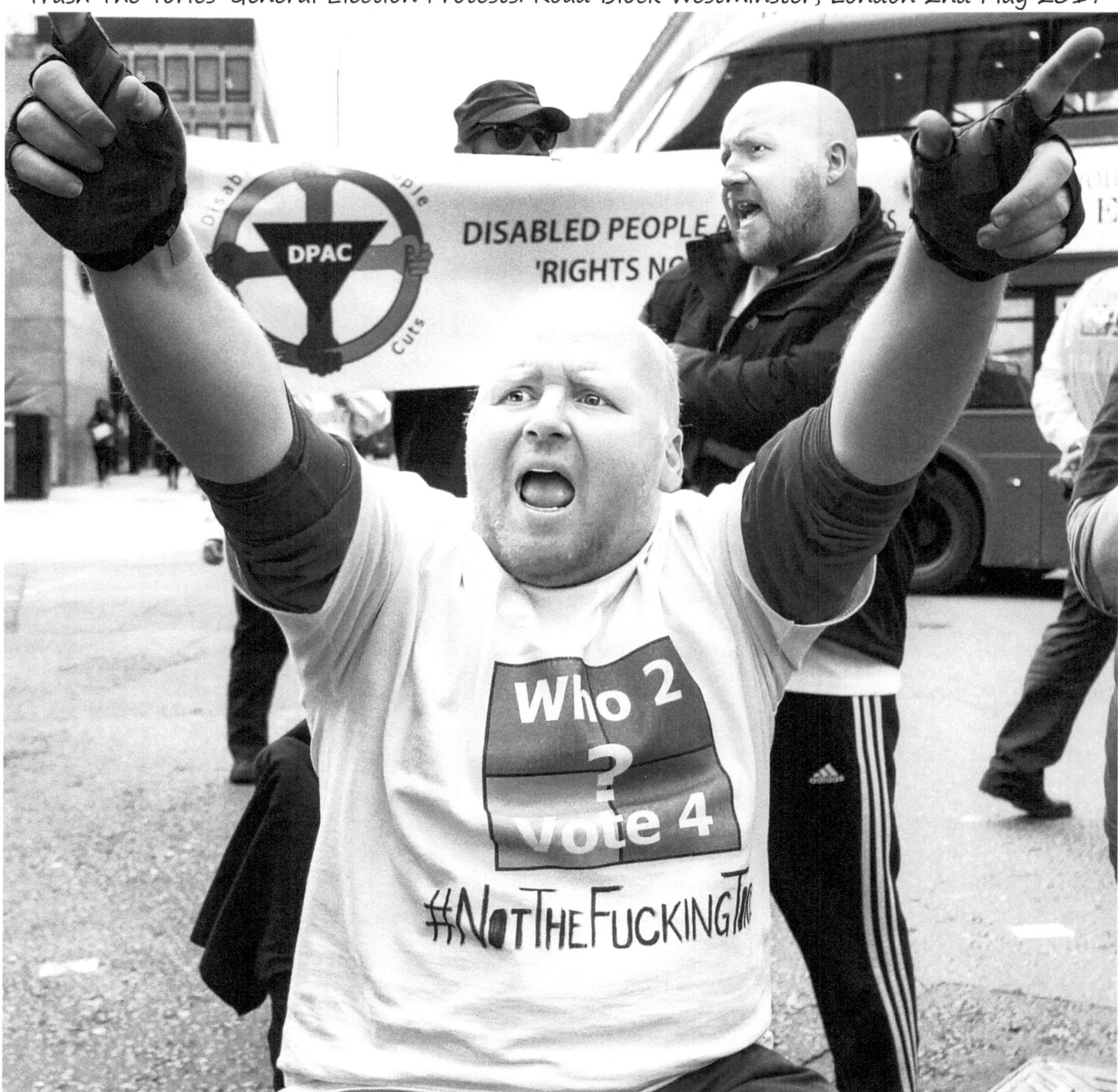

'Trash The Tories' General Election Protests. Road Block Westminster, London 2nd May 2017

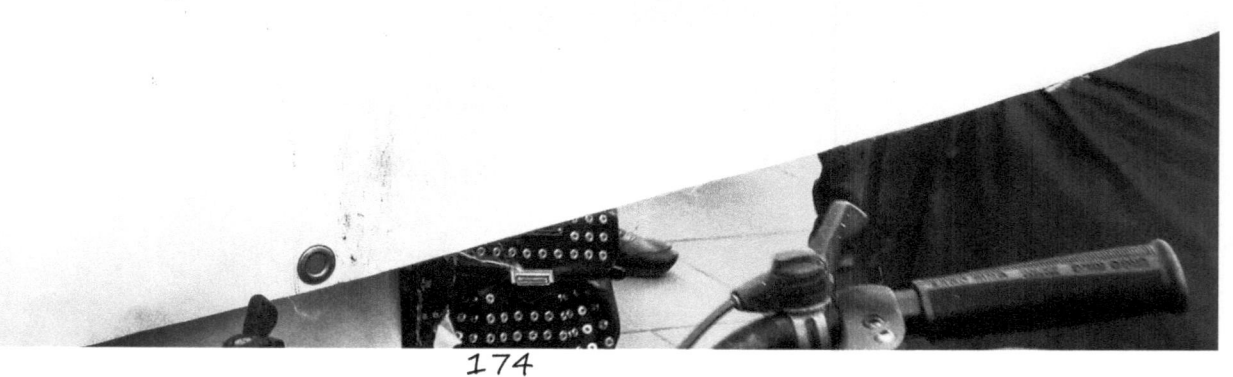

DISABLED PEOPLE AGAINST CUTS
'RIGHTS NOT CHARITY'

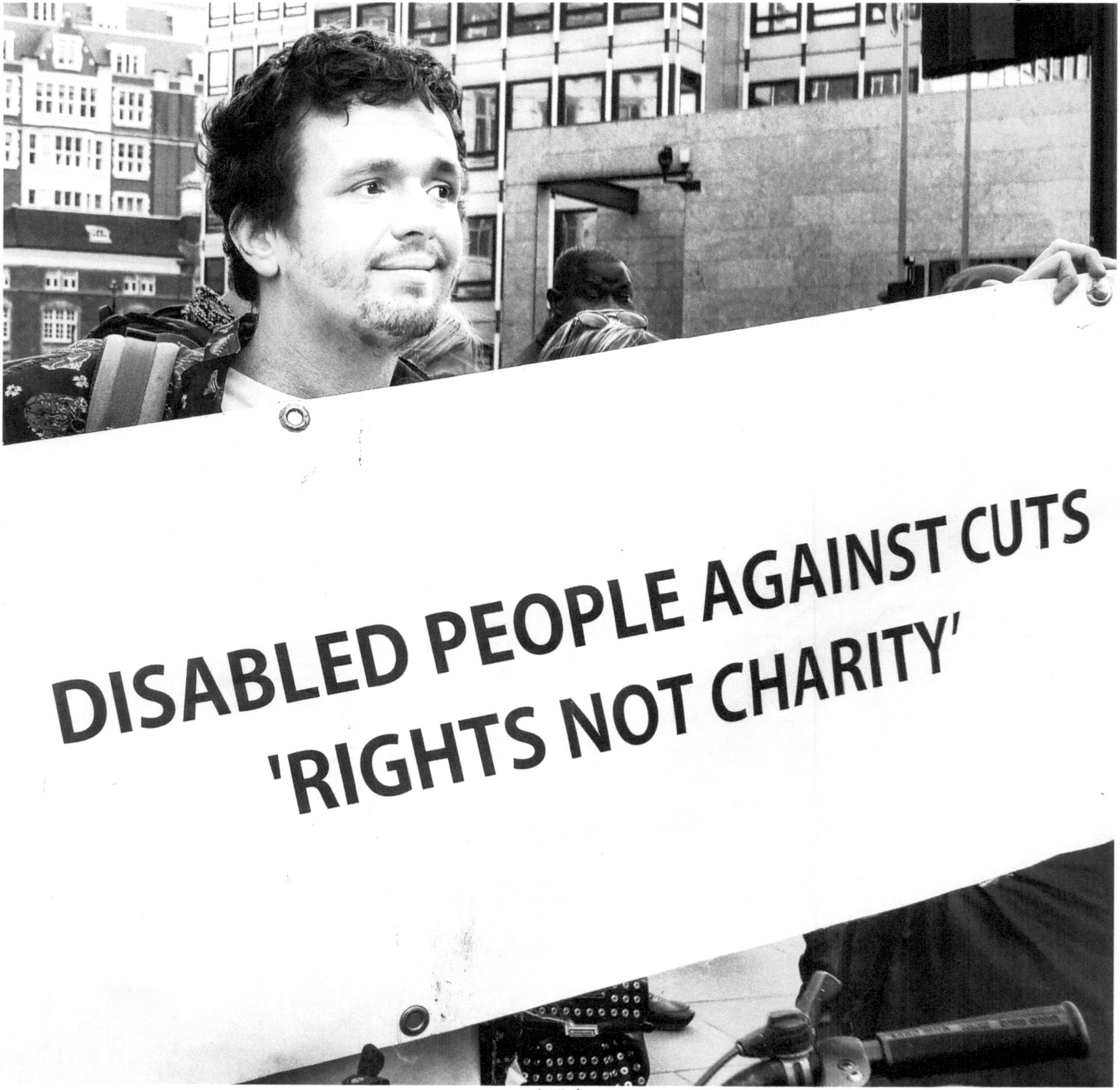

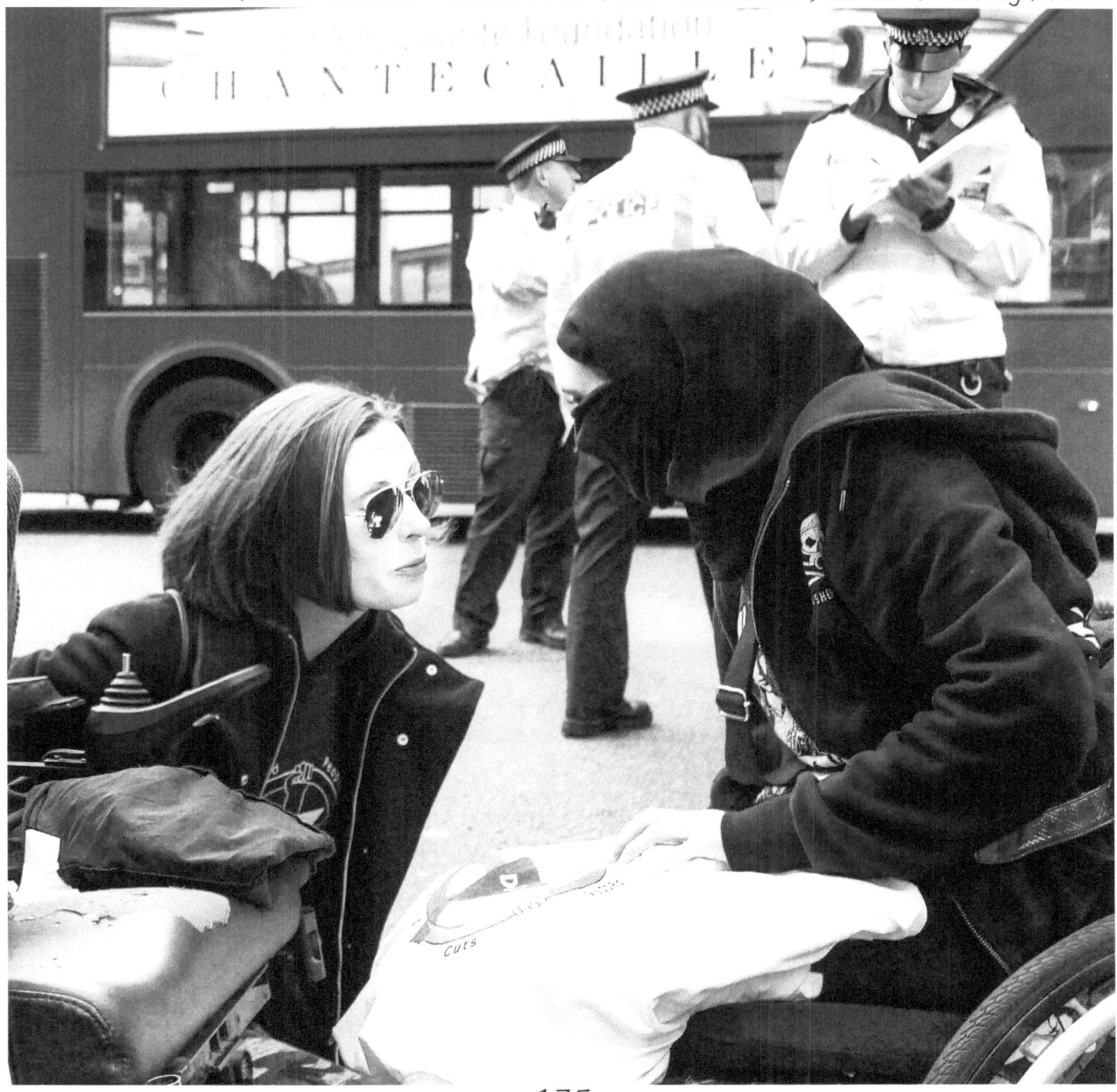

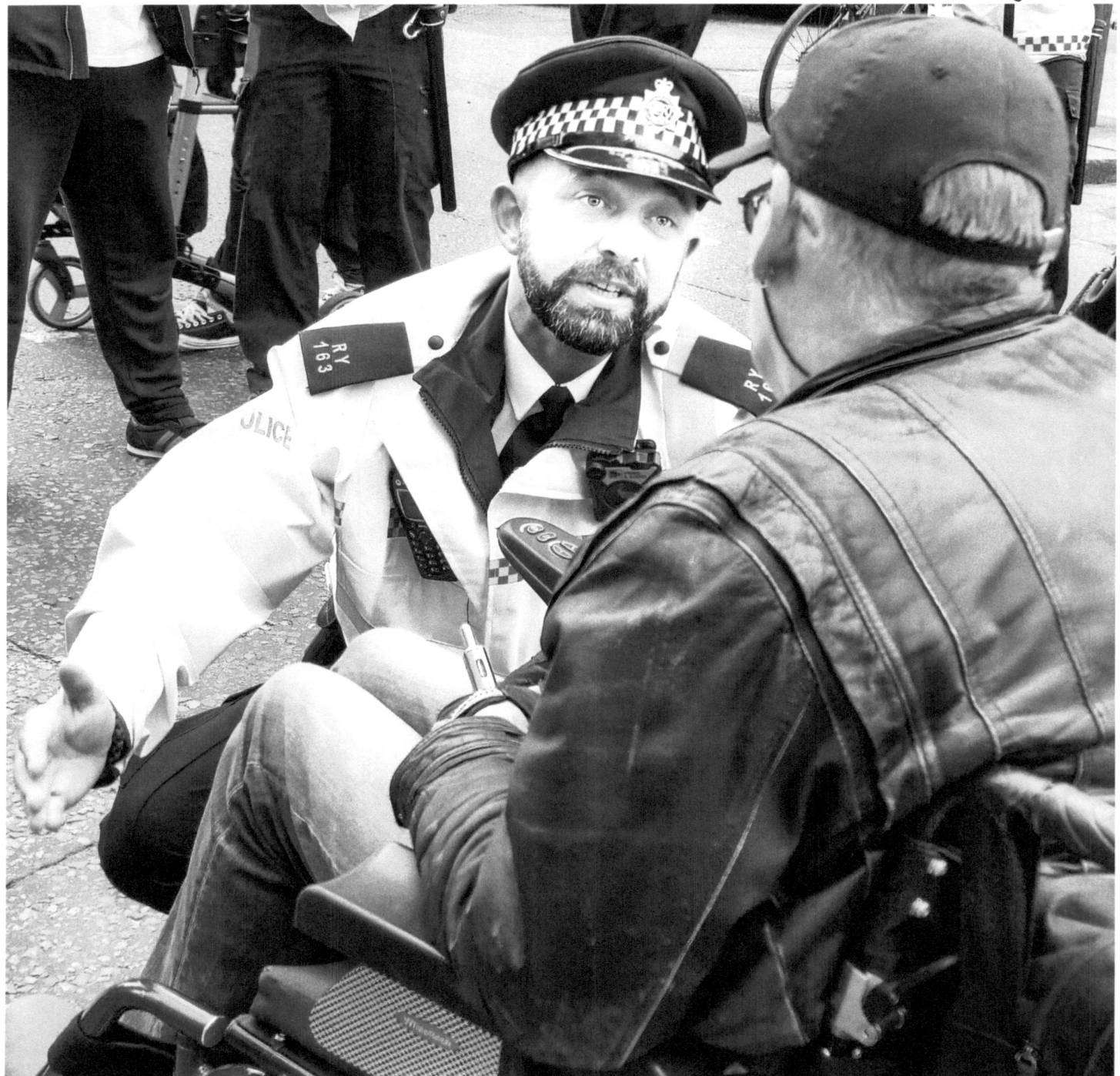

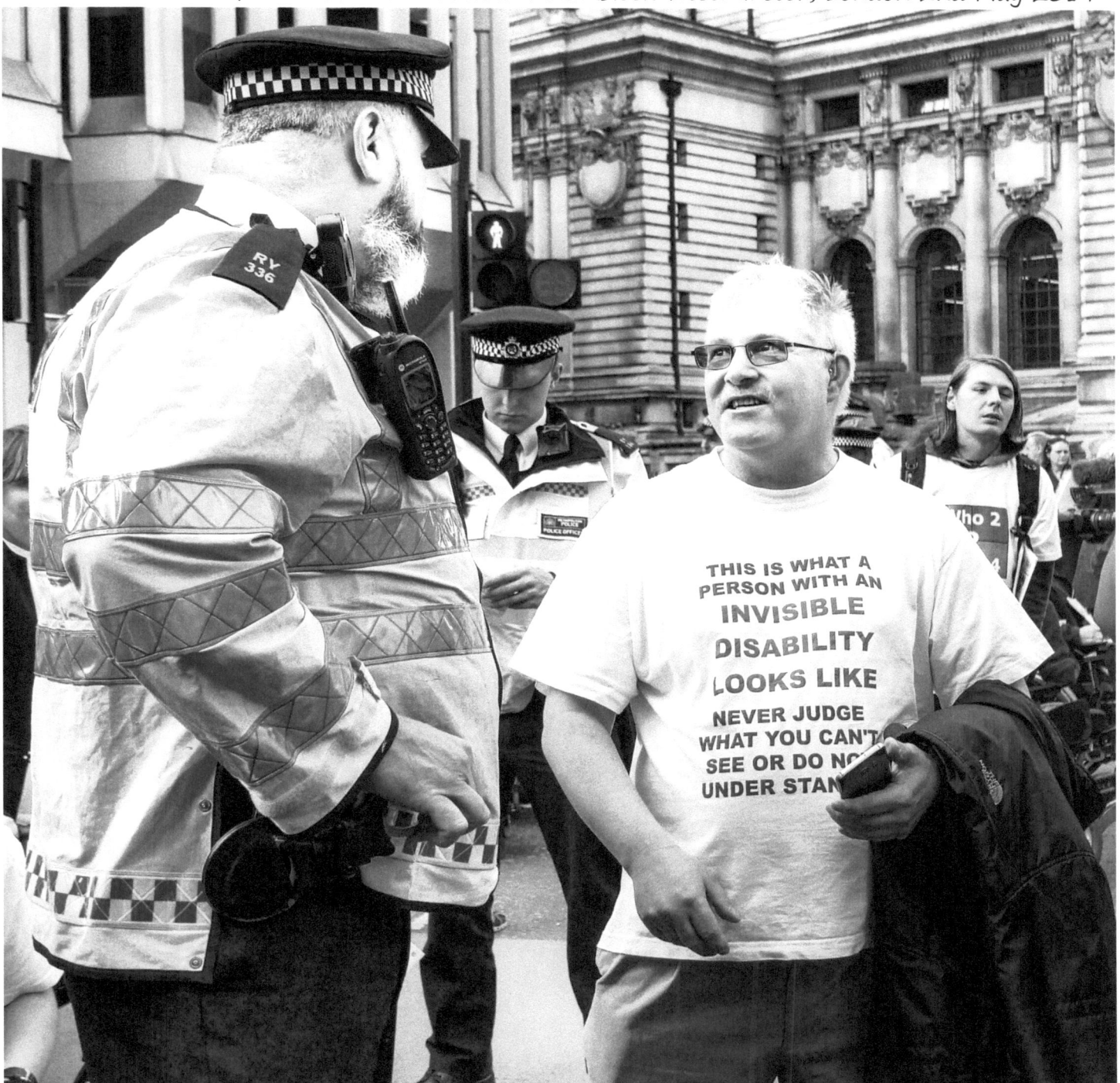

THIS IS WHAT A
PERSON WITH AN
INVISIBLE
DISABILITY
LOOKS LIKE
NEVER JUDGE
WHAT YOU CAN'T
SEE OR DO NOT
UNDER STAND

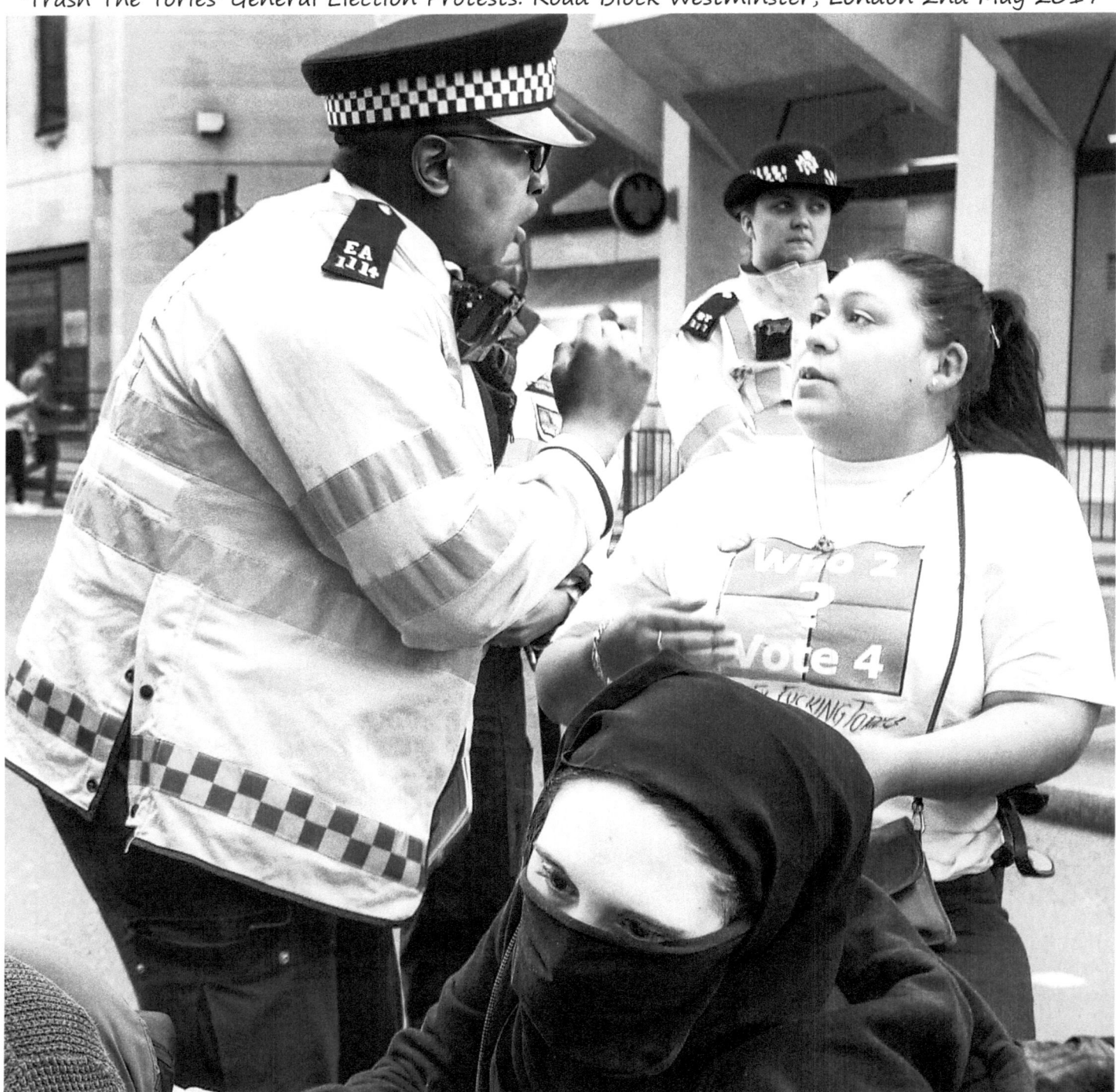

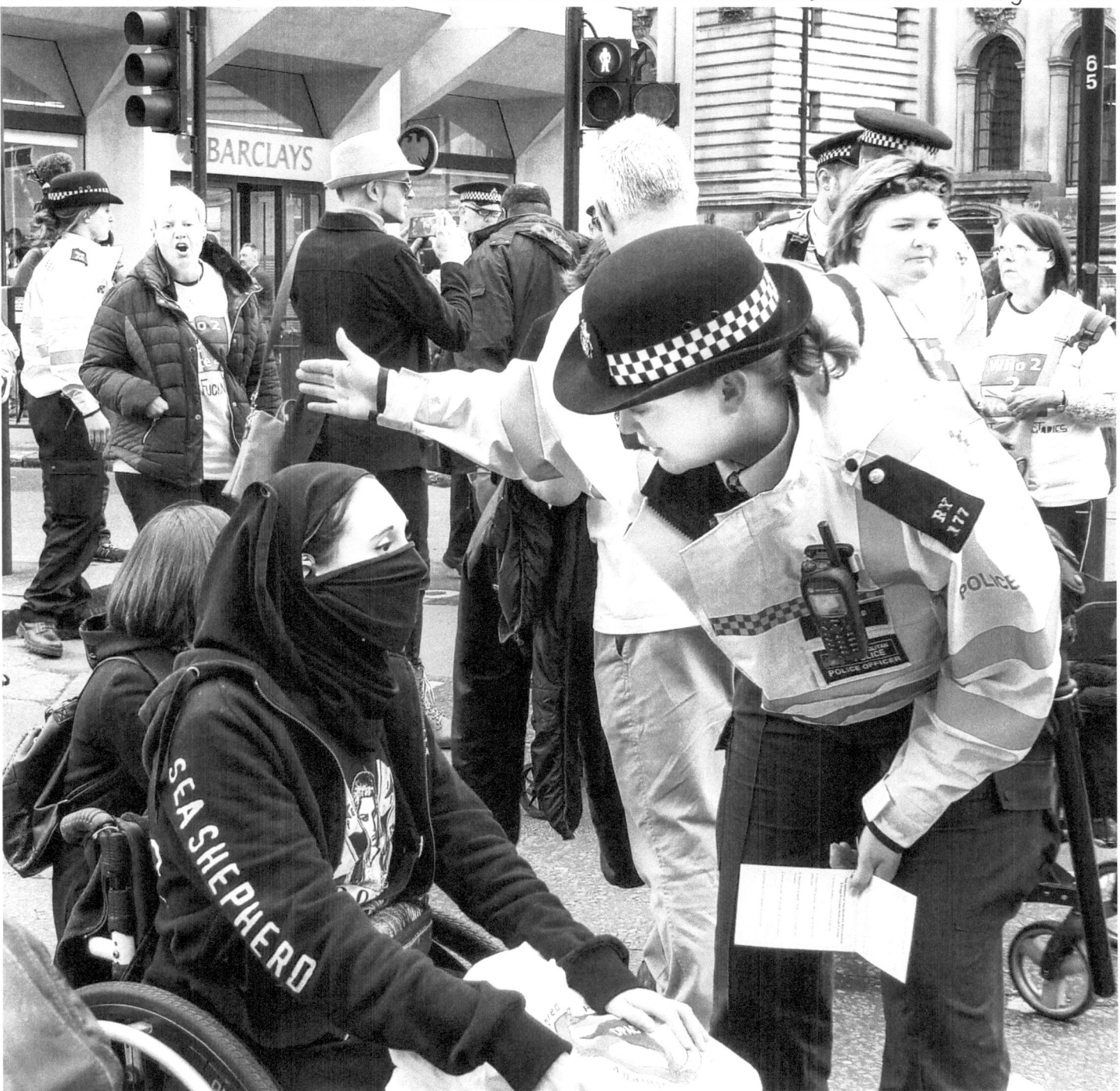

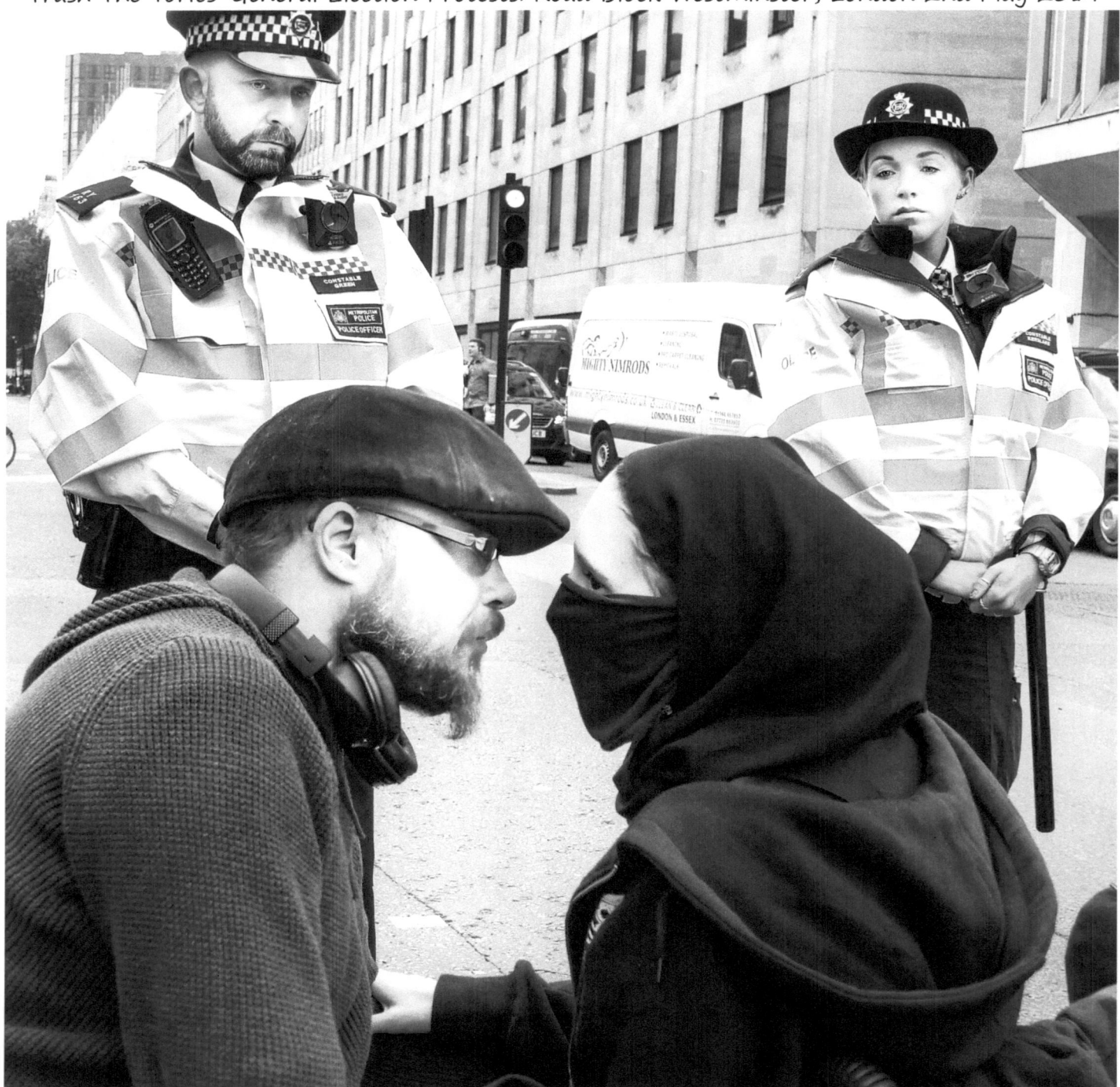

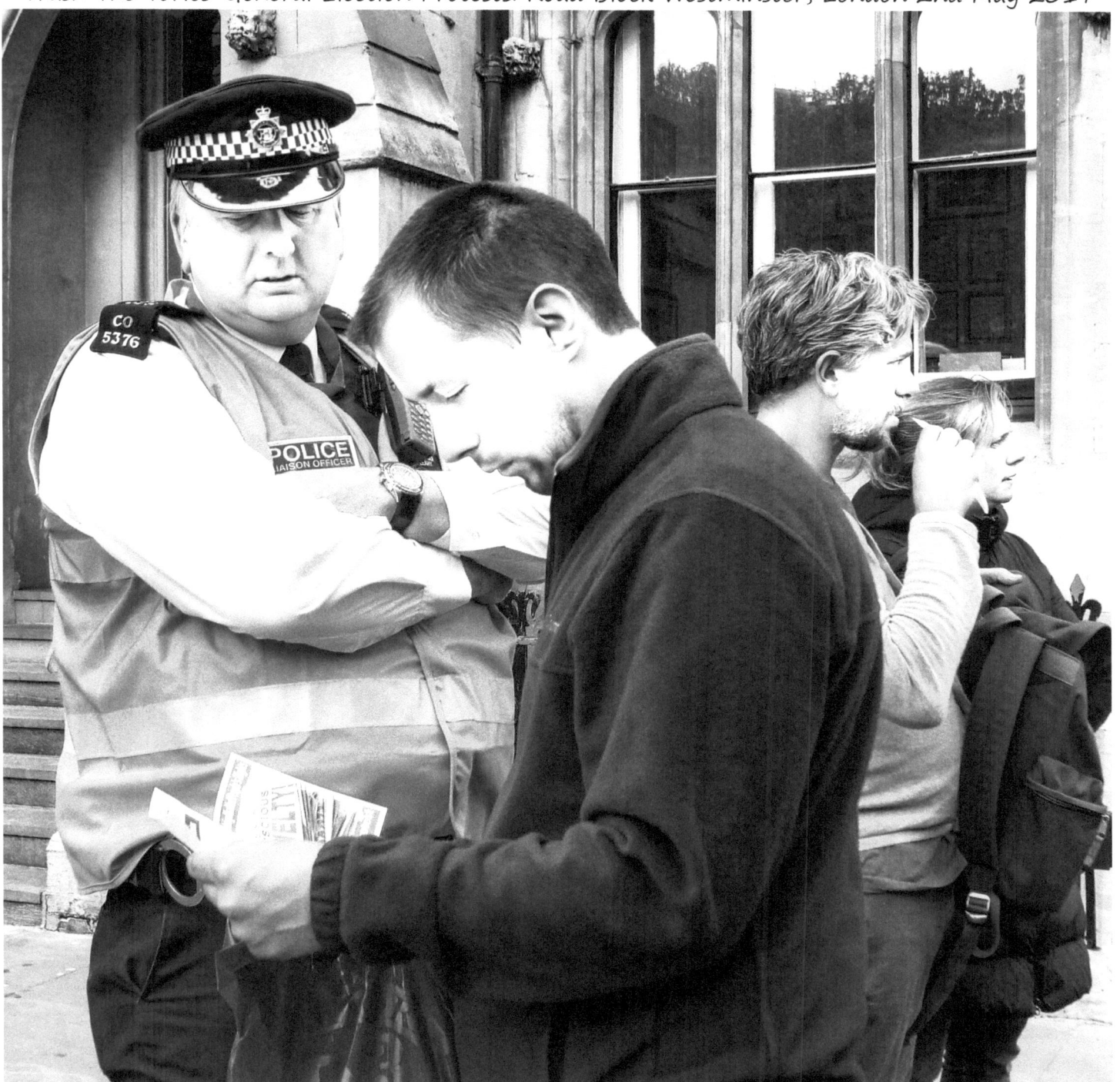

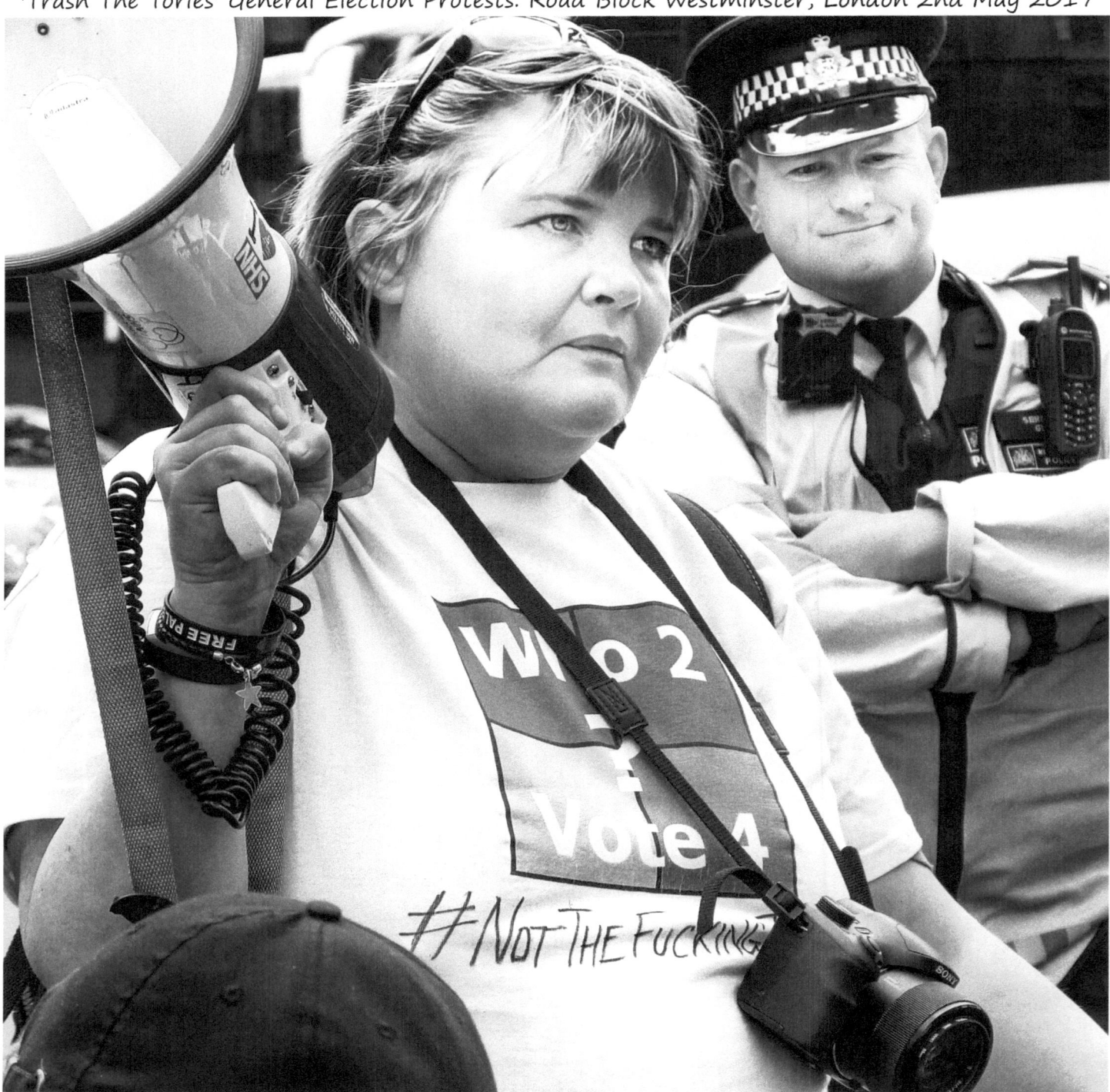

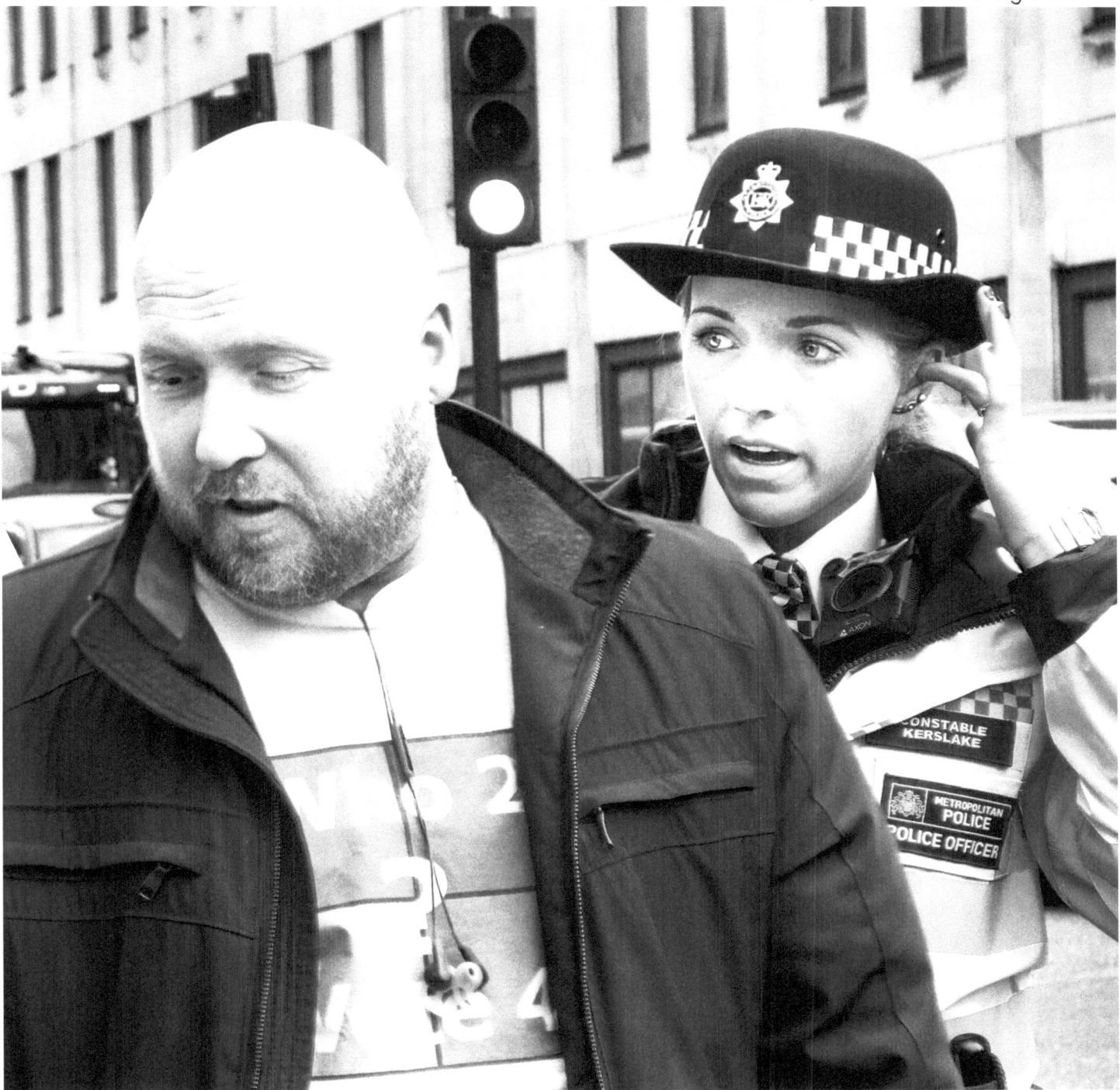

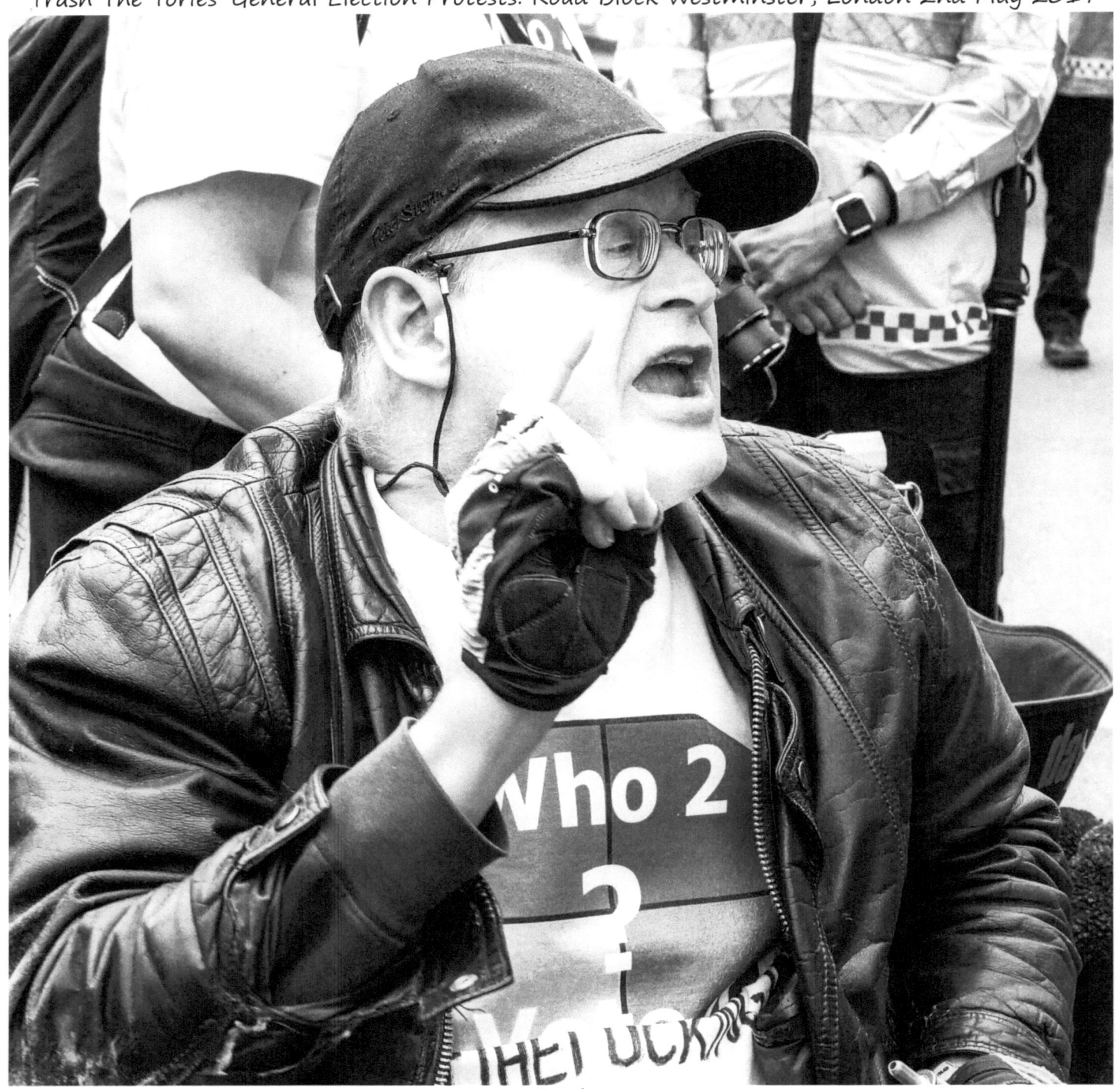

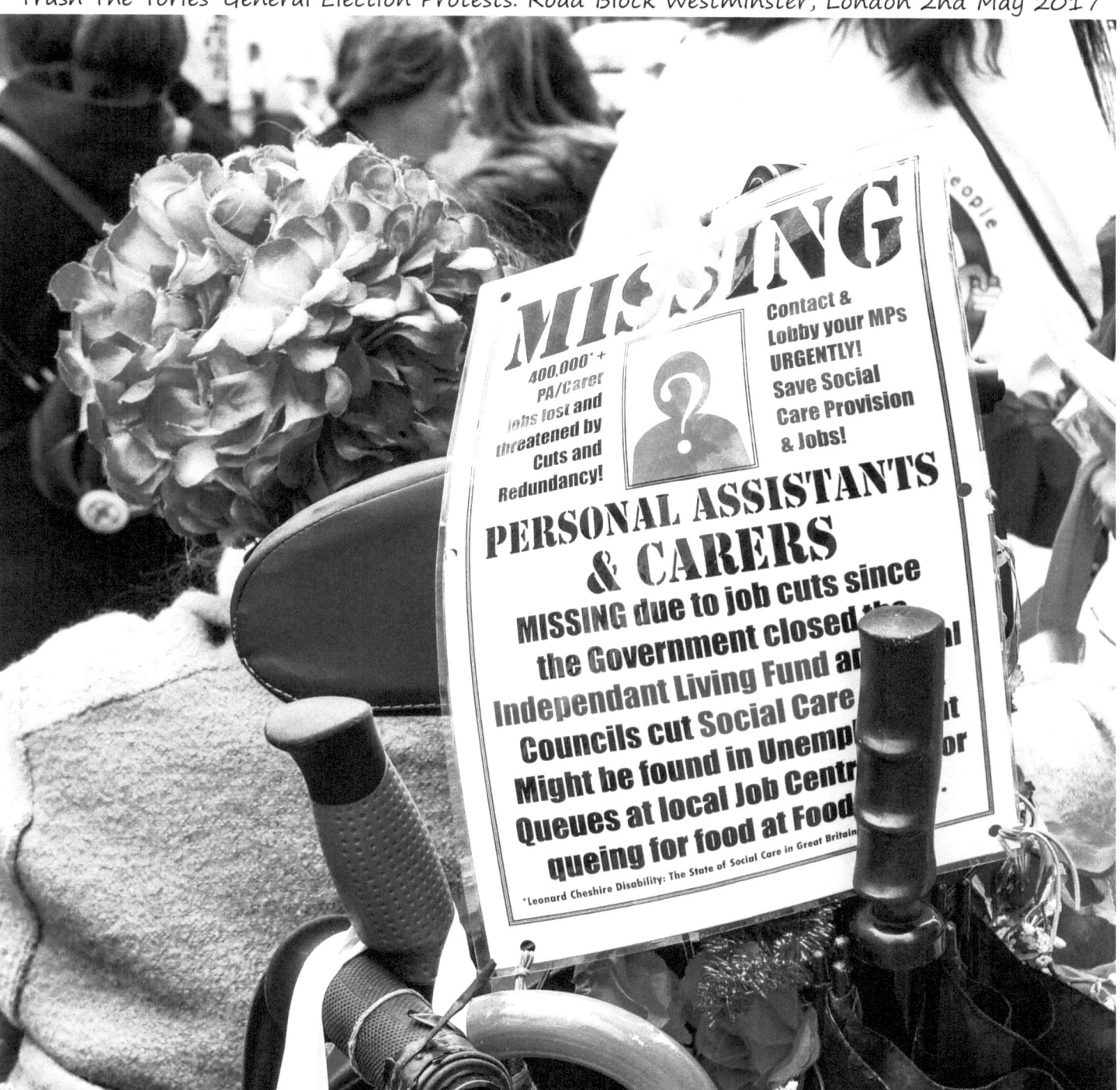

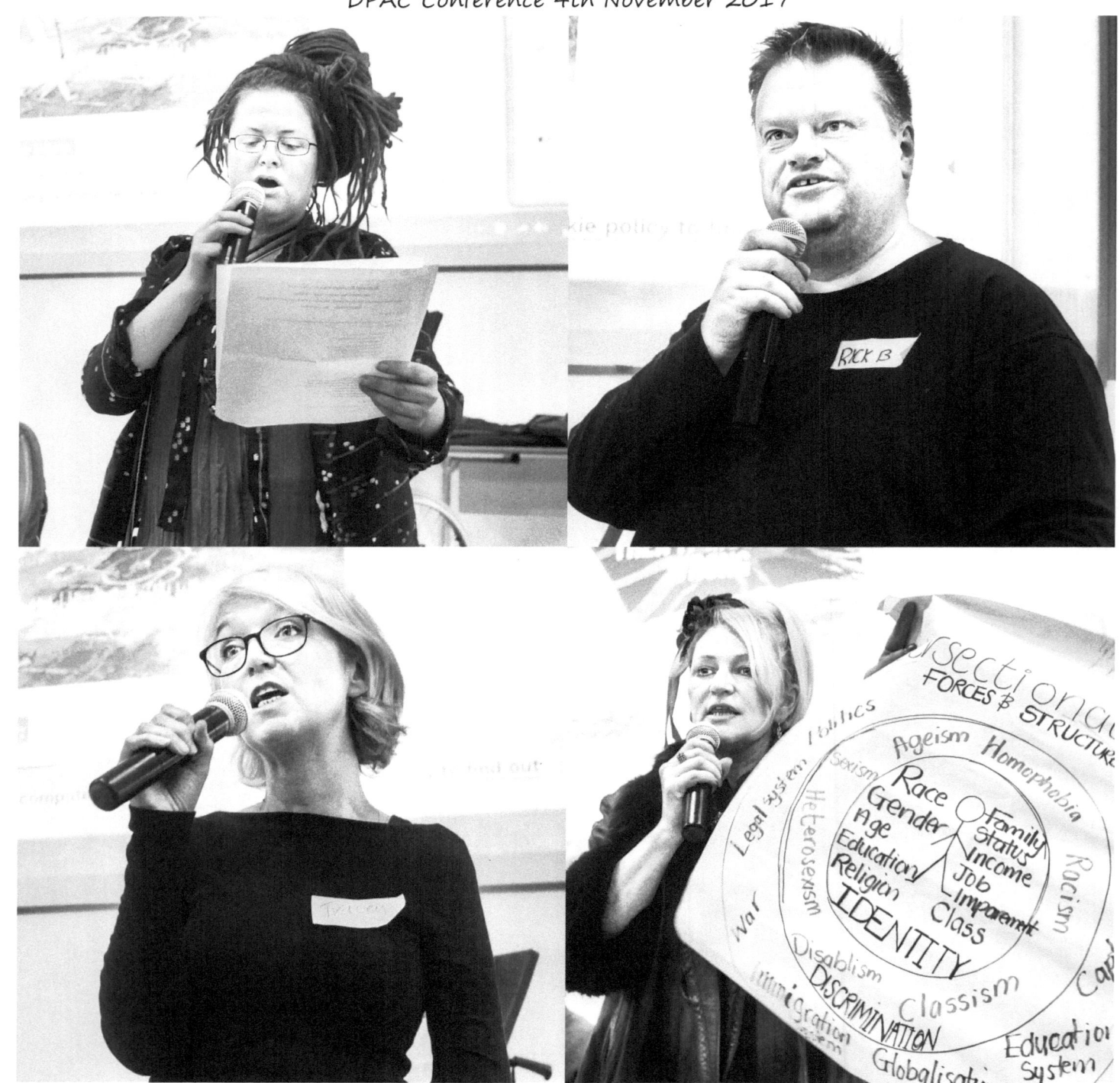

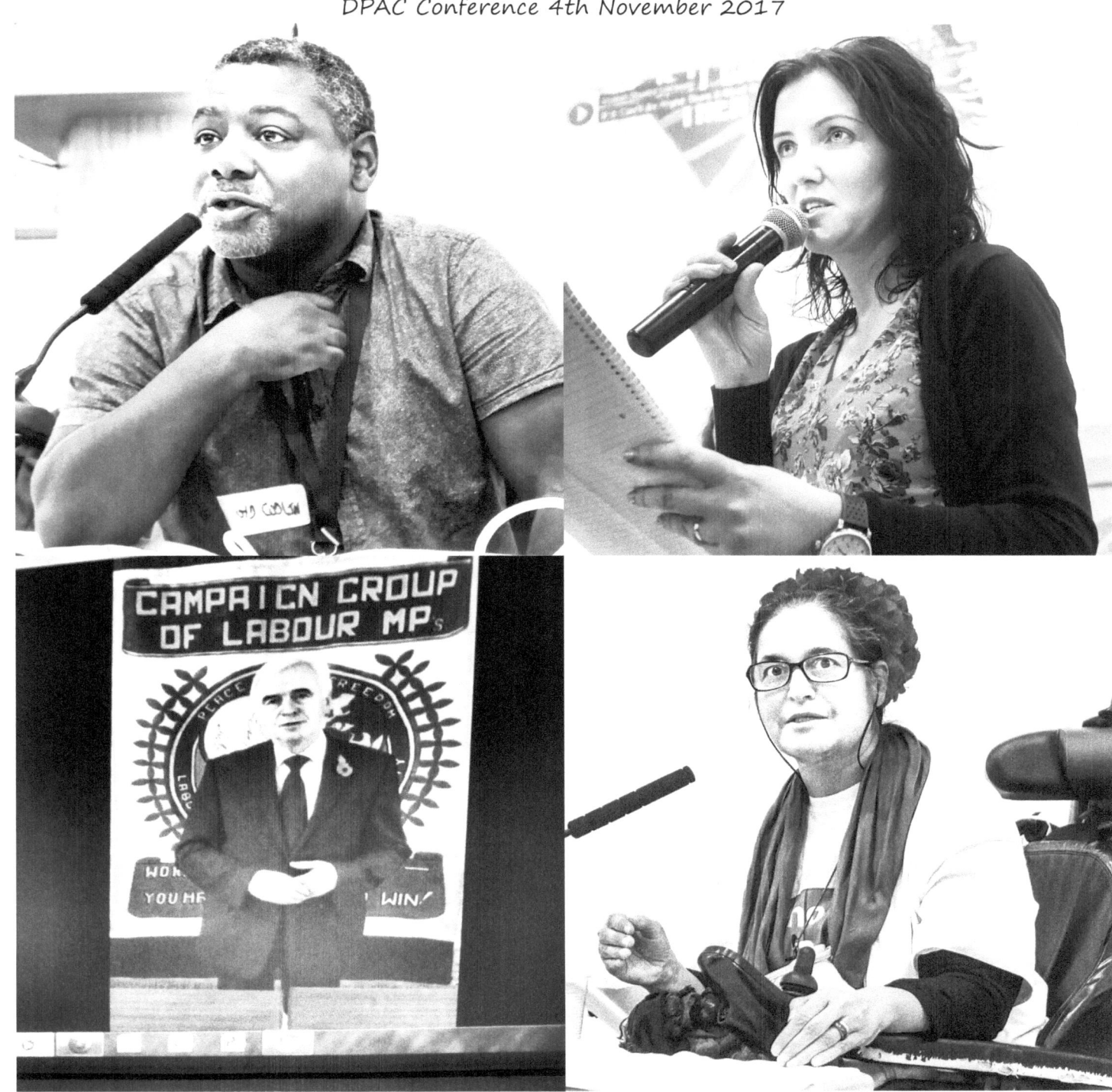

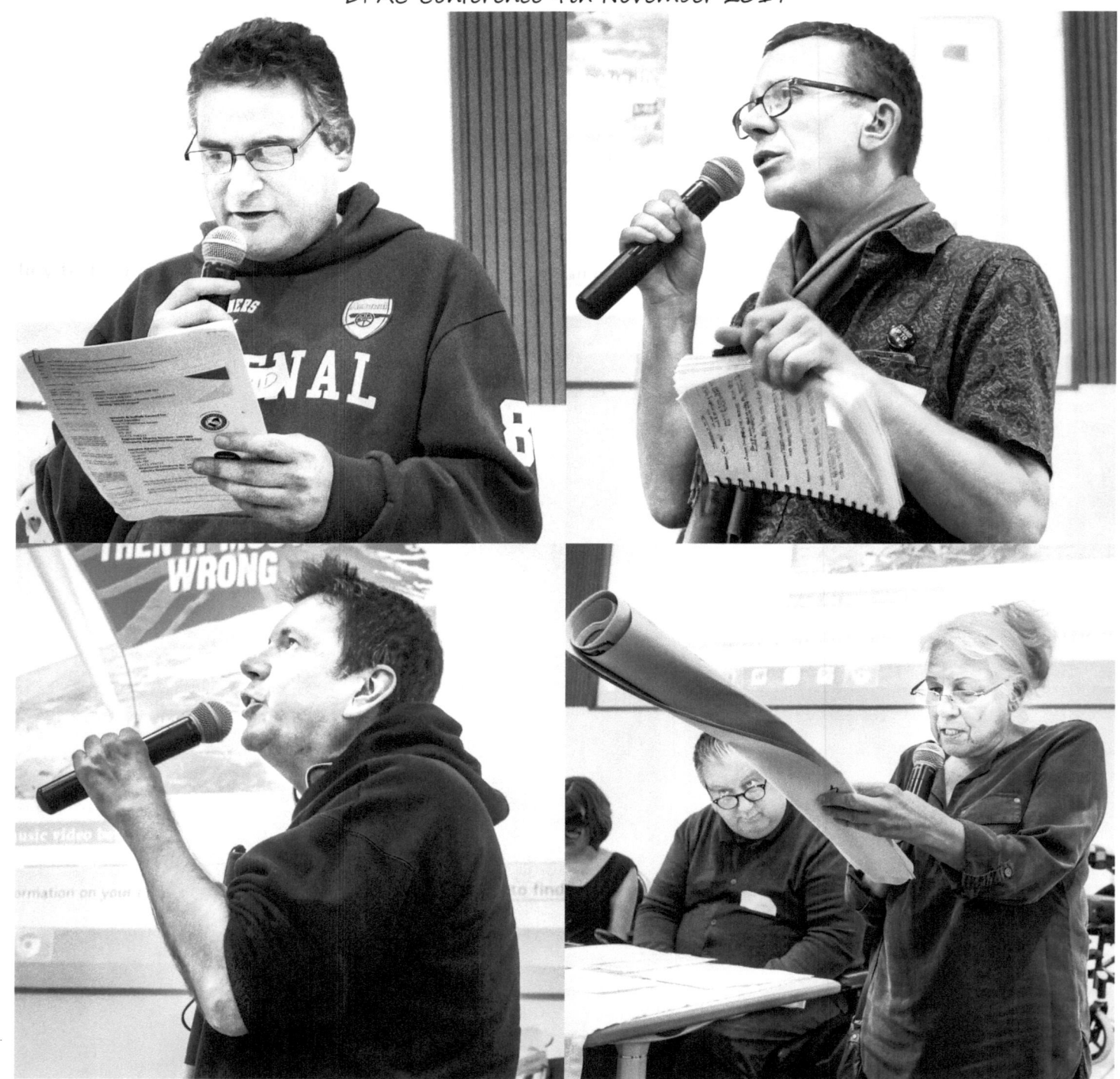

DPAC Stratford Conference 22nd July 2018

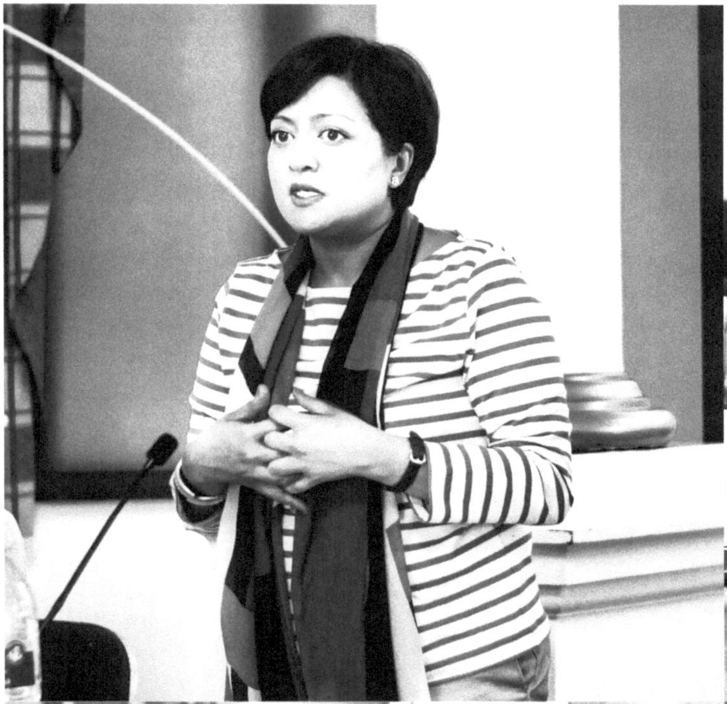

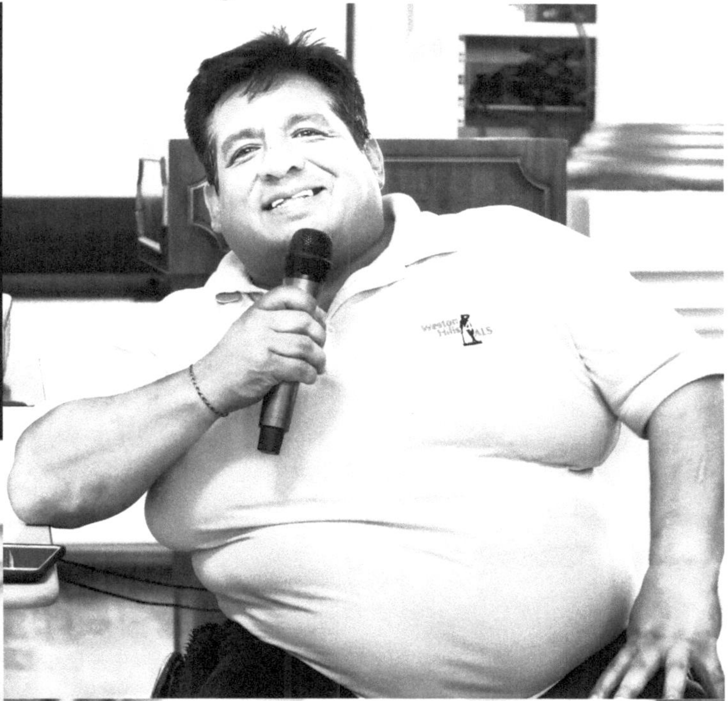

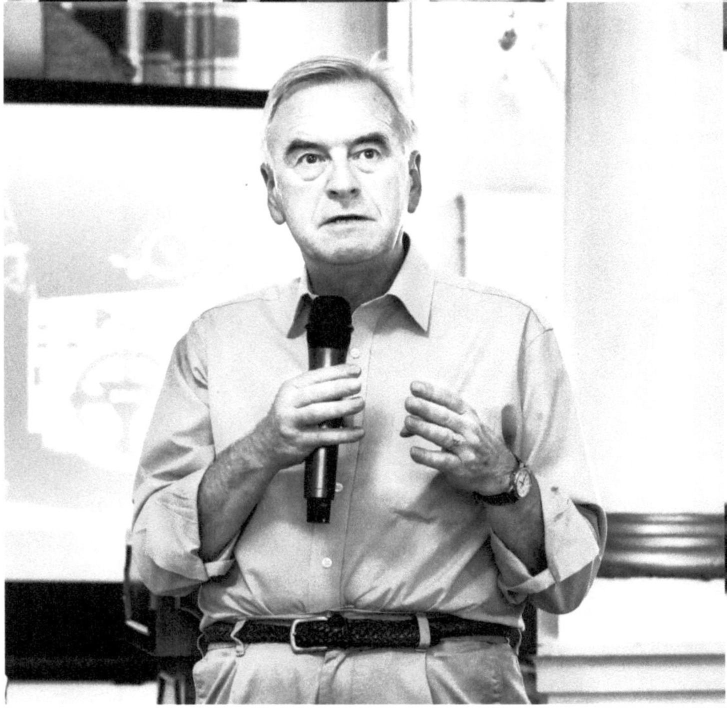

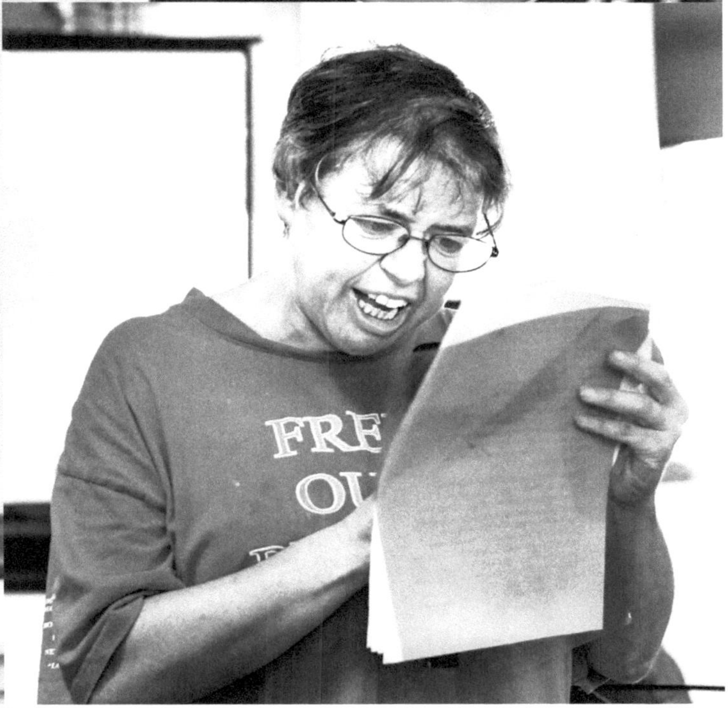

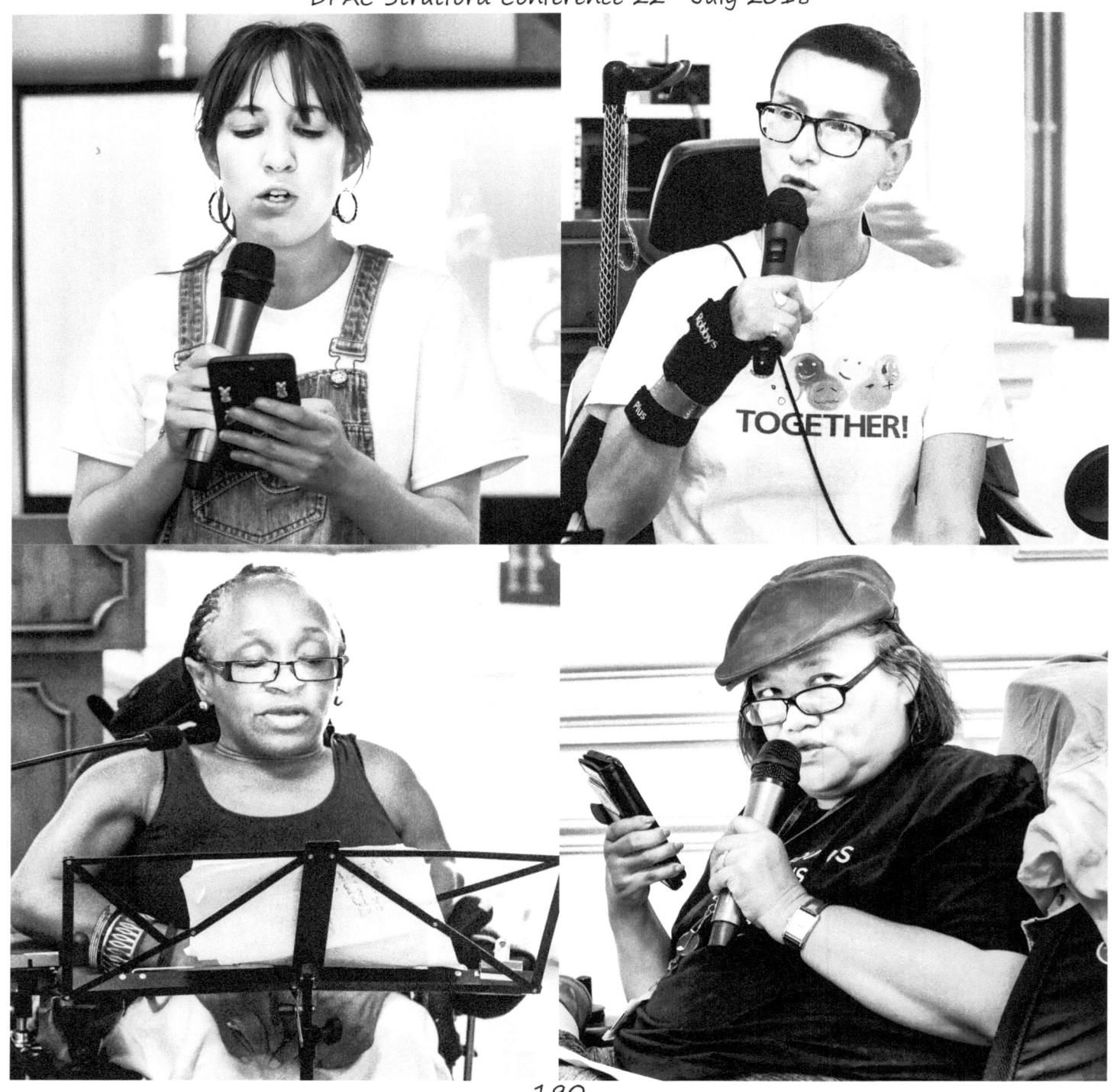

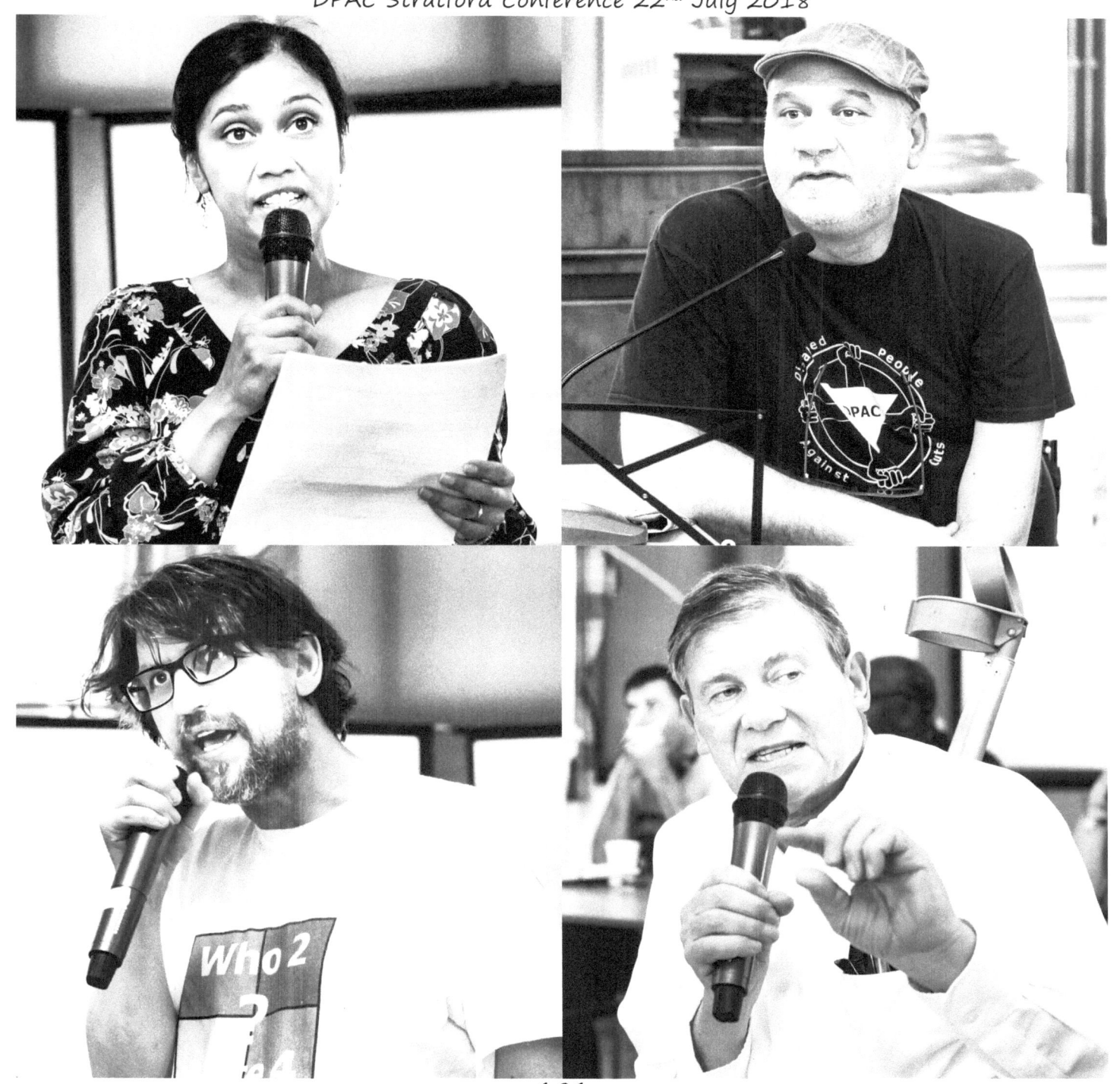

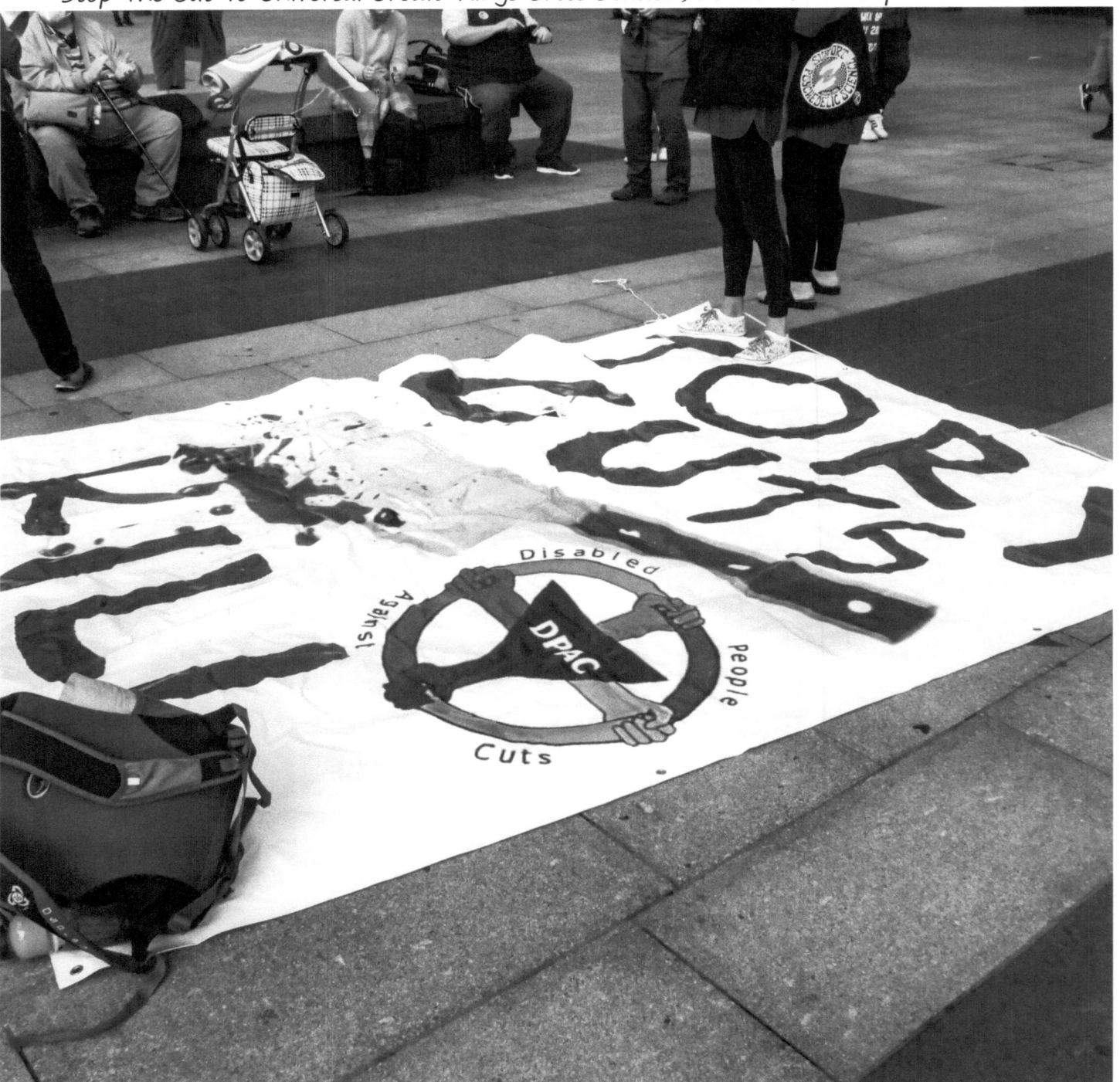

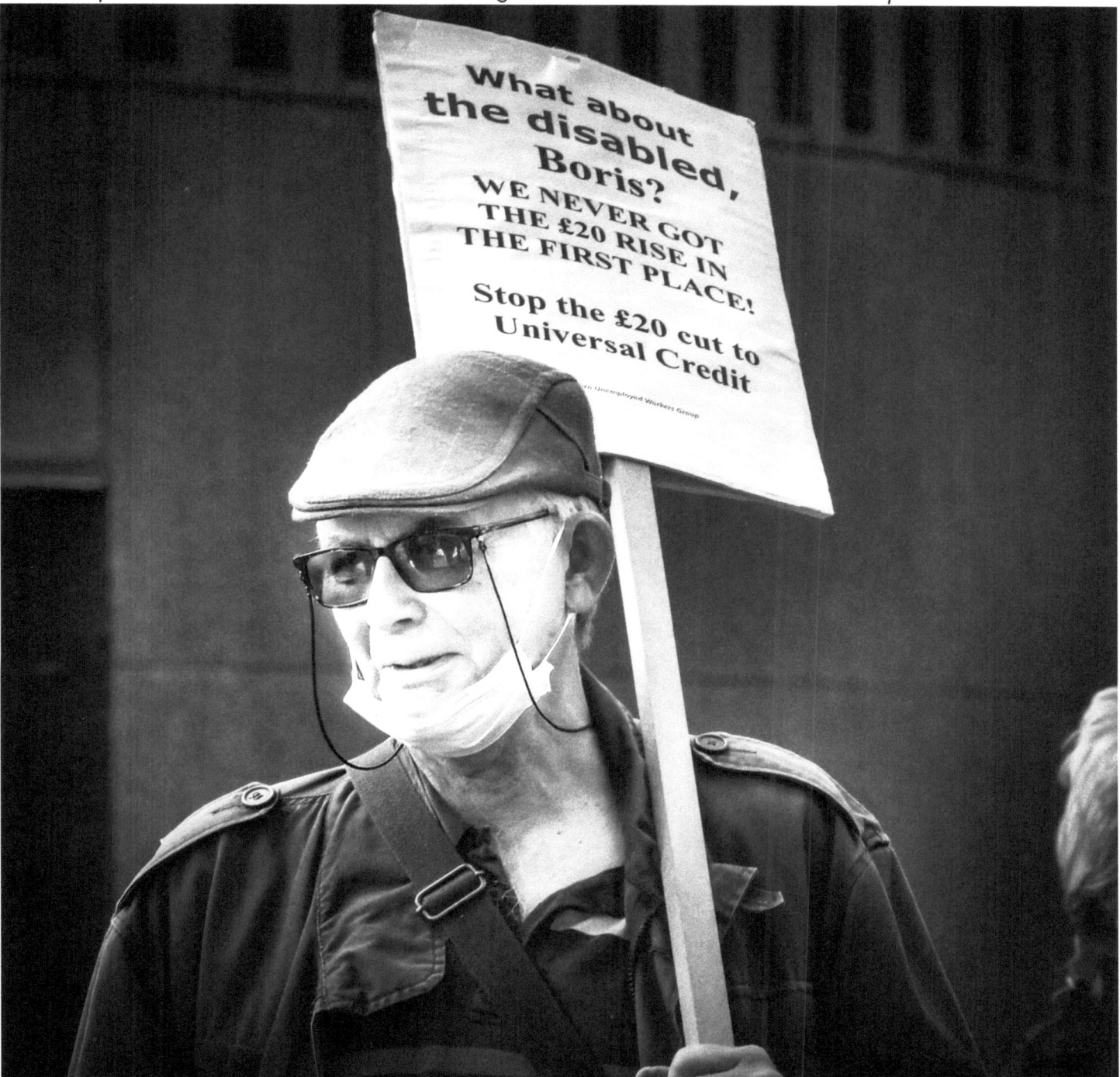

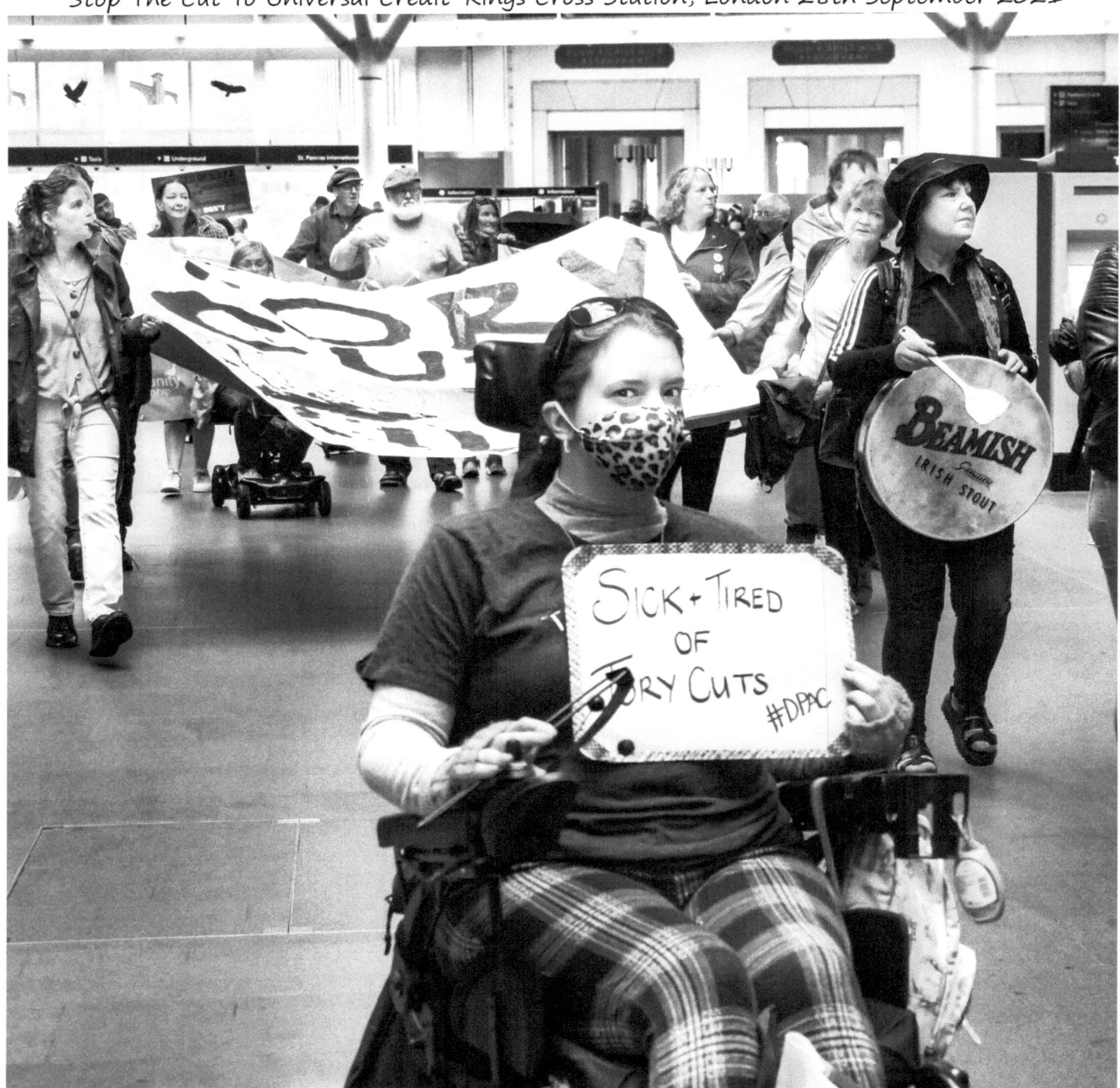

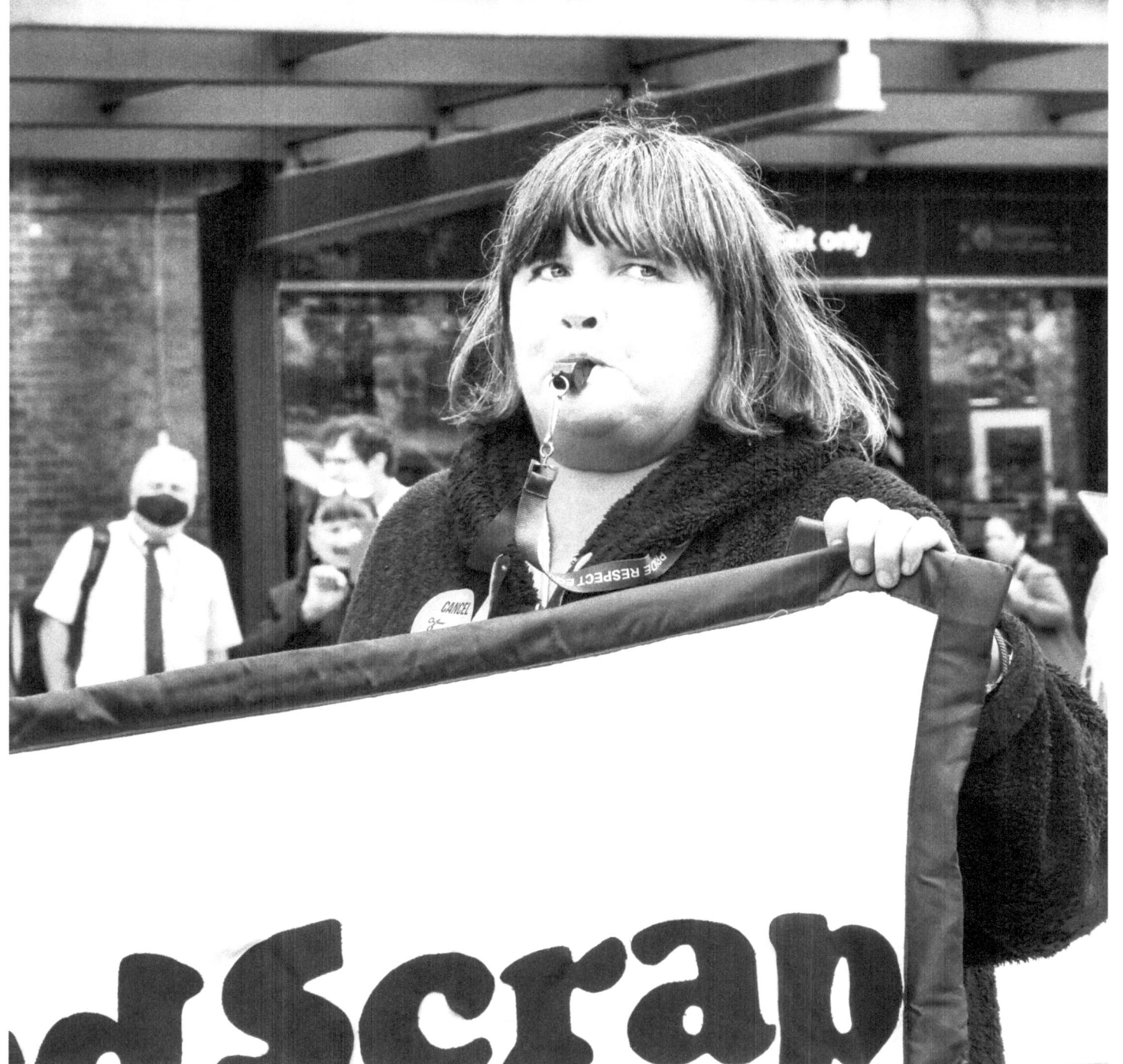

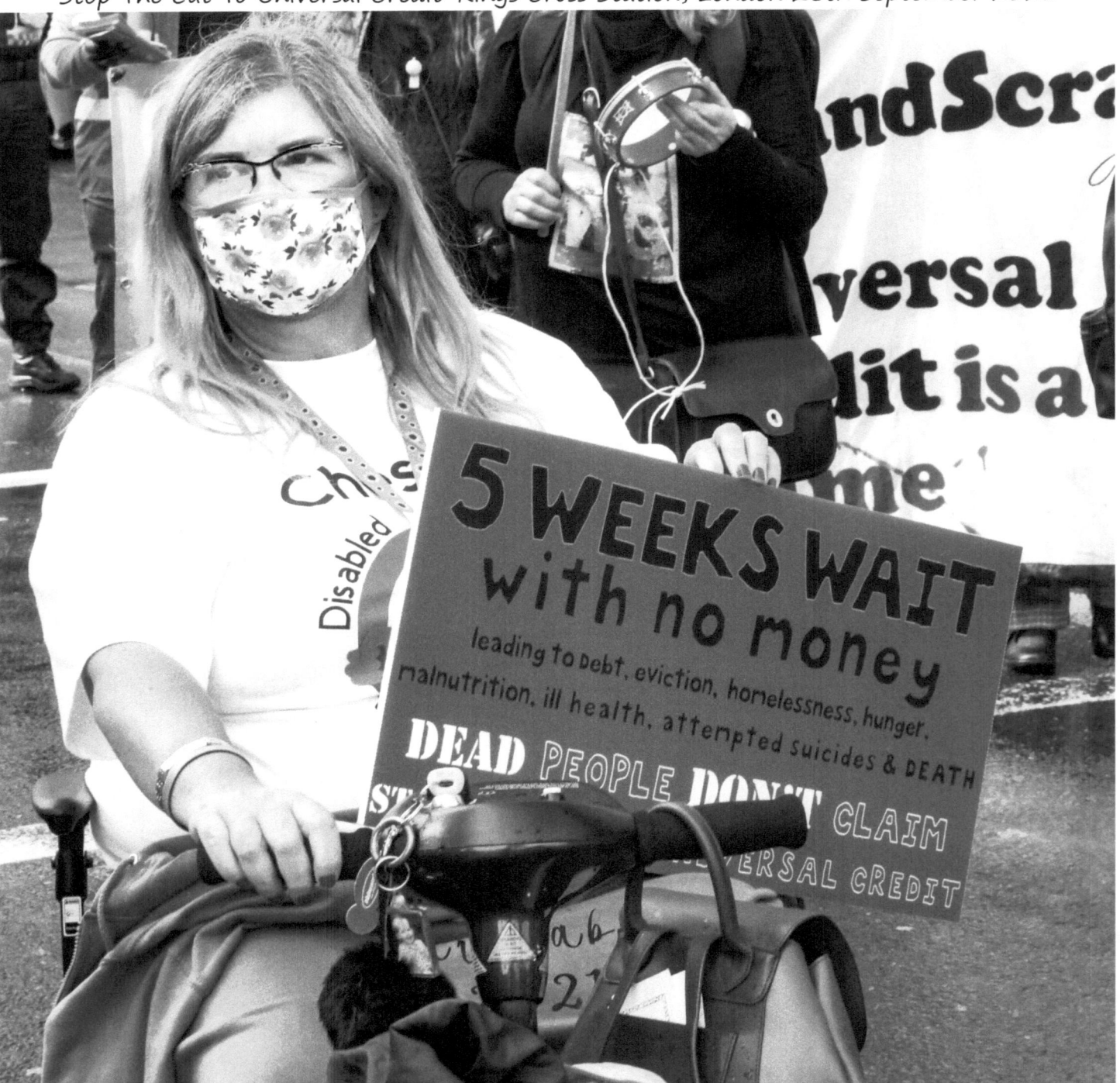

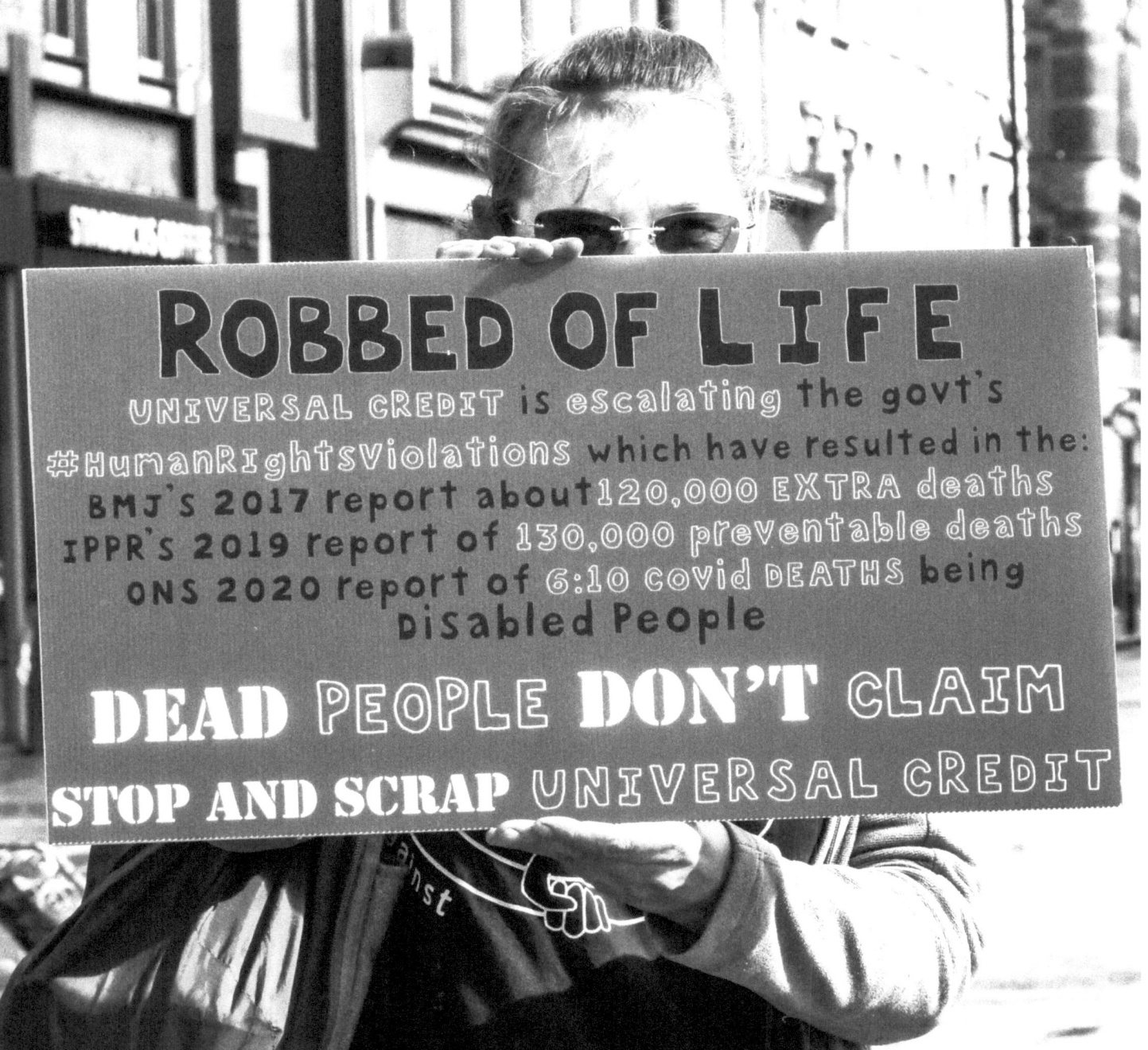

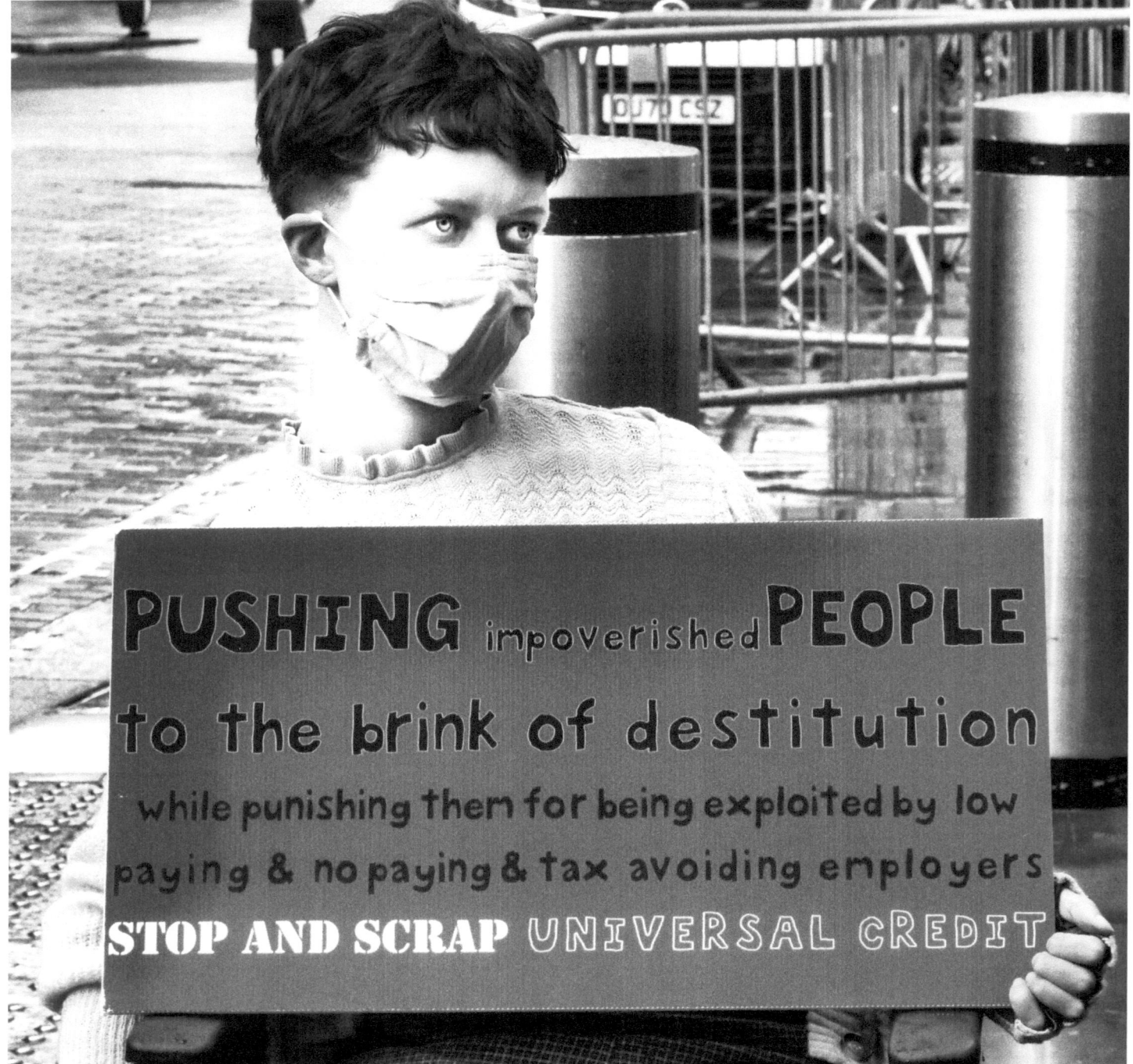

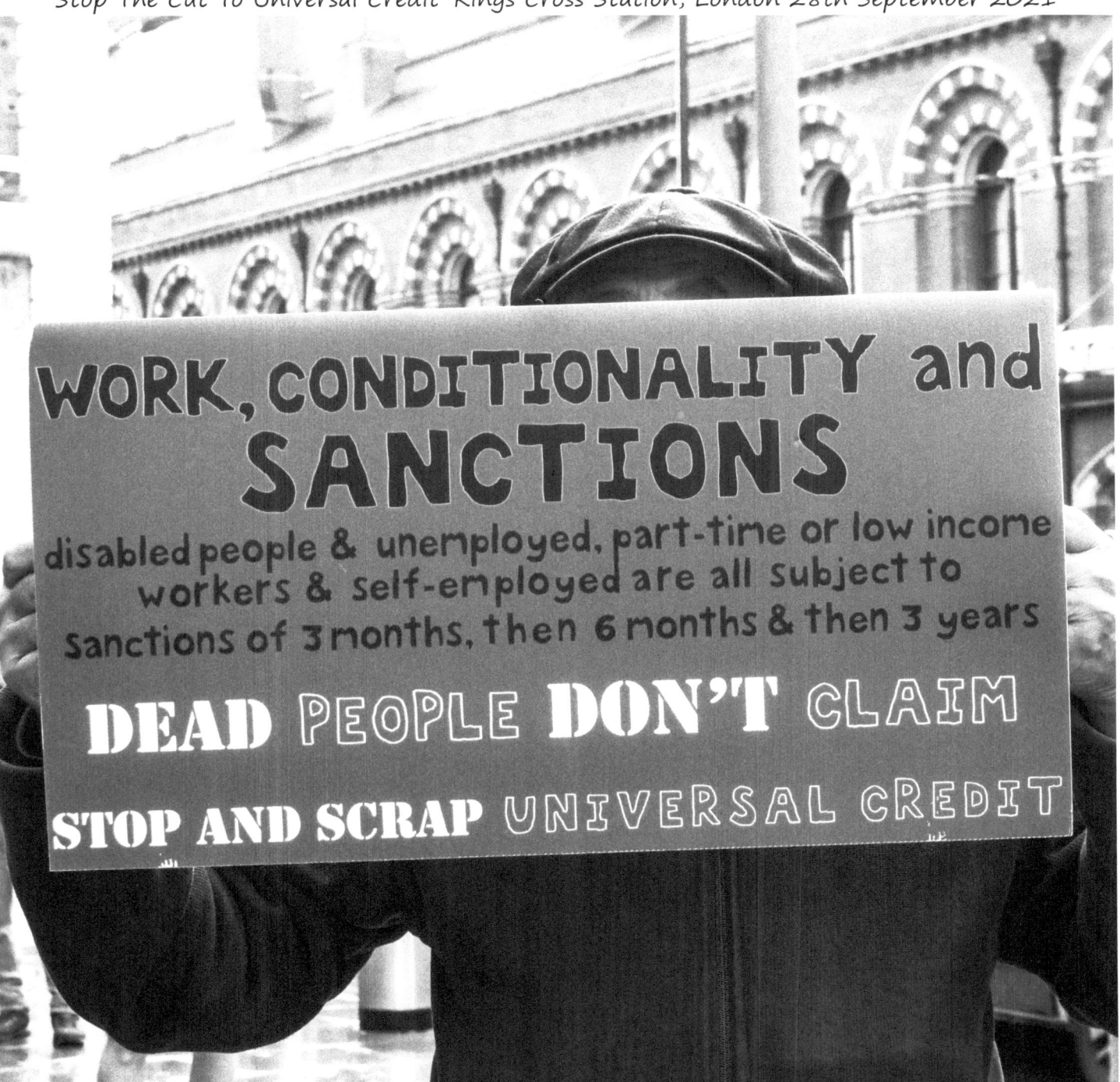

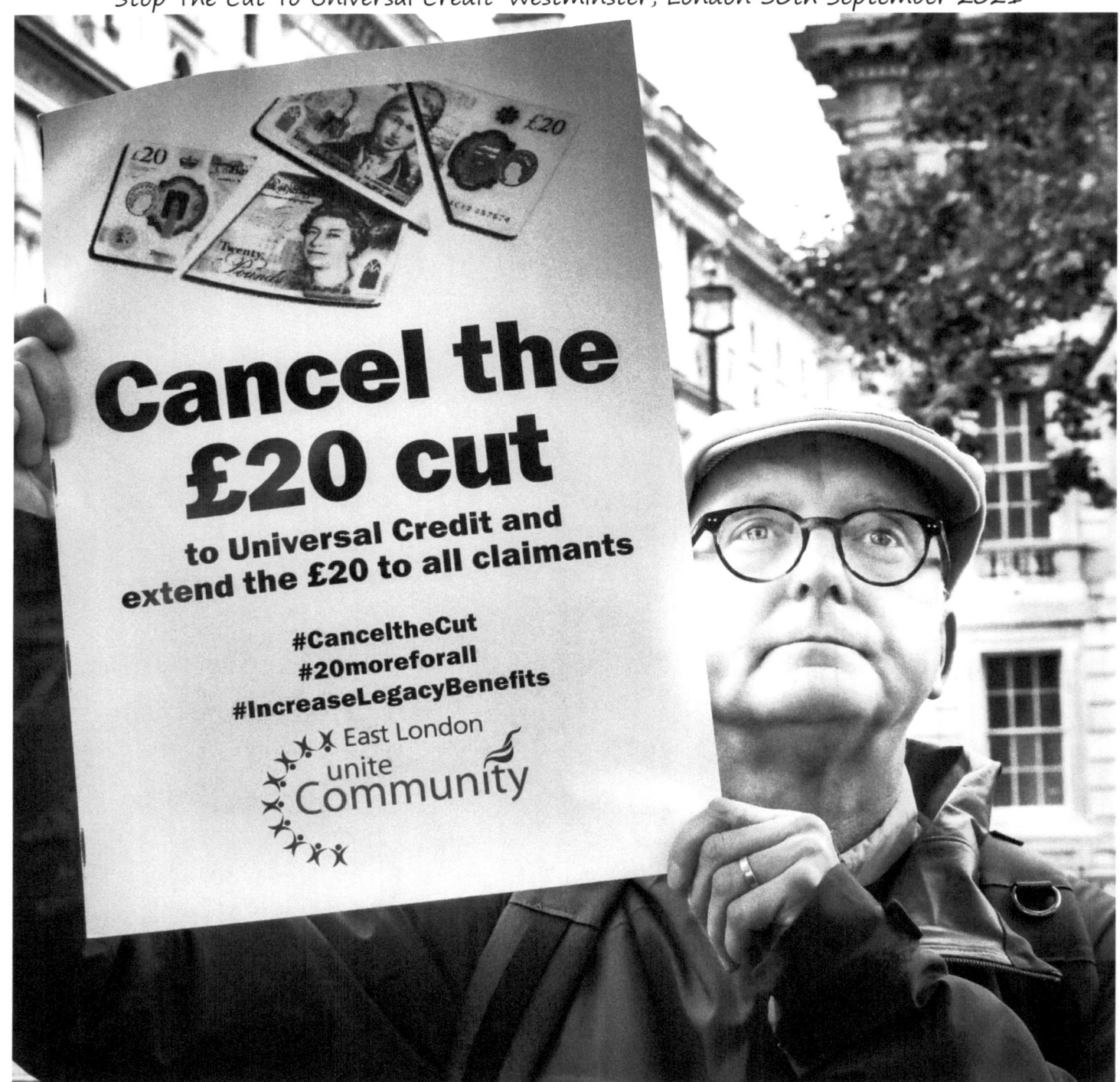

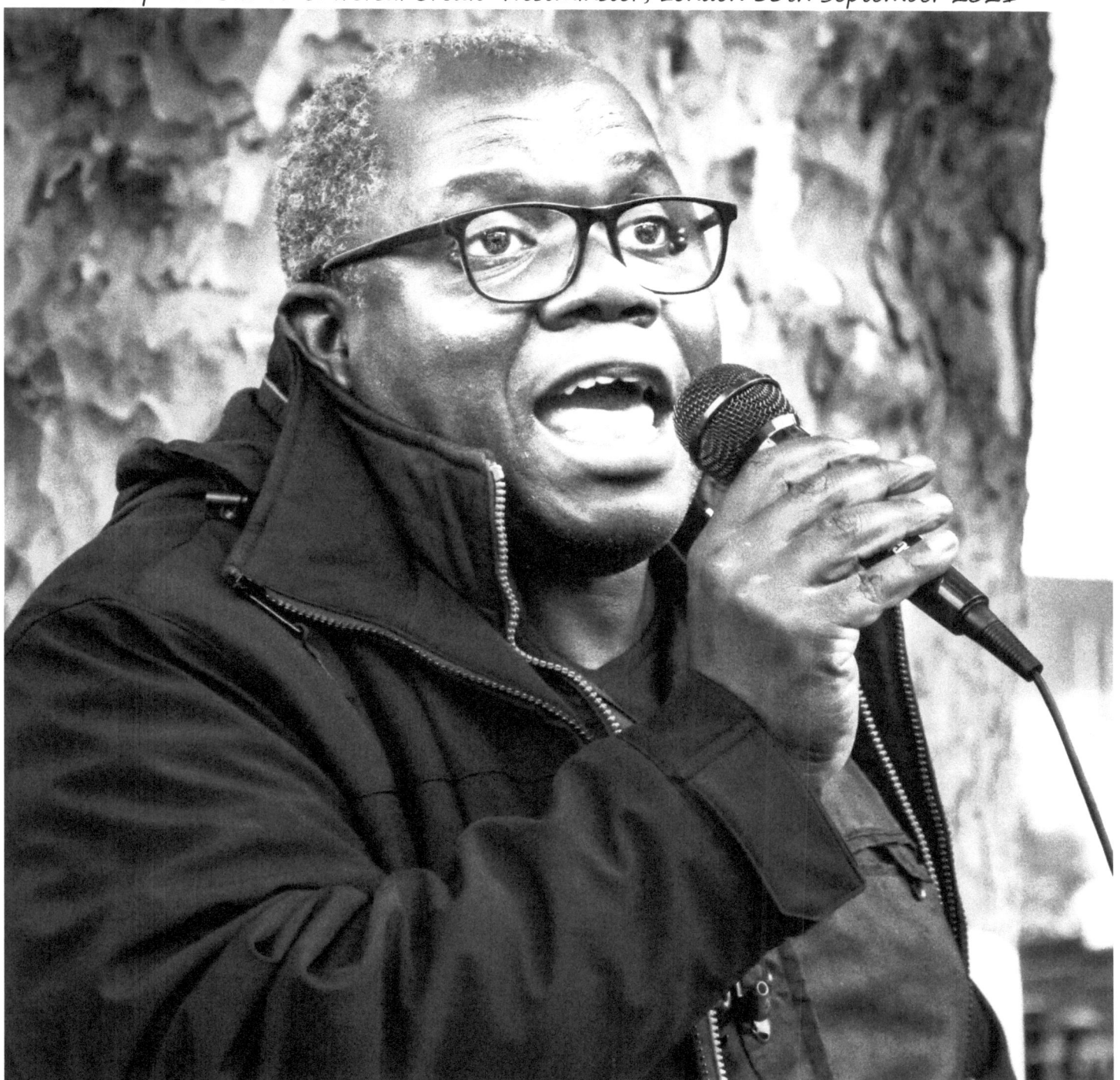

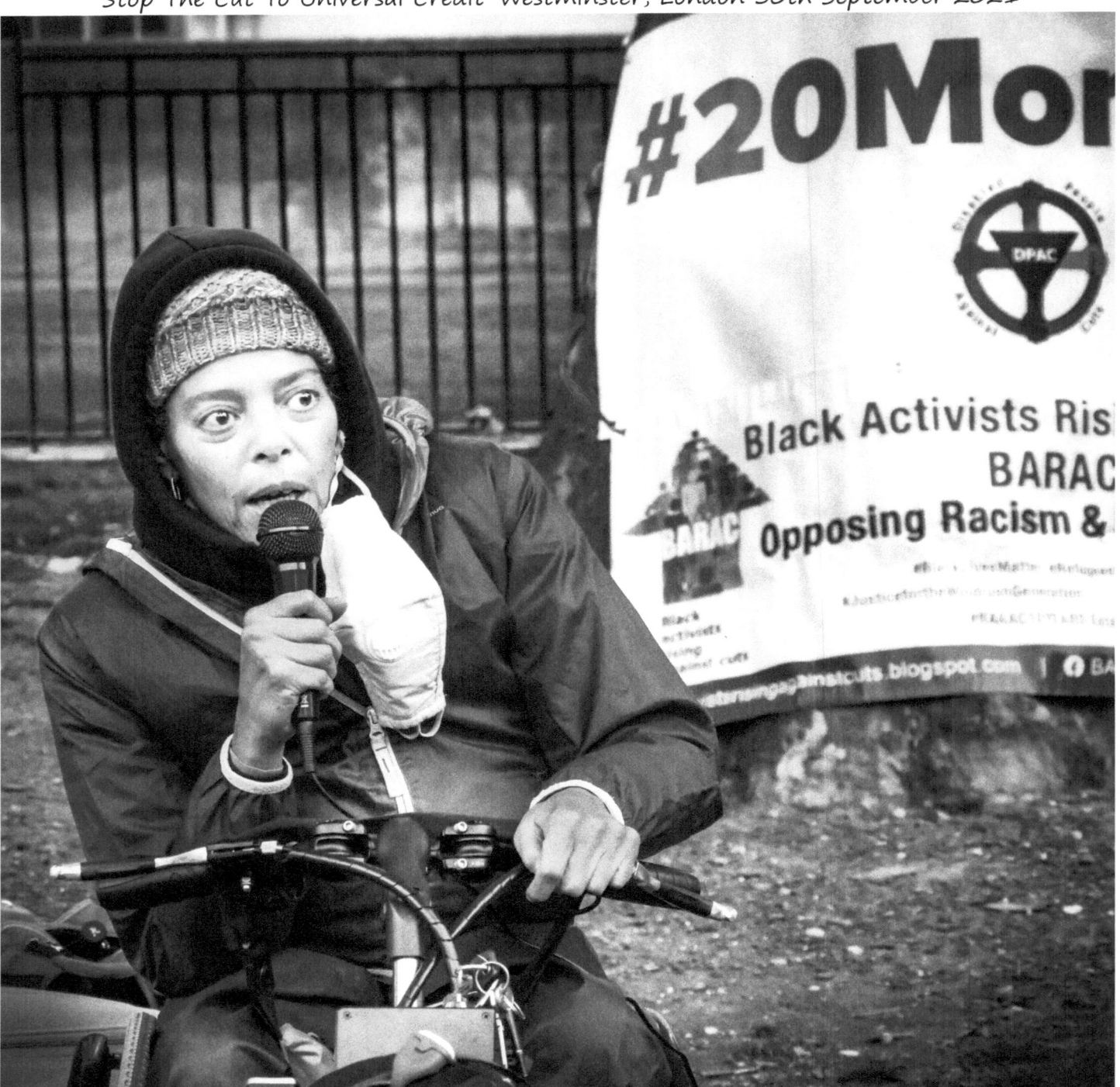

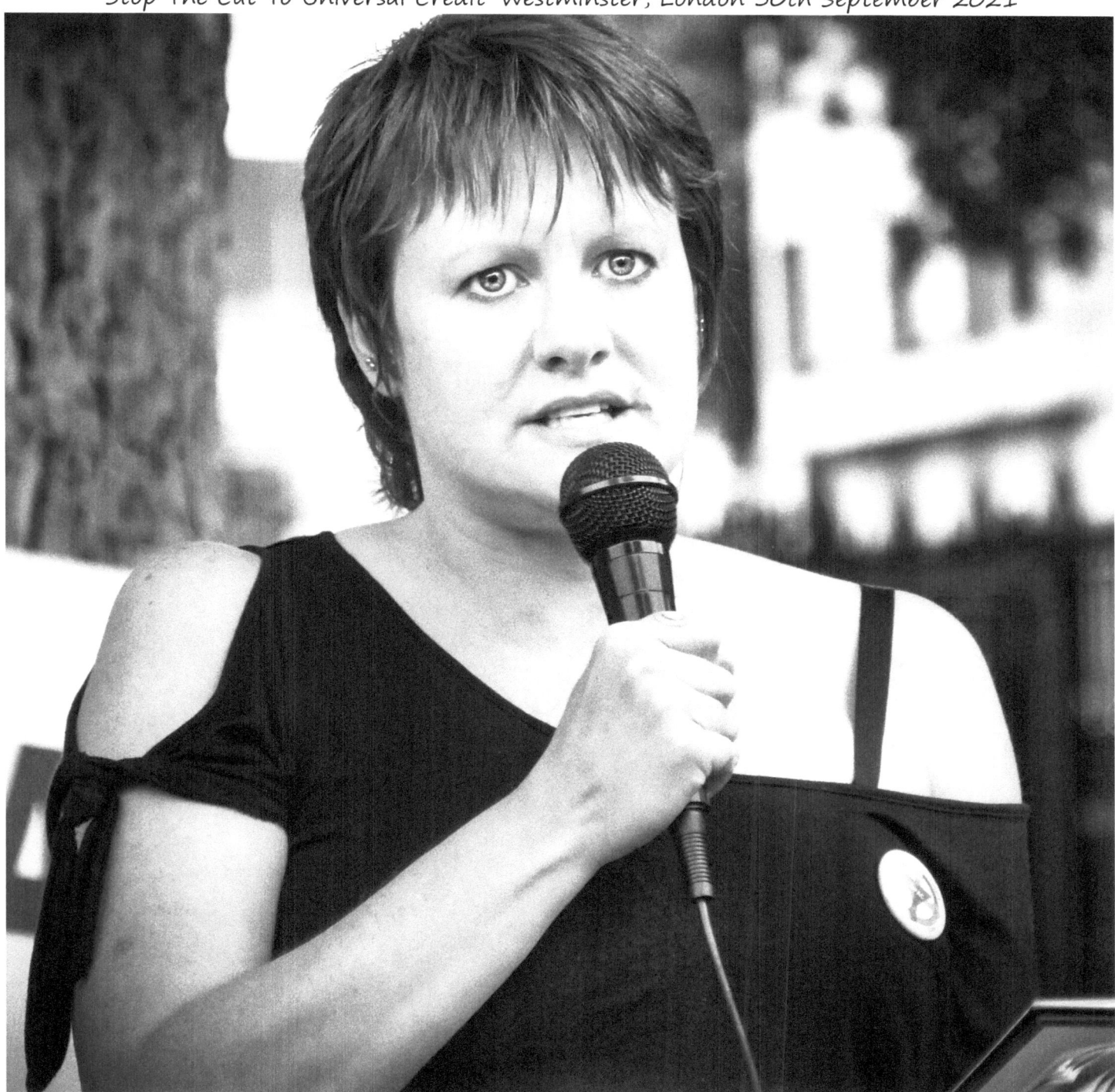

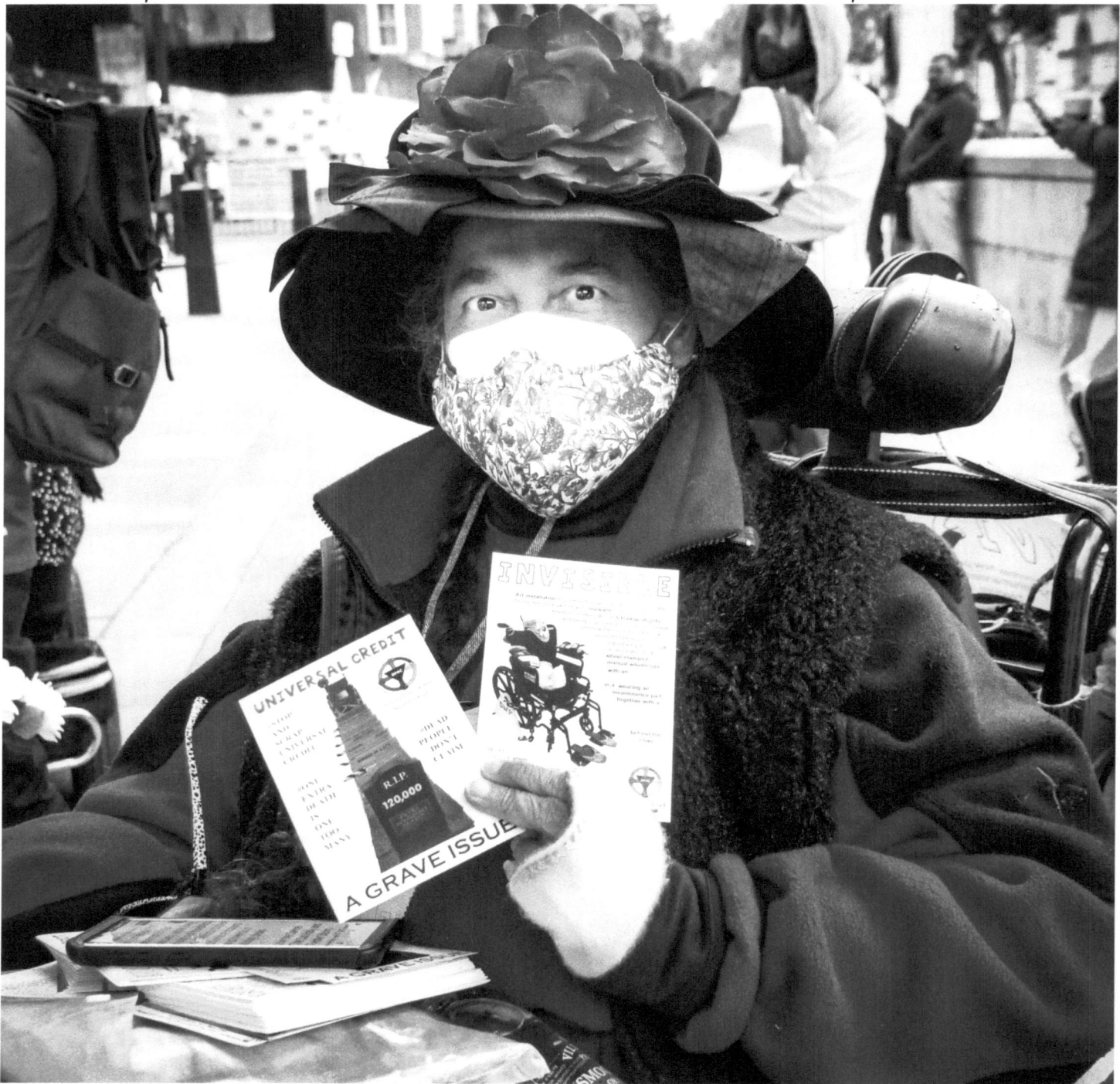

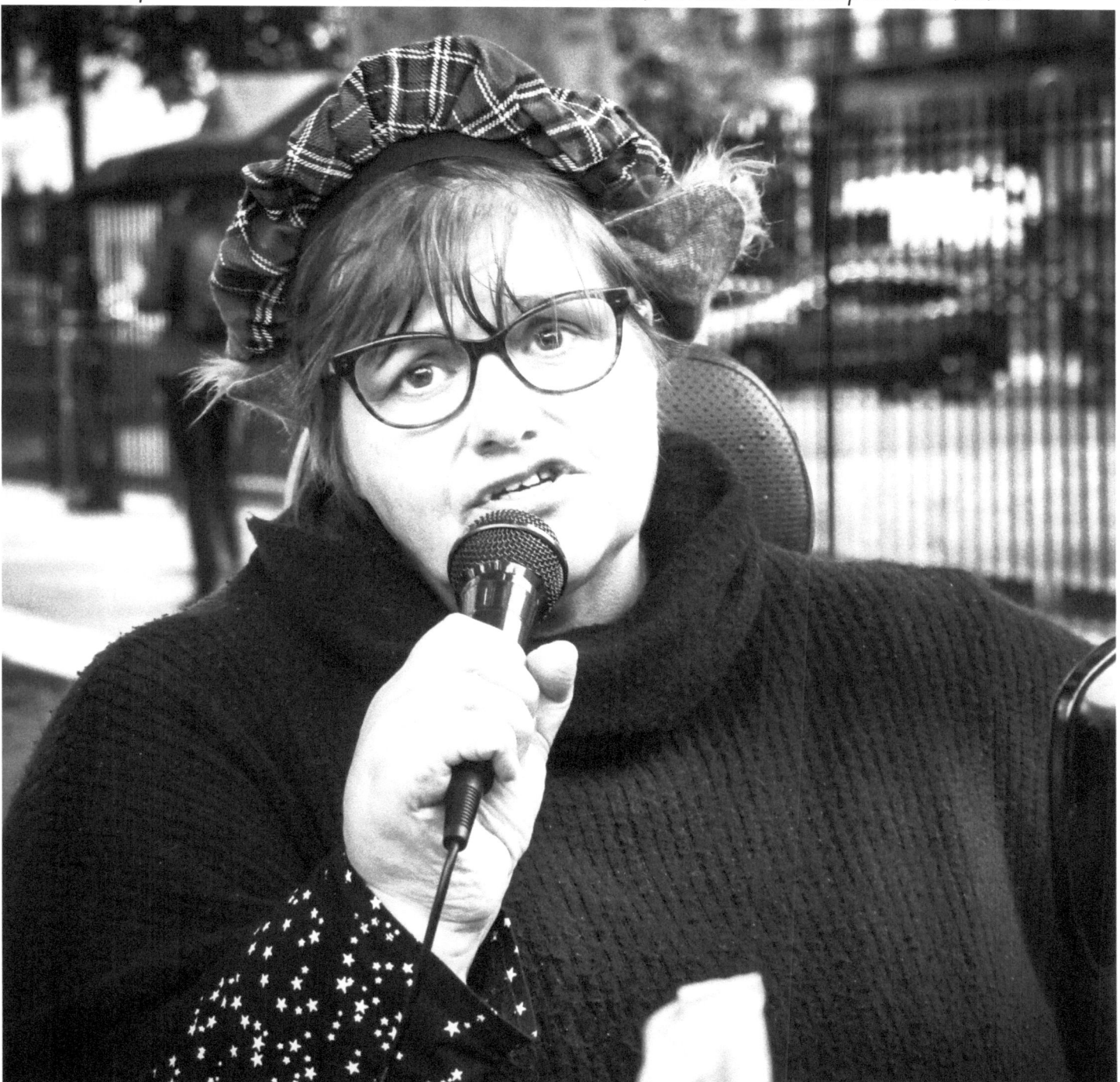

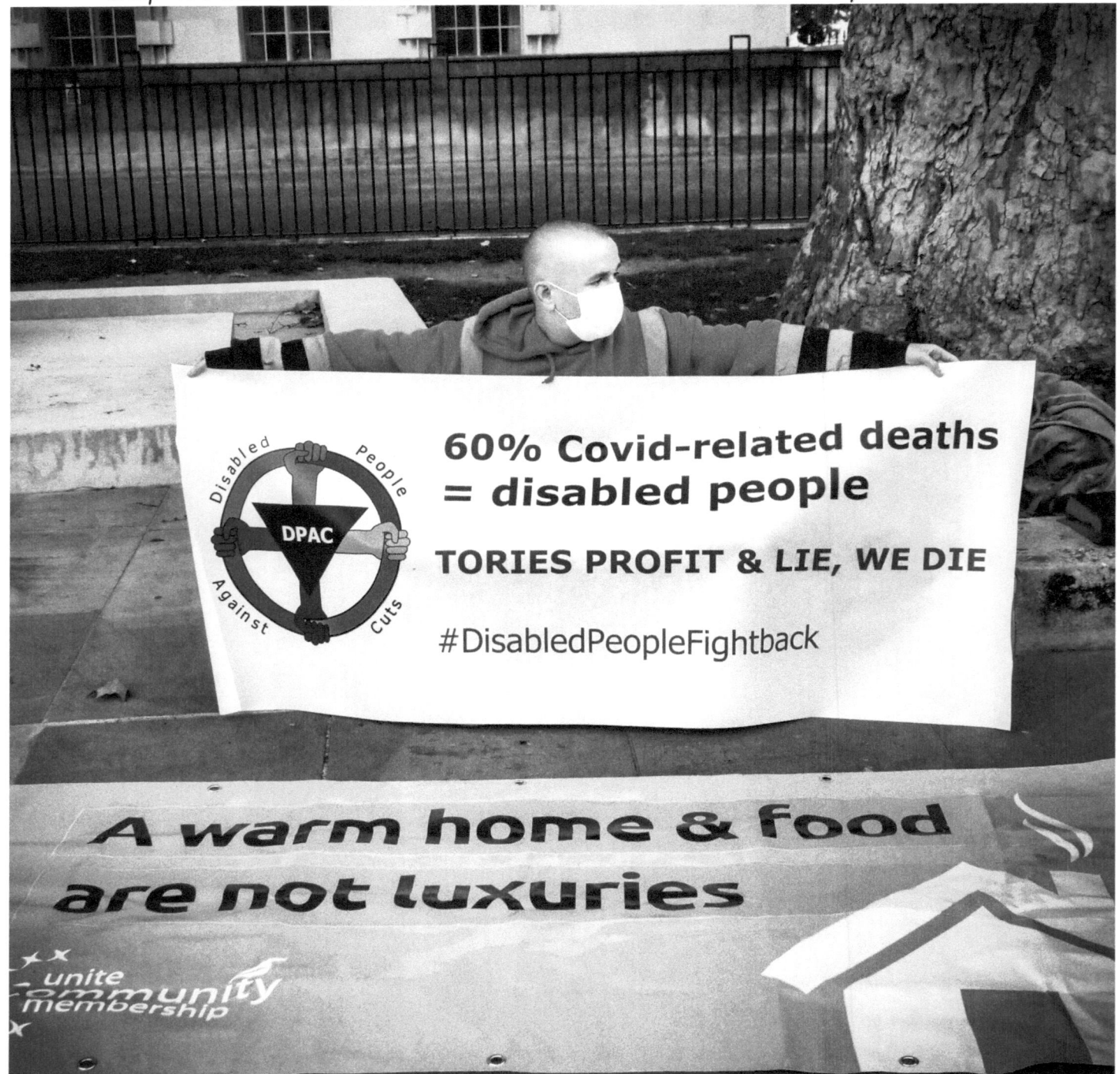

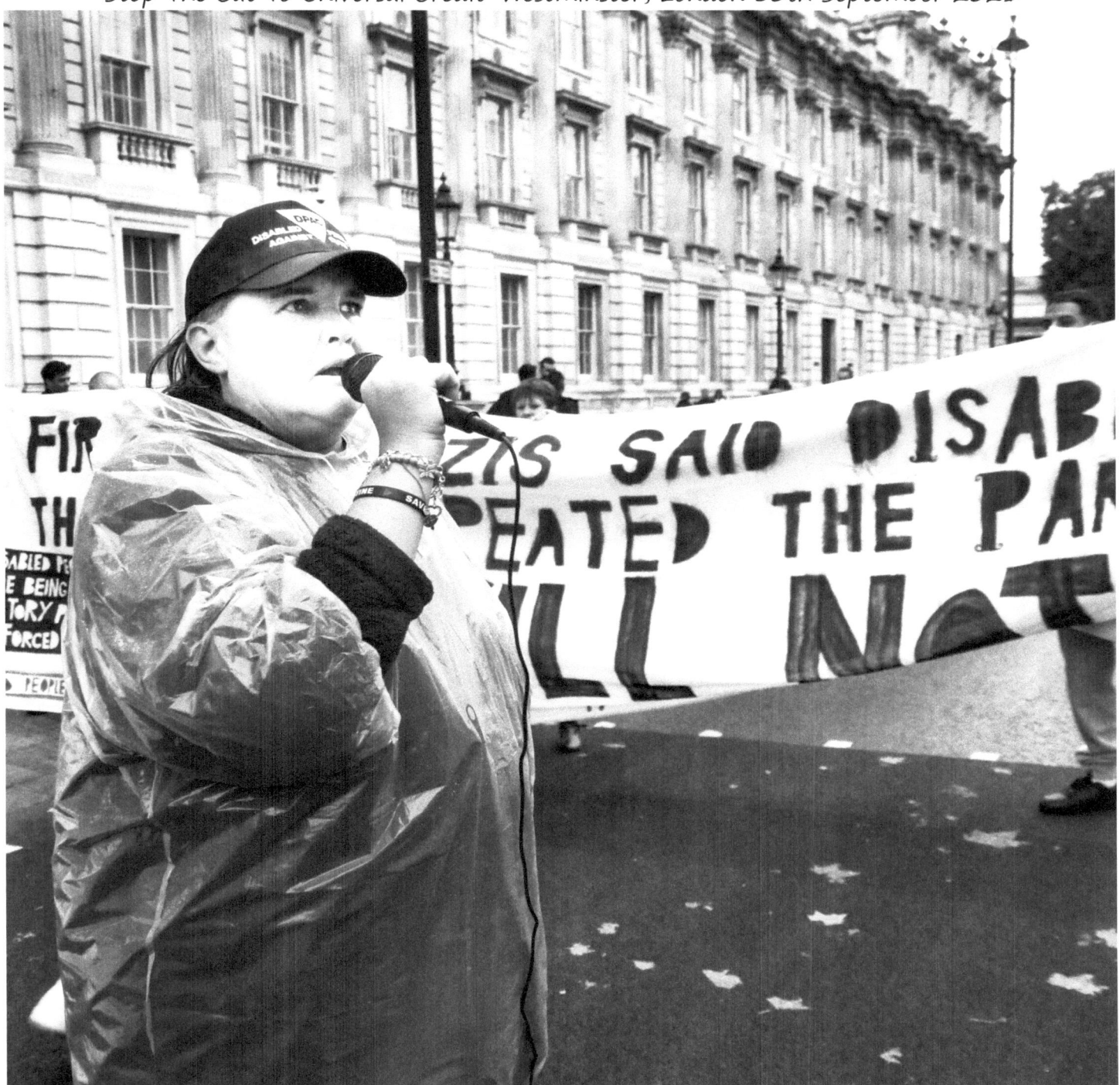

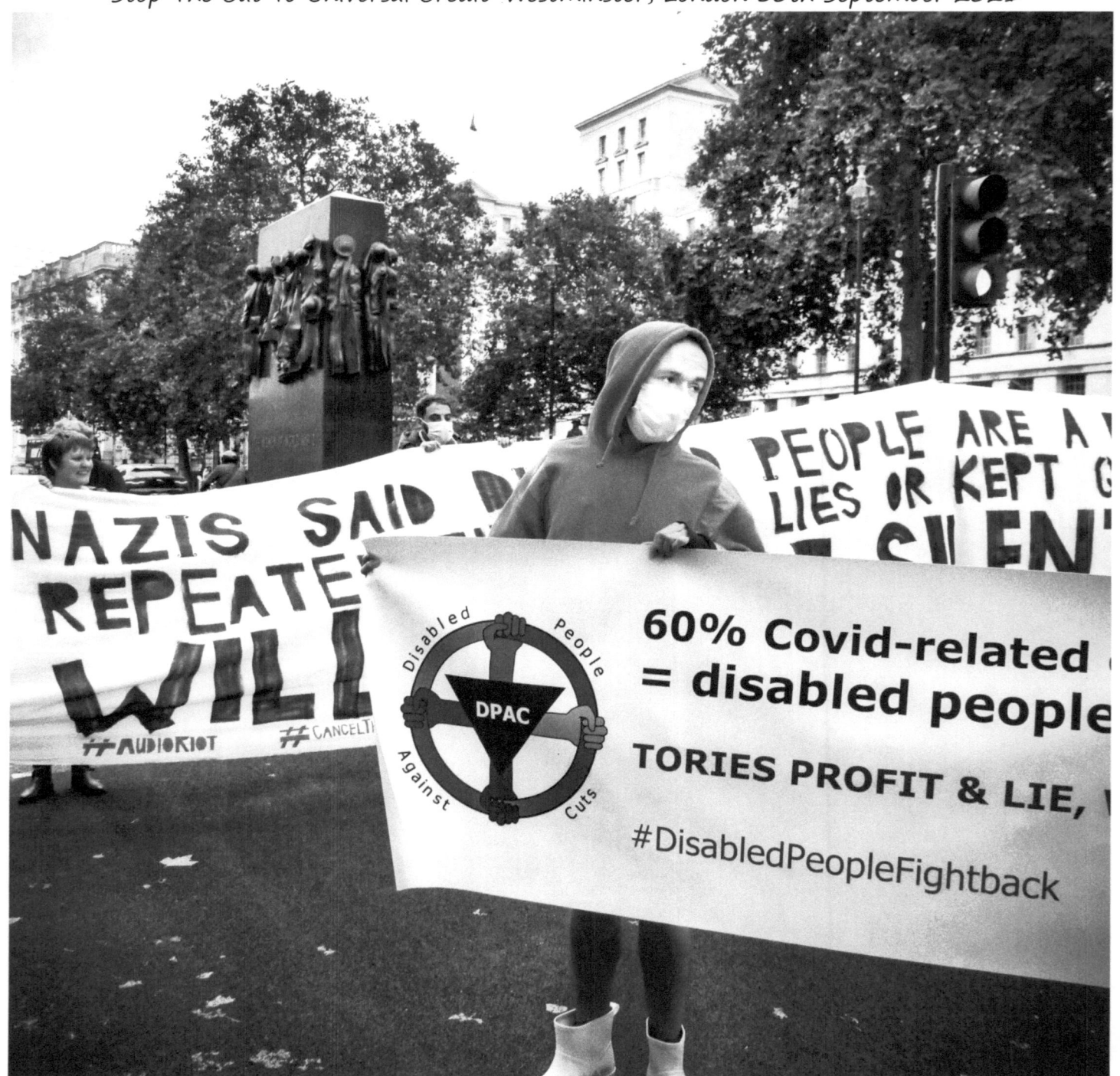

Biography.

Christopher John Ball BA (Hons) MA is a widely exhibited and published, award winning, London based, fine arts photographer, playwright, writer, campaigner, reviewer, publisher, curator, arts juror and lecturer. With over 45 years experience as an artist - his work is held within public and private collections worldwide and he was, together with artist Paul Woods, co-founder of The Association of Erotic Artists - an international academic and campaigning body that was committed to working towards a greater acceptance of the erotic arts whilst defending the genre from the dual threats of censorship and intolerance. Christopher is a passionate advocate for the rights of artists and for the preservation of public arts funding.

After several years within a commercial photographic background, including running his own studio, Chris became increasingly drawn to the use of photography as a fine arts medium and this, along with exploring the role of the arts within the community and education, has been the direction his work has taken him. In the 1980's Chris was a founder member of 'Action Factory' - a community arts group, based in Lancashire, created with the aim of democratising and expanding the role of the arts within the community - in particular amongst disadvantaged groups.

Given that he has been disabled since youth - Chris maintains an active role in the campaign to promote disability awareness and rights. He is particularly focused upon fighting the pernicious impact of the anti-disabled policies of the UK Conservative government. Said policies have been condemned by the UN, via the Convention on the Rights of Persons with Disabilities, as having created a 'human catastrophe'. In November 2016, the UN Committee released a critical report that found that the UK government had systematically discriminated against disabled people in their rights to living standards, social protection, work and employment and independent living.

His art work, views and opinions are very much in demand and he has contributed articles on photography, the arts, politics, philosophy and other topics for various international publications and media outlets including radio and television. His images have been showcased in British, Italian, German, Spanish, Hong Kong and mainland Chinese publications.

Christopher was selected as a juror for both the 2008/09 'Erotic Signature' annual international arts competition and the 'Erotic Review Photographer of the Year Prize 2009.' In 2011 Chris sat on the international Jury for the 2011 '12 inches of Sin' competition and juried exhibition sponsored by the Sin City Gallery, Las Vegas and organised by Dr Laura Henkel. The '12 inches of Sin' juried exhibitions/competitions were repeated each year, for 6 years, from 2012 through to 2017, again with Chris sitting on the selection committee. Several volumes based on the artworks submitted to '12 Inches of Sin' were published, with Chris writing introductions to the books.

He has also worked in film and theatre. "Throwing Stones: What's in your family album?" was co-written by Christopher John Ball and Dean Sipling. Performed in 2005 at the Greenwich Playhouse, a revised version of 'Throwing Stones' was published in November 2013.

Christopher is proud to be involved in the 'Film is Fabulous!' initiative, a vital new project dedicated to preserving the UK's rich film heritage. Film is a fragile medium, and many films are lost each year due to neglect, deterioration, or simply being disposed of in landfills. Launched in 2023 by film collectors, cinema lovers, and vintage television enthusiasts, 'Film is Fabulous!' encourages collectors to create a list of their films and to add this with clear instructions to their Will, so that their collections can be preserved and enjoyed by future generations.

'Film Is Fabulous' is supported by a number of important organisations, including De Montfort University's Cinema and Television History Institute (CATHI) and the Media Archive for Central England (MACE). Its first event was held at Leicester's Phoenix Cinema and Arts Centre, in October 2023, with a series of live panel discussions on film collecting, film collectors and film archivists.

Christopher's work explores social, political, and environmental issues through the human condition, body representation, and the relationship between humanity and nature. Upcoming projects include exhibitions, a book about London's experience of the COVID-19 pandemic, two monographs (one on his photo series of discarded objects and one on British seaside towns in the 1980s), and more fine art photography books.

Other Publications

"Mid-life male photographer meets young, nubile female student-cum-artistic muse - so far it's old hat. But photographer turned playwright Christopher John Ball and co-writer Dean Sipling, whose background is film and television, bring the pairing into a thoroughly contemporary world of intercepted emails, sinister insinuation and sharp retorts. Their 'guilty until proved innocent' plot … is thoroughly watchable and believable - perhaps as a result of Ball's professional insights and DS Dom Lucas' services as police advisor to the production." Barbara Lewis – The Stage

Throwing Stones - 'What's in your family album' a play by Christopher John Ball and Dean Sipling.
ISBN - 978-0-9926899-0-2

'Blackburn - A Town And Its People - A Photographic Essay' by Christopher John Ball
ISBN - 978-0-9926899-5-7

'The Bodies Untamed - Fine Art Nude Photography' by Christopher John Ball
ISBN - 978-0-9926899-1-9

'This Is The Room - Fine Art Nude Photography' by Christopher John Ball
ISBN - 978-0-9926899-2-6

'The Chair - Fine Art Nude Photography' by Christopher John Ball
ISBN - 978-0-9926899-3-3

'Corrupted From Memory - Fine Art Nude Photography' by Christopher John Ball
ISBN - 978-0-9926899-6-4

Social Media

Visit www.christopherjohnball.co.uk for news of future publications, exhibitions, talks and details on how to purchase signed prints.

Regular photography, philosophy and political videos can be found at www.youtube.com/cjballphotographer

Follow Chris on X (Formerly known as Twitter) at https://twitter.com/cjball_london

Visit Chris's Redbubble Store www.redbubble.com/people/cjballphoto/shop

Acknowledgments

Special thanks to Dean Sipling, Carrie White, Ian Davies, Nina Dougall, Sharon Barnes, Emma Barnes-Marriott, Angela Spencer, David Ball, Alan and Karen Gregory, Ian (H) Hodgson, Ewan Butler, Debbie Abrahams MP, John McDonnell MP, Jeremy Corbyn MP, Paula Peters, Linda Burnip, Rick Burgess, John Pring, Andy Greene, Ellen Clifford, Dr Frances Ryan, Pete Eastwood, Jo Ann Taylor, Sam Bosworth, Rachel Curtis, Rose Matthews, Anita Bellows, Dr Amy Kavanagh, Richard Amm, Dr Hannah Barham-Brown, Greg Judge, Simon John Duffy, Rachel Charlton-Dailey, Helen Sims, Francesca Hughes, Dr Mark D'Arcy, Dan White, Bernard Dowdall, Bruce Wilkinson, Alex Tiffin, Stephen Adamson, Nicola Jeffery, Steve Topple, Nikki Clarke, Aditya Chakrabortty, Katherine Birkett, Bernadette Meaden, Del Strain, Michelle Maher

Along with everybody at

Disabled People Against Cuts (DPAC)
www.dpac.uk.net

Black Triangle
www.blacktrianglecampaign.org

Without your invaluable support, encouragement and advice this book would not have been possible.

www.ingramcontent.com/pod-product-compliance
Lightning Source LLC
Chambersburg PA
CBHW050711180526
45159CB00003B/1003